Recent Advances in Linear and Nonlinear Optics

Recent Advances in Linear and Nonlinear Optics

Editors

Christophe Humbert
Thomas Noblet

MDPI • Basel • Beijing • Wuhan • Barcelona • Belgrade • Manchester • Tokyo • Cluj • Tianjin

Editors

Christophe Humbert
Université Paris-Saclay
France

Thomas Noblet
University of Liège
Belgium

Editorial Office
MDPI
St. Alban-Anlage 66
4052 Basel, Switzerland

This is a reprint of articles from the Special Issue published online in the open access journal *Symmetry* (ISSN 2073-8994) (available at: https://www.mdpi.com/journal/symmetry/special_issues/Recent_Advances_Linear_Nonlinear_Optics).

For citation purposes, cite each article independently as indicated on the article page online and as indicated below:

LastName, A.A.; LastName, B.B.; LastName, C.C. Article Title. *Journal Name* **Year**, *Volume Number*, Page Range.

ISBN 978-3-0365-4117-4 (Hbk)
ISBN 978-3-0365-4118-1 (PDF)

Contents

About the Editors

Christophe Humbert

Christophe Humbert is an expert in nonlinear optical vibrational spectroscopy. He obtained his PhD degree in 2003 from the University of Namur (Belgium) by pioneering Two-Colour Sum-Frequency generation (SFG) applied to the structural analysis of the vibrational and electronic properties of interfaces made of molecular monolayers adsorbed on metal surfaces. During a post-doc as a FNRS (Fonds National de la Recherche Scientifique, Belgium) researcher at the French LURE synchrotron in Orsay (France), he successfully contributed to the temporal coupling of the CLIO Free-Electron Laser (FEL) with a table-top 2C-SFG setup at the picosecond scale within the working team of Dr. Abderrahame Tadjeddine. He was recruited as a CNRS (Centre National de la Recherche Scientifique, France) researcher in 2006 for a permanent position at the Institut de Chimie Physique (Orsay, France). The unique worldwide 2C-SFG setup coupled to the CLIO FEL was exploited until 2017, giving rise to several experimental firsts in applications related to functionalized catalytic (gas–solid), electrochemical (liquid–solid) and metal (nanoparticles) or semiconductor (quantum dots) nanostructured interfaces. He became CNRS Research Director in 2020. He has been leading the TEMiC (Electron Transfer in Condensed Phase) research group from 2017 at the Institut de Chimie Physique. The TEMiC group is specialized in chemistry under radiation (ELYSE National Platform and panoramic irradiator) and photo-electro-catalysis for the synthesis, characterization and application of advanced nanomaterials exploited for green energy production and storage and water and soil depollution.

Thomas Noblet

Thomas Noblet works in the fields of photoluminescence and nonlinear vibrational spectroscopies and specifically studies semiconductor quantum dots. He obtained his PhD degree in 2019 from the University of Paris-Saclay (France) thanks to his optical study of the vibroelectronic coupling at the interface between semiconductor quantum dots and organic molecules. This work has been awarded three thesis prizes, one of which was granted by the Chancellery of the Universities of Paris. In addition to the experimental demonstration of the dipole–dipole interaction coupling quantum dots and molecules, he notably took up the challenge of developing a new diagrammatic formalism to model the optical hyperpolarizabilities of nanostructured composite systems and then account for such nanoparticle/molecule interactions. Recruited as a Post-Doc Researcher within the University of Liège (Belgium) in the group of GRASP-Biophotonics, he is now coordinating a research project funded by the SPW (Service Public de Wallonie) implying both academic and industrial partners. This project aims at the design of quantum-dot-based biosensors for neonatal diagnostics.

Editorial

Special Issue of Symmetry: "Recent Advances in Linear and Nonlinear Optics"

Thomas Noblet [1,2] and Christophe Humbert [1,*]

1 Université Paris-Saclay, CNRS, Institut de Chimie Physique, UMR 8000, 91405 Orsay, France; t.noblet@uliege.be
2 GRASP-Biophotonics, CESAM, University of Liege, Institute of Physics, Allée du 6 août 17, 4000 Liège, Belgium
* Correspondence: christophe.humbert@universite-paris-saclay.fr

Citation: Noblet, T.; Humbert, C. Special Issue of Symmetry: "Recent Advances in Linear and Nonlinear Optics". *Symmetry* 2022, *14*, 495. https://doi.org/10.3390/sym14030495

Received: 22 February 2022
Accepted: 24 February 2022
Published: 28 February 2022

Publisher's Note: MDPI stays neutral with regard to jurisdictional claims in published maps and institutional affiliations.

In this Special Issue, invited researchers elaborate on 'Recent Advances in Linear and Nonlinear Optics', demonstrating how sensitive light–matter interactions are concerning symmetry. Through research articles and reviews, physicists, chemists, experimenters and theoreticians here exploit the (non)linearities of the dielectric response of molecules and nanostructures to probe their chemical features or, in return, to shape the light.

The symmetry sensitivity and the subsequent surface specificity of (non)linear optical techniques arise from the tensor structure of the dielectric response functions which relate the excitation electric field(s) with the polarization of matter [1]. Contrary to scalar functions describing isotropic phenomena, the mathematics of tensors conceptually enables the description of the response of matter in any direction (in 3D space) as a combination of different electric field contributions associated with different light beams and light polarization states. Researchers explicitly show how UV-visible, IR, Sum-Frequency Generation (SFG) and Raman spectroscopies all derive from the same tensor formalism, and then draw the consequences for experiments in terms of symmetry-related selection rules.

Henceforth, it is possible to assess the orientation and to identify the composition of a mixture of molecules adsorbed on surfaces by IR, Raman and SFG spectroscopies [2], and to quantify the sensitivity of each regarding their abilities to unmix the spectral signatures of the different chemical species. There is thus evidence that polarized Raman spectra are the most sensitive when the polarity of the molecular orientation is known, while even-order processes like SFG are required when there is ambiguity in the orientation polarity. Researchers here account for the complementarity between polarized Raman scattering, which gives access to numerous spatial projections due to its rank-4 third-order tensor response function, and sum-frequency generation, intrinsically surface-specific and symmetry-sensitive as a second-order dielectric response.

Interestingly, the symmetry-related selection rules that proper to second-order processes like SFG can be bypassed as soon as the sum-frequency generation results from the quadrupolar response of matter, instead of the dipolar one. This is the case in Second Harmonic Scattering (SHS). Typically, dipolar SHS is physically forbidden within centrosymmetrical materials, contrary to quadrupolar SHS. It is therefore possible to benefit from the competition between the two processes in order to differentiate liquid suspensions of molecular dyes on the basis of their (non-) centrosymmetric spatial arrangement [3]. By modeling the molecules as point-like nonlinear dipoles, researchers are able to account for experimentally characterized suspensions of dye aggregates, thus describing the collective organisation of molecular systems at the nanoscale.

In parallel, at the molecular scale, theoreticians benefit from Density Functional Theory (DFT) to study the second-order hyperpolarizability of complex molecules like polyoxometalates [4]. Such theoretical studies provide useful insights for experimenters as it enables the identification of the chemical features which significantly contribute to the nonlinear behavior of the molecules. Especially, the donor/acceptor character of the functional groups,

1

as well as the hybridization states of the composite atoms and the subsequent nature of the chemical bonds (σ, π), critically influence the strength of the second-order response. This paves the way for studying the coupling of two molecules and more to draw near to real systems, like colloidal suspensions and adsorbed molecules.

Subsequently, at the nanoscale, it is possible to perform a quantitative analysis of composite or hybrid systems made of molecules/nanoparticles interfaces designed for optical (bio or chemical) sensing with an improved detection threshold at a low cost. By taking profit of quantum properties of small CdTe Quantum dots (QDs~3.4 nm diameter), researchers use advanced nonlinear optical Two-Colour Sum-Frequency Generation (2C-SFG) spectroscopy to check the hypothesis of the existence of a dipolar coupling from QD excitons to vibrations in their molecular environment to explain enhanced molecular sensitivity [5]. They demonstrate this physical process by comparing the dipolar coupling strength between the close chemical ligands of QDs with a farther molecular monolayer by highlighting $1/r^3$ spatial dependence compatible with dipole–dipole interactions.

As a matter of fact, plasmonics remains a growing research field for sensing thanks to the manufacturing of various metal nanomaterials, by adjusting at will the symmetry properties of plasmonic devices as discussed by researchers: rhombohedral arrays of nanoparticles, nanoholes (elliptical and circular). Recent developments in nonlinear plasmonics based on nanosystems in this review [6] show that symmetry breaking of their electronic properties increases dramatically the molecular sensitivity of nonlinear second-order processes such as those encountered in SHG and SFG spectroscopies. Another prominent developing research field related to symmetry breaking of electronic properties lies in chiral plasmonics based on (meta)materials allowing to specifically probe Left-circular or Right-circular light polarization taking account of bi-dimensional or three-dimensional effects. A comparison of the performances of various plasmonic devices is equally presented and discussed.

Conversely, by using plasmonic nanostructures of various sizes and shapes, it is possible to tune the light polarisation as a function of the LSPR response in favored directions. Researchers report in an extensive way the importance of the choice of a specific axis of symmetry for nanomaterials of increasing size and apply it to selected applications [7]: single nanosphere and dimers, trimers, nanorods, nanowires, nanoholes and nanoellipses, nanoprisms and nanotriangles, nanocrescents, hybrid plasmonic nanostructures. The monitoring of light polarisation states is therefore addressed through multifunctional metamaterials allowing polarisation conversion, from linear to: cross polarisation, left and right circular polarisation with chiral materials such as helical metamaterials. It allows us to design novel devices for real-life applications or overcome fundamental size and bandwidth limitations encountered in engineering based on conventional optics. Finally, a section is dedicated to the role of polarisation in magnetic-plasmonic nanosotructures, considering multiple potential applications based on magneto-optics and magnetoplasmonics: Faraday effect and Inverse Faraday effect, magneto-optics Kerr effect, Magnetic plasmon resonances, SHG, magnetic circular dichroism.

Author Contributions: T.N. and C.H. wrote the Editorial draft. All authors have read and agreed to the published version of the manuscript.

Acknowledgments: The authors acknowledge all the editorial staff of Symmetry journal for their constant support during all the processing of this Special Issue.

Conflicts of Interest: The authors declare no conflict of interest.

References

1. Humbert, C.; Noblet, T. A Unified Mathematical Formalism for First to Third Order Dielectric Response of Matter: Application to Surface-Specific Two-Colour Vibrational Optical Spectroscopy. *Symmetry* **2021**, *13*, 153. [CrossRef]
2. Chen, F.; Gozdzialski, L.; Hung, K.-K.; Stege, U.; Hore, D.K. Assessing the Molecular Specificity and Orientation Sensitivity of Infrared, Raman, and Vibrational Sum-Frequency Spectra. *Symmetry* **2021**, *13*, 42. [CrossRef]

3. Revillod, G.; Duboisset, J.; Russier-Antoine, I.; Benichou, E.; Jonin, C.; Brevet, P.-F. Second Harmonic Scattering of Molecular Aggregates. *Symmetry* **2021**, *13*, 206. [CrossRef]
4. Rtibi, E.; Champagne, B. Density Functional Theory Study of Substitution Effects on the Second-Order Nonlinear Optical Properties of Lindquist-Type Organo-Imido Polyoxometalates. *Symmetry* **2021**, *13*, 1636. [CrossRef]
5. Noblet, T.; Dreesen, L.; Tadjeddine, A.; Humbert, C. Spatial Dependence of the Dipolar Interaction between Quantum Dots and Organic Molecules Probed by Two-Color Sum-Frequency Generation Spectroscopy. *Symmetry* **2021**, *13*, 294. [CrossRef]
6. Barbillon, G.; Ivanov, A.; Sarychev, A.K. Applications of Symmetry Breaking in Plasmonics. *Symmetry* **2020**, *12*, 896. [CrossRef]
7. Khan, P.; Brennan, G.; Lillis, J.; Tofail, S.A.M.; Liu, N.; Silien, C. Characterisation and Manipulation of Polarisation Response in Plasmonic and Magneto-Plasmonic Nanostructures and Metamaterials. *Symmetry* **2020**, *12*, 1365. [CrossRef]

Review

A Unified Mathematical Formalism for First to Third Order Dielectric Response of Matter: Application to Surface-Specific Two-Colour Vibrational Optical Spectroscopy

Christophe Humbert and Thomas Noblet *,†

Université Paris-Saclay, CNRS, Institut de Chimie Physique, UMR8000, 91405 Orsay, France;
christophe.humbert@universite-paris-saclay.fr
* Correspondence: t.noblet@uliege.be
† Current address: GRASP-Biophotonics, CESAM, University of Liege, Institute of Physics, Allée du 6 août 17, 4000 Liège, Belgium.

Abstract: To take advantage of the singular properties of matter, as well as to characterize it, we need to interact with it. The role of optical spectroscopies is to enable us to demonstrate the existence of physical objects by observing their response to light excitation. The ability of spectroscopy to reveal the structure and properties of matter then relies on mathematical functions called optical (or dielectric) response functions. Technically, these are tensor Green's functions, and not scalar functions. The complexity of this tensor formalism sometimes leads to confusion within some articles and books. Here, we do clarify this formalism by introducing the physical foundations of linear and non-linear spectroscopies as simple and rigorous as possible. We dwell on both the mathematical and experimental aspects, examining extinction, infrared, Raman and sum-frequency generation spectroscopies. In this review, we thus give a personal presentation with the aim of offering the reader a coherent vision of linear and non-linear optics, and to remove the ambiguities that we have encountered in reference books and articles.

Keywords: non-linear optics; centrosymmetry; spectroscopy; selection rules; infrared; Raman; sum-frequency generation; interfaces; molecules; nanoparticles

Citation: Humbert, C.; Noblet, T. A Unified Mathematical Formalism for First to Third Order Dielectric Response of Matter: Application to Surface-Specific Two-Colour Vibrational Optical Spectroscopy. *Symmetry* **2021**, *13*, 153. https://doi.org/10.3390/sym13010153

Received: 29 December 2020
Accepted: 15 January 2021
Published: 19 January 2021

Publisher's Note: MDPI stays neutral with regard to jurisdictional clai-ms in published maps and institutio-nal affiliations.

1. Introduction

Within the field of chemical physics, optical spectroscopies are mainly used to characterize the structural and chemical composition of materials. Among the most common techniques, we count UV–visible and infrared extinction spectroscopies, fluorescence emission, Raman scattering and sum-frequency generation (SFG). On a theoretical point of view, they all arise from electromagnetism and quantum mechanics, which enable to implement light–matter interactions. As characterized by its dipole moments, a material is able to couple with light at different orders. Extinction spectroscopies are first order phenomena, while SFG is a second order process, and fluorescence emission and Raman scattering are third order processes. The former fall within the scope of linear optics, whereas the latter constitute the core of non-linear optics. Mathematically, an optical process is qualified as an nth-order process when the material is described by a dipole moment density $\mathbf{P}$, so-called polarization, whose amplitude depends on the nth power of the light electric field amplitude: $|\mathbf{P}| \sim |\mathbf{E}|^n$. The proportionality coefficient is then characteristic of the inner properties of the material: crystal structure, molecular vibrations, electronic density, chemical composition, internal symmetries and so on. This response factor is denoted $\chi^{(n)}$. It must be handled with care: the relation between the polarization $\mathbf{P}$ of the material and the electric field $\mathbf{E}$ of the light is not as simple as $\mathbf{P} = \chi^{(n)}\mathbf{E}^n$: first, the nth power of $\mathbf{E}$ is not necessarily a vector (e.g., $\mathbf{E}^2$ is a number), while $\mathbf{P}$ is a vector; second, each component P_i of $\mathbf{P}$ may depend on all the components E_x, E_y and E_z of the electric field, so that the response factor is actually a tensor [1]; and third, the frequencies of **P** and of the different spectral contributions to **E** must be explicitly written. In order to properly describe optical spectroscopies, the response functions $\chi^{(n)}$ must be well defined on a mathematical point of view: dimension of the tensor, number of frequency arguments, relation with the polarization and the electric field. Given that it is not the case in many articles, we dwell on that point through this review.

To begin, we must distinguish the response functions, which are temporal functions, from the associated susceptibilities, which are spectral functions. The first ones describe how the polarization of the material evolves along time with respect to the time profile of the light excitation, whereas the second ones give the spectral distribution of all the frequencies which compose the dipolar response of the material. Since then, we often encounter two important ambiguities. First, some authors use complex exponential functions to express the physical quantities instead of Fourier transforms. They assume in this way that the signals are monochromatic and hide all the effects which are related to polychromaticity. For instance, strictly speaking, SFG does not combine a visible and an IR beam, both characterized by their own electric field, but all the couples of frequencies available within the Fourier spectrum of the total electric field. This difference of point of view is schemed in Figure 1. Second, while nth-order dielectric response functions $\chi^{(n)}(t_1, \cdots, t_n)$ are always defined as functions of n time variables, the associated susceptibilities are incoherently written as functions of $(n+1)$ frequency variables: $\chi^{(n)}(\omega_{n+1}; \omega_1, \cdots, \omega_n)$. This confusion derives actually from the previous one, when authors illegitimately assume the fields are monochromatic. Such $(n+1)$-argument functions indeed exist mathematically and make sense, but they cannot be assigned to n-argument optical susceptibilities. Section 3.1 of this paper sheds light on these two difficulties. Furthermore, it is not unusual to read misleading interpretations of non-linear processes. For instance, sum-frequency generation is commonly described as a combination of infrared and Raman spectroscopies, but we show that it is not correct (Section 4.5). Another example relates to Raman scattering, which is sometimes considered as a first order phenomenon because the light power of the Raman signal linearly depends on the input light power. There is a difference between the behaviour of the polarization **P** of a material and that of the emitted/scattered light power $\langle |\mathbf{P}|^2 \rangle$. As explained in Section 4.4, this comes from quantum mechanics.

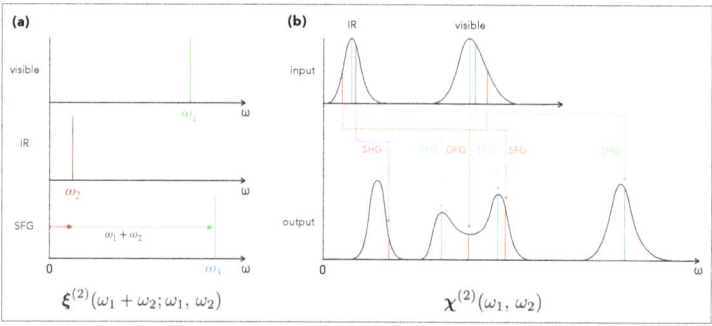

Figure 1. Mono- and polychromatic picture of second order response functions. (a) Common description of sum-frequency generation (SFG) from a monochromatic point of view, considered to derive from a 3-argument function. (b) Description of second order processes (SFG, DFG, SHG) from a polychromatic point of view, considered to derive from the 2-argument second order susceptibility $\chi^{(2)}(\omega_1, \omega_2)$ combining any input frequencies ω_1 and ω_2.

In other words, optical spectroscopies are based on a mathematical formalism which exhibit numerous subtleties. From an experimental point of view, they are extensively used in analytical and physical chemistry to study molecular systems. It is then important to clarify the formalism and to make it accessible to all experimentalists. Hence, this review first recalls the foundations of linear response theory, leading to refraction, absorption, scattering and extinctions processes. Second, we formally introduce the response functions and dielectric susceptibilities as defined to account for second- and third-order processes. We especially dwell on the case of two-dimension SFG spectroscopy, as it is a powerful tool to combine visible (i.e., electronic) and infrared (i.e., vibrational) spectroscopies. Third, we show how it is concretely applied to vibrational spectroscopies. Taking the example of hybrid organic/inorganic systems made of nanostructured interfaces grafted by functional molecules, we evidence the power of two-dimension non-linear spectroscopies for examining vibroelectronic couplings between nanostructures and organic molecules.

2. Linear Response Theory

Most of the experimental studies which aim to probe the physicochemical properties of matter are well described by the theory of linear response. This is indeed the case when samples are probed by low power light excitations. Under the dipolar approximations, atoms, molecules, nanoparticles and solid-state materials are characterized by their electric dipole moments. We recall in this section its definition and develop the consequences on the optical refraction, absorption and extinction processes.

2.1. Polarization of Matter and Optical Response Function

Within neutral matter, the electric polarity of microscopic components is first characterized by their dipole moments μ. For atoms, as for molecules, which have an electronic cloud of charge $-q$, we commonly define $\mu \triangleq q\mathbf{d}$, where $\mathbf{d}$ denotes the vector connecting the barycentre of the negative charges (of the electronic cloud) to the barycentre of the positive charges (of the nucleus). In this context, reducing the behaviour of matter to that of the dipole moment alone is an approximation. When this is necessary (which will not be our case), we may have to consider quadrupole and octupole moments. It is then possible to define for any macroscopic material system the local polarization $\mathbf{P}$ as the volume density of dipole moments:

$$\mathbf{P} \triangleq \sum_i \frac{\mu_i}{V} = N\langle \mu \rangle. \tag{1}$$

The sum over the integers i describes the set of microscopic components of dipole moment μ_i involved in the system. We note V the volume of the total system, N the density of atoms or molecules (considered as uniform) and $\langle \mu \rangle$ the mean dipole moment calculated over the entire system.

At equilibrium and in the absence of an external electric field, the microscopic components may, (i), not be polarized ($\forall i$, $\mu_i = 0$) or else, (ii), have a permanent dipole moment ($\forall i$, $\mu_i \neq 0$). In the first case, the polarization at equilibrium is clearly zero: $\mathbf{P} = 0$. In the second one, it may turn out to be non-zero. However, we often observe an average dipole moment reduced to zero, due to the isotropic orientation distribution of these moments: $\langle \mu \rangle = 0$.

As a matter of fact, materials can most frequently be polarized only thanks to the presence of an external electric field $\mathbf{E}(t)$. As far as we are concerned, we will consider this field to be uniform across the system. For instance, in the case of metallic or semiconductor nanoparticles, this approximation remains quite reasonable. Their radius R is indeed much smaller than the wavelength of the light (visible and infrared) which probes them: $\lambda \gtrsim 400$ nm $\gg R \sim 10$ nm. We therefore define the first order optical response function $t \mapsto \chi^{(1)}(t)$ as the 2nd rank tensor (i.e., 2D matrix) which links the induced polarization $\mathbf{P}(t)$ to the excitation $\mathbf{E}(t')$ [2–5]:

$$\mathbf{P}(t) \triangleq \varepsilon_0 \, \chi^{(1)} * \mathbf{E}(t) = \varepsilon_0 \int_{\mathbb{R}} dt' \, \chi^{(1)}(t - t') \, \mathbf{E}(t'). \tag{2}$$

In other words, $\forall i \in \{x, y, z\}$:

$$P_i(t) = \varepsilon_0 \sum_{j=x,y,z} \int_{\mathbb{R}} dt' \, \chi_{ij}^{(1)}(t - t') E_j(t'). \tag{3}$$

This phenomenological relation reflects the fact that the polarization of the system at time t depends on the excitation at any previous time t'. Moreover, if the material is anisotropic, each component P_i of the polarization can depend on the three components $\{E_j\}_{j=x,y,z}$ of the electric field. The response function is actually a tensor which consists of a 3×3 matrix of response functions $\chi_{ij}^{(1)}(t)$. In Fourier space, the convolution product of Equation (2) can be simply written as a matrix product:

$$\mathbf{P}(\omega) = \varepsilon_0 \, \chi^{(1)}(\omega) \, \mathbf{E}(\omega), \tag{4}$$

where the Fourier transforms are here defined for any function f by:

$$f(\omega) \triangleq \int_{\mathbb{R}} f(t) \, e^{i\omega t} \, \mathrm{d}t \quad \text{and} \quad f(t) \triangleq \int_{\mathbb{R}} f(\omega) \, e^{-i\omega t} \, \frac{\mathrm{d}\omega}{2\pi}. \tag{5}$$

The functions $\chi_{ij}^{(1)}(\omega)$, so called first order dielectric susceptibilities, are the Fourier transforms of the response functions $\chi_{ij}(t)$. In the case of an isotropic material, $\chi^{(1)} = \chi^{(1)}\mathbf{1}$:

$$\mathbf{P}(\omega) = \varepsilon_0 \, \chi^{(1)}(\omega) \, \mathbf{E}(\omega). \tag{6}$$

A single scalar susceptibility is thus enough to describe the optical response of the system. Generally speaking, polarization can be considered as a secondary source of electric field. As oscillating dipoles, the microscopic components of moments $\boldsymbol{\mu} = \mathbf{P}(\omega)/N$ emit their own field, in-phase or out-of-phase with respect to the incident source field, and thereby affect the propagation of the latter. Hence, the response functions govern the propagation of electromagnetic waves in materials and are naturally involved in the description of refraction and absorption phenomena.

2.2. Refraction and Absorption

The propagation of light waves in dielectric materials is commonly described by the D'Alembert Equation [6]:

$$\nabla^2 \mathbf{E}(\mathbf{r}, \omega) + \frac{\omega^2}{c^2} \epsilon(\omega) \mathbf{E}(\mathbf{r}, \omega) = \mathbf{0}, \tag{7}$$

here given in Fourier space. It involves the dielectric permittivity of the material:

$$\epsilon(\omega) \triangleq 1 + \chi^{(1)}(\omega). \tag{8}$$

Considering the case of a wave propagating in an isotropic medium along the x direction, we show that [6]:

$$\mathbf{E}(\mathbf{r}, \omega) = \mathbf{E}_0(\omega) \, e^{iq(\omega)x} \text{ with } q^2(\omega) \triangleq \frac{\omega^2}{c^2}\epsilon(\omega). \tag{9}$$

The complex quantity $q(\omega) = q'(\omega) + iq''(\omega)$ gives rise to a propagation factor $e^{iq'(\omega)x}$ and a damping factor $e^{-q''(\omega)x}$. Actually, $q'(\omega)$ can be seen as the wave vector of light within the medium, which defines *the refractive index* of the material:

$$q'(\omega) \triangleq \frac{\omega}{c} n(\omega), \quad \text{with} \quad n(\omega) = \mathrm{Re}\left(\sqrt{\epsilon(\omega)}\right) = \mathrm{Re}\left(\sqrt{1 + \chi^{(1)}(\omega)}\right), \tag{10}$$

while $q''(\omega)$ characterizes the ability of the material to absorb light:

$$q''(\omega) = \frac{\omega \, \chi''(\omega)}{2c \, n(\omega)}. \tag{11}$$

The imaginary part of the linear susceptibility $\chi^{(1)} = \chi' + i\chi''$ is indeed involved in the absorbance of materials. As light intensity is given by $I = \langle |\mathbf{E}|^2 \rangle$, Equation (9) leads to the Beer–Lambert law for single-photon absorption:

$$I(x, \omega) = I(0, \omega)\, e^{-2q''(\omega)x} \implies \mathcal{A}(\omega) \doteq -\log \frac{I(x, \omega)}{I(0, \omega)} = \frac{x}{c \ln 10} \frac{\omega \chi''(\omega)}{n(\omega)}, \qquad (12)$$

relating in this way the absorbance $\mathcal{A}(\omega)$ of the system (along an optical path of length x) to the dielectric susceptibility. This relationship will be used in particular to extract the analytical expression of the susceptibility of materials from their absorption spectrum obtained by UV–visible spectrophotometry.

As a matter of fact, if the imaginary part $\chi''(\omega)$ of the susceptibility governs the phenomenon of absorption, its real part $\chi'(\omega)$ governs the phenomena of refraction and dispersion, that is to say all the phenomena of propagation without phase shift:

$$\chi'(\omega) \in \mathbb{R} \implies \arg\big(\varepsilon_0 \chi'(\omega) E_i(\omega)\big) = \arg(E_i(\omega)), \qquad (13)$$

while the imaginary part introduces a $\frac{\pi}{2}$ phase shift:

$$i\chi''(\omega) \in i\mathbb{R} \implies \arg\big(\varepsilon_0 i\chi''(\omega) E_i(\omega)\big) = \arg(E_i(\omega)) + \frac{\pi}{2}, \qquad (14)$$

for any component E_i of the electric field. Figure 2 shows the effect of this phase shift on the field transmitted by a dielectric material. This field results from the superposition of two contributions: the field $\mathbf{E}_r(\omega) \propto \mathbf{P}_r(\omega) \doteq \varepsilon_0 \chi'(\omega)\mathbf{E}(\omega)$, resulting from optical refraction, and the field $\mathbf{E}_a(\omega) \propto \mathbf{P}_a(\omega) \doteq \varepsilon_0 i\chi''(\omega)\mathbf{E}(\omega)$, resulting from absorption. Taking into account the $\frac{\pi}{2}$ phase shift which exists between the field $\mathbf{E}$ and the polarization $\mathbf{P}_a$, the field $\mathbf{E}_a$ is phase-shifted of π ($= 2 \times \frac{\pi}{2}$) compared to the field $\mathbf{E}_r$:

$$\mathbf{E} \xrightarrow{+0} \mathbf{P}_r \xrightarrow{+0} \mathbf{E}_r, \qquad \mathbf{E} \xrightarrow{+\pi/2} \mathbf{P}_a \xrightarrow{+\pi/2} \mathbf{E}_a. \qquad (15)$$

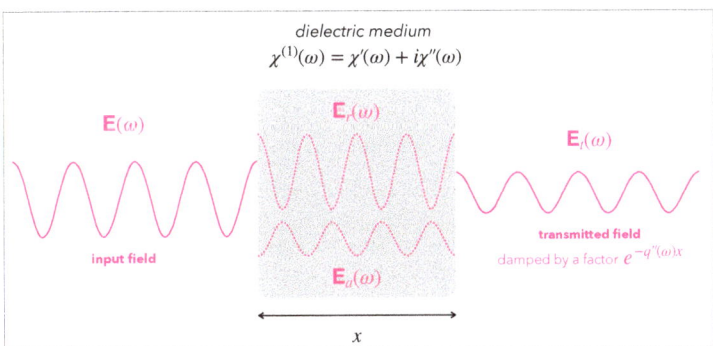

Figure 2. Wave propagation in a dielectric medium. Illustration of refraction and absorption phenomena within a dielectric system of susceptibility $\chi^{(1)}(\omega)$. The incident electric field $\mathbf{E}(\omega)$ generates a polarization $\mathbf{P}(\omega) = \varepsilon_0 \chi'(\omega)\mathbf{E}(\omega) + \varepsilon_0 i\chi''(\omega)\mathbf{E}(\omega)$. The real part of $\chi(\omega)$ results in the appearance of a field $\mathbf{E}_r(\omega)$ in phase with the incident electric field, while the imaginary part leads to the generation of an electric field $\mathbf{E}_a(\omega)$ in phase opposition. The destructive interference thus occurring gives rise to a transmitted electric field $\mathbf{E}_t(\omega)$ of weaker amplitude (damped by a factor $e^{-q''(\omega)x}$).

Therefore, these two electric fields add up in a destructive way. From the point of view of wave optics, absorption can thus be described as resulting from destructive interference. In other words, the function $\chi^{(1)}(\omega)$ measures the coherence of light as it propagates through a dielectric medium.

2.3. Scattering and Extinction

In the case of the propagation of electromagnetic waves through a population of spherical dielectric particles, some part of the light is not only affected by absorption and is deflected in all directions of space. We then speak of scattering [4,7]. From the point of view of geometric optics, this deviation can be explained by multiple reflections and refractions occurring at the particle boundary, as shown in Figure 3a. However, this approach is not realistic. It is indeed necessary to adopt the wave formalism of electromagnetism and to study Mie's theory to explain this scattering phenomenon [8], as shown schematically in Figure 3b.

When a light beam of incident intensity I_0 propagates through a population of particles of density N, some of the photons are absorbed while others are scattered. These are all lost photons, not indeed transmitted in the beam propagation direction. Since light intensity measures the photon flow within a beam, this results in an extinction cross-section σ_{ext} defined so that [7]:

$$\frac{\mathrm{d}I}{\mathrm{d}x} = -N\sigma_{\text{ext}}I(x), \quad \text{i.e.,} \quad I(x) = I(0)\,e^{-N\sigma_{\text{ext}}x}. \tag{16}$$

σ_{ext} actually measures the probability that a photon is absorbed or scattered by a particle:

$$\sigma_{\text{ext}} = \sigma_a + \sigma_s. \tag{17}$$

It is clear that Equation (16) generalizes the Beer–Lambert law. We can also identify the absorption cross-section:

$$\sigma_a(\omega) = \frac{2q''(\omega)}{N}. \tag{18}$$

Mie's theory tells us that the scattering cross-section of a spherical particle depends on the wavevector $q'(\omega)$ and on the polarizability $\alpha(\omega)$ of the particle [7]:

$$\sigma_s(\omega) = \frac{[q'(\omega)]^4}{6\pi}|\alpha(\omega)|^2. \tag{19}$$

As a reminder, this polarizability is nothing other than the microscopic counterpart of susceptibility:

$$\mathbf{P}(\omega) = \varepsilon_0\chi^{(1)}(\omega)\mathbf{E}(\omega) \longleftrightarrow \boldsymbol{\mu}(\omega) = \boldsymbol{\alpha}(\omega)\mathbf{E}_\ell(\omega), \tag{20}$$

where $\mathbf{E}_\ell$ denotes the local field applied to the particle of dipole moment $\boldsymbol{\mu}$.

Like diffraction, scattering significantly manifests itself when the wavelength is about the order of magnitude of the particle radius: $\lambda \lesssim R$. In the case of quantum dots, $\lambda \gg R \sim$ 1–10 nm. Thus, for the same reasons that it is possible to assume a uniform electric field at the nanoscale, we can reasonably neglect scattering with respect to absorption, provided that particles do not agglomerate to form scattering centres of a few hundred nanometers.

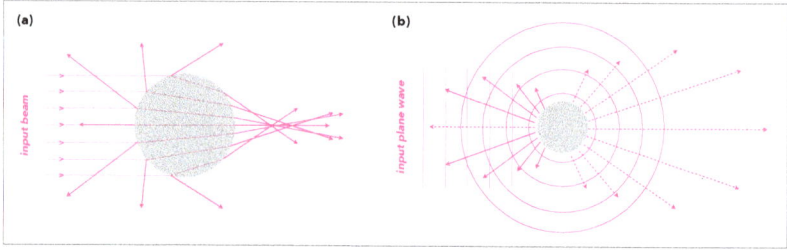

Figure 3. Geometric and wave description of light scattering. Sketch of the scattering process, (**a**) from geometric optics and, (**b**) from wave optics. The dotted arrows represent the intensity of the scattered light according to the scattering angle.

2.4. Extinction Spectroscopies

UV–visible and infrared spectroscopies are generally presented as absorption spectroscopies. To be quite rigorous, these are extinction spectroscopies. When the particles are large enough to scatter light, the Beer–Lambert law of absorbance must be adapted:

$$\mathcal{A}(\omega) \neq -\log \frac{I(x,\omega)}{I(0,\omega)} = \mathcal{A}(\omega) + \mathcal{S}(\omega). \tag{21}$$

While $\mathcal{A}(\omega) = \sigma_a(\omega) N x / \ln 10$ corresponds to absorbance, $\mathcal{S}(\omega)$ would be the 'scatterance' (term not used in the literature and defined here for the sake of clarity):

$$\mathcal{S}(\omega) \triangleq \frac{\sigma_s(\omega) N x}{\ln 10}. \tag{22}$$

This means that UV–visible and infrared spectroscopies, which consist of measuring the quantity $-\log \frac{I(x,\omega)}{I(0,\omega)}$ as a function of the wavelength $\lambda = 2\pi c/\omega$ or the wavenumber $\sigma = 1/\lambda$, are sensitive to light scattering. For instance, UV–visible spectroscopy allows highlighting and quantifying the aggregation of metallic or semiconductor nanoparticles when this indeed occurs [9,10].

3. Non-Linear Response of Anisotropic Media

The linear response theory satisfactorily describes the dielectric properties of matter when light does not excite the system into an anharmonic regime. In short, the excitation is not powerful enough to make the electrons and the nuclei explore potential energy surfaces far from their equilibrium (which is precisely characterized by harmonic potential wells). In contrast, when we probe matter with pulsed lasers, it is possible to achieve this new dielectric regime. It is therefore necessary to expand the optical response at higher orders of polarization.

3.1. Second Order Non-Linear Optical Processes

The phenomenological Relation (2) linking the polarization to the electric field can be considered as a first order truncated series expansion. Here, we introduce the second order term involved in the polarization:

$$\mathbf{P}(t) = \varepsilon_0 \, \chi^{(1)} * \mathbf{E}(t) + \mathbf{P}^{(2)}(t), \tag{23}$$

where the second order polarization $\mathbf{P}^{(2)}$ is quadratically dependent on the electric field. This non-linear term is often treated inappropriately, even in reference books [2,3,11]. It is often defined in frequency space (with complex exponential functions) whereas its true definition can only refers to the time evolution of the system, as written in Equation (23). The frequency spectrum of $\mathbf{P}^{(2)}(t)$ then truly derives from its Fourier transform.

First, the quadratic dependence of $\mathbf{P}^{(2)}(t)$ on the electric field results in a double convolution product involving a new response function $(t,t') \mapsto \chi^{(2)}(t,t')$ [4,5]:

$$\mathbf{P}^{(2)}(t) \triangleq \varepsilon_0 \, \chi^{(2)} * \mathbf{E} \otimes \mathbf{E}(t) = \varepsilon_0 \iint_{\mathbb{R}^2} dt_1 \, dt_2 \, \chi^{(2)}(t-t_1, t-t_2) \, \mathbf{E}(t_1) \otimes \mathbf{E}(t_2). \tag{24}$$

$\chi^{(2)}(t,t')$ is a third-rank tensor, i.e., a $3 \times 3 \times 3$ hyper-matrix of second order response functions $\chi_{ijk}^{(2)}(t,t')$. The tensor product $\otimes$ allows the compact writing of the relation:

$$P_i^{(2)}(t) = \varepsilon_0 \sum_{j,k=x,y,z} \iint_{\mathbb{R}^2} dt_1 \, dt_2 \, \chi_{ijk}^{(2)}(t-t_1, t-t_2) \, E_j(t_1) E_k(t_2). \tag{25}$$

As 2-argument functions, the second order response functions are associated to 2-argument susceptibilities deduced from double Fourier transforms [4,5]:

$$\chi^{(2)}(\omega_1, \omega_2) \triangleq \iint_{\mathbb{R}^2} d\tau_1 \ d\tau_2 \ \chi^{(2)}(\tau_1, \tau_2) \ e^{i(\omega_1 \tau_1 + \omega_2 \tau_2)}. \tag{26}$$

However, the transposition of equation (24) into Fourier space is not as obvious as in the linear case, for which we simply had $\mathbf{P}(\omega) = \varepsilon_0 \chi^{(1)}(\omega) \mathbf{E}(\omega)$. Here:

$$\mathbf{P}^{(2)}(\omega) = \int_{\mathbb{R}} dt \ \mathbf{P}^{(2)}(t) \ e^{i\omega t}, \tag{27}$$

giving:

$$\mathbf{P}^{(2)}(\omega) = \int_{\mathbb{R}} dt \iint_{\mathbb{R}^2} dt_1 \ dt_2 \ \varepsilon_0 \ \chi^{(2)}(t - t_1, t - t_2) \ \mathbf{E}(t_1) \otimes \mathbf{E}(t_2) \ e^{i\omega t}. \tag{28}$$

To simplify this expression, we choose to define the auxiliary function $\xi^{(2)}(\omega; t_1, t_2)$ as a (simple) Fourier transform of the response function $t \mapsto \chi^{(2)}(t - t_1, t - t_2)$:

$$\xi^{(2)}(\omega; t_1, t_2) \triangleq \int_{\mathbb{R}} dt \ \chi^{(2)}(t - t_1, t - t_2) \ e^{i\omega t} \tag{29}$$

In this case, Equation (28) becomes

$$\mathbf{P}^{(2)}(\omega) = \varepsilon_0 \iint_{\mathbb{R}^2} dt_1 \, dt_2 \ \xi^{(2)}(\omega; t_1, t_2) \ \mathbf{E}(t_1) \otimes \mathbf{E}(t_2) \tag{30}$$

$$= \varepsilon_0 \iint_{\mathbb{R}^2} \frac{d\omega_1}{2\pi} \frac{d\omega_2}{2\pi} \ \xi^{(2)}(\omega; \omega_1, \omega_2) \ \mathbf{E}(\omega_1) \otimes \mathbf{E}(\omega_2), \tag{31}$$

where $\xi^{(2)}(\omega; \omega_1, \omega_2)$ is nothing but the double Fourier transform of $\xi^{(2)}(\omega; t_1, t_2)$, with respect to the temporal variables t_1 and t_2. Equation (31) means that the wave generated by the medium at the frequency ω, via $\mathbf{P}^{(2)}(\omega)$, derives from a coupling governed by the tensor $\xi^{(2)}(\omega; \omega_1, \omega_2)$ between all the frequencies (ω_1, ω_2) available in the spectrum of $\mathbf{E}$. In other words, the non-linearity of the material makes it possible to couple two different frequencies (ω_1 and ω_2) into a third one (ω). This non-linearity therefore allows the system to generate new frequencies, which is prohibited by the theory of linear response. This property characterizes moreover all the non-linear processes: they are always *inelastic* (the output frequency is different from the input frequency).

While most of the reference books and articles confuse $\xi^{(2)}(\omega; \omega_1, \omega_2)$ and $\chi^{(2)}(\omega_1, \omega_2)$ [2–4,11], here we make explicit the mathematical relation between them and establish the rigorous description of the non-linear second order optical response (Figure 1). By combining Equations (26) and (29), we get:

$$\xi^{(2)}(\omega; t_1, t_2) = \iint_{\mathbb{R}^2} \frac{d\omega_1}{2\pi} \frac{d\omega_2}{2\pi} \ \chi^{(2)}(\omega_1, \omega_2) \ e^{i(\omega_1 t_1 + \omega_2 t_2)} \underbrace{\int_{\mathbb{R}} dt e^{i(\omega - \omega_1 - \omega_2)t}}_{= 2\pi\delta(\omega - \omega_1 - \omega_2))}. \tag{32}$$

From the definition of $\xi^{(2)}(\omega; \omega_1, \omega_2)$ as a double Fourier transform of $\xi^{(2)}(\omega; t_1, t_2)$, we therefore identify:

$$\xi^{(2)}(\omega; \omega_1, \omega_2) = 2\pi \, \chi^{(2)}(\omega_1, \omega_2) \, \delta(\omega - \omega_1 - \omega_2). \tag{33}$$

Therefore, the tensor $\xi^{(2)}(\omega; \omega_1, \omega_2)$ can be interpreted as the spectral weight associated with the generation of the frequency ω by the non-linear coupling of frequencies ω_1 and ω_2, so that $\omega = \omega_1 + \omega_2$. It is not equal to the susceptibility $\chi^{(2)}(\omega_1, \omega_2)$, which encodes for its part all the possible ways to couple two frequencies ω_1 and ω_2 available in the input light spectrum. As shown in Figure 4, the dielectric medium radiates in this way new fields at the frequencies:

- $\omega = \omega_1 + \omega_2$, via $\chi^{(2)}(\omega_1, \omega_2)$: for SFG, sum-frequency generation;

- $\omega = \omega_1 - \omega_2$, via $\chi^{(2)}(\omega_1, -\omega_2)$: for DFG, difference-frequency generation;
- $\omega = 2\omega_i$, via $\chi^{(2)}(\omega_i, \omega_i)$, for SHG, second harmonic generation;
- $\omega = 0$, via $\chi^{(2)}(\omega_i, -\omega_i)$, corresponding to optical rectification.

Finally, Equations (31) and (33) allow us to give a synthetic description of the non-linear second order optical processes. These are governed by:

$$\mathbf{P}^{(2)}(\omega) = \int_{\mathbb{R}} \frac{d\omega'}{2\pi} \, \mathbf{P}^{(2)}(\omega', \omega - \omega'), \tag{34}$$

with:

$$\mathbf{P}^{(2)}(\omega_1, \omega_2) \doteq \varepsilon_0 \, \chi^{(2)}(\omega_1, \omega_2) \, \mathbf{E}(\omega_1) \otimes \mathbf{E}(\omega_2). \tag{35}$$

This last equation constitutes the quadratic counterpart of the linear constitutive relation $\mathbf{P}(\omega) = \varepsilon_0 \chi^{(1)}(\omega) \mathbf{E}(\omega)$.

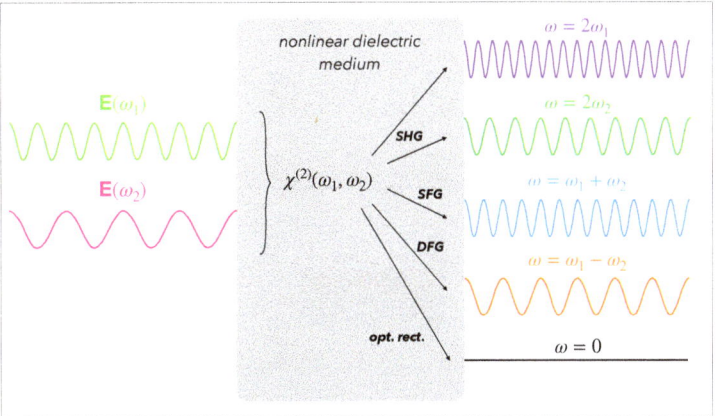

Figure 4. Second order non-linear optical processes. Sketch of the processes of second harmonic generation (SHG), sum-frequency generation (SFG) and difference-frequency generation (DFG). These are driven by the second order dielectric susceptibility $\chi^{(2)}(\omega_1, \omega_2)$ of the material, which couples two input frequencies ω_1 and ω_2 to generate new signals.

3.2. Symmetry Rules

While all dielectric materials exhibit a linear response to optical excitation, they do not necessarily all respond non-linearly. Within the electric dipole approximation, to have a non-zero susceptibility $\chi^{(2)}$, the material must not be centrosymmetric [2–5]. Indeed, let us examine the case of a centrosymmetric system for which $\mathbf{P}^{(2)}(\omega_1, \omega_2) = \varepsilon_0 \, \chi^{(2)}(\omega_1, \omega_2) \, \mathbf{E}(\omega_1) \otimes \mathbf{E}(\omega_2)$. The physical transformation which reverses the orientation of the electric field:

$$\phi : \begin{cases} \mathbb{R}^3 & \longrightarrow & \mathbb{R}^3 \\ \mathbf{E} & \longmapsto & -\mathbf{E}' \end{cases} \tag{36}$$

similarly transforms the polarization, by centrosymmetry of causes and effects: $\phi(\mathbf{P}) = -\mathbf{P}$. However, at the same time:

$$
\begin{aligned}
\phi(\mathbf{P})^{(2)}(\omega_1, \omega_2) &= \varepsilon_0 \, \chi^{(2)}(\omega_1, \omega_2) \, \phi(\mathbf{E})(\omega_1) \otimes \phi(\mathbf{E})(\omega_2) \\
&= \varepsilon_0 \, \chi^{(2)}(\omega_1, \omega_2) \, [-\mathbf{E}(\omega_1)] \otimes [-\mathbf{E}(\omega_2)] \\
&= \varepsilon_0 \, \chi^{(2)}(\omega_1, \omega_2) \, \mathbf{E}(\omega_1) \otimes \mathbf{E}(\omega_2) \\
&= \mathbf{P}^{(2)}(\omega_1, \omega_2).
\end{aligned} \tag{37}
$$

We must therefore both satisfy centrosymmetry, which implies $\phi(\mathbf{P})^{(2)} = -\mathbf{P}^{(2)}$, and Equation (38), which implies $\phi(\mathbf{P})^{(2)} = \mathbf{P}^{(2)}$. In other words, $\mathbf{P}^{(2)} = 0$, and $\chi^{(2)} = 0$: centrosymmetric materials cannot be the site of second order non-linear processes.

Apart from the case of anisotropic crystals and chiral structures which often constitute good non-linear materials, second order non-linearities can arise, first, at the interface between two dielectric media (given the breakdown of symmetry implied by this geometry) or, second, from the quadrupolar response of bulk materials. This is also why sum-frequency generation is very useful for the study of metal [12] and semiconductor [13] nanoparticles. Deposited on a substrate probed by pulsed lasers (Figure 5a), these nanoparticles can be analysed in a fine way given that the SFG signal is specific and characteristic of the interface: the would-be pollutants distributed in volume do not contribute to the signal. In addition, as nanoparticles are chemically functionalized on their surface (Figure 5b), it is also possible to examine the interactions at the interface between them and their surrounding molecules [14].

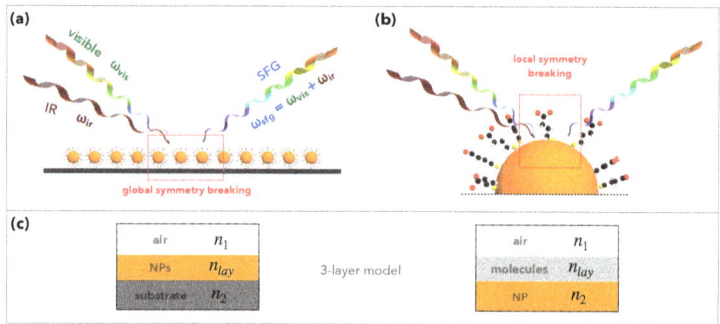

Figure 5. Sum-frequency generation at nanostructured interfaces. Schematic representation of the SFG process in the case of functionalized nanoparticles grafted on a solid substrate. The two input frequencies belong to the visible ($\omega_1 = \omega_{\mathrm{vis}}$) and the infrared ($\omega_2 = \omega_{\mathrm{IR}}$) spectral ranges. This configuration is characterized by (**a**) a breaking of the global centrosymmetry at the macroscopic scale of the substrate and (**b**) a breaking of the local centrosymmetry at the surface of nanoparticles. (**c**) These two interfaces can be modelled as a 3-layer surface characterized by three refractive indices n_1, n_2 and n_{lay}.

3.3. Sum-Frequency Generation at Interfaces

Since the SFG process is specific to interfaces, we choose to base this Review on the above-mentioned example of recent studies of nanoparticles [12,13] deposited on solid substrates, as represented in Figure 5. The aim of this section is therefore to establish the practical equations which allow us to interpret the SFG measurements carried out on such flat samples.

If we consider the generic situation presented in Figure 6, we notice that the sample geometry is invariant by any translation in the plane (x, y) and any azimuthal rotation around the z-axis. Therefore, the tensor $\chi^{(2)}$ of the system exhibit only four non-zero and independent coefficients for symmetry reasons [15,16]:

$$(\mathrm{i})\ \chi^{(2)}_{zzz},\ (\mathrm{ii})\ \chi^{(2)}_{xxz} = \chi^{(2)}_{yyz},\ (\mathrm{iii})\ \chi^{(2)}_{zxx} = \chi^{(2)}_{zyy}\ \mathrm{and}\ (\mathrm{iv})\ \chi^{(2)}_{xzx} = \chi^{(2)}_{yzy}. \tag{38}$$

Indeed, as the z-axis is the axis along which the centrosymmetry is broken, all the components $\chi^{(2)}_{ijk}$ which do not contain at least one z index are zero: 8 components are first removed. Owing to invariance of translation and isotropy within the plane (x, y), all the components containing x and y as indices are zero: 6 more components are removed. Since every plane containing the z-axis is a plane of symmetry and that $(-E_z)^2 = E_z^2$, all the components with two z indices are zero: we get rid of 6 other components. Thus remains $27 - 8 - 6 - 6 = 7$ components, among which the permutation $(x \leftrightarrow y)$ is an identity, due to the 2D-isotropy of the planar geometry. As a result, Equation (38) enumerates the 4 interesting terms.

Moreover, this translational invariance implies a phase matching condition on the parallel components (with respect to the surface plane) of the wavevectors of the two visible and infrared beams which probe the surface [17]:

$$\mathbf{q}_{\|,\mathrm{vis}} + \mathbf{q}_{\|,\mathrm{ir}} = \mathbf{q}_{\|,\mathrm{sfg}}, \tag{39}$$

where we write $\mathbf{q}_{\mathrm{vis}}$, $\mathbf{q}_{\mathrm{ir}}$ and $\mathbf{q}_{\mathrm{sfg}}$, the respective wavevectors of the visible, infrared and SFG beams. In general, we will always denote wavevectors by the letter $\mathbf{q}$. They are defined by their norm, by virtue of Equation (10):

$$|\mathbf{q}| \doteq q'(\omega) = \frac{\omega}{c} n(\omega), \tag{40}$$

and directed according to the direction of propagation of the wave. The momentum $\hbar\mathbf{q}$ is the physical quantity which must be conserved when there is translational invariance, hence the condition of phase agreement (39). This allows us to determine the angle θ_{sfg} under which the SFG signal is emitted by reflection:

$$\theta_{\mathrm{sfg}} = \arcsin \frac{\omega_{\mathrm{vis}} \sin \theta_{\mathrm{vis}} + \omega_{\mathrm{ir}} \sin \theta_{\mathrm{ir}}}{\omega_{\mathrm{vis}} + \omega_{\mathrm{ir}}}, \tag{41}$$

As the beams propagate though air, we consider that $n(\omega) = 1$.

During SFG spectroscopy measurements, we commonly select two particular polarizations of the incident beams: the polarization $\mathcal{P}$, for which the electric field is parallel to the plane of incidence (x, z), and the polarization $\mathcal{S}$ (from the German senkrecht, meaning perpendicular), for which the electric field is normal to the plane of incidence. These polarizations are depicted in the Figure 6 and characterized by the unit vectors:

$$\mathbf{u}_{\mathcal{P}}(\theta_u) = \cos \theta_u \, \mathbf{u}_x + \sin \theta_u \, \mathbf{u}_z \text{ and } \mathbf{u}_{\mathcal{S}}(\theta_u) = \mathbf{u}_y, \tag{42}$$

where the index u refers to the visible or the infrared. The SFG signal can be detected in polarization $\mathcal{P}$ or $\mathcal{S}$:

$$\mathbf{u}_{\mathcal{P}}(\theta_{\mathrm{sfg}}) = \cos \theta_{\mathrm{sfg}} \, \mathbf{u}_x + \sin \theta_{\mathrm{sfg}} \, \mathbf{u}_z \text{ and } \mathbf{u}_{\mathcal{S}}(\theta_{\mathrm{sfg}}) = \mathbf{u}_y. \tag{43}$$

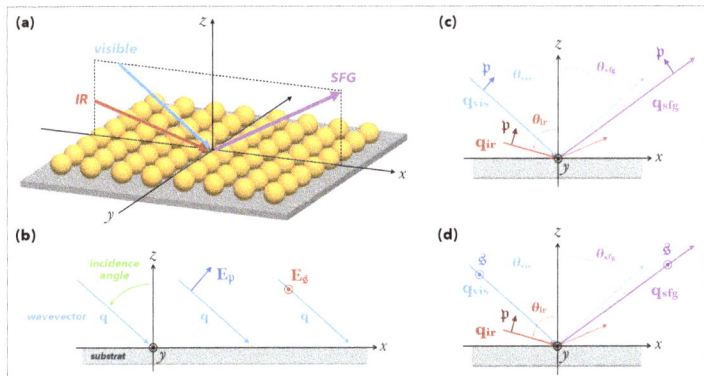

Figure 6. SFG process at flat interfaces. (a) Schematic representation of SFG at the surface of a nanostructured sample. The visible, IR and SFG beams belong to the same plane of incidence (x, z). (b) Definition of the $\mathcal{P}$ and $\mathcal{S}$ polarizations, with respect to the plane of incidence (x, z). (c) Directions and polarizations of the beams in $[\mathcal{P} : \mathcal{P}\mathcal{P}]$ configuration. (d) Directions and polarizations of the beams in $[\mathcal{S} : \mathcal{S}\mathcal{P}]$ configuration.

As far as we are concerned, we are only interested in the two configurations given in Figure 6c,d, namely the configuration $[\mathcal{P} : \mathcal{PP}]$, for which all the beams are $\mathcal{P}$-polarized, and the configuration $[\mathcal{S} : \mathcal{SP}]$, for which the visible is $\mathcal{S}$-polarized, the infrared $\mathcal{P}$-polarized and SFG detected in $\mathcal{S}$ polarization. The choice of these polarization triplets actually depends on the nature of the sample substrate: to obtain an optimum SFG signal, it is important to use the configuration which maximizes the substrate reflectivity, as we usually acquire the SFG signal reflected by the surface.

In $[\mathcal{P} : \mathcal{PP}]$ polarization scheme (SFG, Vis and IR beams, respectively), the laser excitation consists of the superposition of two monochromatic visible and infrared waves polarized according to $\mathbf{u}_{\mathcal{P}}$:

$$\mathbf{E}(t) = E_{\text{vis}} \cos(\omega_{\text{vis}} t) \, \mathbf{u}_{\mathcal{P}}(\theta_{\text{vis}}) + E_{\text{ir}} \cos(\omega_{\text{ir}} t) \, \mathbf{u}_{\mathcal{P}}(\theta_{\text{ir}}), \tag{44}$$

while in $[\mathcal{S} : \mathcal{SP}]$ configuration:

$$\mathbf{E}(t) = E_{\text{vis}} \cos(\omega_{\text{vis}} t) \, \mathbf{u}_{\mathcal{S}}(\theta_{\text{vis}}) + E_{\text{ir}} \cos(\omega_{\text{ir}} t) \, \mathbf{u}_{\mathcal{P}}(\theta_{\text{ir}}). \tag{45}$$

In the first case, we measure the $\mathcal{P}$-component of the SFG field generated by the 2nd order polarization. Therefore, the intensity of the SFG signal in $[\mathcal{P} : \mathcal{PP}]$ is determined by the scalar quantity:

$$P^{(2)}_{\mathcal{P}:\mathcal{PP}}(\omega_{\text{sfg}}) \triangleq \mathbf{u}_{\mathcal{P}}(\theta_{\text{sfg}}) \cdot \mathbf{P}^{(2)}(\omega_{\text{sfg}}). \tag{46}$$

Taking into account the expression of the electric field (45), with Equations (34) and (35) relating $\mathbf{P}^{(2)}(\omega)$ to the electric field via the second order susceptibility, we obtain:

$$P^{(2)}_{\mathcal{P}:\mathcal{PP}}(\omega_{\text{sfg}}) = \frac{\pi \varepsilon_0}{2} \, E_{\text{vis}} E_{\text{ir}} \, \chi^{(2)}_{\mathcal{P}:\mathcal{PP}}(\omega_{\text{vis}}, \omega_{\text{ir}}), \tag{47}$$

involving the effective second order susceptibility:

$$
\begin{aligned}
\chi^{(2)}_{\mathcal{P}:\mathcal{PP}}(\omega_{\text{vis}}, \omega_{\text{ir}}) \;=\; & -\cos\theta_{\text{sfg}} \left(\cos\theta_{\text{vis}} \sin\theta_{\text{ir}} \, \chi^{(2)}_{xxz}(\omega_{\text{vis}}, \omega_{\text{ir}}) + \sin\theta_{\text{vis}} \cos\theta_{\text{ir}} \, \chi^{(2)}_{xzx}(\omega_{\text{vis}}, \omega_{\text{ir}}) \right) \\
& + \sin\theta_{\text{sfg}} \left(\cos\theta_{\text{vis}} \cos\theta_{\text{ir}} \, \chi^{(2)}_{zxx}(\omega_{\text{vis}}, \omega_{\text{ir}}) + \sin\theta_{\text{vis}} \sin\theta_{\text{ir}} \, \chi^{(2)}_{zzz}(\omega_{\text{vis}}, \omega_{\text{ir}}) \right).
\end{aligned}
$$

This result is consistent with the literature [17], with the difference that we have not taken into account the Local Field correction factors $L_{ijk}(\omega_{\text{vis}}, \omega_{\text{ir}})$ which must strictly multiply $\chi^{(2)}_{ijk}(\omega_{\text{vis}}, \omega_{\text{ir}})$. These Local Field correction factors account for the reflectivity and optical dispersion of the sample. They are introduced in the next section. In the case of the $[\mathcal{S} : \mathcal{SP}]$ configuration, the equations are simplified:

$$P^{(2)}_{\mathcal{S}:\mathcal{SP}}(\omega_{\text{sfg}}) = \frac{\pi \varepsilon_0}{2} \, E_{\text{vis}} E_{\text{ir}} \, \chi^{(2)}_{\mathcal{S}:\mathcal{SP}}(\omega_{\text{vis}}, \omega_{\text{ir}}), \tag{48}$$

with:

$$\chi^{(2)}_{\mathcal{S}:\mathcal{SP}}(\omega_{\text{vis}}, \omega_{\text{ir}}) = \sin\theta_{\text{ir}} \, \chi^{(2)}_{xxz}(\omega_{\text{vis}}, \omega_{\text{ir}}). \tag{49}$$

The SFG intensity is then proportional to the square norm of the scalar polarization, which results in [17]:

$$I(\omega_{\text{sfg}}) \;\propto\; \frac{\omega_{\text{sfg}}^2}{\cos^2\theta_{\text{sfg}}} \, |\chi^{(2)}_{\text{eff}}(\omega_{\text{vis}}, \omega_{\text{ir}})|^2 \, I(\omega_{\text{vis}}) \, I(\omega_{\text{ir}}), \tag{50}$$

where $\chi^{(2)}_{\text{eff}} = \chi^{(2)}_{\mathcal{P}:\mathcal{PP}}$ or $\chi^{(2)}_{\mathcal{S}:\mathcal{SP}}$, depending on the polarization configuration, and $I(\omega_{\text{vis}})$ and $I(\omega_{\text{ir}})$ designate the intensities of the two incident beams. The measurement of the

SFG intensity thus enables to extract the square norm of the effective susceptibility $\chi_{\text{eff}}^{(2)}$, but not directly the susceptibilities $\chi_{ijk}^{(2)}$.

3.4. Local Field Correction Factors: Light Intensity Modulation by Interface Symmetry

To be completely rigorous in our interpretations, we must take into account the influence of Local Field correction factors on the SFG response. We have omitted them so far, but their contribution is generally not negligible. In $[\mathcal{P} : \mathcal{PP}]$ configuration, these factors, noted L_{ijk}, modulate the susceptibilities $\chi_{ijk}^{(2)}$ as follows:

$$
\begin{aligned}
\chi_{\mathcal{P}:\mathcal{PP}}^{(2)} = \quad & -L_{xxz} \, \cos\theta_{\text{sfg}} \, \cos\theta_{\text{vis}} \, \sin\theta_{\text{ir}} \, \chi_{xxz}^{(2)} \\
& -L_{xzx} \, \cos\theta_{\text{sfg}} \, \sin\theta_{\text{vis}} \, \cos\theta_{\text{ir}} \, \chi_{xzx}^{(2)} \\
& +L_{zxx} \, \sin\theta_{\text{sfg}} \, \cos\theta_{\text{vis}} \, \cos\theta_{\text{ir}} \, \chi_{zxx}^{(2)} \\
& +L_{zzz} \, \sin\theta_{\text{sfg}} \, \sin\theta_{\text{vis}} \, \sin\theta_{\text{ir}} \, \chi_{zzz}^{(2)}.
\end{aligned}
\tag{51}
$$

They account for the refraction and reflection processes between the different layers of which the interface is made. In the case of typical interfaces, we use the 3-layer model, as shown in Figure 5c. Hence, the Fresnel coefficients can be factorized in the form $L_{ijk}(\omega_{\text{vis}}, \omega_{\text{ir}}) = F_{ii}(\omega_{\text{vis}} + \omega_{\text{ir}}) \, F_{jj}(\omega_{\text{vis}}) \, F_{kk}(\omega_{\text{ir}})$, with [17]:

$$
F_{xx}(\omega_u) = \frac{2 \, n_1(\omega_u) \cos\theta_u^{\text{T}}}{n_1(\omega_u) \cos\theta_u^{\text{T}} + n_2(\omega_u) \cos\theta_u},
\tag{52}
$$

$$
F_{yy}(\omega_u) = \frac{2 \, n_1(\omega_u) \cos\theta_u}{n_1(\omega_u) \cos\theta_u + n_2(\omega_u) \cos\theta_u^{\text{T}}},
\tag{53}
$$

and:

$$
F_{zz}(\omega_u) = \frac{2 \, n_2(\omega_u) \cos\theta_u}{n_1(\omega_u) \cos\theta_u^{\text{T}} + n_2(\omega_u) \cos\theta_u} \left(\frac{n_1(\omega_u)}{n_{\text{lay}}(\omega_u)} \right)^2.
\tag{54}
$$

The indices u refer to the visible, infrared or SFG. It is worth noting that:

$$
\theta_{\text{vis}} = 55°, \quad \theta_{\text{ir}} = 65°, \quad \theta_{\text{sfg}} = \arcsin\left(\frac{\omega_{\text{vis}} \sin\theta_{\text{vis}} + \omega_{\text{ir}} \sin\theta_{\text{ir}}}{\omega_{\text{vis}} + \omega_{\text{ir}}} \right),
\tag{55}
$$

and the transmission angle of each beam is deduced from Snell-Descartes laws:

$$
\theta_u^{\text{T}} = \arcsin\left(\frac{n_1(\omega_u) \sin\theta_u}{n_2(\omega_u)} \right).
\tag{56}
$$

3.5. Third Order Non-Linear Optical Processes

Beyond second order, the optical processes of the third order are no longer governed by the geometry of the dielectric media and do not require any particular breaking of centrosymmetry: all materials can exhibit a third order contribution. In addition, most of the 3rd order processes are scattering processes since they do not involve phase matching condition, which is quite different from the 2nd order processes.

These processes include Raman scattering and fluorescence [2–4], which are concomitant processes. In both cases, a pump beam at frequency ω_p excites the system. The spectrum $J(\omega)$ of the light emitted by inelastic process ($\omega \neq \omega_p$) is measured to obtain electronic (fluorescence) or vibrational (Raman, in the framework of Figure 7 for molecular optical spectroscopy) information. Formally, for a three-state system $|g\rangle, |v\rangle$ and $|e\rangle$, illustrated in Figure 7, the susceptibility $\chi^{(3)}$ which governs inelastic processes of order 3 actually involves two factors [4]:

$$\chi^{(3)}(\omega_p, -\omega_p, \omega) \propto \underbrace{\frac{1}{\omega_{ev} - \omega + \imath\gamma_{ev}}}_{\substack{\text{fluorescence :} \\ \text{Lorentzian resonance}}} \left(\text{constant} - \underbrace{\frac{i}{\omega_{vg} - (\omega_p - \omega) - \imath\gamma_{vg}}}_{\text{Raman scattering}} \right), \tag{57}$$

where γ_{ev} and γ_{vg} denote the relaxation rates associated with the transitions $(e \to v)$ and $(v \to g)$. The first factor is resonant for $\omega = \omega_{ev}$: the measured optical signal corresponds to the transition from the electronic state $|e\rangle$ (excited) to the vibrational state $|v\rangle$ (fundamental), characteristic of a relaxation by fluorescence (Figure 7a). The second factor resonates at $\omega = \omega_p - \omega_{vg}$: the associated signal corresponds to a vibrational excitation of the system; the pump transfers a part of its energy ω_p, in this case the quantity ω_{vg}, to stimulate the vibrational state $|v\rangle$ (Figure 7b). This is the Stokes Raman process, from which we distinguish the anti-Stokes Raman process, described by $\chi^{(3)}(\omega_p, -\omega_p, -\omega)$ and giving a signal at $\omega = \omega_p + \omega_{vg}$ (Figure 7c). While fluorescence is a process that occurs between real electronic states, Raman scattering involves virtual states. As such, fluorescence can be qualified as a resonant scattering process whereas Raman scattering is a non-electronically resonant process.

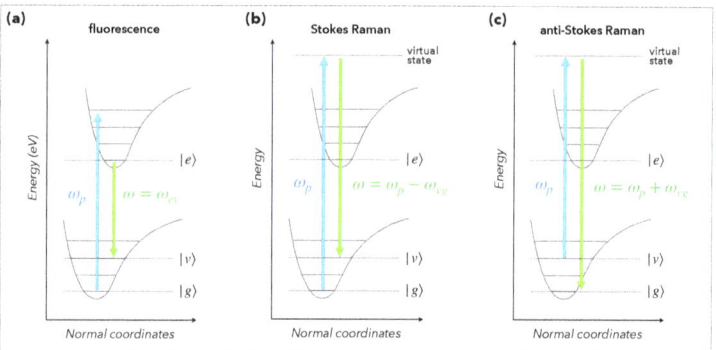

Figure 7. Fluorescence and Raman scattering. Illustration of third order non-linear processes: (**a**) fluorescence, (**b**) Stokes Raman scattering and (**c**) anti-Stokes Raman scattering. We note $|g\rangle$ the ground state, $|v\rangle$ a vibrational state within the ground state, and $|e\rangle$ an electronic excited state. The definition of normal coordinates is given in Section 4.1 in the case of molecules.

Furthermore, there are other third order non-linear processes, among which we count the optical Kerr effect, two-photon absorption (via $\chi^{(3)}(\omega, -\omega, \omega)$), third harmonic generation (via $\chi^{(3)}(\omega, \omega, \omega)$) and sum-frequency generation under static field (via $\chi^{(3)}(\omega_1, \omega_2, 0)$) [2–4,18,19].

4. Vibrational Spectroscopies

In physical chemistry, molecular SFG vibrational spectroscopy was established experimentally in 1987 by Y.R. Shen at Berkeley (USA) through its three seminal papers published on pentadecanoic acid [20,21] and coumarin monolayers [22]. SFG spectroscopy is used in many applications such as (but not only) for the study of electrochemical [23–26] and catalytic [27–29] processes at liquid/solid and gas/solid interfaces. In the recent literature, SFG spectroscopy is intensively performed for the study of the water/air interface [30–32] or water/solid interface [33,34]. SFG allows in particular to examine the molecular organization of these interfaces, in presence or absence of organic pollutants [35,36], the formation of micellar complexes at the surface during the addition of various surfactants [37], or even the ultra-fast dynamics of water molecules near the free surface [38]. This opens up the

SFG to the study of biological systems (among which lipid layers are emblematic [39–41]), with the objective to obtain structural information on the biological molecules (for peptides and proteins, see a recent exhaustive review [42]) located at the liquid/air or liquid/solid interfaces (e.g., conformational order, orientation of functional groups and chirality [43–46]).

SFG spectroscopy is a technique dedicated to the study of vibroelectronic couplings [47–55]. Indeed, it combines a visible excitation, which stimulates electronic transitions in materials such as metals or semiconductors, and an infrared excitation, which allows to simultaneously perform vibrational spectroscopy of organic species. SFG spectroscopy (2nd order process) therefore comes within the scope of vibrational spectroscopies, alongside infrared absorption (linear or 1st order process) and Raman scattering (3rd order process). We recall here the formalism used to describe the vibration modes of molecules and, in order to contextualize the particular place occupied by SFG spectroscopy, we compare these three spectroscopic probes.

4.1. Molecular Vibrations

Molecules can be mathematically described as a collection of N elastically bonded atoms. We denote by $\mathbf{r}_p = (x_p, y_p, z_p)$, $p \in [\![1, N]\!]$, the displacement vector of the p-th atom in the reference frame of the centre of mass of the molecule. This vector is defined with respect to the equilibrium position of each atom. To describe the vibrations of the molecule, a first change of coordinates must be done. We use the mass-weighted Cartesian coordinates $\{q_n\}_{n=1}^{3N}$ [56]:

$$
\begin{aligned}
q_1 &= \sqrt{m_1}x_1 \quad q_4 = \sqrt{m_2}x_2 \\
q_2 &= \sqrt{m_1}y_1 \quad q_5 = \sqrt{m_2}y_2 \quad \cdots \\
q_3 &= \sqrt{m_1}z_1 \quad q_6 = \sqrt{m_2}z_2
\end{aligned}
\tag{58}
$$

These mass-weighted coordinates make it possible to easily express the kinetic energy:

$$
T(\{q_n\}) = \frac{1}{2}\sum_n \dot{q}_n^2.
\tag{59}
$$

The elastic bond between the atoms of the molecule results from the limited development of their potential interaction energy in the vicinity of their equilibrium positions [56]:

$$
V(\{q_n\}) = V(\{0\}) + \sum_n \left(\frac{\partial V}{\partial q_n}\right)_{\{0\}} q_n + \frac{1}{2}\sum_{n,m}\left(\frac{\partial^2 V}{\partial q_n \partial q_m}\right)_{\{0\}} q_n q_m.
\tag{60}
$$

By setting the zero energy such that $V(\{0\}) = 0$, and since the potential energy reaches its minimum at equilibrium, i.e., $\left(\frac{\partial V}{\partial q_n}\right)_{\{0\}} = 0$:

$$
V(\{q_n\}) = \frac{1}{2}\sum_{n,m} f_{nm}\, q_n q_m \text{ with } f_{nm} \triangleq \left(\frac{\partial^2 V}{\partial q_n \partial q_m}\right)_{\{0\}}.
\tag{61}
$$

The Euler–Lagrange dynamic equation thus leads to $3N$ coupled differential equations:

$$
\frac{\mathrm{d}}{\mathrm{d}t}\left(\frac{\partial T}{\partial \dot{q}_j}\right) + \frac{\partial V}{\partial q_j} = 0 \implies \ddot{q}_n(t) + \sum_m f_{nm}\, q_m(t) = 0,
\tag{62}
$$

which admit solutions of the form $q_n^v(t) = q_{n,0}^v \cos(\omega_v t)$, where ω_v^2 is an eigenvalue of the matrix $f = (f_{nm})$, i.e., $\sum_m f_{nm} q_m = \omega_v^2 q_n$, and $q_{n,0}^v$ a constant depending on the initial conditions. The scalar quantities ω_v correspond to the vibration frequencies of the normal modes $|v\rangle = \{q_n^v\}_{n=1}^{3N}$ which diagonalize the matrix f of inter-atomic interactions. These are also associated with the normal coordinates $\{Q_v\}$ defined so that the potential energy explicitly reflects the existence of an elastic interaction between the atoms of the molecule:

$$
V = \frac{1}{2}\sum_v \omega_v^2 Q_v^2.
\tag{63}
$$

It can also be shown that these normal coordinates are linear combinations of the mass-weighted coordinates [56]. By noting $l = (l_{nv})$ the basis change matrix:

$$Q_v = \sum_n l_{nv} q_n \propto \cos(\omega_v t). \tag{64}$$

This means that each specific vibration mode consists of a collective oscillation of its atoms. When a molecule vibrates, all of its atoms oscillate at the same frequency and pass through their equilibrium position at the same time. We generally distinguish two classes of normal modes, represented in Figure 8: stretching and angular distorsion. In the cases of hydrogen, carbon, nitrogen and oxygen, which are light atoms abundant in organic species, the modes of angular distorsion, whose wavenumbers do not exceed 1500 cm^{-1}, are much less energetic than the stretching modes, which can be around 4000 cm^{-1} (Figure 9).

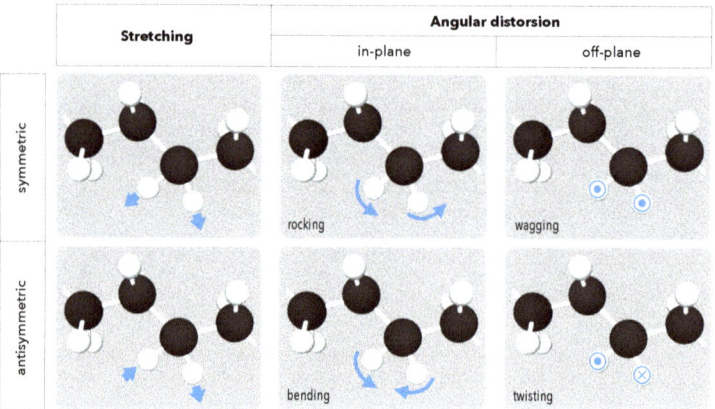

Figure 8. Normal vibration modes. Schematic representation of the different vibration modes observed within molecules. Here we take the example of CH$_2$ chemical group.

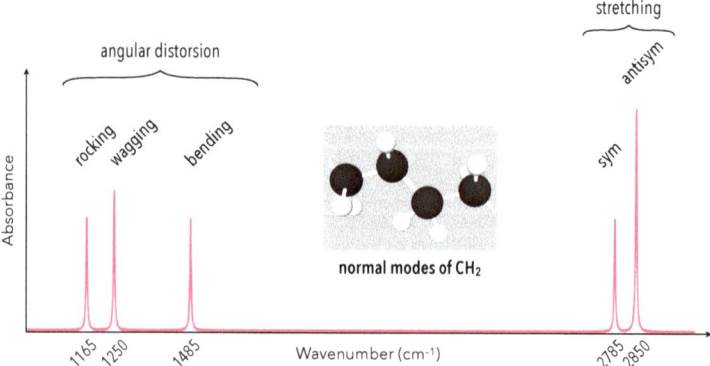

Figure 9. Infrared spectroscopy of methylene. Typical shape of the IR spectrum associated with C−H vibration modes within CH$_2$ groups.

4.2. Transition Dipole Moments and Susceptibility

Until now, we have only considered the classical definition of the dipole moment μ. In quantum mechanics, this physical quantity has a corresponding operator described by the matrix (μ_{nm}), where n and m label the set of quantum states:

$$\mu_{nm} \triangleq \langle n|\mu|m \rangle. \tag{65}$$

We speak in this case of transition dipole moment, each μ_{nm} corresponding to the dipole moment that the system acquires when it is promoted from state $|n\rangle$ to state $|m\rangle$. The selection rules of the different spectroscopies directly derive from these transition dipole moments, allowing or prohibiting certain optical transitions. In the case of a molecular vibration $|v\rangle$, the dipole moment $\mu(t)$ can be expanded in the vicinity of the equilibrium position $Q_v = 0$ as follows:

$$\mu(t) = \mu^{(0)} + \left(\frac{\partial\mu}{\partial Q_v}\right)_0 Q_v(t). \tag{66}$$

Denoting the ground state by $|0\rangle$, and assuming that the equilibrium is characterized by a zero dipole moment, i.e., $\langle 0|\mu^{(0)}|v\rangle = 0$, we see that the transition moments only depend on the variation of μ with respect to the normal coordinates [56]:

$$\mu_{0v} = \left(\frac{\partial\mu}{\partial Q_v}\right)_0 \langle 0|Q_v(t)|v\rangle = \sqrt{\frac{\hbar}{2\omega_v}}\left(\frac{\partial\mu}{\partial Q_v}\right)_0. \tag{67}$$

For a quantum system, the linear susceptibility $\chi^{(1)}(\omega)$ depends on the transition moments. Kubo's theorem (which results from the quantum treatment of the theory of linear response via the density matrix formalism) indeed gives [57]:

$$\chi_{ij}^{(1)}(t) = iN\theta(t)\langle[\mu_i(t), \mu_j]\rangle_0, \tag{68}$$

where $\theta(t)$ is the Heaviside function. The mean value is defined with respect to the density matrix $\rho^{(0)}$ characterizing the statistic of the system at equilibrium. For any operator A:

$$\langle A\rangle_0 \hat{=} \mathrm{tr}\left(\rho^{(0)}A\right). \tag{69}$$

This leads to the well-known expression [2–4,58]:

$$\chi_{ij}^{(1)}(\omega) = -\frac{N}{\hbar\varepsilon_0}\sum_{n,m}\rho_{mm}^{(0)}\left[\frac{\mu_{mn}^i\mu_{nm}^j}{\omega - \omega_{nm} + i\gamma_{nm}} - \frac{\mu_{nm}^i\mu_{mn}^j}{\omega - \omega_{mn} + i\gamma_{mn}}\right], \tag{70}$$

which relates the transition dipole moments to the linear susceptibility. Taking into account Equation (67), molecular systems are characterized by the tensor relation:

$$\chi^{(1)} \propto \mu_{0v} \otimes \mu_{v0} \propto \left(\frac{\partial\mu}{\partial Q_v}\right)_0 \otimes \left(\frac{\partial\mu}{\partial Q_v}\right)_0. \tag{71}$$

This is quite logical and substantial. On the one hand, the transition moments $(\partial\mu/\partial Q_v)_0$ are 1st rank tensors (i.e., vectors). The product of two 1st rank tensors does indeed give a new 2nd rank tensor: here $\chi^{(1)}$ [59]. On the other hand, $(\partial\mu/\partial Q_v)_0$ describes the zero order of the dielectric response (We use here the notation of Landau $O(E^n)$ proper to Taylor expansion. For polarization, we typically have: $P = \chi^{(0)}E^0 + \chi^{(1)}E^1 + \cdots + \chi^{(n-1)}E^{n-1} + O(E^n)$, where E denotes the scalar amplitude of the electric field. Saying that a response function is in $O(E^n)$ means that it describes the response to the order $n-1$, and dominates all terms of order greater than or equal to n.), behaving like $O(E)$, which means that $\chi^{(1)}$ describes the dielectric response to order 1, behaving like $O(E) \times O(E) = O(E^2)$ as expected. These remarks will prove to be very enlightening thereafter.

4.3. Infrared Spectroscopy

The first vibrational spectroscopy technique relies on infrared absorption [56,60,61]. It is a linear optical process driven by the susceptibility $\chi^{(1)}(\omega_{ir})$ of the medium. This technique is widely used for the identification of molecular species, each molecule having its own infrared response, according to its modes of vibration. As soon as the energy $\hbar\omega_{ir}$ brought by the excitation matches the frequency ω_v of a vibrational eigenmode, we observe an absorption band, as described in Figure 9. The vibration modes of a molecule are not systematically detectable by infrared spectroscopy. In particular, the dipole moment μ of the molecule must vary when the molecule vibrates [2,3,56,62]:

$$\left(\frac{\partial \boldsymbol{\mu}}{\partial Q_v}\right)_0 \neq \mathbf{0}. \tag{72}$$

Indeed, Section 2.2 taught us that absorption was governed by the imaginary part of the linear susceptibility. Equations (67) and (70) lead then to the infrared absorbance [63]:

$$\mathcal{A}(\omega_{ir}) \propto \operatorname{Im} \chi_{ij}^{(1)}(\omega_{ir}) = \frac{N}{2\varepsilon_0 \omega_v}\left(\frac{\partial \mu_i}{\partial Q_v}\right)_0\left(\frac{\partial \mu_j}{\partial Q_v}\right)_0 \frac{\gamma_v}{(\omega_v - \omega_{ir})^2 + \gamma_v^2}. \tag{73}$$

As announced, the intensity of the infrared signal directly depends on the dipole moment variation with respect to the normal coordinates, which confirms the selection rule (72). Especially, this rule explains that the antisymmetric normal modes absorb more efficiently than the symmetric modes (Figure 9), the former being generally accompanied by a greater increase in the dipole moment. Equation (73) also tells us that each active vibration mode gives rise to a Lorentzian resonance in the absorption spectrum, which justifies the shape of the spectrum presented in Figure 9.

4.4. Raman Spectroscopy

As said in Section 3.5, the Raman process consists of the inelastic scattering of a pump beam $\mathbf{E}(t) = \mathbf{E}_0 \cos(\omega_p t)$ by the vibration modes ω_v of the medium. By measuring the frequency ω'_p of the scattered light, it is thus possible to retrieve the value of the eigen-frequencies, given by $\omega_v = |\omega_p - \omega'_p|$, and to identify the present molecular species [64], provided that the associated vibration modes are Raman active. While the selection rules for infrared absorption is related to the transition dipole moments, the Raman selection rules are based on the polarizability $\boldsymbol{\alpha}$, which we expand to the first order in Q_v [4,65]:

$$\boldsymbol{\alpha}(t) = \boldsymbol{\alpha}^{(0)} + \left(\frac{\partial \boldsymbol{\alpha}}{\partial Q_v}\right)_0 Q_v(t). \tag{74}$$

Assuming that the vibration mode v is potentially activated within the molecule (by thermal agitation in particular), Q_v is a sinusoidal function of frequency ω_v and amplitude Q_m: $Q_v(t) = Q_m \cos(\omega_v t)$. Using then the relation $\boldsymbol{\mu}(t) = \boldsymbol{\alpha}(t)\mathbf{E}(t)$, although it is not very rigorous, we get:

$$\boldsymbol{\mu}(t) = \boldsymbol{\alpha}^{(0)}\mathbf{E}_0 \cos(\omega_p t) \tag{75}$$

$$+ \frac{Q_m}{2}\left(\frac{\partial \boldsymbol{\alpha}}{\partial Q_v}\right)_0 \mathbf{E}_0 \cos[(\omega_p - \omega_v)t] \tag{76}$$

$$+ \frac{Q_m}{2}\left(\frac{\partial \boldsymbol{\alpha}}{\partial Q_v}\right)_0 \mathbf{E}_0 \cos[(\omega_p + \omega_v)t]. \tag{77}$$

Thus, we identify the elastic Rayleigh scattering at the frequency ω_p (75), the inelastic Stokes Raman scattering at the frequency $\omega_p - \omega_v$ (76) and the inelastic anti-Stokes Raman scattering at the frequency $\omega_p + \omega_v$ (77). Although its use is common, this presentation is not satisfactory. Formally, Equations (75)–(77) show Raman scattering as a linear process, which is obviously not the case (since inelastic). This mathematical contradiction actually translates our inability to describe by classical electromagnetism the incoherent processes of Raman scattering and fluorescence [66]. These two processes are indeed spontaneous and random, so that each photon scattered in Raman (or emitted in fluorescence) has a random phase. Consequently, they give rise to incoherent fields, whose value is zero in average. Moreover, it is because of this inconsistency, characterized by the absence of a phase matching condition, that the scattered and incident powers maintain a linear relation [58] (as described in Equations (75)–(77)), despite the non-linearity of the optical process. The classical approach that we have just presented here predicts formally the

Stokes and anti-Stokes Raman processes, and justifies also the selection rule specific to Raman spectroscopy, that is:

$$\left(\frac{\partial \boldsymbol{\alpha}}{\partial Q_v}\right)_0 \neq \mathbf{0}. \tag{78}$$

As demonstrated elsewhere in quantum mechanics [2,3,58,62,67], a vibration mode is Raman active if the polarizability of the molecule depends on the normal mode coordinate. It is not a coincidence if the polarizability is involved in the Raman process. As a 3rd order non-linear process, Raman spectroscopy is driven by [63,68,69]:

$$\chi^{(3)} \propto \left(\frac{\partial \boldsymbol{\alpha}}{\partial Q_v}\right)_0 \otimes \left(\frac{\partial \boldsymbol{\alpha}}{\partial Q_v}\right)_0. \tag{79}$$

Like the tensor Relation (71), Equation (79) mathematically manifests the non-linearity of the physical phenomenon. First, the polarizability $\boldsymbol{\alpha} = (\alpha_{ij})$ is a 2nd rank tensor. The product of two 2nd rank tensors gives a 4th rank tensor: $\chi^{(3)} = (\chi^{(3)}_{ijkl})$. Second, $\boldsymbol{\alpha}$ describes the 1st order dielectric response, behaving like $O(E^2)$, which is consistent with the fact that $\chi^{(3)}$ describes the 3rd order response, behaving like $O(E^2) \times O(E^2) = O(E^4)$. Analogously to infrared spectroscopy, the Raman spectrum of scattered light is then represented by [63]:

$$\text{Im } \chi^{(3)}_{ijkl}(\omega_p, -\omega_p, \omega) = \frac{N}{2\varepsilon_0 \omega_v} \left(\frac{\partial \alpha_{ij}}{\partial Q_v}\right)_0 \left(\frac{\partial \alpha_{kl}}{\partial Q_v}\right)_0 \frac{\gamma_v}{[\omega_v - (\omega_p - \omega)]^2 + \gamma_v^2}. \tag{80}$$

As the foundations of infrared and Raman spectroscopies are now established, it is possible to present the specificities of SFG spectroscopy and understand its interest in the study of vibroelectronic couplings within matter.

4.5. SFG Spectroscopy

We commonly read in the literature that SFG spectroscopy is a combination of infrared and Raman spectroscopies. Figure 10 illustrates this point of view by considering the case of a three-state quantum system. For purely molecular systems, this enables to justify the SFG selection rules. In this case, the non-linear susceptibility $\chi^{(2)}$, behaving like $O(E^3)$, is proportional to the transition polarizability, behaving like $O(E^2)$, and the transition dipole moment, behaving like $O(E)$ [2,3,63]:

$$\chi^{(2)}(\omega_{\text{vis}}, \omega_{\text{ir}}) \propto \left(\frac{\partial \boldsymbol{\alpha}}{\partial Q_v}\right)_0 \otimes \left(\frac{\partial \boldsymbol{\mu}}{\partial Q_v}\right)_0. \tag{81}$$

This relation tells us that a vibration mode is active in SFG spectroscopy if it is active in both infrared absorption and Raman scattering. However, we cannot ignore that the infrared and Raman processes are driven by the tensor Relations (71) and (79), which logically means that their combination would give rise to a 5th order optical process: $\chi^{(5)} \propto \left(\frac{\partial \boldsymbol{\alpha}}{\partial Q_v}\right)_0 \otimes \left(\frac{\partial \boldsymbol{\alpha}}{\partial Q_v}\right)_0 \otimes \left(\frac{\partial \boldsymbol{\mu}}{\partial Q_v}\right)_0 \otimes \left(\frac{\partial \boldsymbol{\mu}}{\partial Q_v}\right)_0$, much different from SFG. Considering sum-frequency generation as a combination of infrared and Raman processes is thus misleading: $\chi^{(2)}_{\text{sfg}} \neq \chi^{(1)}_{\text{ir}} \otimes \chi^{(3)}_{\text{Raman}}$. The only way to formally link $\chi^{(2)}$ to $\chi^{(1)}$ and $\chi^{(3)}$ is by defining contracted tensors [59], even though it is fundamentally and conceptually improper to describe SFG as a combination of IR and Raman spectroscopies.

To understand the specificity of SFG spectroscopy, we compare it to infrared and Raman spectroscopies in Table 1. Especially, SFG is resonant with respect to the infrared, and consists in a coherent emission (which is hardly the case of Raman). Another advantage of SFG is its surface specificity and that it can be doubly resonant [70]: in addition to its resonant character in the infrared, inherited from IR absorption, the SFG signal can be resonant in the visible. This situation is shown in Figure 10, where the visible and SFG frequencies match electronic transitions.

Table 1. Comparison of vibrational spectroscopies. Comparative table of the three vibrational spectroscopies: infrared absorption, Raman scattering and SFG. [†] Raman scattering can be resonant in the visible spectral range when the frequency of the pump beam coincides with an electronic transition (the excited state is therefore not virtual but indeed real, as illustrated in Figure 10). [‡] SFG can be doubly resonant, with respect to the infrared and visible beams, as shown in Figure 10.

IR Absorption	Raman Scattering	SFG
$\chi^{(1)}(\omega_{ir})$	$\chi^{(3)}(\omega_{vis}, -\omega_{vis}, \omega)$	$\chi^{(2)}(\omega_{vis}, \omega_{ir})$
$\left(\frac{\partial\mu}{\partial Q_v}\right)_0 \neq 0$	$\left(\frac{\partial\alpha}{\partial Q_v}\right)_0 \neq 0$	$\left(\frac{\partial\alpha}{\partial Q_v}\right)_0 \otimes \left(\frac{\partial\mu}{\partial Q_v}\right)_0 \neq 0$
ω_{ir}-resonant	non ω_{ir}-resonant	ω_{ir}-resonant
non ω_{vis}-resonant	(ω_{vis}-resonant) [†]	(ω_{vis}-resonant) [‡]
coherent	incoherent	coherent
directional	diffused	directional
non surface-specific	non surface-specific	surface specific

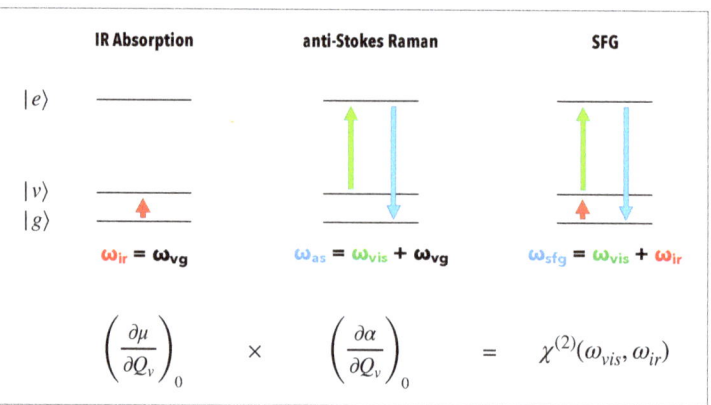

Figure 10. Vibrational spectroscopies. Comparison between the three techniques of vibrational spectroscopy: infrared absorption, anti-Stokes Raman scattering and sum-frequency generation. We represent three quantum states $|g\rangle$, $|v\rangle$ and $|e\rangle$ for the system, with the same meaning than Figure 7.

Therefore, three spectroscopic approaches can be employed. The first one is conventional: it consists in measuring the intensity of the SFG signal for a given visible excitation (i.e., at a fixed frequency ω_{vis}) by varying the frequency ω_{ir} of the infrared excitation [9,71]. The corresponding spectra carry the vibrational information of the probed system (Figure 11a). In a less conventional way, it is possible to compare several vibrational SFG spectra obtained for different visible excitations (Figure 11b) and thereby deduce the influence of the electronic properties of the system on the expression of its vibrational fingerprint [13,72]. Eventually, in a last unconventional manner, a third approach consists of measuring the SFG intensity for a given infrared excitation, preferably matching a vibration mode (i.e., $\omega_{ir} = \omega_v$), by varying the frequency ω_{vis} of the visible excitation (Figure 11c) [14,73].

When we exploit SFG spectroscopy in its vibrational dimension, by fixing ω_{vis} and by varying ω_{ir}, the spectrum is described by [3,63]:

$$\chi_{ijk}^{(2)}(\omega_{vis}, \omega_{ir}) = \frac{N}{2\varepsilon_0\omega_v}\left(\frac{\partial\alpha_{ij}}{\partial Q_v}\right)_0\left(\frac{\partial\mu_k}{\partial Q_v}\right)_0\frac{1}{\omega_{ir} - \omega_v + i\gamma_v}. \tag{82}$$

This equation reflects the vibrational response of the molecular system, obviously resonant in the infrared range when the excitation frequency ω_{ir} coincides with the eigenfrequency ω_v. In the typical case of functionalized nanoparticles grafted on a solid substrate, it is also necessary to take into account the SFG response of the substrate and the nanoparticles. Generally, these components do not exhibit vibration modes over the probed infrared spectral range. The SFG spectra are then modelled by an effective susceptibility of the form [72,74]:

$$\chi_{\text{eff}}^{(2)}(\omega_{\text{vis}}, \omega_{\text{ir}}) = A\, e^{i\Phi} + \sum_v \frac{a_v\, e^{i\varphi_v}}{\omega_{\text{ir}} - \omega_v + i\gamma_v}. \tag{83}$$

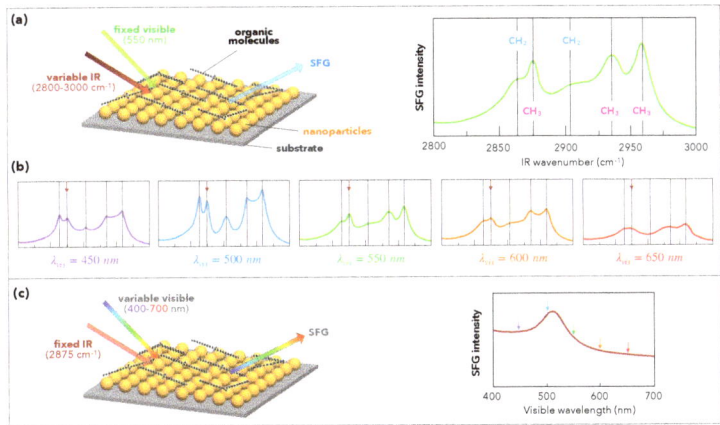

Figure 11. Principle of 2-dimension sum-frequency generation. (**a**) Conventional use of SFG spectroscopy on a nanostructured sample functionalized by organic molecules. The SFG spectrum consists in measuring the SFG intensity as a function of the IR wavenumber for a fixed visible wavelength ($\lambda_{\text{vis}} = 550$ nm). (**b**) Comparison of five vibrational SFG spectra obtained for five different visible wavelengths. For each vibration mode, the variation of the intensity from a visible wavelength to another is characteristic of electronic structure of the system (nanoparticles). (**c**) Unconventional use of SFG spectroscopy at variable visible wavelength. The spectrum is acquired at a fixed IR wavenumber that coincides with the vibration mode indicated on the spectra of Figure 11b.

The first term corresponds to the non-resonant response (with respect to the infrared) of the inorganic components (i.e., substrate and nanoparticles). The amplitude A and the phase Φ can possibly depend on the electronic response of these objects, hence:

$$A = A(\omega_{\text{vis}}) \in \mathbb{R}^+ \text{ and } \Phi = \Phi(\omega_{\text{vis}}) \in [0, 2\pi[. \tag{84}$$

The sum over v describes the vibrational resonances associated with each of the molecular vibration modes of eigenfrequencies ω_v. These are complex Lorentzian functions, as suggested by Equation (82). In the general case of hybrid organic/inorganic interfaces, the amplitudes of vibration a_v can be conditioned by the electronic activity of the inorganic components. As such, they potentially admit a dependence on the visible frequency:

$$a_v = a_v(\omega_{\text{vis}}) \in \mathbb{R}^+ \text{ and } \varphi_v = \varphi_v(\omega_{\text{vis}}) \in [0, 2\pi[. \tag{85}$$

As the terms of Equation (83) are complex numbers, this experimentally results in interference patterns on the SFG spectra. Figure 12 illustrates this point. According to Equation (50), the SFG intensity is proportional to the square norm of the effective second order susceptibility. Considering the case of a single mode of vibration:

$$
\begin{aligned}
|\chi_{\text{eff}}^{(2)}|^2 \;=\;& A^2 \\
+\;& \frac{a_v^2}{(\omega_{\text{ir}} - \omega_v)^2 + \gamma_v^2} \\
+\;& \frac{2Aa_v}{\sqrt{(\omega_{\text{ir}} - \omega_v)^2 + \gamma_v^2}} \cos\!\left(\varphi_v - \Phi - 2\arctan\frac{\gamma_v}{\omega_{\text{ir}} - \omega_v + \sqrt{(\omega_{\text{ir}} - \omega_v)^2 + \gamma_v^2}}\right).
\end{aligned}
\tag{86}
$$

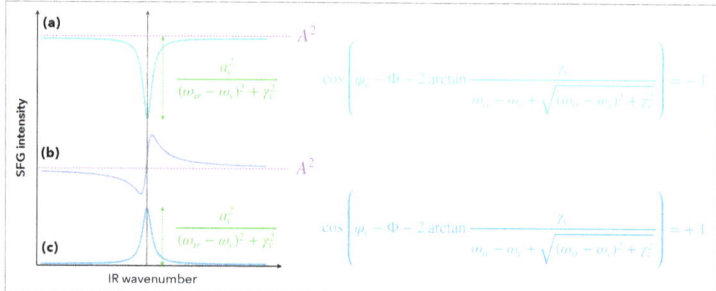

Figure 12. Interference profiles of SFG spectra. Typical profiles of the vibrational SFG spectra: (**a**) in the destructive case, (**b**) in an intermediate case, (**c**) in the constructive case. The quantity A^2 corresponds to the non-resonant background. It is not specific to the molecular species but to the inorganic components of the system.

The first term defines what is called the non-resonant background of the SFG signal. The second term is the vibrational resonance, and the third is an interference term between the substrate and the adsorbate. In the constructive case, the vibration appears as a peak on the SFG spectrum (Figure 12c); in the destructive case, it appears as a dip (Figure 12a). The above-mentioned description of the SFG response of an interface is phenomenological and easy to use for data fitting. In addition, it is worth noting that recent theoretical and analytical models developed for doubly resonant SFG and DFG spectroscopies give a quantified description of complex phenomena related to vibronic couplings inside molecules [75,76].

4.6. Prospects in SFG Spectroscopy and Microscopy

Beyond the mathematical formalism introduced here and applied to surface-specific Two-colour SFG spectroscopy, we emphasize that the intrinsic symmetry properties of SFG spectroscopy allow to relate its susceptibility chiral components to the broader concept of vibrational optical activity (VOA) already developed for infrared and Raman spectroscopy, widening the field of investigation not only for any type of surface or (buried) interface but also for bulk materials (in volume). Nowadays, chiral SFG spectroscopy is a potential powerful local probe aimed at playing specifically with (bio)molecular symmetry rules in primary, secondary and ternary biological structures. In fact, it is the object of numerous experimental developments and studies [77], constituting the utmost probe of VOA [78,79] for both interfacial and bulk samples, which is counter-intuitive at first glance for non-linear 2nd order optical probes in the latter case. Moreover, chiral SFG allows to distinguish between non-zero susceptibility components as a function of the sample symmetry at the molecular, nanometer and microscopic scale: it allows therefore to discriminate chiral interface, chiral bulk, achiral interface and achiral bulk properties, respectively. In these conditions, it is clear that SFG sensitivity is greatly enhanced as a function of the selected polarization combination triplet (x, y, z) for $\chi_{ijk}^{(2)}$ in the 3-dimensional space. It can therefore be applied to distinguish different enantiomers in racemic mixtures, analyse the geometry inside polymer thin films or a the air/proteins interfaces. More exciting for the future, it could be also applied to selectively detect complementary DNA strands in the development of biosensors for medical purposes. A dedicated theoretical formalism for VOA SFG has to be developed in the future and our contribution could constitute a solid foundation for such a demanding task.

Finally, promising developments show that it is possible to use SFG in microscopy imaging [80–83], thus offering the possibility of probing interfaces at least with 100 nm spatial resolution.

5. Conclusions

In this review, by revisiting past and current literature on the fundamentals of linear (first order) and non-linear optics (second and third orders), we have established a coherent and unified mathematical description for the major optical vibrational and electronic spectroscopies thanks to a progressive description of their own characteristics and interest field: absorption, scattering, fluorescence, infrared, Raman and sum-frequency generation (SFG) processes, compatible with the current and past experimental observations. This made it possible to remove the ambiguities observed in literature for the description of the susceptibilities of materials. The emblematic case of SFG spectroscopy has been addressed in details because it relies on the selection and exclusion rules of infrared and Raman spectroscopies, strictly correlated to (centro)symmetry properties of interface and bulk materials. While nowadays SFG spectroscopy is mainly aimed at probing surfaces and interfaces at multiscale, from the atomic to the biological scale, the presence of chiral parameters in the design of complex hybrid organic/inorganic systems opens the door to a bright and exciting future in the analysis of their physico-chemical properties: a new age of non-linear spectroscopy is on the edge!

Author Contributions: C.H. and T.N. prepared, wrote, edited and reviewed the paper. T.N. draw all the figures of the paper. All authors have read and agreed to the published version of the manuscript.

Funding: This research received no external funding.

Institutional Review Board Statement: Not relevant to this Review.

Informed Consent Statement: Not applicable.

Data Availability Statement: Not applicable.

Conflicts of Interest: The authors declare no conflict of interest.

Abbreviations

The following abbreviations are used in this manuscript:

SFG	Sum-frequency generation
DFG	Difference-frequency generation
SHG	Second harmonic generation
VOA	Vibrational optical activity

References

1. Battaglia, F.; George, T.F. Tensors: A guide for undergraduate students. *Am. J. Phys.* **2013**, *81*, 498–511. [CrossRef]
2. Shen, Y.R. *The Principles of Nonlinear Optics*; Wiley-Interscience: New York, NY, USA, 1984.
3. Boyd, R.W. *Nonlinear Optics*, 2nd ed.; Academic Press: Cambridge, MA, USA, 2003.
4. Hache, F. *Optique Non Linéaire*; EDP Sciences: Les Ulis, France, 2016.
5. He, G.S. *Nonlinear Optics and Photonics*; Oxford University Press: Oxford, UK, 2015.
6. Haug, H.; Koch, S. *Quantum Theory of the Optical and Electronic Properties of Semiconductors*, 5th ed.; World Scientific: Singapore, 2009.
7. Bohren, C.F.; Huffman, D.R. *Absorption and Scattering of Light by Small Particles*; Wiley: Hoboken, NJ, USA, 1983.
8. Mie, G. Beiträge zur Optik trüber Medien, speziell kolloidaler Metallösungen. *Ann. Phys.* **1908**, *330*, 377–445. [CrossRef]
9. Dalstein, L.; Haddada, M.B.; Barbillon, G.; Humbert, C.; Tadjeddine, A.; Boujday, S.; Busson, B. Revealing the Interplay between Adsorbed Molecular Layers and Gold Nanoparticles by Linear and Nonlinear Optical Properties. *J. Phys. Chem. C* **2015**, *119*, 17146–17155. [CrossRef]
10. Hottechamps, J.; Noblet, T.; Brans, A.; Humbert, C.; Dreesen, L. How quantum dots aggregation enhances Förster Resonant Energy Transfer. *ChemPhysChem* **2020**, *21*, 853–862. [CrossRef] [PubMed]
11. Bloembergen, N. *Nonlinear Optics*, 4th ed.; World Scientific: Singapore, 1965.
12. Dalstein, L.; Humbert, C.; Haddada, M.B.; Boujday, S.; Barbillon, G.; Busson, B. The Prevailing Role of Hotspots in Plasmon-Enhanced Sum-Frequency Generation Spectroscopy. *J. Phys. Chem. Lett.* **2019**, *10*, 7706–7711. [CrossRef]
13. Noblet, T.; Dreesen, L.; Boujday, S.; Méthivier, C.; Busson, B.; Tadjeddine, A.; Humbert, C. Semiconductor quantum dots reveal dipolar coupling from exciton to ligand vibration. *Commun. Chem.* **2018**, *1*, 76. [CrossRef]

14. Noblet, T.; Boujday, S.; Méthivier, C.; Erard, M.; Hottechamps, J.; Busson, B.; Humbert, C. Two-Dimensional Layers of Colloidal CdTe Quantum Dots: Assembly, Optical Properties, and Vibroelectronic Coupling. *J. Phys. Chem. C* **2020**, *124*, 25873–25883. [CrossRef]

15. Fumi, F.G. The direct-inspection method in systems with a principal axis of symmetry. *Acta. Cryst.* **1952**, *5*, 691–694. [CrossRef]

16. Sioncke, S.; Verbiest, T.; Persoons, A. Second-order nonlinear optical properties of chiral materials. *Mater. Sci. Eng. Rep.* **2003**, *42*, 115–155. [CrossRef]

17. Zhuang, X.; Miranda, P.B.; Kim, D.; Shen, Y.R. Mapping molecular orientation and conformation interfaces by surface nonlinear optics. *Phys. Rev. B* **1999**, *59*, 12632–12640. [CrossRef]

18. Vidal, F.; Busson, B.; Tadjeddine, A. Probing electronic and vibrational properties at the electrochemical interface using SFG spectroscopy: Methanol electro-oxidation on Pt(110). *Chem. Phys. Lett.* **2005**, *403*, 324–328. [CrossRef]

19. Joutsuka, T.; Hirano, T.; Sprikb, M.; Morita, A. Effects of third-order susceptibility in sum frequency generation spectra: A molecular dynamics study in liquid water. *Phys. Chem. Chem. Phys.* **2018**, *20*, 3040. [CrossRef] [PubMed]

20. Hunt, J.; Guyot-Sionnest, P.; Shen, Y. Observation of C-H stretch vibrations of monolayers of molecules optical sum-frequency generation. *Chem. Phys. Lett.* **1987**, *133*, 189–192. [CrossRef]

21. Guyot-Sionnest, P.; Hunt, J.; Shen, Y. Sum-frequency vibrational spectroscopy of a Langmuir film: Study of molecular orientation of a two-dimensional system. *Phys. Rev. Lett.* **1987**, *59*, 1597–1600. [CrossRef] [PubMed]

22. Zhu, X.; Suhr, H.; Shen, Y. Surface vibrational spectroscopy by infrared-visible sum frequency generation. *Phys. Rev. B* **1987**, *35*, 3047–3050. [CrossRef] [PubMed]

23. Nicolau, B.G.; Garcia-Rey, N.; Dryzhakov, B.; Dlott, D.D. Interfacial Processes of a Model Lithium Ion Battery Anode Observed, in Situ, with Vibrational Sum-Frequency Generation Spectroscopy. *J. Phys. Chem. C* **2015**, *119*, 10227–10233. [CrossRef]

24. Yang, S.; Noguchi, H.; Uosaki, K. Electronic Structure of the CO/Pt(111) Electrode Interface Probed by Potential-Dependent IR/Visible Double Resonance Sum Frequency Generation Spectroscopy. *J. Phys. Chem. C* **2015**, *119*, 26056–26063. [CrossRef]

25. Braunschweig, B.; Mukherjee, P.; Haan, J.L.; Dlott, D.D. Vibrational sum-frequency generation study of the CO_2 electrochemical reduction at Pt/EMIM-BF_4 solid/liquid interfaces. *J. Electroanal. Chem.* **2017**, *800*, 144–150. [CrossRef]

26. Garcia-Rey, N.; Dlott, D.D. Studies of electrochemical interfaces by broadband sum frequency generation. *J. Electroanal. Chem.* **2017**, *800*, 114–125.

27. Feng, R.; Liu, A.; Liu, S.; Shi, J.; Zhang, R.; Ren, Z. In Situ Studies on the Dissociation and Photocatalytic Reactions of CH_3OH on TiO_2 Thin Film by Sum Frequency Generation Vibrational Spectroscopy. *J. Phys. Chem. C* **2015**, *119*, 9798–9804. [CrossRef]

28. Vanselous, H.; Stingel, A.M.; Petersen, P.B. Interferometric 2D Sum Frequency Generation Spectroscopy Reveals Structural Heterogeneity of Catalytic Monolayers on Transparent Materials. *J. Phys. Chem. Lett.* **2017**, *8*, 825–830. [CrossRef] [PubMed]

29. Ouvrard, A.; Wang, J.; Ghalgaoui, A.; Nave, S.; Carrez, S.; Zheng, W.; Dubost, H.; Bourguignon, B. CO Adsorption on Pd(100) Revisited by Sum Frequency Generation: Evidence for Two Adsorption Sites in the Compression Stage. *J. Phys. Chem. C* **2014**, *118*, 19688–19700. [CrossRef]

30. Morita, A.; Hynes, J.T. A Theoretical Analysis of the Sum Frequency Generation Spectrum of the Water Surface. II. Time-Dependent Approach. *J. Phys. Chem. B* **2002**, *106*, 673–685. [CrossRef]

31. Medders, G.R.; Paesani, F. Dissecting the Molecular Structure of the Air/Water Interface from Quantum Simulations of the Sum-Frequency Generation Spectrum. *J. Am. Chem. Soc.* **2016**, *138*, 3912–3919. [CrossRef] [PubMed]

32. Chiang, K.Y.; Dalstein, L.; Wen, Y.C. Affinity of Hydrated Protons at Intrinsic Water/Vapor Interface Revealed by Ion-Induced Water Alignment. *J. Phys. Chem. Lett.* **2020**, *11*, 679–701. [CrossRef] [PubMed]

33. Khatib, R.; Backus, E.H.G.; Bonn, M.; Perez-Haro, M.J.; Gaigeot, M.P.; Sulpizi, M. Water orientation and hydrogen-bond structure at the fluorite/water interface. *Sci. Rep.* **2016**, *6*, 24287. [CrossRef] [PubMed]

34. Urashima, S.; Myalitsin, A.; Nihonyanagi, S.; Tahara, T. The Topmost Water Structure at a Charged Silica/Aqueous Interface Revealed by Heterodyne-Detected Vibrational Sum Frequency Generation Spectroscopy. *J. Phys. Chem. Lett.* **2018**, *9*, 4109–4114. [CrossRef]

35. Tuladhar, A.; Piontek, S.M.; Borguet, E. Insights on Interfacial Structure, Dynamics, and Proton Transfer from Ultrafast Vibrational Sum Frequency Generation Spectroscopy of the Alumina(0001)/Water Interface. *J. Phys. Chem. C* **2017**, *121*, 5168–5177. [CrossRef]

36. Kusaka, R.; Ishiyama, T.; Nihonyanagi, S.; Morita, A.; Tahara, T. Structure at the air/water interface in the presence of phenol: A study using heterodyne-detected vibrational sum frequency generation and molecular dynamics simulation. *Phys. Chem. Chem. Phys.* **2018**, *20*, 3002. [CrossRef]

37. Nguyen, K.T.; Nguyen, A.V.; Evans, G.M. Interfacial Water Structure at Surfactant Concentrations below and above the Critical Micelle Concentration as Revealed by Sum Frequency Generation Vibrational Spectroscopy. *J. Phys. Chem. C* **2015**, *119*, 15477–15481. [CrossRef]

38. Nihonyanagi, S.; Yamaguchi, S.; Tahara, T. Ultrafast Dynamics at Water Interfaces Studied by Vibrational Sum Frequency Generation Spectroscopy. *Chem. Rev.* **2017**, *117*, 10665–10693. [CrossRef] [PubMed]

39. Toledo-Fuentes, X.; Lis, D.; Cecchet, F. Structural Changes to Lipid Bilayers and Their Surrounding Water upon Interaction with Functionalized Gold Nanoparticles. *J. Phys. Chem. C* **2016**, *120*, 21399–21409. [CrossRef]

40. Saha, A.; SenGupta, S.; Kumar, A.; Naik, P.D. Interaction of L-Phenylalanine with Lipid Monolayers at Air-Water Interface at Different pHs: Sum-Frequency Generation Spectroscopy and Surface Pressure Studies. *J. Phys. Chem. C* **2018**, *122*, 3875–3884. [CrossRef]

41. Zhang, J.; Yang, W.; Tanab, J.; Ye, S. In situ examination of a charged amino acid-induced structural change in lipid bilayers by sum frequency generation vibrational spectroscopy. *Phys. Chem. Chem. Phys.* **2018**, *20*, 5657. [CrossRef] [PubMed]
42. Hosseinpour, S.; Roeters, S.; Bonn, M.; Peukert, W.; Woutersen, S.; Weidner, T. Structure and Dynamics of Interfacial Peptides and Proteins from Vibrational Sum-Frequency Generation Spectroscopy. *Chem. Rev.* **2020**, *120*, 3420–3465. [CrossRef]
43. Laaser, J.E.; Skoff, D.R.; Ho, J.J.; Joo, Y.; Serrano, A.L.; Steinkruger, J.D.; Gopalan, P.; Gellman, S.H.; Zanni, M.T. Two-Dimensional Sum-Frequency Generation Reveals Structure and Dynamics of a Surface-Bound Peptide. *J. Am. Chem. Soc.* **2014**, *136*, 956–962. [CrossRef]
44. Yan, E.C.Y.; Fu, L.; Wang, Z.; Liu, W. Biological Macromolecules at Interfaces Probed by Chiral Vibrational Sum Frequency Generation Spectroscopy. *Chem. Rev.* **2014**, *114*, 8471–8498. [CrossRef]
45. Schmüser, L.; Roeters, S.; Lutz, H.; Woutersen, S.; Bonn, M.; Weidner, T. Determination of Absolute Orientation of Protein α-Helices at Interfaces Using Phase-Resolved Sum Frequency Generation Spectroscopy. *J. Phys. Chem. Lett.* **2017**, *8*, 3101–3105. [CrossRef]
46. Xiao, M.; Wei, S.; Li, Y.; Jasensky, J.; Chen, J.; Brooks, C.L.; Chen, Z. Molecular interactions between single layered MoS_2 and biological molecules. *Chem. Sci.* **2018**, *9*, 1769. [CrossRef]
47. Raab, M.; Becca, J.C.; Heo, J.; Lim, C.K.; Baev, A.; Jensen, L.; Prasad, P.N.; Velarde, L. Doubly resonant sum frequency spectroscopy of mixed photochromic isomers on surfaces reveals conformation-specific vibronic effects. *J. Chem. Phys.* **2019**, *150*, 114704. [CrossRef]
48. Peremans, A.; Caudano, Y.; Thiry, P.A.; Dumas, P.; Zhang, W.Q.; Rille, A.L.; Tadjeddine, A. Electronic Tuning of Dynamical Charge Transfer at an Interface: K Doping of C_{60}/Ag(111). *Phys. Rev. Lett.* **1997**, *78*, 2999–3002. [CrossRef]
49. Caudano, Y.; Silien, C.; Humbert, C.; Dreesen, L.; Mani, A.A.; Peremans, A.; Thiry, P.A. Electron-phonon couplings at C_{60} interfaces: a case study by two-color, infrared-visible sum-frequency generation spectroscopy. *J. Electron Spectrosc. Relat. Phenom.* **2003**, *129*, 139–147. [CrossRef]
50. Elsenbeck, D.; Das, S.K.; Velarde, L. Substrate influence on the interlayer electron-phonon couplings in fullerene films probed with doubly-resonant SFG spectroscopy. *Phys. Chem. Chem. Phys.* **2017**, *19*, 18519. [CrossRef] [PubMed]
51. Chou, K.C.; Westerberg, S.; Shen, Y.R.; Ross, P.N.; Somorjai, G.A. Probing the charge-transfer state of CO on Pt(111) by two-dimensional infrared-visible sum frequency generation spectroscopy. *Phys. Rev. B* **2004**, *69*, 153413. [CrossRef]
52. Bozzini, B.; D'Urzo, L.; Mele, C.; Busson, B.; Humbert, C.; Tadjeddine, A. Doubly Resonant Sum Frequency Generation Spectroscopy of Adsorbates at an Electrochemical Interface. *J. Phys. Chem. C* **2008**, *112*, 11791–11795. [CrossRef]
53. Dreesen, L.; Humbert, C.; Celebi, M.; Lemaire, J.J.; Mani, A.A.; Thiry, P.A.; Peremans, A. Influence of the metal electronic properties on the sum-frequency generation spectra of dodecanethiol self-assembled monolayers on Pt(111), Ag(111) and Au(111) single crystals. *Appl. Phys. B* **2002**, *74*, 621–625. [CrossRef]
54. Lis, D.; Caudano, Y.; Henry, M.; Demoustier-Champagne, S.; Ferain, E.; Cecchet, F. Selective Plasmonic Platforms Based on Nanopillars to Enhance Vibrational Sum-Frequency Generation Spectroscopy. *Adv. Opt. Mater.* **2013**, *1*, 244–255. [CrossRef]
55. Hayashi, M.; Lin, S.H.; Raschke, M.B.; Shen, Y.R. A Molecular Theory for Doubly Resonant IR-UV-vis Sum-Frequency Generation. *J. Phys. Chem. A* **2002**, *106*, 2271–2282. [CrossRef]
56. Wilson, E.B.; Decius, J.C.; Cross, P.C. *Molecular Vibrations: The Theory of Infrared and Raman Vibrational Spectra*; Dover Publications: New York, NY, USA, 1955.
57. Mahan, G.D. *Many-Particle Physics*, 2nd ed.; Plenum Press: New York, NY, USA, 1990.
58. Albrecht, A.C. On the Theory of Raman Intensities. *J. Chem. Phys.* **1961**, *34*, 1476. [CrossRef]
59. Chen, F.; Gozdzialski, L.; Hung, K.K.; Stege, U.; Hore, D.K. Assessing the Molecular Specificity and Orientation Sensitivity of Infrared, Raman, and Vibrational Sum-Frequency Spectra. *Symmetry* **2021**, *13*, 42. [CrossRef]
60. Atkins, P.W. *Physical Chemistry*, 5th ed.; Oxford University Press: Oxford, UK, 1994.
61. Lin-Vien, D.; Colthup, N.B.; Fateley, W.G.; Grasselli, J.G. *The Handbook of Infrared and Raman Characteristic Frequencies of Organic Molecules*; Academic Press: Cambridge, MA, USA, 1991.
62. Porezag, D.; Pederson, M.R. Infrared intensities and Raman-scattering activities within density-functional theory. *Phys. Rev. B* **1996**, *54*, 7830–7836. [CrossRef] [PubMed]
63. Hung, K.K.; Stege, U.; Hore, D.K. IR Absorption, Raman Scattering, and IR-Vis Sum-Frequency Generation Spectroscopy as Quantitative Probes of Surface Structure. *Appl. Spec. Rev.* **2015**, *50*, 351–376. [CrossRef]
64. Veilly, E.; Roques, J.; Jodin-Caumon, M.C.; Humbert, B.; Drot, R.; Simoni, E. Uranyl interaction with the hydrated (001) basal face of gibbsite: A combined theoretical and spectroscopic study. *J. Chem. Phys.* **2008**, *129*, 244704. [CrossRef] [PubMed]
65. Kakkar, R. *Atomic and Molecular Spectroscopy: Basic Concepts and Applications*; Cambridge University Press: Cambridge, UK, 2015.
66. Lakowicz, J.R. *Principles of Fluorescence Spectroscopy*, 3rd ed.; Springer: Berlin/Heidelberg, Germany, 2006.
67. Polavarapu, P.L. Ab Initio Vibrational Raman and Raman Optical Activity Spectra. *J. Chem. Phys.* **1990**, *94*, 8106–8112. [CrossRef]
68. Potma, E.O.; Mukamel, S. *Coherent Raman Scattering Microscopy*; CRC Press: Boca Raton, FL, USA, 2012.
69. Roy, S.; Beutier, C.; Hore, D.K. Combined IR-Raman vs vibrational sum-frequency heterospectral correlation spectroscopy. *J. Mol. Struct.* **2018**, *1161*, 403–411. [CrossRef]
70. Huang, J.H.; Shen, Y.R. Theory of doubly resonant infrared-visible sum-frequency and difference-frequency generation from adsorbed molecules. *Phys. Rev. A* **1994**, *49*, 3973–3981. [CrossRef]

71. Humbert, C.; Noblet, T.; Dalstein, L.; Busson, B.; Barbillon, G. Sum-Frequency Generation Spectroscopy of Plasmonic Nanomaterials: A Review. *Materials* **2019**, *12*, 836. [CrossRef] [PubMed]
72. Humbert, C.; Dahi, A.; Dalstein, L.; Busson, B.; Lismont, M.; Colson, P.; Dreesen, L. Linear and nonlinear optical properties of functionalized CdSe quantum dots prepared by plasma sputtering and wet chemistry. *J. Colloid Interface Sci.* **2015**, *445*, 69–75. [CrossRef] [PubMed]
73. Dreesen, L.; Humbert, C.; Sartenaer, Y.; Caudano, Y.; Volcke, C.; Mani, A.A.; Peremans, A.; Thiry, P.A.; Hanique, S.; Frère, J.M. Electronic and Molecular Properties of an Adsorbed Protein Monolayer Probed by Two-Color Sum-Frequency Generation Spectroscopy. *Langmuir* **2004**, *20*, 7201–7207. [CrossRef] [PubMed]
74. Yang, W.C.; Hore, D.K. Determining the Orientation of Chemical Functional Groups on Metal Surfaces by a Combination of Homodyne and Heterodyne Nonlinear Vibrational Spectroscopy. *J. Phys. Chem. C* **2017**, *121*, 28043–28050. [CrossRef]
75. Busson, B. Doubly resonant SFG and DFG Spectroscopies: An analytic model for data analysis including distorted and rotated vibronic levels. I. Theory. *J. Chem. Phys.* **2020**, *153*, 174701. [CrossRef] [PubMed]
76. Busson, B. Doubly resonant SFG and DFG Spectroscopies: An analytic model for data analysis including distorted and rotated vibronic levels. II. Applications. *J. Chem. Phys.* **2020**, *153*, 174702. [CrossRef] [PubMed]
77. Ishibashi, T.A.; Okuno, M. Chapter 9—Heterodyne-detected chiral vibrational sum frequency generation spectroscopy of bulk and interfacial samples. In *Molecular and Laser Spectroscopy*; Gupta, V., Ozaki, Y., Eds.; Elsevier: Amsterdam, The Netherlands, 2020; pp. 315–348.
78. Nafie, L. Vibrational optical activity: From discovery and development to future challenges. *Chirality* **2020**, *32*, 667–692. [CrossRef] [PubMed]
79. Fujisawa, T.; Unno, M. Chapter 2—Vibrational optical activity spectroscopy. In *Molecular and Laser Spectroscopy*; Gupta, V., Ozaki, Y., Eds.; Elsevier: Amsterdam, The Netherlands, 2020; pp. 41–82.
80. Lee, C.M.; Kafle, K.; Huang, S.; Kim, S.H. Multimodal Broadband Vibrational Sum Frequency Generation (MM-BB-V-SFG) Spectrometer and Microscope. *J. Phys. Chem. B* **2016**, *120*, 102–116. [CrossRef] [PubMed]
81. Allgeyer, E.S.; Sterling, S.M.; Gunewardene, M.S.; Hess, S.T.; Neivandt, D.J.; Mason, M.D. Combining Total Internal Reflection Sum Frequency Spectroscopy Spectral Imaging and Confocal Fluorescence Microscopy. *Langmuir* **2015**, *31*, 987–994. [CrossRef] [PubMed]
82. Fang, M.; Santos, G.; Chen, X.; Baldelli, S. Roles of oxygen for methanol adsorption on polycrystalline copper surface revealed by sum frequency generation imaging microscopy. *Surf. Sci.* **2016**, *648*, 35–41. [CrossRef]
83. Wang, H.; Gao, T.; Xiong, W. Self-Phase-Stabilized Heterodyne Vibrational Sum Frequency Generation Microscopy. *ACS Photonics* **2017**, *4*, 1839–1845. [CrossRef]

MDPI

Article

Assessing the Molecular Specificity and Orientation Sensitivity of Infrared, Raman, and Vibrational Sum-Frequency Spectra

Fei Chen [1], Lea Gozdzialski [2], Kuo-Kai Hung [2], Ulrike Stege [2] and Dennis K. Hore [1,2]*

[1] Department of Computer Science, University of Victoria, Victoria, BC V8P 5C2, Canada; feichen@uvic.ca
[2] Department of Chemistry, University of Victoria, Victoria, BC V8W 3V6, Canada; lgozdzialski@uvic.ca (L.G.); kaigary@uvic.ca (K.-K.H.); ustege@uvic.ca (U.S.)
* Correspondence: dkhore@uvic.ca

Abstract: Linear programming was used to assess the ability of polarized infrared absorption, Raman scattering, and visible–infrared sum-frequency generation to correctly identify the composition of a mixture of molecules adsorbed onto a surface in four scenarios. The first two scenarios consisted of a distribution of species where the polarity of the orientation distribution is known, both with and without consideration of an arbitrary scaling factor between candidate spectra and the observed spectra of the mixture. The final two scenarios have repeated the tests, but assuming that the polarity of the orientation is unknown, so the symmetry-breaking attributes of the second-order nonlinear technique are required. The results indicate that polarized Raman spectra are more sensitive to orientation and molecular identity than the other techniques. However, further analysis reveals that this sensitivity is not due to the high-order angle dependence of Raman, but is instead attributed to the number of unique projections that can be measured in a polarized Raman experiment.

Keywords: molecular orientation; spectral unmixing; infrared absorption; visible-infrared sum-frequency generation; Raman scattering; linear programming

Citation: Chen, F.; Gozdzialski, L.; Stege, U.; Hore, D. Assessing the Molecular Specificity and Orientation Sensitivity of Infrared, Raman, and Vibrational Sum-Frequency Spectra. *Symmetry* **2021**, *13*, 42. https://doi.org/10.3390/sym13010042

Received: 17 December 2020
Accepted: 25 December 2020
Published: 30 December 2020

1. Introduction

The structural characterization of ordered systems has been a cornerstone of chemistry. Understanding the orientation of molecules with respect to each other, and with respect to a macroscopic entity such as a crystal structure, material profile, or surface can inform on the physical and chemical properties of the system. Molecular arrangements have been studied by X-ray and neutron scattering, nuclear magnetic resonance, and optical spectroscopy. Among the optical methods [1], vibrational techniques are of particular interest due to their ability to access sub-molecular information from the characteristic vibrational frequencies associated with specific chemical functional groups, thereby providing local bond-level orientation information, in addition to revealing markers of molecular conformation. The general idea exploits the relationship between transition dipole moment and electric field, as the strength of the interaction depends on the angle between these two vector quantities [2]. Combining these ideas, the use of polarized light in vibrational spectroscopy has long been used to qualitatively and quantitatively assess the identity and orientation of molecules [3].

The theory of polarized infrared (IR) absorption [4–12] and polarized Raman scattering [13–20] to elucidate the orientation of molecules in bulk materials, thin films, and on surfaces has been well-established. When dealing with monolayers on surfaces, infrared absorption experiments in either transmission or reflection geometry are challenging due to the low value of absorbance (in the 10^{-4} range), but are possible. Spontaneous Raman scattering from such a low number density is more of a challenge but has been addressed, primarily through the use of resonance Raman techniques [21–24]. Visible-infrared sum-frequency generation (SFG) spectroscopy [25–32], on the other hand, is ideally suited for the study of surfaces since sufficient signal may be detected even for monolayers. The niche application of SFG is the study of surfaces whose constituent molecules are the same as those in the bulk—for example the water vapour–liquid interface [33,34]. In such cases, only molecules at the surface contribute to the measured signal as a result of the inversion symmetry-breaking requirement of SFG [25,35]. In the present discussion, however, we can keep the application general, exploring the ability of these techniques to discriminate between different molecules in different orientations regardless of whether the assembly is two- or three-dimensional. Typical sample and experimental conditions will often limit the applicability of these three techniques but, in an idealized comparison, we can assess their sensitivity based on the nature of the response functions alone. In this work, we consider a mixture of six molecules with varying composition and orientations. This would, for example, describe a surface that is exposed to a solution of molecules. Even if we know the proportion of molecules in the bulk solution state, we cannot know in advance the composition of the surface due to variability in the surface preference. Furthermore, each species may adsorb with a preferred orientation; there are of course bulk analogies as well. As the assessment of molecular specificity and orientation requires the evaluation of thousands of combinations of spectra in a highly multi-dimensional parameter space, we employ linear programming to be guaranteed of the exact solution to the spectral unmixing problem that encodes the structural information we seek.

2. Background

2.1. Molecular and Ensemble Response Functions

When light with a time-varying j-polarized electric field E_j interacts with a molecule, the ij element of the linear polarizability $\alpha^{(1)}$ determines the magnitude and phase of the resulting time-varying induced dipole moment, whose Cartesian component i is given by $p_i = \alpha_{ij}^{(1)} E_j$. In general, higher order polarizabilities (the so-called hyperpolarizabilities) can contribute through the expansion [35,36]

$$p_i = \alpha_{ij}^{(1)} E_j + \frac{1}{2}\alpha_{ijk}^{(2)} E_j E_k + \frac{1}{6}\alpha_{ijk\ell}^{(3)} E_j E_k E_\ell + \cdots + \frac{1}{n!}\alpha^{(n)} E^n \tag{1}$$

where we have used Einstein notation for implicit summation over repeated indices. It is simplest to describe the above interactions when the induced dipole moment, electric fields, and polarizability tensors are all in the same coordinate system. We will use the indices i, j, k, ℓ as placeholders for any of the molecule-fixed (x, y, z) Cartesian coordinates as shown in Figure 1.

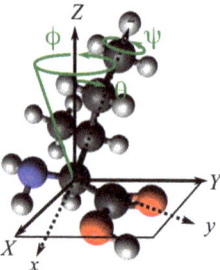

Figure 1. Illustration of the molecule-fixed (x, y, z) and laboratory frame (X, Y, Z) coordinates, related through three Euler angles. Here θ is the tilt angle that projects the molecular long axis z onto the surface normal Z, ϕ is the azimuthal angle that describes rotation about Z and ψ is the twist angle that describes rotation about z. The surface is represented by the (X, Y)-plane.

However, this is not a practical description in reality, since the input and measured fields are in the laboratory frame. Now using I, J, K, L as placeholders for any of the lab frame (X, Y, Z) coordinates, we can write an expression for the polarization (dipole moment per unit volume)

$$P_I = \varepsilon_0 \left(\chi_{IJ}^{(1)} E_j + \frac{1}{2} \chi_{IJK}^{(2)} E_J E_K + \frac{1}{6} \chi_{IJKL}^{(3)} E_J E_K E_L + \cdots + \frac{1}{n!} \chi^{(n)} E^n \right). \tag{2}$$

These expressions are related by the molecular number density N and the average over participating molecular orientations. For example, in a molecular dynamics simulation where the orientation of each molecule can be tracked independently, $\chi_{IJ}^{(1)} = \sum_{\text{molecules}}^{N} \alpha_{IJ}^{(1)} / \varepsilon_0$. In an experiment, we do not have access to such information, and instead work with the ensemble average

$$\chi_{IJ}^{(1)} = \frac{N}{\varepsilon_0} \langle \alpha_{IJ}^{(1)} \rangle. \tag{3}$$

The point to note is that, before the ensemble average can be considered in Equation (3), it is required to project $\alpha_{ij}^{(1)}$ from the molecular frame in which it is defined into the laboratory frame to arrive at $\alpha_{IJ}^{(1)}$, thereby encoding the molecular orientation. The manner in which these projections are performed is related to the light–matter interaction accompanying each of the $\alpha^{(n)}$ processes. As a result, different spectroscopic techniques have different symmetry properties, sensitivity to molecular orientation, and fingerprinting abilities.

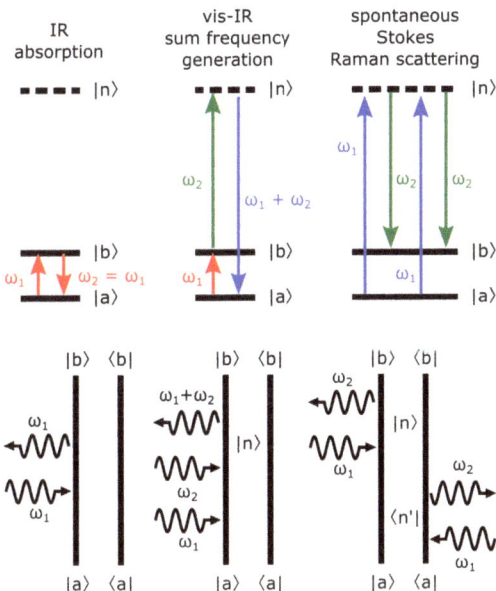

Figure 2. Energy level and double-sided Feynman diagrams of the IR absorption, visible–infrared sum-frequency generation, and spontaneous Stokes Raman scattering processes.

Figure 2 provides energy level and double-sided Feynman diagrams illustrating the interactions associated with the three spectroscopic techniques that we consider in this comparison. The first case illustrates that IR absorption spectroscopy is a probe of the linear polarizability $\alpha^{(1)}$. Absorption of an IR photon causes a transition from the ground vibrational state $|a\rangle$ to an excited vibrational state $|b\rangle$. The emitted photon has the same frequency, polarization, and wavevector as the exciting photon, and hence this self-heterodyne experiment provides direct access to $\mathbb{Im}\{\chi^{(1)}\}$. In visible–infrared sum-frequency generation, a broadband or tuneable IR beam is spatially and temporally overlapped with a typically fixed frequency visible beam. In the absence of inversion symmetry, this generates light at the sum of the two input frequencies, proportional to the second-order susceptibility $\chi^{(2)}$, through interaction with a non-resonant electronic virtual state $|n\rangle$. Intensity-only detection schemes measure a signal proportional to $|\chi^{(2)}|^2$, while phase-sensitive detection provides access to $\mathbb{Im}\{\chi^{(2)}\}$ [37–42]. Of the large family of Raman scattering probes, we consider the case of spontaneous Raman scattering where the Stokes-shifted wavelengths are detected. Although the intensity of the detected light (frequency ω_2 in Figure 2) is linearly proportional to the intensity of the pump beam (frequency ω_1) [43], the observables commonly associated with Raman spectroscopy reveal that this is in fact a probe of $\mathbb{Im}\{\chi^{(3)}\}$, and is associated with four light-matter interactions [44,45].

2.2. Accessing Elements of the Response Functions Using Polarized Light

IR absorption. In an infrared absorption experiment, one measures diagonal elements of the rank-2 tensor $\mathbb{Im}\{\chi^{(1)}_{II}\}$ that originates from a sum and orientational average over $\mathbb{Im}\{\alpha^{(1)}_{II}\}$. As shown in Figure 3, these quantities have nine elements, but can almost always be diagonalized into three principle components. This is the origin of the typically single-subscripted refractive index and absorption coefficient. If we consider $\mathbf{D}(\theta, \phi, \psi)$ to be the 3×3 direction cosine matrix (DCM) incorporating the Euler angles θ, ϕ, and ψ defined in Figure 1, we can then carry out the projection [26,46]

$$\chi^{(1)}_{IJ}(\theta, \phi, \psi) = N \sum_{\ell} \sum_{m} D_{Ii}(\theta, \phi, \psi) \cdot D_{Jj}(\theta, \phi, \psi) \cdot \alpha^{(1)}_{ij}. \tag{4}$$

If we were to use the contracted version, such as the 3-element transition dipole moment vector, we would use

$$|\langle b_I|\overline{\mu}|a_J\rangle|^2 = \left| \sum_{\ell} D_{Ii}(\theta, \phi, \psi) \cdot \langle b_j|\overline{\mu}|a_i\rangle \right|^2, \tag{5}$$

where $\overline{\mu}$ is the dipole moment operator. Note that, even though we are now using a single application of the the direction cosine matrix to transform a vector (tensor of rank 1) from the molecule-fixed to the laboratory-fixed coordinate system, the square results in the same angle-dependence. For the present demonstration, we assume an isotropic distribution of azimuthal angles ϕ and twist angles ψ (see Figure 1) so the the only orientation is that between the molecular reference axis and the laboratory z-axis. In the case of molecules adsorbed to surfaces, this is the often-encountered situation in which there is no preferred orientation in the (x, y) plane of the surface, and θ is the polar angle between the molecular long axis **c** and the surface normal **z**. This may be realized by integrating over ϕ and ψ to obtain

$$\begin{aligned} \chi^{(1)}_{II}(\theta) &= \frac{1}{4\pi^2} \int_0^{2\pi} \int_0^{2\pi} \chi^{(1)}_{II}(\theta, \phi, \psi) \, \mathrm{d}\phi \, \mathrm{d}\psi \\ &= \frac{1}{4\pi^2} \int_0^{2\pi} \int_0^{2\pi} |\langle b_I|\overline{\mu}|a_I\rangle|^2 \, \mathrm{d}\phi \, \mathrm{d}\psi. \end{aligned} \tag{6}$$

The main point is that, regardless of whether we use the rank 2 tensor $\chi^{(1)}$, or the vector $\langle b_I|\overline{\mu}|a_I\rangle$, the θ-dependence of the resulting function is the same. Furthermore, when this integration is carried out over all Cartesian coordinates, we find that there are only two unique elements; these are $\chi^{(1)}_{XX} = \chi^{(1)}_{YY}$ (due to azimuthal symmetry of the surface) and $\chi^{(1)}_{ZZ}$. A polarized IR absorption experiment is therefore carried out with a single polarizer placed before the sample. Owing to the symmetry of specific normal modes of vibration, the molecular frame $\alpha^{(1)}_{ii}$ may have a simple form, for example $\alpha^{(1)}_{xx} = \alpha^{(1)}_{yy} \ll \alpha^{(1)}_{zz}$ for a methyl symmetric stretch. In general, however, we can consider $\alpha^{(1)}_{xx} \neq \alpha^{(1)}_{yy} \neq \alpha^{(1)}_{zz}$, as these molecular values will be determined from electronic structure calculations. Regardless of any inherent symmetries in $\alpha_{ij}^{(1)}$, we can always write the result as

$$\chi_{II}^{(1)}(\theta) = c_0 + c_1 \cos^2 \theta \tag{7}$$

which, in turn, enables the polarized IR absorption spectra to be expressed in terms of an order parameter $\langle P_2 \rangle$ derived from the second-order Legendre polynomial $P_2(\cos \theta) = \frac{3}{2}\langle \cos^2 \theta \rangle - \frac{1}{2}$ [47].

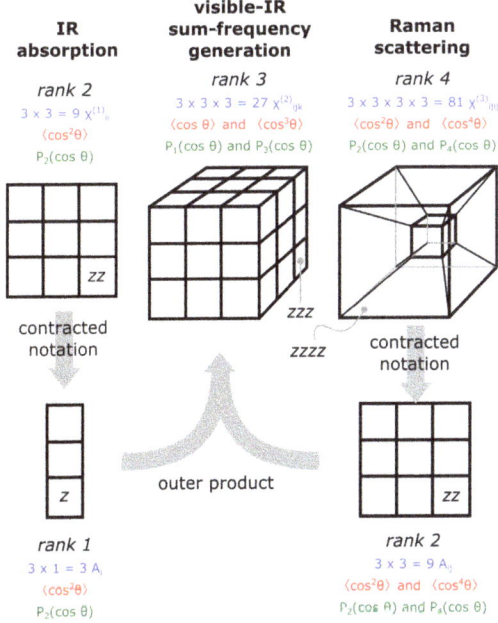

Figure 3. The tensoral nature of the IR absorption, visible–infrared sum-frequency generation, and Raman scattering processes illustrated. In the top row, the material response is arranged according to the rank of the process. In the bottom row, the most-often used contracted notation for an absorption process and Raman scattering are illustrated.

Sum frequency generation. In a vibrational SFG experiment, we can independently control the polarization of the incoming visible and infrared beams, and select a component of the emitted SFG field polarization. This enables measurement of all non-zero components of the 27-element rank-3 tensor $\chi_{IJK}^{(2)}$. From the molecular response, we can again project into the laboratory frame to obtain

$$\chi_{IJK}^{(2)}(\theta, \phi, \psi) = N \sum_\ell \sum_m \sum_n D_{Ii}(\theta, \phi, \psi) \cdot D_{Jj}(\theta, \phi, \psi) \cdot D_{Kk}(\theta, \phi, \psi) \cdot \alpha_{ijk}^{(2)} \tag{8}$$

this time employing three direction cosine matrix elements to compute each element of $\chi_{IJK}^{(2)}$ as this is a rank 3 tensor. We are interested in the result

$$\chi_{IJK}^{(2)}(\theta) = \frac{1}{4\pi^2} \int_0^{2\pi} \int_0^{2\pi} \chi_{IJK}^{(2)}(\theta, \phi, \psi) \, d\phi \, d\psi$$
$$= c_1 \cos \theta + c_3 \cos^3 \theta. \tag{9}$$

We note that, unlike the case of IR absorption, this function has odd symmetry with respect to θ. We can therefore express the solution in terms of the order parameters $\langle P_1 \rangle$ and $\langle P_3 \rangle$. Among the methods we discuss, SFG is the only technique that is capable of distinguishing molecules oriented in the quadrant $0° \leq \theta \leq 90°$ from those in the quadrant $90° \leq \theta \leq 180°$. That is, $\mathrm{Im}\{\chi^{(2)}\}(\theta) = -\mathrm{Im}\{\chi^{(2)}\}(180° - \theta)$. In the most commonly-encountered case of electronic non-resonance, this integration results in only seven non-zero elements, of which three are unique. These are $\chi^{(2)}_{XXZ} = \chi^{(2)}_{YYZ}$, $\chi^{(2)}_{XZX} = \chi^{(2)}_{YZY} = \chi^{(2)}_{ZXX} = \chi^{(2)}_{ZYY}$, and $\chi^{(2)}_{ZZZ}$.

Raman scattering. The Raman scattering process is the most complex and interesting among the techniques we compare, owing to the four-dimension response function. In a spontaneous Raman experiment, although we probe components of the 81-element rank-3 tensor $\chi^{(3)}_{IJKL}$, only the elements $\chi^{(3)}_{IJIJ}$ are accessible. This readily lends itself to the contracted notation as shown in Figure 3, where the transition polarizability $\bar{\alpha}$ (a rank 2 tensor with dimensions 3×3 are used. In analogy to our description of the IR absorption experiment, we note that the transformation from molecular to laboratory coordinates can then be carried out on $\alpha^{(3)}$ directly [48]:

$$\chi^{(3)}_{IJIJ}(\theta, \phi, \psi) = N \sum_i \sum_j \sum_k \sum_\ell D_{Ii}(\theta, \phi, \psi) \cdot D_{Jj}(\theta, \phi, \psi) \cdot D_{Kk}(\theta, \phi, \psi) \cdot D_{L\ell}(\theta, \phi, \psi) \cdot \alpha^{(3)}_{ijk\ell}.$$

(10)

If we were to use the contracted version corresponding to the the transition polarizability matrix, we would use

$$|\langle b_I | \bar{\alpha} | a_J \rangle|^2 = \left| \sum_i \sum_j D_{Ii}(\theta, \phi, \psi) \cdot D_{Jj}(\theta, \phi, \psi) \cdot \langle b_i | \bar{\alpha} | a_j \rangle \right|^2.$$

(11)

Once again, we emphasize that, regardless of whether the rank 4 or rank 2 representation of the Raman response is used, the same angle dependence results, noting that the square of the transition polarizability must be used when determining the orientational average. Integrating over the angles that we consider to be uniformly distributed provides the tilt angle dependence

$$\begin{aligned} \chi^{(3)}_{IJIJ}(\theta) &= \frac{1}{4\pi^2} \int_0^{2\pi} \int_0^{2\pi} \chi^{(3)}_{IJIJ}(\theta, \phi, \psi)\, \mathrm{d}\phi\, \mathrm{d}\psi \\ &= \frac{1}{4\pi^2} \int_0^{2\pi} \int_0^{2\pi} |\langle b_I | \bar{\alpha} | a_J \rangle|^2\, \mathrm{d}\phi\, \mathrm{d}\psi \\ &= c_0 + c_2 \cos^2 \theta + c_4 \cos^4 \theta. \end{aligned}$$

(12)

The resulting functional form shares the same symmetry characteristics as IR absorption (insensitive to the polarity of the tilt angle distribution), but now includes a higher-order contribution as we can probe the average $\langle \cos^4 \theta \rangle$, and therefore also have access to the order parameter $\langle P_4 \rangle$. Further symmetry and electronic non-resonance reduce the probed elements to $\chi^{(3)}_{XXXX} = \chi^{(3)}_{YYYY}$, $\chi^{(3)}_{XYXY} = \chi^{(3)}_{YXYX}$, $\chi^{(3)}_{XZXZ} = \chi^{(3)}_{ZXZX}$, and $\chi^{(3)}_{ZZZZ}$. In practice, all of the above-mentioned tensor elements are obtained using one or more polarization schemes, but those experimental details are not relevant to the current discussion. Instead, we focus on the maximum information content available from each experiment as a consequence of the symmetry of the relevant susceptibility tensor.

3. Methods

3.1. Generation of the Candidate Spectra

Methods for the calculation of infrared transition dipole moments $\langle b | \bar{\mu} | a \rangle$, Raman transition polarizabilities $\langle b | \bar{\alpha} | a \rangle$, and their coupling to estimate vibrational hyperpolarizabilities $\alpha^{(2)} = \langle b | \bar{\alpha} | a \rangle \otimes \langle b | \bar{\mu} | a \rangle$ (direct product as illustrated in Figure 3) have been previously described [26,49]. In brief, calculations were carried out using GAMESS [50] at the B3LYP/6-31G(d,p) level, using a finite difference approach to determine the transition matrix elements from the dipole moment frequency dependent polarizability variation with respect to the normal mode coordinates. It has been established this basis set reproduces vibrational spectra of amino acids [51]. A polarizable continuum model was used to simulate adsorbed states in an aqueous solution. A frequency scaling factor of 0.96 has been applied [52]. We consider the six amino acids methionine (Met), leucine (Leu), isoleucine (Ile), alanine (Ala), threonine (Thr) and valine (Val). We have previously demonstrated the manner in which the spectral lineshape is calculated from these quantum mechanical properties [46]. In the case of infrared spectroscopy, the absorbance is proportional to

$$\mathbb{Im}\{\chi_{II}^{(1)}\}(\omega_{IR}) = N \sum_q \frac{\langle b_I|\overline{\mu}|a_I\rangle_q^2 \Gamma_q}{(\omega_q - \omega_{IR})^2 + \Gamma_q^2} \tag{13}$$

where ω_q and Γ_q are the frequency and homogeneous linewidth of the qth normal mode. For a mixture of $n = 6$ molecules each oriented at a different angle θ according to the weighting factor $f(n, \theta)$, the overall IR spectrum of the mixture, hereafter referred to as the target spectrum, is given by

$$T_{II} = \sum_{n=1}^{6} \sum_\theta f(n,\theta) \cdot \mathbb{Im}\{\chi_{II}^{(1)}\}(n,\theta), \tag{14}$$

imposing the normalization condition

$$\sum_n \sum_\theta f(n,\theta) = 1. \tag{15}$$

The lineshape for the polarized heterodyne-detected SFG spectrum of a single molecule at a single tilt angle is given by

$$\mathbb{Im}\{\chi_{IJK}^{(2)}\}(\omega_{IR}) = N \sum_q \frac{\langle a_I|\overline{\alpha}|b_J\rangle_q \langle b_K|\overline{\mu}|a_K\rangle_q \Gamma_q}{(\omega_q - \omega_{IR})^2 + \Gamma_q^2} \tag{16}$$

and the collection of molecules has the target spectrum

$$T_{IJK} = \sum_{n=1}^{6} \sum_\theta f(n,\theta) \cdot \mathbb{Im}\{\chi_{IJK}^{(2)}\}(n,\theta). \tag{17}$$

The Raman spectra of individual candidate molecules are obtained from

$$\mathbb{Im}\{\chi_{IJIJ}^{(3)}\}(\Delta\omega) = N \sum_q \frac{\langle b_I|\overline{\alpha}|a_J\rangle_q^2 \Gamma_q}{(\omega_q - \Delta\omega)^2 + \Gamma_q^2} \tag{18}$$

where $\Delta\omega$ is the Stokes shift with respect to the incident light frequency. We assume that the mixture of molecules then has an overall measured Raman spectrum given by

$$T_{IJIJ} = \sum_{n=1}^{6} \sum_\theta f(n,\theta) \cdot \mathbb{Im}\{\chi_{IJIJ}^{(3)}\}(n,\theta). \tag{19}$$

Note that, with the exception of the hyperpolarizabilities $\alpha^{(n)}$ and susceptibilities $\chi^{(n)}$, we will not explicitly specify the nth order quantities with superscripts and instead rely on the $n + 1$ Cartesian coordinates in subscripts such as T_{IJIJ} to indicate that this is an element of rank 4 tensor representing a third-order response function.

3.2. Linear Programming

Linear programming (LP) belongs to the class of convex optimization techniques that is known to provide exact solutions to problems that are challenging to solve using other methods, either due to the inherent complexity of the function to be minimized, or due to the number of local minima in the multidimensional parameter/error space [53–56]. In addition, LP can provide solutions in $\mathcal{O}(n)$ time, compared to traditional techniques [57–59] that can require $\mathcal{O}(n!)$ time. An example of a small LP problem that is convenient to visualize is minimization of the two-dimensional objective function

$$f(x, y) = 2y - x + 8 \tag{20}$$

subject to the constraints

$$-x + 2y \leq 4 \tag{21a}$$
$$x + y \leq 8 \tag{21b}$$
$$y < 5 \tag{21c}$$
$$x > 0 \tag{21d}$$
$$y > 0. \tag{21e}$$

The region of the solution space is illustrated as the shaded region in Figure 4. The fundamental theorem of LP states that the minimum exists at the boundary of the convex polyhedron that defines the feasible region of the solution space. It can be shown that the solution is further restricted to the vertices of this polyhedron. In this simple two-dimensional example, there are only four vertices at $(0,0)$, $(8,0)$, $(4,4)$ and $(0,2)$. It is straightforward to evaluate the value of the function at each of these locations to select the vertex with the minimum value. In practice, for more difficult problems, the task of vertex finding and evaluation may be performed by algorithms such as simplex [60], and there are existing packages for this task. We used the GNU linear programming toolkit [61] to identify the LP solutions.

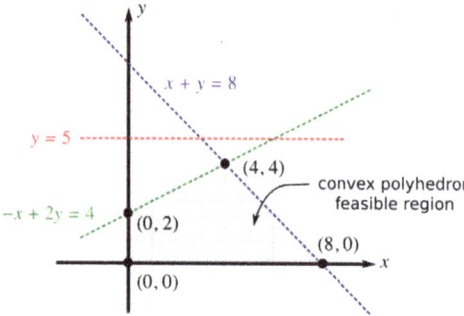

Figure 4. A two-dimensional example of a minimization problem subject to constraints whose linear programming solution can be visualized graphically.

In order to apply LP to spectroscopy problems, we need to have an appropriate formulation of the objective function to be minimized. For each polarization of the IR spectrum, we can a component of the objective function as

$$S_{II} = \min \sum_{p=1}^{\text{points}} \left| T_{II,p} - \sum_{c=1}^{\text{candidates}} f_c \cdot \mathbb{Im}\{\chi_{II}^{(1)}\}_{c,p} \right|, \tag{22}$$

where f_c are the unknown fractions of the candidate, the decision variables returned by the LP solver; p is the number of points selected along the wavenumber axis, both for candidates and target spectra; c is the number of candidates. We can then include both projections that come from the two unique polarization schemes identified in our problem by combining them in

$$S_{IR} = S_{XX} + S_{ZZ}. \tag{23}$$

Further details on the formulation of the objective function and its solution are given in Ref. [62]. In brief, the absolute residual between the target spectrum and the one composed by the decision variables is calculated for each data point. The objective function minimizes the sum of the absolute residuals over all the data points. Note that the LP model exactly describes our problem to be solved, yielding the target composition if we can provide precise enough data. Recall that if the solution space of an LP instance is feasible and bounded, then there is a unique optimum solution.

Analogous versions of the objective function in Equation (22) exist for the SFG data as S_{IJK}, from which

$$S_{SFG} = S_{XXZ} + S_{XZX} + S_{ZZZ} \tag{24}$$

is calculated, and S_{IJIJ} for the Raman spectra from which

$$S_{Raman} = S_{XXXX} + S_{XYXY} + S_{XZXZ} + S_{ZZZZ} \tag{25}$$

may be determined.

3.3. Construction of Test Cases

IR (2 polarizations), SFG (3 polarizations), and Raman (4 polarizations) spectra for each molecule were calculated as a function of tilt angle from $\theta = 0°$ to $\theta = 180°$ with a step size of $10°$ and stored, so subsequent calculations and spectra of mixtures could be computed quickly. A random number generator was then used to determine the composition of the mixture, and the result is normalized so the fraction of all candidates together does not exceed 100%. An independently-seeded random number generator determined the tilt angle of each amino acid in the mixture. An example of the semi-discrete parameter space is shown in Figure 5. Linear programming is then used to decipher the composition of the mixture, using all available polarization data, but possibly a subset of the experimental techniques in the following cases: IR data only, SFG data only, Raman data only, IR and SFG data combined, IR and SFG, SFG and Raman, and the combination of all data employing IR and SFG and Raman spectra. Each test case was then run 100 times in order to remove potential bias that may result from insufficient statistics.

4. Results and Discussion

The results of all test cases are summarized in Table 1. Instead of describing individual outcomes (that would appear as indicated in Figure 5) corresponding to a randomly selected distribution of molecules, we report on whether LP was able to determine the correct composition of the mixture (molecular identity of the species and tilt angle of each component) from data obtained in all trials. The advantage of LP is that we can be assured of finding the global minimum solution. In cases where we were not able to recover the target composition, the local minima and global minimum have identical scores S.

4.1. Known Scaling Factors

The first set of cases we considered corresponds to the scenario in which the absolute intensity scaling (absorbance in the case of IR, and intensity with respect to a reference sample in the case of SFG and Raman, or expressed in terms of absolute units of $\chi^{(2)}$ and $\chi^{(3)}$) is known. Although this is certainly possible, it is not common practice to go through this effort, especially for Raman data. Nevertheless, it is an important set of data for us to discuss first, as it represents the simplest case where all techniques can readily be compared on equal footing. We further divide this data set into cases where the polarity of the orientation of each molecule is known in advance (whether the tilt angle lies in the range $0° \le \theta \le 90°$ or $90° \le \theta \le 180°$) or is unknown ($0° \le \theta \le 180°$) and therefore needs to be resolved through the spectral interpretation. For simplicity, we can consider the known polarity as corresponding to tilt angles restricted to the quadrant $0° \leq \theta \leq 90°$, since it is always possible to redefine the orientation of the molecular long axis to suit this definition. From an experimental perspective, this is equivalent to using chemical intuition to identify which end of the molecule is closest to the surface. In this case, column a of Table 1 indicates that IR data taken alone can return the correct composition of the mixture, but either SFG or Raman are able to do this. Immediately, two conclusions come to mind: SFG and Raman contain higher order response functions, sensitive to $\langle \cos^3 \theta \rangle$ and $\langle \cos^4 \theta \rangle$, and more unique polarization schemes compared to the $\langle \cos^2 \theta \rangle$ sensitivity of IR spectra and the two unique polarizations it offers. We will further comment on the origins of the molecular specificity and orientation sensitivity below. We note that determinations using combinations of the methods are moot within this set, as the results are predictable from the success of individual methods. This is indicated by the parenthetical ($\checkmark$) in Table 1 representing successful spectral unmixing from an unnecessary combination of data.

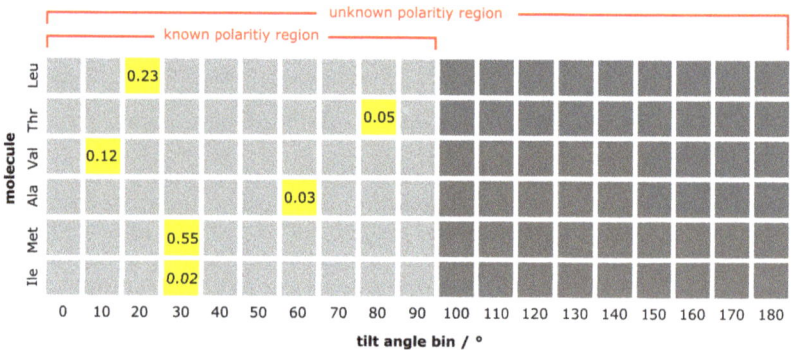

Figure 5. An illustration of the semi-discrete parameter space that comprises a single mixture. In the case of molecules with known polarity, we consider the range $\theta = 0°$ to $\theta = 90°$ in discrete steps of $10°$. In the case of unknown polarity, the tilt angles in the range $\theta = 0°$ to $\theta = 180°$ may be selected for each molecule. A fraction of each molecule (yellow squares) is then chosen as a weighting factor to generate the mixture. The mixture in the example shown contains 55% methionine tilted at 30° as its largest component, and 2% isoleucine tilted at 30° as its smallest component.

Table 1. A summary of the evaluated test cases indicating the ability of the spectral data to reveal the target composition in terms of the identity and orientation of the constituent molecules. An ✗ indicates that the data set was insufficient to determine the target composition. A ✓ indicates that sufficient data was available for spectral unmixing, while a parenthetical ($\checkmark$) indicates success, but a data set that is unnecessary since a subset of the data has been shown to be sufficient.

	Known Scaling Factors		Arbitrary Scaling Factors	
Spectral Data	**(a) Known Polarity**	**(b) Unknown Polarity**	**(c) Known Polarity**	**(d) Unknown Polarity**
IR only	✗	✗	✗	✗
SFG only	✓	✗	✗	✗
Raman only	✓	✗	✓	✗
IR + Raman	(✓)	✗	(✓)	✗
IR + SFG	(✓)	✓	✗	✗
SFG + Raman	(✓)	✓	(✓)	✓
IR + SFG + Raman	(✓)	(✓)	(✓)	(✓)

We next consider the interesting case where each molecule in the mixture can lie in any of the two quadrants covered by the tilt angle cones. These results, summarized in column b of Table 1. The fact that IR and Raman data, either alone or in combination, cannot resolve the tilt angle is expected, since the even powers of cosine are symmetric about $\theta = 90°$ (the plane of the surface). We therefore anticipate requiring SFG data to answer any question that requires such symmetry breaking. It is interesting to see, however, that SFG spectra alone cannot consistently return the correct target composition, and so we label its data as insufficient. When SFG is combined with either IR or Raman data, the spectral unmixing then succeeds. We will return to the discussion of this result after considering the remaining cases.

4.2. Arbitrary Scaling Factors

In the data described above, we have used electronic structure calculations to determine the spectra of various molecules at particular tilt angles, created a linear combination of these results, and then evaluated the ability of different spectroscopic data to aid in the unmixing. We therefore had significant help from the fact that the candidate spectra and the target spectrum were on the same scale. In a real experiment, there are two factors that prevent such information from being available in most cases. One is that the response in SFG and particularly Raman is typically not calibrated through the use of a reference material. Furthermore, since we are not dealing with isotropic mixtures, it would be difficult to obtain oriented samples in order to know the response from each species. Hence the use of electronic structure calculations is valuable. This, however, poses the second challenge: the spectra predicted by any calculation will necessarily be on a different scale from the measured target spectrum. Furthermore, the arbitrary scaling factor differs in the case of IR absorption, SFG, and Raman scattering. Fortunately, linear programming enables us to readily consider such scaling factors by introducing slack variables. A detailed example on the use of slack variables with application to unmixing Raman data is provided in Ref. [62]. Here we introduce separate slack variables for IR, SFG, and Raman data thereby acknowledging that the scaling factors are constant within an experiment when changing only the beam/detector polarization (which still requires calibration, but is easy to achieve in practice), but is not related across the techniques. This is obviously a more challenging problem to solve, with the results indicated in column c of Table 1. In the case of molecular orientations restricted to a single known quadrant of the tilt angle, now only Raman data (and no longer SFG alone) can accurately reveal the molecular identities and orientations. Naturally, any combination with Raman also works, but provides no additional benefit. When we increase the complexity of the problem by lifting the polarity restriction, column d shows that the needed SFG data must now be combined with Raman data (as an IR complement to SFG is no longer sufficient).

4.3. Exploring the Origins of Orientation Sensitivity

As we have noted, many of the results presented above have displayed the trend Raman > SFG > IR in terms of the abilities of the techniques to resolve the components of the mixture including proper identification of the tilt angles of each component. Based on this information alone, one is curious about the origins of displayed sensitivities. On the one hand, this sequence follows from $\langle \cos^4 \theta \rangle$ being more sensitive than $\langle \cos^3 \theta \rangle$ which is in turn more sensitive to small differences in the tilt angle than $\langle \cos^2 \theta \rangle$. On the other hand, the techniques based on higher-order response functions necessarily have more unique elements of the response tensor that can be probed with different polarizations. The two features are intrinsically linked through the transformations between molecular and laboratory coordinates as illustrated. Nevertheless, in an attempt to further comment on the relative utility of multiple projections compared to higher angle sensitivity of individual spectroscopies, we have performed a separate comparison using only z-polarized version of each technique. In other words, the $\chi_{ZZ}^{(1)}$ response from IR absorption with a z-polarized input light field; the $\chi_{ZZZ}^{(2)}$ element of the SFG response (that typically needs to be separated from a combination of terms when all beams are p-polarized), and $\chi^{(3)}_{ZZZZ}$ that is measured in a Raman experiment with a z-polarized input field and the selection of the z-polarized scattered light for detection. For this evaluation, we consider all pairs of neighbouring angles that are separated by $10°$, for example $(0°, 10°)$, $(10°, 20°)$, up to $(70°, 80°)$. The specific angle $\theta = 90°$ is avoided since it results in zero intensity for SFG due to the isotropy of the twist and azimuthal distributions. We then compute the pairwise Pearson's correlation coefficient

$$c_P = \frac{\sum\limits_{i=1}^{N} (\omega_i - \overline{\omega}) \left(\mathbb{Im}\{\chi^{(n)}\}_i - \overline{\mathbb{Im}\{\chi^{(2)}\}} \right)}{\sqrt{\sum\limits_{i=1}^{N} (\omega_i - \overline{\omega})^2} \sqrt{\sum\limits_{i=1}^{N} \left(\mathbb{Im}\{\chi^{(n)}\}_i - \overline{\mathbb{Im}\{\chi^{(2)}\}} \right)^2}} \tag{26}$$

where ω refers to ω_{IR} in the case of IR and SFG spectra, and to the Stokes shift $\Delta\omega$ in the case of Raman spectra. When results from all pairs of angles were averaged over all six molecules, we obtained the result $c_P = 0.99$ for the set of z-polarized IR spectra, $c_P = 0.97$ for the set of z-polarized SFG spectra, and $c_P = 0.98$ for the z-polarized Raman spectra. These coefficients are invariant to scale, so we can compare across techniques without normalizing the spectra. We anticipate $c_P \approx 1$ in all cases, as the spectral features for the same molecule tilted by an additional $10°$ are small. Nevertheless, the result is counter-intuitive as the largest difference (smallest c_P) is not seen for the Raman spectra. There is in fact no trend in this data that is consistent with the results from LP that we have reported.

Further insight into this result may be obtained by plotting the spectrum obtained by averaging over all tilt angles (blue traces in Figure 6) along with the standard deviation about the mean (grey trace in Figure 6. Vector normalized spectra are used to allow for comparison between the three techniques. Visual inspection alone suggests that for all molecules the SFG spectra display the highest spectral variation across all tilt angles. This is numerically highlighted with the spectral deviation averaged over all frequencies $\overline{\sigma}$, where SFG is the highest in all cases. Otherwise, the averaged standard deviation does not reveal any consistent trend between IR and Raman. For example, for the case of isoleucine (Ile) we obtain $\overline{\sigma} = 0.0009$ for the set of z-polarized IR spectra, $\overline{\sigma} = 0.0042$ for the set of z-polarized SFG spectra, and $\overline{\sigma} = 0.0017$ for the z-polarized Raman spectra. In this case we may conclude that spectral variation follows the trend of SFG > Raman > IR. For methionine (Met), this changes to SFG > IR > Raman, indicating that there is no general trend. Regardless, the point is that the largest variation is not observed in the Raman spectra, supporting the conclusion made using the Pearson's correlation coefficient.

We now return to the earlier result revealed by LP that, in the case where molecules can lie in any of the two tilt angle quadrants, SFG is needed but SFG alone is not sufficient to return the complete mixture composition for all 100 randomly chosen samples. In the case where no additional scaling factor was introduced, the SFG data needed to be combined with either IR or Raman data to ensure success in all tests. It was intriguing that IR could complement the SFG data since it is, in theory, less sensitive to changes in tilt angle. This was an early indication that the additional projections in form of unique polarized spectra are potentially more valuable than higher-order response functions, a point that is now confirmed through the examination of these spectral differences.

A final point concerns the utility of higher-order techniques for molecular orientation determination. In the cases we have considered in this work, all molecules are assumed to be aligned at a fixed angle θ_0, with no spread in angles. In other words, we have considered an orientation distribution described by $f(\theta) = \delta(\theta - \theta_0)$. A more realistic system has a spread of tilt angles, and the goal of any complete orientation analysis is to reconstruct the orientation distribution from experimental data. In the next simplest case, where it is assumed that the distribution is Gaussian, experimental data must then provide the value of the mean tilt angle θ_0 and the width of the tilt distribution σ. Data from IR absorption alone cannot provide even these two parameters, regardless of whether the polarity of the orientation is known. In such cases, one exploits the true power of higher-order spectroscopies [63–65]. Nevertheless, many experimental systems are either too complex for detailed analysis, or have too many undermined parameters. In such cases, it is common to assume a narrow distribution of tilt angles. This work has demonstrated how information obtained from different experiments can aid in these pursuits.

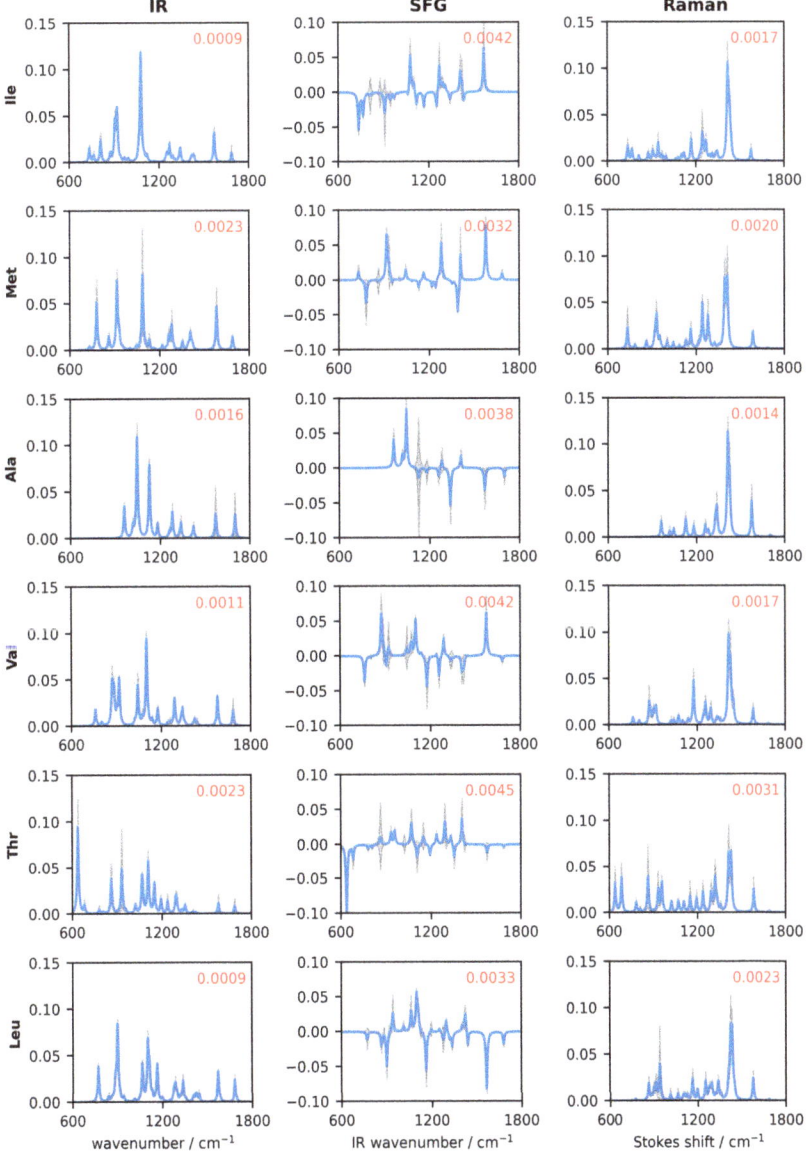

Figure 6. Average spectra (blue) computed from all tilt angles in the range 0°–80° and the standard deviation (grey) about the mean. The extent of the vertical axis is the same in all plots, as the spectra are vector normalized for this comparison only. The standard deviation averaged over all frequencies is indicated in red in the inset of each panel.

5. Conclusions

This work has addressed the challenging problem of a mixture of molecules in solution whose component molecules may preferentially adsorb to a surface and adopt a preferential orientation in their adsorbed state. We have theoretically investigated the ability of three spectroscopic techniques to unmix the spectral signatures in order to determine the composition and structure of the system. These included IR absorption spectroscopy, based on the rank 2 response function derived from the linear susceptibility; visible-infrared sum-frequency spectroscopy that is based on the rank 3 response of the second-order susceptibility; spontaneous Raman scattering that, although linear in its dependence on the incident light intensity, encodes information characteristic of a rank 4 third-order response function. Linear programming is ideally suited to this investigation as it is a convex optimization technique and hence can return the global minimum. The results indicate that polarized Raman scattering is always the preferred technique that is capable of returning the correct distribution of species and orientations, provided that there is no ambiguity in the polarity of the orientation. In cases where polarity resolution is required, one must incorporate a technique with an even-order response function (such as sum-frequency generation), but SFG alone cannot accurately describe complex mixtures without the aid of IR and, in the most general case, Raman data. Our analysis of these results indicates that it is the additional projections afforded by the unique elements of the response tensors that are responsible for the sensitivity of Raman spectroscopy.

Author Contributions: Conceptualization, U.S. and D.K.H.; methodology, F.C., K.-K.H. and L.G.; software, F.C. and L.G.; writing, L.G., U.S., and D.K.H.; funding acquisition, U.S. and D.K.H. All authors have read and agreed to the published version of the manuscript.

Funding: We thank the Natural Sciences and Engineering Research Council of Canada (NSERC) for support of this science with Discovery Grants to D.K.H. and U.S. F.C. is grateful to the University of Victoria for a graduate fellowship. LG is partially supported by an NSERC Canada Graduate Scholarship, and a Chemistry Graduate Award for Research Excellence.

Institutional Review Board Statement: Not applicable.

Informed Consent Statement: Not applicable.

Data Availability Statement: The data presented in this study are available on request from the corresponding author.

Conflicts of Interest: The authors declare no conflict of interest. The funders had no role in the design of the study; in the collection, analyses, or interpretation of data; in the writing of the manuscript, or in the decision to publish the results.

Abbreviations

The following abbreviations are used in this manuscript:

DCM	direction cosine matrix
IR	infrared
LP	linear programming
SFG	sum-frequency generation

References

1. Ward, I.M. Determination of Molecular Orientation by Spectroscopic Techniques. *Adv. Poly. Sci.* **1985**, *66*, 81–115.
2. McHale, J.L. *Molecular Spectroscopy*; Pearson Education: New York, NY, USA, 2008.
3. Kliger, D.S.; Lewis, J.W.; Randal, C.E. *Polarized light in optics and spectroscopy*; Academic Press, Inc.: San Diego, CA, USA, 1990.
4. Pelletier, I.; Laurin, I.; Buffeteau, T.; Pézolet, M. Determination of Molecular Orientation in Biaxially Oriented Ultrathin Films. *J. Phys. Chem. B* **2004**, *108*, 7162–7169. [CrossRef]
5. Umemura, J.; Kamata, T.; Kawai, T.; Takenaka, T. Quantitative Evaluation of Molecular Orientation in Thin Langmuir–Blodgett Films by FT-IR Transmission and Reflection-Absorption Spectroscopy. *J. Phys. Chem.* **1990**, *94*, 62–67. [CrossRef]
6. Brunner, H.; Mayer, U.; Hoffmann, M. External Reflection Infrared Spectroscopy of Aniostropic Adsorbate Layers on Dielectric Substrates. *Appl. Spectrosc.* **1997**, *51*, 209–217. [CrossRef]

7. Chollet, P.A.; Messier, J.; Rosilio, C. Infrared Determination of the Orientation of Molecules in Stearamide Monolayers. *J. Chem. Phys.* **1976**, *64*, 1042–1050. [CrossRef]

8. Debe, M.K. Extracting Physical Structure Information from Thin Film Organic Films with Reflection Absorption Infrared Spectroscopy. *J. Appl. Phys.* **1984**, *55*, 3354–3366. [CrossRef]

9. Dluhy, R.A. Quantitative External Reflection Infrared Spectroscopic Analysis of Insoluble Monolayers Spread at the Air–Water Interface. *J. Phys. Chem.* **1986**, *90*, 1373–1379. [CrossRef]

10. Greenler, R.G. Infrared study of adsorbed molecules on metal surfaces by reflection techniques. *J. Chem. Phys.* **1966**, *44*, 310–315. [CrossRef]

11. Hasegawa, T.; Takeda, S.; Kawaguchi, A.; Umemura, J. Quantitative Analysis of Uniaxial Molecular Orientation in Langmuir-Blodgett Films by Infrared Reflection Spectroscopy. *Langmuir* **1995**, *11*, 1236–1243. [CrossRef]

12. Mendelson, R.; Brauner, J.W.; Gericke, A. External Infrared Absorption Spectrometry of Monolayer Films at the Air-Water Interface. *Annu. Rev. Phys. Chem.* **1995**, *46*, 305–333. [CrossRef]

13. Sourisseau, C. Polarization Measurements in Macro- and Micro-Raman Spectoscopies: Molecular Orientations in Thin Films and Azo-Dye Polymer Systems. *Chem. Rev.* **2004**, *104*, 3851–3892. [CrossRef] [PubMed]

14. Tanaka, M.; Young, R.J. Polarised Raman Spectroscopy for the Study of Molecular Orientation Distributions in Polymers. *J. Mater. Sci.* **2006**, *41*, 963–991. [CrossRef]

15. Bower, D.I. Investigation of Molecular Orientation Distributions by Polarized Raman Scattering and Polarized Fluorescence. *J. Poly. Sci.* **1972**, *10*, 2135–2153. [CrossRef]

16. Lagugné Labarthet, F. Polarized Measurements in Raman Microscopy. *Annu. Rep. Prog. Chem.* **2007**, *103*, 326–350. [CrossRef]

17. Richard-Lacroix, M.; Pellerin, C. Novel Method for Quantifying Molecular Orientation by Polarized Raman Spectroscopy: A Comparative Simulations Study. *Appl. Spectrosc.* **2013**, *67*, 409–419. [CrossRef] [PubMed]

18. Richard-Lacroix, M.; Pellerin, C. Accurate New Method for Molecular Orientation Quantification Using Polarized Raman Spectroscopy. *Macromolecules* **2013**, *46*, 5561–5569. [CrossRef]

19. Tsuboi, M.; Benevides, J.M.; Tomas, G.J., Jr. Raman Tensors and their Application in Structural Studies of Biological Systems. *Proc. Jpn. Acad. Ser. B* **2009**, *85*, 83–97. [CrossRef]

20. Yang, S.; Michielsen, S. Orientation Distribution Functions Obtained via Polarized Raman Spectroscopy of Poly(ethylene terephthalate) Fibers. *Macromolecules* **2003**, *36*, 6484–6492. [CrossRef]

21. Takenaka, T.; Fukuzaki, H. Resonance Raman Spectra of Insoluble Monolayers Spread on a Water Surface. *J. Raman Spectrosc.* **1979**, *8*, 151–154. [CrossRef]

22. Takenaka, T.; Nakanaga, T. Resonance Raman Spectra of Monolayers Adsorbed at the Interface between Carbon Tetrachloride and an Aqueous Solution of a Surfactant and a Dye. *J. Phys. Chem.* **1976**, *80*, 475–480. [CrossRef]

23. Takenaka, T. Effect of Electrolyte on the Molecular Orientation in Monolayers Adsorbed at the Liquid–Liquid Interface: Studies by Resonance Raman Spectra. *Chem. Phys. Lett.* **1978**, *55*, 515–518. [CrossRef]

24. Nakanaga, T.; Takenaka, T. Resonance Raman Spectra of Monolayers of a Surface–Active Dye Adsorbed at the Oil–Water Interface. *J. Phys. Chem.* **1977**, *81*, 645–649. [CrossRef]

25. Morita, A. *Theory of Sum Frequency Generation Spectroscopy*; Springer: Singapore, 2018.

26. Hall, S.A.; Jena, K.C.; Covert, P.A.; Roy, S.; Trudeau, T.G.; Hore, D.K. Molecular-Level Surface Structure from Nonlinear Vibrational Spectroscopy Combined with Simulations. *J. Phys. Chem. B* **2014**, *118*, 5617–5636. [CrossRef] [PubMed]

27. Richmond, G.L. Molecular Bonding and Interactions at Aqueous Surfaces as Probed by Vibrational Sum Frequency Spectroscopy. *Chem. Rev.* **2002**, *102*, 2693–2724. [CrossRef] [PubMed]

28. Bain, C.D. Sum-Frequency Vibrational Spectroscopy of the Solid/Liquid Interface. *J. Chem. Soc. Faraday Trans.* **1995**, *91*, 1281–1296. [CrossRef]

29. Lambert, A.G.; Davies, P.B.; Neivandt, D.J. Implementing the Theory of Sum Frequency Generation Vibrational Spectroscopy: A Tutorial Review. *Appl. Spectrosc. Rev.* **2005**, *40*, 103–145. [CrossRef]

30. Vidal, F.; Tadjeddine, A. Sum-Frequency Generation Spectroscopy of Interfaces. *Rep. Prog. Phys.* **2005**, *68*, 1095–1127. [CrossRef]

31. Buck, M.; Himmelhaus, M. Vibrational Spectroscopy of Interfaces by Infrared-Visible Sum Frequency Generation. *J. Vac. Sci. Technol. A* **2001**, *19*, 2717–2736. [CrossRef]

32. Shen, Y.R. Basic Theory of Surface Sum-Frequency Generation. *J. Phys. Chem. C* **2012**, *116*, 15505–15509. [CrossRef]

33. Pezzotti, S.; Serva, A.; Gaigeot, M.P. 2D-HB Network at the Air–Water Interface: A Structural and Dynamical Characterization by Means of ab initio and Classical Molecular Dynamics Simulations. *J. Chem. Phys.* **2018**, *148*, 174701. [CrossRef]

34. Ojha, D.; Kühne, T.D. "On-The-Fly" Calculation of the Vibrational Sum-Frequency Generation Spectrum at the Air-Water Interface. *Molecules* **2020**, *25*, 3939. [CrossRef] [PubMed]

35. Shen, Y.R. Surfaces Probed by Nonlinear Optics. *Surf. Sci.* **1994**, *299–300*, 551–562. [CrossRef]

36. Boyd, R.W. *Nonlinear Optics*, 2nd ed.; Academic Press: San Diego, CA, USA, 2003.

37. Superfine, R.; Huang, J.Y.; Shen, Y.R. Phase Measurement For Surface Infrared-Visible Sum-Frequency Generation. *Opt. Lett.* **1990**, *15*, 1276–1278. [CrossRef] [PubMed]

38. Shen, Y.R.; Ostroverkhov, V. Sum-frequency Vibrational Spectroscopy on Water Interfaces: Polar Orientation of Water Molecules at Interfaces. *Chem. Rev.* **2006**, *106*, 1140–1154. [CrossRef] [PubMed]

39. Mondal, J.; Nihonyanagi, S.; Yamaguchi, S.; Tahara, T. Structure and Orientation of Water at Charged Lipid Monolayer/Water Interfaces Probed by Heterodyne-Detected Vibrational Sum Frequency Generation Spectroscopy. *J. Am. Chem. Soc.* **2010**, *132*, 10656–10657. [CrossRef] [PubMed]

40. Nihonyanagi, S.; Yamaguchi, S.; Tahara, T. Direct Evidence for Orientational Flip–Flop of Water Molecules at Charged Interfaces: A Heterodyne-Detected Vibrational Sum Frequency Generation Study. *J. Chem. Phys.* **2009**, *130*, 204704.

41. Jena, K.; Hung, K.K.; Schwantje, T.; Hore, D.K. Methyl groups at dielectric and metal surfaces studied by sum-frequency generation in co- and counter-propagating configurations. *J. Chem. Phys.* **2011**, *135*, 044704. [CrossRef]

42. Jena, K.C.; Covert, P.A.; Hore, D.K. Phase Measurement in Non-Degenerate Three-Wave Mixing Spectroscopy. *J. Chem. Phys.* **2011**, *134*, 044712. [CrossRef]

43. Long, D.A. *The Raman Effect: A Unified Treatment of The Theory of Raman Scattering by Molecules*; John Wiley & Sons: Hoboken, NJ, USA, 2002.

44. Potma, E.O.; Mukamel, S. *Coherent Raman Scattering Microscopy*; CRC Press: Boca Raton, FL, USA, 2013; Chapter 1. pp. 3–42.

45. Mukamel, S. *Principles of Nonlinear Optical Spectroscopy*; Oxford University Press: New York, NY, USA, 1995.

46. Hung, K.K.; Stege, U.; Hore, D.K. IR Absorption, Raman Scattering, and IR-Vis Sum-Frequency Generation Spectroscopy as Quantitative Probes of Surface Structure. *Appl. Spectrosc. Rev.* **2015**, *50*, 351–376. [CrossRef]

47. Lagugné Labarthet, F.; Buffeteau, T.; Sourisseau, C. Orientation Distribution Functions in Uniaxial Systems Centered Perpendicularly to a Constraint Direction. *Appl. Spectrosc.* **2000**, *54*, 699–705. [CrossRef]

48. Wang, Y.; Cui, Z.F.; Wang, H.F. Experimental Observables and Macroscopic Susceptibility/Microscopic Polarizability Tensors for Third and Fourth-Order Nonlinear Spectroscopy of Ordered Molecular System. *Chin. J. Chem. Phys.* **2007**, *20*, 449–460. [CrossRef]

49. Hall, S.A.; Hickey, A.D.; Hore, D.K. Structure of Phenylalanine Adsorbed on Polystyrene From Nonlinear Vibrational Spectroscopy Measurements and Electronic Structure Calculations. *J. Phys. Chem. C* **2010**, *114*, 9748–9757. [CrossRef]

50. Schmidt, M.W.; Baldridge, K.K.; Boatz, J.A.; Elbert, S.T.; Gordon, M.S.; Jensen, J.H.; Koseki, S.; Matsunaga, N.; Nguyen, K.A.; Su, S.; et al. General atomic and molecular electronic structure system. *J. Comput. Chem.* **1993**, *14*, 1347–1363. [CrossRef]

51. Linder, R.; Nispeal, M.; Häber, T.; Kleinermanns, K. Gas-phase FT-IR spectra of natural amino acids. *Chem. Phys. Lett.* **2005**, *409*, 260–264. [CrossRef]

52. Merrick, J.R.; Moran, D.; Radom, L. An Evaluation of Harmonic Vibrational Frequency Scale Factors. *J. Phys. Chem. A* **2007**, *111*, 11683–11700. [CrossRef]

53. Matousek, J.; Gärtner, B. *Understanding and Using Linear Programming*; Springer: Heidelberg/Berlin, Germany, 2007.

54. Dantzig, G.B. Reminiscences about the origins of linear programming. *Oper. Res. Lett.* **1982**, *1*, 43–48. [CrossRef]

55. Karmarkar, N. A new polynomial-time algorithm for linear programming. *Combinatorica* **1984**, *4*, 373–395. [CrossRef]

56. Chvatal, V. *Linear Programming*; W. H. Freeman and Company: New York, NY, USA, 1983.

57. Roy, R.; Sevick-Muraca, E. Truncated Newton's Optimization Scheme for Absorption and Fluorescence Optical Tomography: Part I Theory and Formulation. *Opt. Exp.* **1999**, *4*, 353–371. [CrossRef]

58. Partovi-Azar, P.; Kühne, T.D.; Kaghazchi, P. Evidence for the Existence of Li_2S_2 clusters in Lithium-Sulfur Batteries: *ab initio* Raman spectroscopy simulation. *Phys. Chem. Chem. Phys.* **2015**, *17*, 22009–22014. [CrossRef]

59. Li, D.H.; Fukushima, M. A Modified BFGS Method and its Global Convergence in Nonconvex Minimization. *J. Comput. Appl. Math.* **2001**, *129*, 15–35. [CrossRef]

60. Cormen, T.H.; Leiserson, C.E.; Livest, R.L.; Stein, C. *Introduction to Algorithms*; MIT Press: Cambridge, MA, USA; McGraw-Hill: New York, NY, USA, 2001; Chapter The Simplex Algorithm, pp. 790–804.

61. GNU Linear Programming Kit, Version 4.64. 2017. Available online: http://www.gnu.org/software/glpk/glpk.html (accessed on 19 February 2015).

62. Chen, F.; Hung, K.K.; Stege, U.; Hore, D.K. Linear Programming Applied to Polarized Raman Data for Elucidating Molecular Structure at Surfaces. *Chemometr. Intell. Lab.* **2020**, *196*, 103898. [CrossRef]

63. Buffeteau, T.; Lagugné Labarthet, F.; Sourisseau, C.; Kostromine, S.; Bieringer, T. Biaxial orientation induced in a photoaddressable azopolymer thin film as evidenced by polarized UV-visible, infrared, and Raman spectra. *Macromolecules* **2004**, *37*, 2880–2889. [CrossRef]

64. Lagugné-Labarthet, F.; Sourisseau, C.; Schaller, R.D.; Saykally, R.J.; Rochon, P. Chromophore orientations in a nonlinear optical azopolymer diffraction grating: even and odd order parameters from far-field Raman and near-field second harmonic generation microscopies. *J. Phys. Chem. B* **2004**, *108*, 17059–17068. [CrossRef]

65. Rodriguez, V.; Lagugné Labarthet, F.; Sourisseau, C. Orientation Distribution Functions based upon both $\langle P_1 \rangle$, $\langle P_3 \rangle$ Order Parameters and upon the Four $\langle P_1 \rangle$ up to $\langle P_4 \rangle$ Values: Application to an Electrically Poled Nonlinear Optical Azopolymer Film. *Appl. Spectrosc.* **2005**, *59*, 322–328. [CrossRef]

Article

Second Harmonic Scattering of Molecular Aggregates

Guillaume Revillod [1], Julien Duboisset [2], Isabelle Russier-Antoine [1], Emmanuel Benichou [1], Christian Jonin [1] and Pierre-François Brevet [1,*]

1   Institut Lumière Matière, Université de Lyon, UMR 5306 CNRS et Université Claude Bernard Lyon 1, Bâtiment Alfred Kastler, 10 Rue Ada Byron, CEDEX, 69622 Villeurbanne, France; grevillo@gmail.com (G.R.); isabelle.russier-antoine@univ-lyon1.fr (I.R.-A.); Emmanuel.Benichou@univ-lyon1.fr (E.B.); Christian.Jonin@univ-lyon1.fr (C.J.)
2   Institut Fresnel, Aix Marseille Université, UMR 6133 CNRS, Centrale Marseille et Aix Marseille Université, Avenue Escadrille Normandie-Niémen, CEDEX, 13013 Marseille, France; Julien.Duboisset@fresnel.fr
*   Correspondence: pfbrevet@univ-lyon1.fr; Tel.:+33-(0)-472-445-873; Fax: +33-(0)-472-445-871

Abstract: A general model is developed to describe the polarization-resolved second harmonic scattering (SHS) response from a liquid solution of molecular aggregates. In particular, the molecular spatial order is introduced to consider the coherent contribution, also known as the retarded contribution, besides the incoherent contribution. The model is based on the description of a liquid suspension of molecular dyes represented by point-like nonlinear dipoles, locally excited by the fundamental field and radiating at the harmonic frequency. It is shown that for a non-centrosymmetrical spatial arrangement of the nonlinear dipoles, the SHS response is very similar to the purely incoherent response, and is of electric dipole origin. However, for centrosymmetrical or close to centrosymmetrical spatial arrangements of the nonlinear dipoles, the near cancellation of the incoherent contribution due to the inversion symmetry rule allows the observation of the coherent contribution of the SHS response, also known as the electric quadrupole contribution. This model is illustrated with experimental data obtained for aqueous solutions of the dye Crystal Violet (CV) in the presence of sodium dodecyl sulfate (SDS) and mixed water-methanol solutions of the dye 4-(4–dihexadecylaminostyryl)-N-methylpyridinium iodide (DiA), a cationic amphiphilic probe molecule with a strong first hyper-polarizability; both CV and DiA form molecular aggregates in these conditions. The quantitative determination of a retardation parameter opens a window into the spatial arrangements of the dyes in the aggregates, despite the small nanoscale dimensions of the latter.

Keywords: molecules; molecular aggregates; second harmonic generation; hyper rayleigh scattering; second harmonic scattering; light polarizatio

Citation: Revillod, G.; Duboisset, J.; Russier-Antoine, I.; Benichou, E.; Jonin, C.; Brevet, P.-F. Second Harmonic Scattering of Molecular Aggregates. *Symmetry* 2021, 13, 206. https://doi.org/10.3390/sym13020206

Academic Editor: Wiesław Leonski
Received: 28 December 2020
Accepted: 22 January 2021
Published: 27 January 2021

1. Introduction

Molecular aggregates are ubiquitous in nature. They may be found on many occasions, especially in the field of soft matter, where structures like micelles, liposomes, or vesicles are often encountered, and can be used as nanoscale probes for nonlinear optics alongside other nanoparticles [1,2]. The organization of the molecules at the microscopic level in these aggregates defines the properties or the function of these nanostructures. Hence, developing new tools and techniques to investigate how molecules arranges at the nanoscale nanostructures is always welcome, but is often hindered by the dimensions of the structures, often of sizes much smaller than the wavelength of light. Hence, one reverts to methods where the wavelength of the probe is of the order of the size of the aggregates, using X-ray or neutron scattering, for instance [3,4]. As a result, linear optical techniques are of limited use because of the diffraction limit rule. Nonlinear optical techniques, however, may offer new strategies in these studies, especially for even order techniques, like second harmonic generation (SHG), obeying the inversion symmetry cancellation rule. This rule states that SHG is forbidden in a medium possessing inversion symmetry within the electric dipole approximation [5]. Hence, when the nonlinear optical sources are strongly correlated, the coherent response from the system is markedly different from that of an assembly of non-correlated sources. Furthermore, when going beyond the electric dipole approximation, a direct view is opened on the molecular organization in the system [6–8]. To investigate this question more thoroughly, the spatial organization in small molecular aggregates has been probed by the frequency doubling conversion process known as second harmonic scattering (SHS). The latter terminology emphasizes that both an incoherent and a coherent response are observed as opposed to hyper-Rayleigh scattering (HRS), where only the incoherent response is observed. The first observation of this process has been reported by R.W. Terhune et al. and discussed by P.D. Maker, S.J. Cyvin et al. and R. Besohn et al. [9–12]. It has then been extensively used in the past to characterize the first hyper-polarizability of molecular compounds, supporting the extensive molecular engineering design of new organic compounds able to act as molecular probes [13–15]. The investigation of elaborated structures, like micelles, liposomes, or even metallic nanoparticles, has also been performed [16–19]. In these systems, the question of the phase retardation in the SHS response must be raised. In particular, in the case of metallic gold nanoparticles, where the diameter of the system can be tuned without changing other properties, this question has turned into the determination of the role of retardation in the electromagnetic fields to correctly describe the polarization-resolved response at the harmonic frequency [20,21].

In this work, we first present a theoretical foundation of the theory of second harmonic scattering of molecular aggregates. This is an extension of the standard theory developed for second harmonic scattering from molecules, also known as the theory of hyper-Rayleigh scattering, to encompass the case of molecular aggregates. In a second step, we illustrate this theory with two specific cases of molecular aggregates, the two cases differing by the internal molecular organization of the aggregate. In particular, we show unambiguously how the experimental data provide a quantitative insight into this aggregate molecular organization.

Hence, a general model for the SHS response of an assembly of a nonlinear dipole is first developed in order to investigate the impact of molecular organization of small molecular aggregates on the polarization-resolved SHS intensity. As a direct consequence, the weight of the dipolar and quadrupolar contributions is determined through a retardation parameter. This parameter describes the retardation effects, namely the spatial dependence of the electromagnetic field over the volume occupied by the aggregate, introduced in order to fully describe the SHS intensity response from aggregates. It is shown that this model encompasses the previous approaches restricted to the electric dipole approximation and used for the analysis of liquid solutions of well-dispersed, non-interacting molecular compounds, which now account for molecular correlations [22,23]. Experimental data are provided to illustrate the model. These data are obtained from aqueous solutions of Crystal Violet (CV), a non-centrosymmetric octupolar dye, in the presence of sodium dodecyl sulfate (SDS) and a mixed water-methanol solution of 4-(4–dihexadecylaminostyryl)-N-methylpyridinium iodide (DiA), a cationic amphiphilic probe molecule with a strong first hyper-polarizability.

2. Experimental

Optics: The optical set-up has already been described elsewhere [24]. Briefly, to perform the SHS measurements, a femtosecond Ti-sapphire oscillator laser providing pulses with 150 fs duration with a repetition rate of 76 MHz was used. The fundamental wavelength was set at 800 nm. The average power was set at about 500 mW. The incident beam was focused into the sample cell. The latter consisted into a standard spectrophotometric cell with quartz windows. The focusing lens was standard consisting in a low numerical aperture microscope objective. The incident beam was linearly polarized and its polarization angle γ defined with a half wave plate. For vertically polarized light, $\gamma = 0$ (also noted v), whereas for horizontally polarized light, $\gamma = \pi/2$ (also noted h). The SHS intensity was collected at a right angle with a 5 cm focal length fused silica lens and sent to a monochromator coupled to a cooled photomultiplier tube. The detection was working in the gated photon counting regime. Owing to the low light level, the beam was chopped to remove noise with periods when the beam is blocked. The scattered harmonic light polarization state was selected with an analyzer. For the analyzer set vertically, the angle of polarization $\Gamma = 0$ (also noted V) was selected for vertical output polarization, whereas the angle $\Gamma = \pi/2$ (also noted H) was selected for horizontal output polarization. Color filters were used to remove any unwanted light along the beam path. The laser power was continuously monitored to account for intensity fluctuations.

Chemistry: The molecular compounds used in these experiments, Crystal Violet (chloride salt, Sigma Aldrich), 4-(4–dihexadecylaminostyryl)-N-methylpyridinium (iodide salt, Fluo Probes Inc.), and sodium dodecyl sulfate (Sigma Aldrich) were used as received. Millipore water (resistivity = 18 MΩ.cm) was used. Methanol (Prolabo) was purchased and used as received.

3. Theory

SHS intensity for molecular aggregates: The electric field amplitude of light scattered by a molecule i located at position $\vec{r}_i'$ at the harmonic frequency $\Omega = 2\omega$, where ω is the fundamental frequency in the direction $\vec{r}$, is $\vec{E}(\vec{r}, \vec{r}_i', \Omega)$, the expression of which is given by [25]:

$$\vec{E}(\vec{r}, \vec{r}_i', \Omega) = \frac{\left(K^{(\Omega)}\right)^2}{4\pi[n(\Omega)]^2 \varepsilon_0} \frac{\exp\left(iK^{(\Omega)}\left|\vec{r} - \vec{r}_i'\right|\right)}{\left|\vec{r} - \vec{r}_i'\right|} \left[\hat{n} \times \vec{p}(\vec{r}_i', \Omega)\right] \times \hat{n} \tag{1}$$

where $K^{(\Omega)} = n(\Omega)\Omega/c$ is the harmonic wave vector modulus, with $n(\Omega)$ being the optical index of the medium at the harmonic frequency, and $\hat{n} = \vec{r}/r$ being the unit vector in the direction of collection. The expression of the nonlinear dipole induced at the harmonic frequency is related to the molecular first hyper-polarizability $\overleftrightarrow{\beta}_m(i)$ through:

$$\vec{p}(\vec{r}_i', \Omega) = \overleftrightarrow{T}(\hat{r}_i') \overleftrightarrow{\beta}_m(i) \vec{E}(\vec{r}', \omega) \vec{E}(\vec{r}', \omega) \tag{2}$$

where $\vec{E}(\vec{r}\prime, \omega)$ is the fundamental wave electric field, with $\hat{e} = \cos\gamma \, \hat{X} + \sin\gamma \, \hat{Y}$ being its polarization vector defined with the polarization angle γ in the plane perpendicular to the propagation OZ direction. The frame transformation tensor $\overleftrightarrow{T}(\hat{r}_i')$, accounting for the transformation of the molecular first hyper-polarizability tensor from the molecular frame to the laboratory frame, is defined with the standard Euler angles according to Figure 1 below.

For an assembly of correlated molecules, the total field amplitude $\vec{E}(\vec{r}, \Omega)$ is the sum of the individual amplitudes given in Equation (1). The m molecules of the aggregate are assumed to be fixed relative to each other in space, hence, in position and orientation. Here, it is therefore simply assumed that the time scale of molecular motion in the aggregate is much longer than the time scale of the nonlinear interaction with the electromagnetic wave. With multiple scattering at both frequencies, and local field factors and molecular interactions neglected, then:

$$\vec{E}(\vec{r}, \Omega) = \frac{\left(K^{(\Omega)}\right)^2}{4\pi[n(\Omega)]^2 \varepsilon_0} \sum_{i=1}^{m} \frac{\exp\left(iK^{(\Omega)}\left|\vec{r} - \vec{r}_i'\right|\right)}{\left|\vec{r} - \vec{r}_i'\right|} \left[\hat{n} \times \vec{p}(\vec{r}_i', \Omega)\right] \times \hat{n} \tag{3}$$

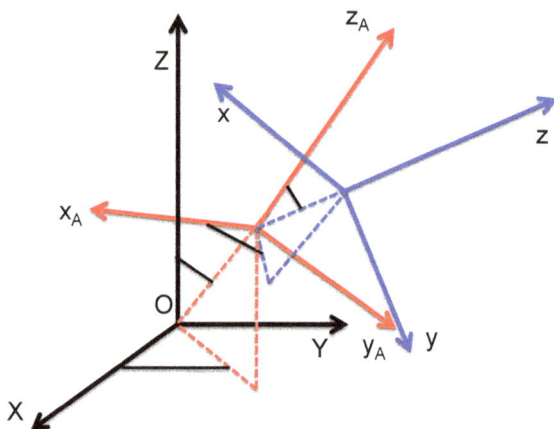

Figure 1. Illustration of the three reference frames required, the molecular one (blue, smallcase labels), the aggregate one (red, A subscripted smallcase labels), and the laboratory one (black, uppercase labels).

This superposition is built as a coherent superposition of the amplitudes scattered by single molecules. For a large number of molecules present in the aggregate, that is, if m is large, the discrete sum may be replaced by a continuous integration. In a liquid suspension, however, the molecules are distributed into many aggregates, and the latter are randomly distributed in the sampled volume in position and orientation. Hence, for N molecules distributed within n aggregates containing m molecules, one has $N = n \times m$, and the total intensity scattered at the harmonic frequency is the incoherent superposition of the intensities scattered by each molecular aggregate.

This intensity is therefore:

$$I^{(\Omega)} = \frac{1}{2}n(\Omega)\varepsilon_0 cn \left\langle \vec{E}(\vec{r},\Omega)\vec{E}^*(\vec{r},\Omega) \right\rangle \tag{4}$$

where the brackets stand for the spatial averaging of the orientation of the aggregate, since it is dispersed in a liquid suspension. This description is the standard theoretical foundation for hyper-Rayleigh scattering.

In the developments of the above foundation for molecular aggregates, it is now important to introduce three distinguished reference frames: the laboratory frame (OXYZ), the molecular frame (Oxyz), and the aggregate frame (Ox$_A$y$_A$z$_A$) (see Figure 1). Indeed, the molecules possess a fixed position and orientation within the aggregate, but the aggregate is randomly distributed in the liquid suspension in position and orientation. Hence, in Equation (4), the averaging procedure is performed on the orientation of the aggregate. Owing to the intermediate frame, the frame transformation from the molecular to the laboratory frame can be performed into two successive steps for a single molecule (see Supplementary File Part A), namely:

$$\overset{\leftrightarrow}{\beta}_L(i) = \overset{\leftrightarrow}{T}_A \overset{\leftrightarrow}{\beta}_A(i) = \overset{\leftrightarrow}{T}_A \overset{\leftrightarrow}{T}(\hat{r}_i')\overset{\leftrightarrow}{\beta}_m(i) \tag{5}$$

with the introduction of the frame transformation tensor from the aggregate to the laboratory frame $\overset{\leftrightarrow}{T}_A$ and the molecular first hyper-polarizability tensor $\overset{\leftrightarrow}{\beta}_A(i)$ of molecule i expressed in the aggregate reference frame.

In order to get a better insight into the different contributions to the scattered intensity, Equation (3) is rewritten using the first order approximation:

$$\left|\vec{r} - \vec{r_i}'\right| \cong r - \hat{n} \cdot \vec{r_i}' \tag{6}$$

for simplicity and later discussion. Hence, keeping only the term in $1/r$, Equation (3) yields:

$$\vec{E}(\vec{r}, \Omega) = \frac{\left(K^{(\Omega)}\right)^2 \exp\left(iK^{(\Omega)}r\right)}{4\pi[n(\Omega)]^2 \varepsilon_0 r} \left(E^{(\omega)}\right)^2$$
$$\times \left[\hat{n} \times \overset{\leftrightarrow}{T}_A \left\{ \int_V \rho(\vec{r}') \exp\left(i\Delta\vec{k} \cdot \vec{r}'\right) \overset{\leftrightarrow}{\beta}_A(\vec{r}')dV \right\} \hat{e}\hat{e}\right] \times \hat{n} \tag{7}$$

with the introduction of the molecular volume density $\rho(\vec{r}')$ within the aggregate and the wave vector mismatch $\Delta\vec{k}$, the expression of which is simply:

$$\Delta\vec{k} = K^{(\Omega)}\hat{n} - 2\vec{k}^{(\omega)} = \frac{4\pi}{\lambda}\left[n(\Omega)\hat{n} - n(\omega)\hat{Z}\right] \tag{8}$$

with the introduction of the fundamental wavelength λ. If the direction of collection is in the forward direction, namely $\hat{n} = \hat{Z}$, then the usual phase matching condition of second harmonic generation (SHG) is recovered. Because the condition $r' \ll \lambda$ is also assumed, i.e., the aggregates are small before the fundamental wavelength, the expansion of the exponential factor of the integral in Equation (7) yields:

$$\vec{E}(\vec{r}, \Omega) = \frac{\left(K^{(\Omega)}\right)^2 \exp\left(iK^{(\Omega)}r\right)}{4\pi[n(\Omega)]^2 \varepsilon_0 r} \left(E^{(\omega)}\right)^2 \left[\hat{n} \times \overset{\leftrightarrow}{T}_A \left\{ \int_V \rho(\vec{r}')\left[1 + i\Delta\vec{k} \cdot \vec{r}'\right] \overset{\leftrightarrow}{\beta}_A(\vec{r}')dV \right\} \hat{e}\hat{e}\right] \times \hat{n} \tag{9}$$

It is therefore convenient to split the harmonic field amplitude into two terms, namely:

$$\vec{E}(\vec{r}, \Omega) = \frac{\left(K^{(\Omega)}\right)^2 \exp\left(iK^{(\Omega)}r\right)}{4\pi[n(\Omega)]^2 \varepsilon_0 r} \left(E^{(\omega)}\right)^2 \left[\hat{n} \times \left(\vec{p}_{eff,L}(\Omega) + i\Delta\vec{k} \cdot \overset{\leftrightarrow}{q}_{eff,L}(\Omega)\right)\right] \times \hat{n} \tag{10}$$

The first term $\vec{p}_{eff,L}(\Omega)$ in Equation (10) is the equivalent of Equation (3) at the level of the aggregate instead of the molecule. Hence, the integrated induced dipole of the aggregate $\vec{p}_{eff,L}(\Omega)$ is simply:

$$\vec{p}_{eff,L}(\Omega) = \overset{\leftrightarrow}{\beta}_{eff,L}\hat{e}\hat{e} = \overset{\leftrightarrow}{T}_A\overset{\leftrightarrow}{\beta}_{eff,A}\hat{e}\hat{e} \tag{11}$$

where the dipolar first hyper-polarizability of the aggregate is given by:

$$\overset{\leftrightarrow}{\beta}_{eff,A} = \int_V \rho(\vec{r}')\overset{\leftrightarrow}{\beta}_A(\vec{r}')dV = \int_V \rho(\vec{r}')\overset{\leftrightarrow}{T}(\hat{r_i}')\overset{\leftrightarrow}{\beta}_m(i)dV \tag{12}$$

i.e., the superposition of the first hyper-polarizabilities of the molecules present in the aggregate. This superposition takes into account both the position and the orientation of the molecules. The second term $\overset{\leftrightarrow}{q}_{eff,L}(\Omega)$ of Equation (10) is the first correction to the non-vanishing spatial extension of the aggregate. Therefore, $\overset{\leftrightarrow}{q}_{eff,L}(\Omega)$ is the integrated induced quadrupole of the aggregate, and is given by:

$$\overset{\leftrightarrow}{q}_{eff,L}(\Omega) = \overset{\leftrightarrow}{\gamma}_{eff,L}\hat{e}\hat{e} = \overset{\leftrightarrow}{T}_A\overset{\leftrightarrow}{\gamma}_{eff,A}\hat{e}\hat{e} \tag{13}$$

with the quadrupolar first hyper-polarizability $\overset{\leftrightarrow}{\gamma}_{eff,A}$ of the aggregate defined through:

$$\overset{\leftrightarrow}{\gamma}_{eff,A} = \int_V \rho(\vec{r}')\vec{r}'\overset{\leftrightarrow}{\beta}_A(\vec{r}')dV = \int_V \rho(\vec{r}')\overset{\leftrightarrow}{T}(\hat{r_i}')\vec{r}'\overset{\leftrightarrow}{T}(\hat{r_i}')\overset{\leftrightarrow}{\beta}_m(i)dV \tag{14}$$

Note that the vector $\vec{r}'$ has to be also transformed into the aggregate reference frame. In the molecular frame, it is simply given by $\vec{r}' = a\hat{z}$. The quadrupolar first hyperpolarizability $\overset{\leftrightarrow}{\gamma}_{eff,A}$ is a fourth rank tensor. Owing to the definition of the wave vector mismatch $\Delta\vec{k}$ in Equation (8) and the geometrical configuration of the experiment, where the direction of incidence of the fundamental wave is along the OZ direction and the collection of the harmonic wave is performed in the OY direction in the laboratory, only the elements of the general form $\gamma_{eff,L,ZIJK}$ and $\gamma_{eff,L,YIJK}$ are involved in Equation (13), but the calculation of these elements entails the transformation from the aggregate frame to the laboratory frame with the definition $\overset{\leftrightarrow}{\gamma}_{eff,L} = \overset{\leftrightarrow}{T}_A \overset{\leftrightarrow}{\gamma}_{eff,A}$. Finally, it is observed that, from Equation (10), the second contribution scales with the parameter r'/λ. Since it has been set beforehand that this parameter is much smaller than unity, this contribution is usually neglected for molecular aggregates, since their average size is much smaller than the fundamental wavelength. Typical aggregates have diameters of the order of a few nanometers, whereas the fundamental wavelength is often in the range of hundreds of nanometers. However, depending on the molecular organization of the aggregate, the induced dipole $\vec{p}_{eff,L}(\Omega)$ may be very small or even vanish. In this case, the quadrupolar contribution may not be negligible any longer, and must be accounted for.

SHS scattered intensity for non-centrosymmetrical aggregates: In the particular case of a non-centrosymmetrical spatial orientational distribution of the molecules in the aggregates, $\vec{p}_{eff,L}(\Omega)$ does not vanish, and possesses three components, namely $p_{eff,L,X}(\Omega)$, $p_{eff,L,Y}(\Omega)$, and $\vec{p}_{eff,L,Z}(\Omega)$. In most cases, this $\vec{p}_{eff,L,Z}(\Omega)$ term will dominate, and this case reverts to the rather well-known case of a single molecule, albeit at the level of the aggregate. The scattered intensity at the harmonic frequency vertically and horizontally polarized, respectively $I^{(\Omega)V}$ and $I^{(\Omega)H}$, is now given by:

$$I^{(\Omega)V} = a^V \cos^4\gamma + b^V \cos^2\gamma\sin^2\gamma + c^V\sin^4\gamma \tag{15a}$$

$$I^{(\Omega)H} = a^H \cos^4\gamma + b^H \cos^2\gamma\sin^2\gamma + c^H\sin^4\gamma \tag{15b}$$

with the conditions $b^V = a^V + c^V$ and $b^H = 2a^H = 2c^H$. The different coefficients are simply:

$$a^\Gamma = Gn\left\langle \beta_{eff,L,IXX}\beta^*_{eff,L,IXX}\right\rangle I^2 \tag{16a}$$

$$b^\Gamma = Gn\left\langle \beta_{eff,L,IXX}\beta^*_{eff,L,IYY} + \beta^*_{eff,L,IXX}\beta_{eff,L,IYY} + 4\beta_{eff,L,IXY}\beta^*_{eff,L,IYY}\right\rangle I^2 \tag{16b}$$

$$c^\Gamma = Gn\left\langle \beta_{eff,L,IYY}\beta^*_{eff,L,IYY}\right\rangle I^2 \tag{16c}$$

with the constant:

$$G = \frac{32n(\Omega)\omega^4}{[4\pi\varepsilon_0]^2[n(\omega)]^2\varepsilon_0 c^5 r^2} \tag{17}$$

and $I = X$ for $\Gamma = V$ and $I = Z$ for $\Gamma = H$. In particular, the depolarization ratio $D = c^V/a^V$ is now an indication of the symmetry of the aggregate, and no longer of the molecule. Furthermore, the total intensity scales linearly with the number of aggregates present in the liquid suspension. Note that the resulting apparent first hyper-polarizability of the aggregates depends now on the orientation of all molecules constituting the aggregate, and can be very large, since it is the superposition of the first hyper-polarizabilities of the m molecules contained in the aggregate. For instance, in a perfect alignment of all molecules, the aggregate first hyperpolarizability is indeed as large as m times that of a single molecule, and hence, the intensity scattered at the harmonic intensity scales with the product nm^2.

A typical graph of the vertically polarized SHS intensity collected in the case of a non-centrosymmetric aggregate with an arbitrary depolarization ratio of $D = 0.4$ is provided in Figure 2 below.

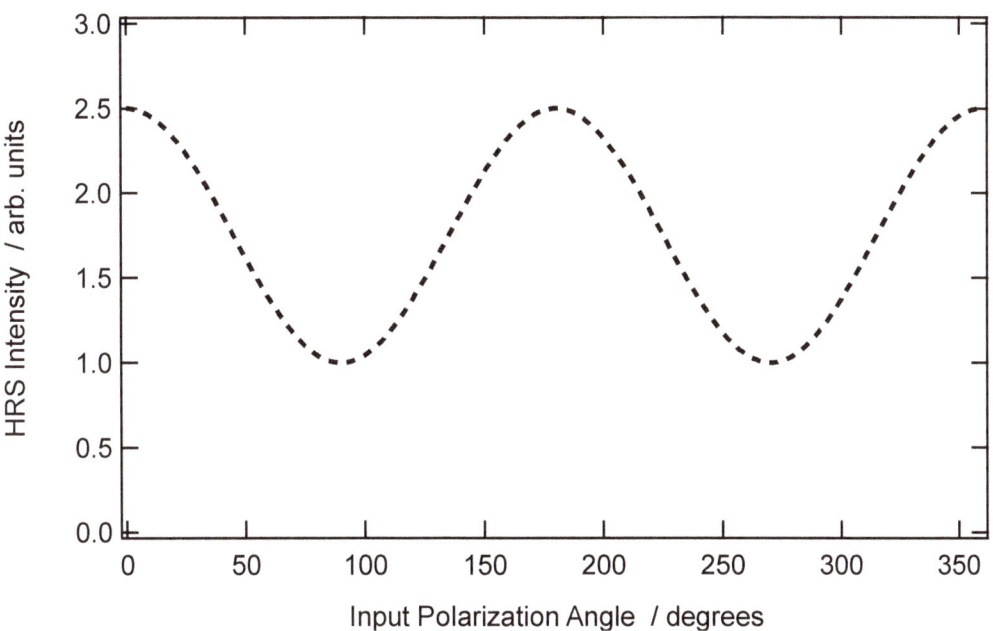

Figure 2. Theoretical vertically polarized SHS intensity as a function of the input polarization angle for a depolarization ratio $D = 0.4$.

SHS scattered intensity for centrosymmetrical aggregates: The second case occurs when the organization of the molecules within the aggregate possesses a center of inversion. This is the organization found in spherical micelles, for instance, or corresponding to a random orientation. As expected for this centrosymmetrical structure, the first contribution vanishes, namely $\vec{p}_{eff,L}(\Omega) = 0$. The scattered amplitude at the harmonic frequency is therefore reduced to the second contribution only, which may be recast as:

$$\vec{E}(\vec{r}, \Omega) = \frac{\left(K^{(\Omega)}\right)^2 i \exp\left(iK^{(\Omega)}r\right)}{4\pi[n(\Omega)]^2 \varepsilon_0 r} \left(E^{(\omega)}\right)^2 \left[\hat{n} \times \left(\Delta \vec{k} \cdot \overset{\leftrightarrow}{q}_{eff,L}(\Omega)\right)\right] \times \hat{n} \qquad (18)$$

Finally, the intensity again takes the expressions given by Equations (15a) and (15b), but this time:

$$a^{\Gamma} = Gn\left\langle \Gamma_{eff,L,IXX}\Gamma^*_{eff,L,IXX} \right\rangle I^2 \qquad (19a)$$

$$b^{\Gamma} = Gn\left\langle \Gamma_{eff,L,IXX}\Gamma^*_{eff,L,IYY} + \Gamma^*_{eff,L,IXX}\Gamma_{eff,L,IYY} + 4\Gamma_{eff,L,IXY}\Gamma^*_{eff,L,IYY} \right\rangle I^2 \qquad (19b)$$

$$c^{\Gamma} = Gn\left\langle \Gamma_{eff,L,IYY}\Gamma^*_{eff,L,IYY} \right\rangle I^2 \qquad (19c)$$

with the constant:

$$G = \frac{32n(\Omega)\omega^4}{[4\pi\varepsilon_0]^2[n(\omega)]^2\varepsilon_0 c^5 r^2}\left(\frac{4\pi}{\lambda}\right)^2 \tag{20}$$

and the effective parameters:

$$\Gamma^\Gamma_{eff,L,IJK} = n(\Omega)\gamma_{eff,L,YIJK} + n(\omega)\gamma_{eff,L,ZIJK} \tag{21}$$

with $I = X$ for $\Gamma = V$ and $I = Z$ for $\Gamma = H$.

The case of spherical micelles of radius a leads to simple expressions for the intensity coefficients of Equations (19a–c). With a uniform distribution of the molecular dye at the aggregate surface, the molecular density is simply:

$$\rho(\vec{r}') = \delta(r' - a) \tag{22}$$

if one assumes that the nonlinear optical chromophore is point-like. The volume integration for the effective quadrupolar first hyper-polarizability elements leads to a dependence of these elements with the third power of the radius of the sphere. Furthermore, the coefficients a^V and c^V for the vertical polarization vanish, whereas b^V does not, and is proportional to $b^V \propto \Delta k^2 m^2 a^2$ (see Figure 3). For the horizontal polarization, one gets $b^H = 2a^H = 2c^H$. Furthermore, for an experimental geometry where the collection is performed along the opposite direction of the OY axis of the laboratory, Equation (21) will involve the difference of $n(\Omega)\gamma_{eff,L,YIJK}$ and $n(\omega)\gamma_{eff,L,ZIJK}$, rather than their sum.

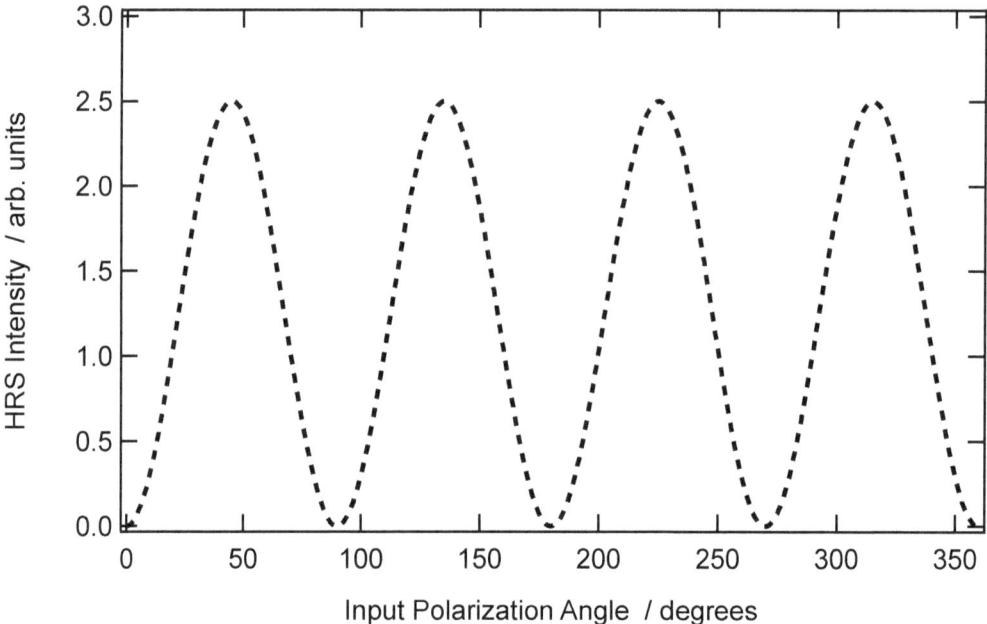

Figure 3. Theoretical vertically polarized SHS intensity as a function of the input polarization angle for centrosymmetric aggregates of radius a, where molecules are organized in a radial orientational distribution.

The perfect centrosymmetry rule is not expected to be strictly fulfilled by aggregates. However, if this symmetry is close to perfect, contributions from the first contribution $\vec{p}_{eff,L}(\Omega)$ will also contribute simultaneously to the total intensity scattered at the harmonic frequency without overwhelming the second one. Therefore, the resulting polarization-resolved plot may take a profile somewhere in between the two contributions presented in Figures 2 and 3. Note also that other orientational distributions may be found, like the azimuthal one, instead of the radial one.

SHS of Molecular Aggregates: To illustrate the problem, we now discuss the case of aggregates constituted by Crystal Violet and DiA, two compound-forming aggregates with different properties depending on the conditions, see below.

Experiments are initially performed for a simple rod-like molecule, 4-(4–dihexadecy-laminostyryl)-N-methylpyridinium (DiA) (see Figure 4), the first hyper-polarizability tensor of which is dominated by a single element. This latter dominating element is $\beta_{m,zzz}(i)$ where the molecular Oz axis is taken along the axis of the charge transfer. Since DiA is rod-like, this molecular axis is nearly oriented along the axis direction of DiA. Since DiA is also amphiphilic due to the two long alkyl chains, it is expected to form micelle-like aggregates, with the Oz axis oriented towards the center of the aggregate. The orientation distribution within the molecular aggregate is therefore expected to closely resemble that of spherical micelles. DiA dissolves in methanol but not in water, and therefore aggregation was induced by varying the volume fraction of water into methanol at a fixed DiA concentration of 12.5 μM [25]. A typical vertically polarized resolved SHS intensity for DiA dispersed in pure methanol is given in Figure 5. This graph allows to immediately identify a^V as $I^V(\gamma=0)$, c^V as $I^V(\gamma=\pi/2)$, and b^V as $4I^V(\gamma=\pi/4)-a^V-c^V$, although an adjustment procedure with Equation (15a) is usually performed, and the condition $b^V = a^V + c^V$ is obeyed.

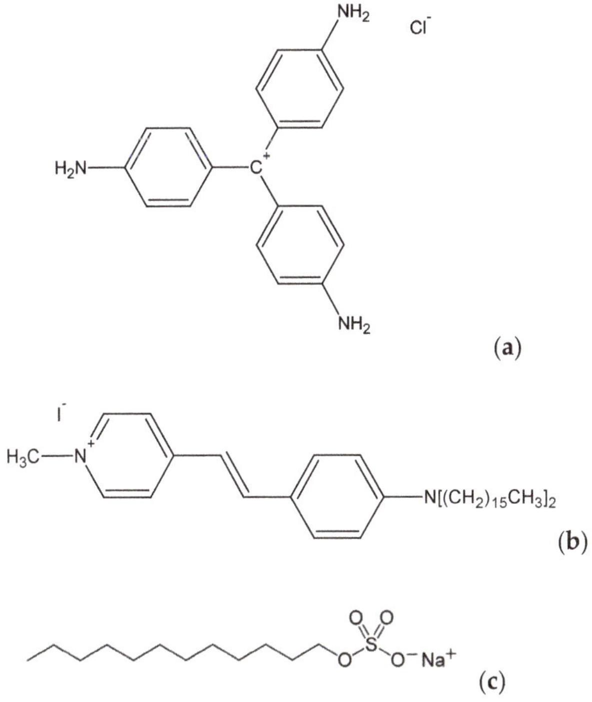

(a)

(b)

(c)

Figure 4. Molecular compounds used in the experiments: (**a**) Crystal Violet, (**b**) DiA, and (**c**) SDS.

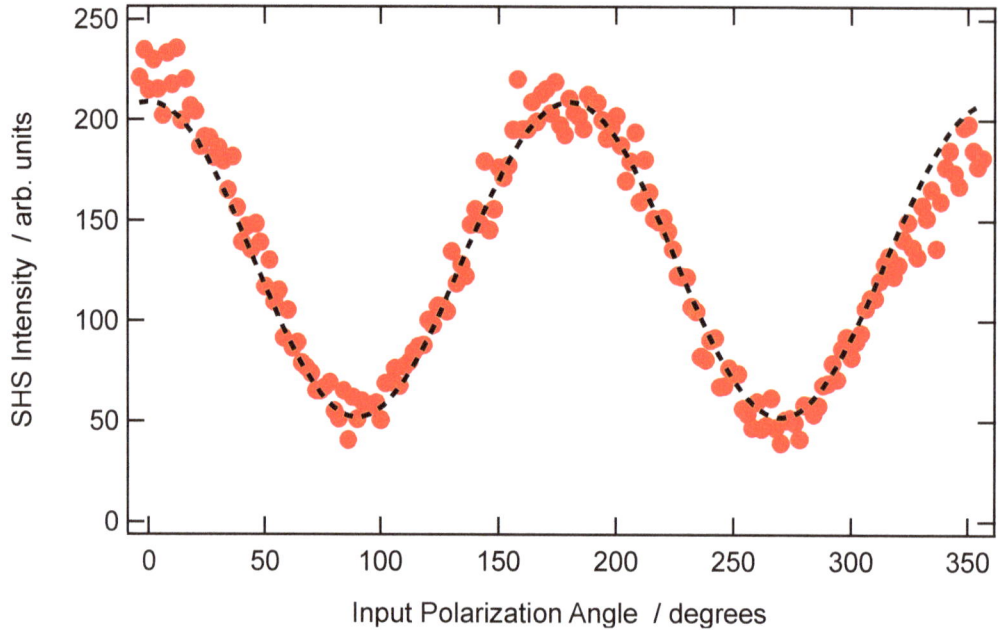

Figure 5. Vertically polarized SHS intensity of a 12.5 µM concentration of DiA dispersed in pure methanol as a function of the incoming polarization angle.

In order to have a quantified characterization of the aggregate, the following ζ^V parameter is defined:

$$\zeta^V = \frac{b^V - a^V - c^V}{b^V} \tag{23}$$

also found as [6]:

$$I_4 = \frac{a^V + c^V - b^V}{b^V + 3a^V + 3c^V} \tag{24}$$

Note in particular the sign inversion between I_4 and ζ^V. As examples, it is immediate to see that the pure dipolar response of a non-centrosymmetric aggregate leads to $\zeta^V = 0$, whereas the purely retarded response of a centrosymmetric aggregate in the shape of a spherical micelle, i.e., with a radial distribution, leads to $\zeta^V = 1$. Interestingly, an azimuthal distribution of the dyes forming a centrosymmetric aggregate leads to a negative value for the retarded parameter ζ^V.

As an illustration of a quantitative analysis of the aggregate structure, one may discuss the results reported in Ref. [25], comparing the vertically polarized SHS intensity obtained for DiA dispersed in pure methanol and in a mixed 5:1 *v/v* water-methanol solution. The depolarization ratio $D = c^V/a^V$ is found to be 0.25, along with a vanishing retardation parameter ζ^V for DiA dispersed in pure methanol (see Figure 5). Oppositely, in a mixed 5:1 *v/v* water-methanol solvent, the depolarization ratio $D = c^V/a^V$ is found to be 0.28, along with a retardation parameter $\zeta^V = 0.41$ [25].

The depolarization ratio obtained for the aggregate is different from the value of +0.25 measured for DiA dissolved in pure methanol and closely associated with a single first hyper-polarizability tensor element compound [25]. It is concluded that some distortion in the electronic structure of DiA occurs in the aggregate, leading to the appearance of contributions from other tensor elements. Furthermore, the retardation parameter, vanishing in the pure methanol solution where DiA is ideally dispersed, now increases, indicating an organization tending to the spherical micellar-like structure, as expected for a compound with two hydrophobic long alkyl chains.

In the case of aqueous solutions of Crystal Violet, the same experiments were performed, this time as a function of SDS concentration, as this anionic surfactant is known to form micelles beyond the critical micelle concentration (CMC) of 7 mM [24]. It is expected that these molecular structures favor adsorption [26]. Figure 6 shows the depolarization ratio D along with the retardation parameter ζ^V as a function of the SDS concentration, below and above the SDS CMC.

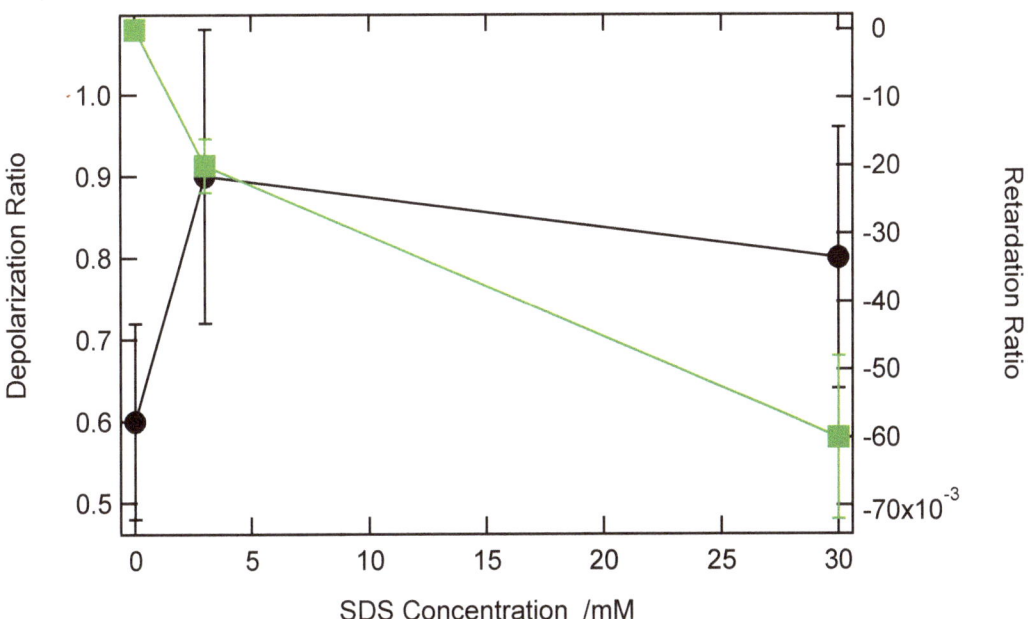

Figure 6. (Black) The depolarization ratio and (Green) retardation parameter for aqueous solutions of CV as a function of the SDS concentration.

The depolarization ratio is 0.6 in the absence of SDS, as expected for the close to planar octupolar symmetry of CV [27]. It increases when SDS is present, but does not change much, indicating a change in symmetry of the whole aggregate compared to the CV monomer. Oppositely, the retardation parameter ζ^V is initially zero, as expected for a compound ideally dissolved in its solvent, but then decreases as SDS is introduced into the solution. The negative value of this parameter is not in agreement with a spherical micellar-like organization, but rather with an azimuthal distribution, i.e., adsorption onto the SDS aggregates. Interestingly, this organization already starts at 3 mM, a value below the SDS CMC, suggesting the appearance of aggregates below the CMC.

4. Conclusions

We have developed a model to describe assemblies of nonlinear dipoles exhibiting two dominating contributions, one of electric dipole origin associated to the non-centrosymmetric organization of the compounds into the aggregates, and one associated with phase retardation, providing a deep insight at the nanoscale into the aggregate spatial organization. Illustration of this model with the two CV and DiA compounds forming aggregates in different conditions shows that, in particular, the sign of the retardation parameter may be crucial in disentangling the aggregate spatial organization.

On a final note, we point out that this model may be applied to other systems, like metallic nanoparticles [28].

Supplementary Materials: The following are available online at https://www.mdpi.com/2073-899 4/13/2/206/s1.

Author Contributions: G.R., J.D., I.R.-A. did the experiments and performed the analysis, E.B. and C.J. performed the analysis, P.-F.B. conceived the experiment and wrote the paper. All authors have read and agreed to the published version of the manuscript.

Funding: This research received no external funding.

Data Availability Statement: All data are available to the corresponding author upon request.

Conflicts of Interest: The authors declare no conflict of interest.

References

1. Ramanathan, M.; Hong, K.; Ji, Q.; Yonamine, Y.; Hill, J.P.; Ariga, K. Nanoarchitectonics of Molecular Aggregates: Science and Technology. *J. Nanosci. Nanotechnol.* **2014**, *14*, 390. [CrossRef] [PubMed]
2. Bonacina, L.; Brevet, P.F.; Finazzi, M.; Celebrano, M. Harmonic Generation at the Nanoscale. *J. Appl. Phys.* **2020**, *127*, 230901. [CrossRef]
3. Bouazizi, S.; Hammami, F.; Nasr, S.; Bellissent-Funel, M.-C. Neutron Scattering Experiments on Aqueous Sodium Chloride Solutions and Heavy Water. Comparison to Molecular Dynamics and X-Ray Results. *J. Mol. Struct.* **2008**, *892*, 47. [CrossRef]
4. Takamuku, T.; Tabata, M.; Yamaguchi, A.; Nishimoto, J.; Kumamoto, M.; Wakita, H.; Yamaguchi, T. Liquid structure of acetonitrile-water mixtures by x-ray diffraction and infrared spectroscopy. *J. Phys. Chem. B* **1998**, *102*, 8880. [CrossRef]
5. Boyd, R.W. *Nonlinear Optics*, 4th ed.; Elsevier: New York, NY, USA, 2020.
6. Duboisset, J.; Brevet, P.F. Salt-Induced Long-to-Short Range Orientational Transition in Water. *Phys. Rev. Lett.* **2018**, *120*, 263001. [CrossRef]
7. Duboisset, J.; Rondepierre, F.; Brevet, P.F. Long-Range Orientational Organization of Dipolar and Steric Liquids. *J. Phys. Chem. Lett.* **2020**, *11*, 9869. [CrossRef]
8. Pardon, A.; Bonhomme, O.; Gaillard, C.; Brevet, P.F.; Benichou, E. Nonlinear Optical Signature of Nanostructural Transition in Ionic Liquids. *J. Mol. Liq.* **2020**, *322*, 114976. [CrossRef]
9. Terhune, R.W.; Maker, P.D.; Savage, C.M. Measurements of Nonlinear Light Scattering. *Phys. Rev. Lett.* **1965**, *14*, 681. [CrossRef]
10. Maker, P.D. Spectral Broadening of Elastic Second-Harmonic Light Scattering in Liquids. *Phys. Rev. A* **1970**, *1*, 923. [CrossRef]
11. Cyvin, S.J.; Rausch, J.E.; Decius, J.C. Theory of Hyper-Raman Effects (Nonlinear Inelastic Light Scattering): Selection Rules and Depolarization Ratios for the Second-Order Polarizability. *J. Chem. Phys.* **1965**, *43*, 4083. [CrossRef]
12. Bersohn, R.; Pao, Y.H.; Frisch, H.L. Double-Quantum Light Scattering by Molecules. *J. Chem. Phys.* **1966**, *45*, 3184. [CrossRef]
13. Zyss, J.; Ledoux, I. Nonlinear Optics in Multipolar Media, Theory and Experiments. *Chem. Rev.* **1994**, *94*, 77. [CrossRef]
14. Zyss, J.; Van, T.C.; Dhenaut, C.; Ledoux, I. Harmonic Rayleigh Scattering from Nonlinear Octupolar Molecular Media: The Case of Crystal Violet. *Chem. Phys.* **1993**, *177*, 281. [CrossRef]
15. Das, P.K. Chemical Applications of Hyper-Rayleigh Scattering in Solution. *J. Phys. Chem. B* **2006**, *110*, 7621. [CrossRef]
16. Ghosh, S.; Krishnan, A.; Das, P.K.; Ramakrishnan, S. Determination of Critical Micelle Concentration by Hyper-Rayleigh Scattering. *J. Am. Chem. Soc.* **2003**, *125*, 1602. [CrossRef] [PubMed]
17. Butet, J.; Brevet, P.F.; Martin, O.J.F. Optical Second Harmonic Generation in Plasmonic Nanostructures: From Fundamental Principles to Advanced Applications. *ACS Nano* **2015**, *9*, 10545. [CrossRef]
18. Dadap, J.I.; Shan, J.; Eisenthal, K.B.; Heinz, T.F. Second-Harmonic Rayleigh Scattering from a Sphere of Centrosymmetric Material. *Phys. Rev. Lett.* **1999**, *83*, 4045. [CrossRef]
19. Nappa, J.; Revillod, G.; Russier-Antoine, I.; Jonin, C.; Benichou, E.; Brevet, P.F. Electric Dipole Origin of the Second Harmonic Generation of Small Metallic Particles. *Phys. Rev. B* **2005**, *71*, 165407. [CrossRef]
20. Butet, J.; Bachelier, G.; Russier-Antoine, I.; Jonin, C.; Benichou, E.; Brevet, P.F. Interference between Selected Dipoles and Octupoles in the Optical Second-Harmonic Generation from Spherical Gold Nanoparticles. *Phys. Rev. Lett.* **2010**, *105*, 077401. [CrossRef]
21. Bachelier, G.; Butet, J.; Russier-Antoine, I.; Jonin, C.; Benichou, E.; Brevet, P.F. Origin of Optical Second Harmonic Generation in Spherical Gold Nanoparticles: Local Surface and Nonlocal Bulk Contributions. *Phys. Rev. B* **2010**, *82*, 235403. [CrossRef]
22. Wang, H.; Yan, E.C.Y.; Borguet, E.; Eisenthal, K.B. Second harmonic generation from the surface of centrosymmetric particles in bulk solution. *Chem. Phys. Lett.* **1996**, *259*, 15. [CrossRef]
23. Shelton, D.A. Hyper-Rayleigh scattering from correlated molecules. *J. Chem. Phys.* **2013**, *138*, 154502. [CrossRef] [PubMed]
24. Revillod, G.; Russier-Antoine, I.; Benichou, E.; Jonin, C.; Brevet, P.F. Investigating the Interaction of Crystal Violet Probe Molecules on Sodium Dodecyl Sulfate Micelles with Hyper-Rayleigh Scattering. *J. Phys. Chem. B* **2005**, *109*, 5383. [CrossRef] [PubMed]
25. Revillod, G.; Duboisset, J.; Russier-Antoine, I.; Benichou, E.; Bachelier, G.; Jonin, C.; Brevet, P.F. Multipolar Contributions to the Second Harmonic Response from Mixed DiA-SDS Molecular Aggregates. *J. Phys. Chem. C* **2008**, *112*, 2723. [CrossRef]

26. Liu, Y.; Yan, E.C.Y.; Eisenthal, K.B. Effects of Bilayer Surface Charge Density on Molecular Adsorption and Transport Across Liposome Bilayers. *Biophys. J.* **2001**, *80*, 1004. [CrossRef]
27. Brasselet, S.; Zyss, J. Multipolar Molecules and Multipolar Fields: Probing and Controlling the Tensorial Nature of Nonlinear Molecular Media. *J. Opt. Soc. Am. B* **1998**, *15*, 257. [CrossRef]
28. Duboisset, J.; Brevet, P.F. Second-Harmonic Scattering-Defined Topological Classes for Nano-Objects. *J. Phys. Chem. C* **2019**, *123*, 25303. [CrossRef]

Article

Spatial Dependence of the Dipolar Interaction between Quantum Dots and Organic Molecules Probed by Two-Color Sum-Frequency Generation Spectroscopy

Thomas Noblet [1,2,*], Laurent Dreesen [2], Abderrahmane Tadjeddine [1] and Christophe Humbert [1]

[1] Université Paris-Saclay, CNRS, Institut de Chimie Physique, UMR 8000, 91405 Orsay, France; abderrahmane.tadjeddine@universite-paris-saclay.fr (A.T.); christophe.humbert@universite-paris-saclay.fr (C.H.)

[2] GRASP-Biophotonics, CESAM, University of Liege, Institute of Physics, Allée du 6 août 17, 4000 Liège, Belgium; laurent.dreesen@uliege.be

* Correspondence: t.noblet@uliege.be

Abstract: Given the tunability of their optical properties over the UV–Visible–Near IR spectral range, ligand-capped quantum dots (QDs) are employed for the design of optical biosensors with low detection threshold. Thanks to non-linear optical spectroscopies, the absorption properties of QDs are indeed used to selectively enhance the local vibrational response of molecules located in their vicinity. Previous studies led to assume the existence of a vibroelectronic QD–molecule coupling based on dipolar interaction. However, no systematic study on the strength of this coupling has been performed to date. In order to address this issue, we use non-linear optical Two-Color Sum-Frequency Generation (2C-SFG) spectroscopy to probe thick QD layers deposited on calcium fluoride (CaF$_2$) prisms previously functionalized by a self-assembled monolayer of phenyltriethoxysilane (PhTES) molecules. Here, 2C-SFG is performed in Attenuated Total Reflection (ATR) configuration. By comparing the molecular vibrational enhancement measured for QD–ligand coupling and QD–PhTES coupling, we show that the spatial dependence of the QD–molecule interactions ($\sim 1/r^3$, with r the QD–molecule distance) is in agreement with the hypothesis of a dipole–dipole interaction.

Keywords: quantum dots; phenyl derivative; UV–Visible spectroscopy; non-linear optics; sum-frequency generation spectroscopy; centrosymmetry; dipole–dipole interaction

Citation: Noblet, T.; Dreesen, L.; Tadjeddine, A.; Humbert, C. Spatial Dependence of the Dipolar Interaction between Quantum Dots and Organic Molecules Probed by Two-Color Sum-Frequency Generation Spectroscopy. *Symmetry* **2021**, *13*, 294. https://doi.org/ 10.3390/sym13020294

Academic Editor: Jorge Segovia

Received: 21 January 2021
Accepted: 5 February 2021
Published: 9 February 2021

Publisher's Note: MDPI stays neutral with regard to jurisdictional clai-ms in published maps and institutio-nal affiliations.

1. Introduction

As semiconductor nanoparticles, colloidal quantum dots (QDs) evince unique optical and electronic properties deriving from the quantum confinement of their laser-excited electron-hole pairs. With diameters ranging between 1 and 10 nm, QDs are able to absorb and emit light over the visible range [1–5]. Hence, they are largely employed within various scientific fields such as photovoltaics [6,7], photocatalysis [8–10], fluorescence spectroscopy [11,12], biomedical imaging [13–15], and biosensing [16–21]. In the later case, QDs are often used as fluorescent probes. Indeed, their spectral and temporal emission properties are highly sensitive to their chemical environment, including capping ligands, solvent, pH, ion concentration, cross-linking molecules, and biomolecules [12,22–29]. As a result, the literature extensively reports how the chemical medium of QDs influence their optical properties, especially within the framework of biosensors.

For some years now, our team has investigated the possibility of a reciprocal coupling enabling to use the optical and electronic behavior of QDs in order to influence their molecular surroundings [29,30]. Since then, the aim is to design biosensors wherein QDs are employed as optoelectronic enhancers instead of fluorescent probes. Thanks to non-linear Two-color Sum-Frequency Generation (2C-SFG) spectroscopy combining a visible and an infrared laser beams, we previously proved that the amplitude of the vibrational response of the ligands (over the IR range) was modulated by the linear optical susceptibility of the QDs (over the visible range), $\chi^{(1)}(\omega_{vis})$ [29]. To evidence such a vibroelectronic correlation, we performed 2C-SFG spectroscopy on thick layers of QDs deposited on CaF$_2$ prisms. From the symmetry rules proper to second-order optical processes [31], 2C-SFG spectroscopy is actually surface-specific and then constitutes an ideal tool to study the interactions occurring at the interface between QDs and molecules, both immobilized on a solid substrate. Besides, CaF$_2$ prisms benefit from favorable Local Field correction factors (reflectivity) in ATR configuration (Figure 1a) as explained in Section 3.1. In this way, we succeeded in measuring the vibrational spectrum of the QD ligands (from 3.2 to 3.6 µm, i.e., 2800 to 3000 cm^{-1}) under a visible excitation whose wavelength varied between 450 and 620 nm. This previous study thus demonstrated a spectral correlation between the ligand vibration amplitudes $a_v(\omega_{vis})$ and $\chi^{(1)}(\omega_{vis})$ [29]. On a theoretical point of view, we assumed it arose from a dipolar interaction between the QDs, on one side, and the molecules, on the other side. However, this assumption has not been experimentally attested so far. Especially, our aim here is to assess the spatial dependence of the vibroelectronic coupling with respect to the distance between QDs and molecules.

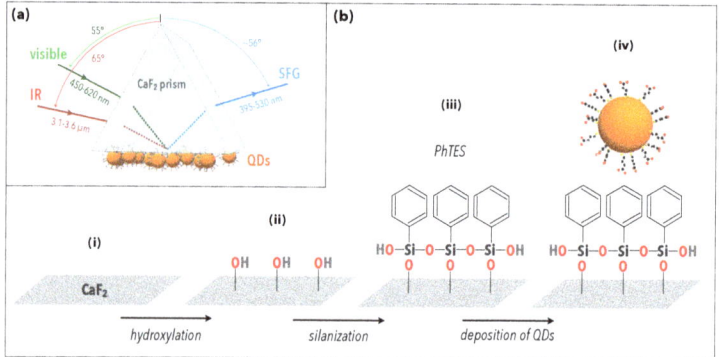

Figure 1. (**a**) Scheme of the experimental configuration used to perform SFG spectroscopy on a quantum dot (QD) layer deposited on a CaF$_2$ prism. The surface of the prism is first functionalized by PhTES molecules. (**b**) Description of the different steps of the chemical preparation of the sample. (i) The prism initially has a surface layer of CaF$_2$, which is mainly oxidized. (ii) Hydroxylation then leads to the activation of silanol groups that serve as the attachment base for (iii) the grafting of PhTES molecules. (iv) The deposition of QDs is then obtained by drop-casting. (See Materials and Methods for details.)

In this paper, we chose to study the interaction between, on the one hand, a thick layer of colloidal CdTe$_{0.25}$S$_{0.75}$ QDs capped with mercaptocarboxylic acids and, on the other hand, a self-assembled monolayer of phenyltriethoxysilane molecules (PhTES), both deposited or grafted on a CaF$_2$ prism. PhTES actually displays two great advantages for our study: first, it can be grafted on CaF$_2$ in the form of a monolayer and be used as a molecular probe to assess the strength and the range of the vibroelectronic coupling induced by the overlying QDs; second, the IR vibrational response of its aromatic rings is characterized by CH stretching modes located at ~3060 cm^{-1} [32], which is out of the range of the QD ligands (from 2800 to 3000 cm^{-1}) [29]. Thanks to this approach, we show that the vibroelectronic coupling already seen between QDs and their ligands, chemically bound to their surface and thus very close to them, can also be observed with molecules which are further from their surface. First, this teaches us that the coupling is not mediated by strong chemical bounds. Second, compared to the ligands, the intensity of the coupling proves to be two times lower in the case of PhTES. This ratio is consistent with a spatial dependence of the coupling following $1/r^3$, where r is the QD–molecule distance, therefore compatible with the hypothesis of a dipole–dipole interaction.

2. Materials and Methods

Preparation of CdTe$_{0.25}$S$_{0.75}$ QD. CdTe (cadmium telluride) QDs were purchased from Sigma-Aldrich (Saint-Quentin-Fallavier, France): Ref. 777935 CdTe core-type 25 mg (www.sigmaaldrich.com/catalog/product/aldrich/777935, accessed on January 2021). These commercial QDs are coated with carboxylic acid functional ligands (COOH) and are provided through water-soluble powders. According to Ref. [33], their mean radius is $R_0 = 1.7 \pm 0.3$ nm. The stock solution was prepared in Milli-Q water (18 MΩ·cm, Millipore, France) for a QD density $N = 3.66\ 10^{20}$ m^{-3} (i.e., ~0.6 μM). Previous works [29,30] have shown that the nanocrystals are CdTe$_{0.25}$S$_{0.75}$ alloys and that the ligands are HS-(CH$_2$)$_n$-COOH, with $n \leqslant 3$.

Preparation of Prism/PhTES/QD interface. To graft PhTES molecules and deposit QDs on an equilateral CaF$_2$ prism (Fichou, flatness: $\lambda/4$ at 633 nm, sample base size: 25 mm), we first washed the prism in acetone (99.8%, Sigma-Aldrich) and ethanol (99.8%, Sigma-Aldrich) using a sonication bath, and then we cleaned it with a piranha solution (H$_2$O$_2$ 30%:H$_2$SO$_4$ 96%, 1:2, Sigma-Aldrich). It was rinsed with Milli-Q water (18 MΩ·cm, Millipore, France) and dried under nitrogen gas flow. For the grafting of the PhTES monolayer, we prepared a 5% solution of phenyltriethoxysilane (679291-50G Triethoxyphenylsilane, ≥98%, Sigma-Aldrich) in anhydrous methanol (MeOH, 99.9%,VWR). One percent solution is equivalent to 1 g of PhTES in 100 mL of methanol. The prism was immersed in 4 mL of this solution for 1 h and 30 min under a fume hood at 20°C, then rinsed in methanol under sonication (four baths of 1 min), and finally dried under nitrogen flow. The result of this process is shown in Figure 1b, step iii. The deposition of QDs then consisted of spreading a droplet (50 μL) of the stock solution on one face of the prism and drying it with nitrogen.

UV–visible spectroscopy. UV–visible absorbance spectra of the Prism/PhTES/QD sample was recorded using a Cary-5000 spectrophotometer (Agilent) in transmission. A bare CaF$_2$ prism was used as reference. The absorbance curve was thus obtained by differential measurement.

Non-linear 2C-SFG spectroscopy. Vibrational SFG spectra were acquired thanks to a home-made setup described in Ref. [32]. A pulsed IR laser source (Nd:YVO$_4$, 1064 nm, 7.5 ps, HighQ laser) was coupled to an acousto-optic modulator (AA Opto-Electronic, 62.5 MHz micropulse repetition rate, 2 μs train, 25 Hz macropulse repetition rate) and underwent a power amplification step based on the successive double round-trip passage of the incident beam through two successive water-cooled Nd:YVO$_4$ crystals (Quantel flash pump laser system); this step temporally widened the pulse up to 12 ps with 1.3 W mean power at the output. The latter was therefore used to pump two optical parametric oscillators (OPO) with a pump power ratio of 35% and 65% for the IR and visible OPOs described, respectively as follows: (i) the IR OPO based on a lithium niobate (LiNBO$_3$) non-linear crystal continuously tunable in the 2500–4000 cm^{-1} spectral range (spectral resolution fixed to 3 cm^{-1} thanks to a Fabry–Perot slide inserted inside the OPO cavity in a direction normal to the beam propagation; output mean power at 3.45 μm: 30 mW) and, (ii) the visible OPO based on a non-linear BBO (β-BaB$_2$O$_4$) crystal continuously tunable between 440 and 710 nm (spectral resolution fixed to 6 cm^{-1} thanks to a Fabry–Perot slide inserted inside the OPO cavity in a direction normal to the beam propagation; output mean power at 520 nm: 20 mW) for which we selected five specific wavelengths in the SFG experiments: 450, 488, 520, 568, and 612 nm, respectively. It is worth noting that the BBO crystal inside the visible OPO cavity was pumped by an ultraviolet beam (wavelength: 355 nm, mean power: 200 mW) obtained after frequency conversion of the pump beam from successive passage through two non-linear crystals: (i) a BBO crystal that converts a part of the incident IR beam (1064 nm) into a green visible beam (532 nm) by frequency doubling, (ii) a LBO (lithium triborate, LiB$_3$O$_5$) crystal that mixes the green beam and the remaining part of the incident IR beam, giving rise to the ultraviolet beam by a sum-frequency generation process. The infrared and visible beams were then coherently mixed at the same point of the functionalized surface of the prism, as illustrated in Figure 1a. Both beams were in Gaussian beam mode with 2 mm diameter on the sample surface in order to avoid sample damage. The two input beams were p-polarized, and the p-component of the SFG output beam was collected by photomultipliers after spatial and spectral filtering through Raman filters (Kaiser Optical Systems, for each of the five incident corresponding visible wavelengths) and a monochromator (Princeton Instruments, Acton SpectraPro SP-2500, 500 nm triple grating imaging spectrometer). Besides, in order to compensate for the intensity fluctuations of the laser source, the SFG signal of a reference ZnS crystal was acquired in the same conditions and used to normalize the SFG intensity of the sample. 2C-SFG measurements were performed at ambient air in a dark experimental room with temperature fixed at 22 °C. All the laser, OPO, and spectroscopic setups were embedded in a protective box on the optical table with a monitored humidity less than 10% thanks to the presence of a circulating nitrogen flow under the box during measurements, which minimized IR OPO absorption in the probed spectral range.

3. Results

3.1. Structural and Chemical Characterizations of the QD/Molecule Interface

In order to probe the vibroelectronic coupling between QDs and phenyltriethoxysilane (PhTES), the CaF_2 prism was first functionalized by an organic monolayer of PhTES, as depicted in Figure 1b (steps i to iii). The QD layer was then deposited through drop-casting, by drying 50 µL of a QD colloidal solution under nitrogen (Figure 1b, step iv). The UV–visible absorption spectrum of this Prism/PhTES/QD sample is given in Figure 2a. The semiconductor gap of the $CdTe_{0.25}S_{0.75}$ QDs was characterized by a first absorption peak located at 488 nm. Thanks to a mathematical model developed in previous works [29,30], it is possible to extract the surface density of QDs, which was here up to 7.68 nm^{-2}, and to estimate a layer thickness of 300 nm. This dense QD layer is expected to contribute to the vibrational SFG signal through the vibration modes of the ligands: mercaptocarboxylic acids, $HS-(CH_2)_n-COOH$, with $n \leqslant 3$. The SFG spectrum of Figure 2b indeed exhibits the five vibration modes of mercaptocarboxylic acids between 2800 and 3000 cm^{-1}. They correspond to [29]: the symmetric (2856 cm^{-1}), asymmetric (2929 cm^{-1}), and exotic (2910 cm^{-1}) stretching modes of CH_2; the symmetric (2883 cm^{-1}) and asymmetric (2871 cm^{-1}) stretching modes of CH_3 [29,34]. This spectrum also shows a new, intense peak located at 3062 cm^{-1} that can be ascribed to the CH stretching modes of PhTES aromatic rings and, thus, proves how efficient the chemical grafting of PhTES on the prism is. Indeed, such aromatic modes revealed to be hardly observable by SFG spectroscopy on metals [32,35], especially compared with CH_2 and CH_3 stretching modes. Here, we show that the combination of the ATR configuration and the QD layer deposition enhanced the signal associated to aromatic CH stretching modes. The ATR configuration allowed the coupling of light with the PhTES/QD layer through the generation of an evanescent electromagnetic wave at the interface. This evanescent wave had a decreasing intensity through the QD layer in the z-direction normal to the sample surface. The ATR coupling configuration is efficient on a distance related to the wavelength of the beams. In the present case, the visible and incident beams were in total reflection, generating two evanescent waves whose the intensity was significant at least until 450 nm deep in the z-direction because it corresponds to the lowest visible beam wavelength used in the process (while the IR one being around 3 µm is 10 times greater). In both cases, the penetration depth was greater than the sample layer thickness of 300 nm mentioned before. ATR configuration is thus of particular interest in SFG spectroscopy because the surface-specificity of the probe relies on the breaking of symmetry induced by the CaF_2 prism in terms of spatial symmetry (existence of an interface) and local electric field symmetry (existence of a dielectric gap), leading thus to evanescent waves at the sample interface [36]. Moreover, given that SFG is sensitive to the symmetry of the sample in the z-direction pointing out of the interface, the presence of such an intense peak means that the PhTES layer is very well ordered, with a great isotropy of the PhTES monolayer in the (x, y) plane parallel to the prism surface. As a result, PhTES constitutes a very good molecular probe to assess the strength and the range of the vibroelectronic coupling induced by the QDs beyond their ligands.

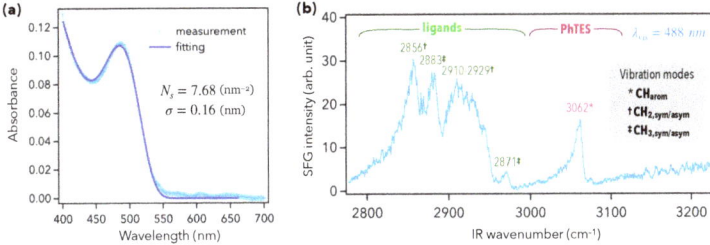

Figure 2. (**a**) UV–visible absorption spectra of the Prism/PhTES/QD sample. The continuous curve is a fit to the data. The fitting procedure is only based on two parameters: the surface density N_s of QDs, and their size dispersion σ (radius). (**b**) Vibrational SFG spectrum of the Prism/PhTES/QD sample performed at a fixed visible wavelength of 488 nm.

3.2. Vibroelectronic Correlation between QDs and Aromatic Rings

Benefiting from a tunable visible laser beam, we acquired five vibrational SFG spectra for five different fixed visible wavelengths: 450, 488, 520, 568, and 612 nm (Figure 3a). In order to get a greater precision on the measurement of the vibration amplitude associated to PhTES at 3062 cm^{-1}, we optimized the spatial overlap between the visible and IR beams, at the sample point, over the range 3000–3100 cm^{-1}. This explains why the amplitudes of the aromatic mode (resp. of the ligand modes) were higher (resp. lower) than those of Figure 2b. As expected, the vibration amplitude a_{ar} of the aromatic CH stretching mode was maximum when the visible wavelength coincided with the first peak of excitonic absorption at 488 nm. It evidences that the vibroelectronic coupling previously observed with the ligands (chemically bound to the QD surface) was also efficient and above all quantifiable according to the distance, with molecules which are not located within the direct chemical environment of the QDs (and not chemically bound to their surface) as calculated below in Section 4. This was not possible to be calculated in disorganized monolayers made of APTES (3-aminopropyltriethoxysilane) [30]. Here again, the vibration amplitude of the aromatic rings was driven by the linear susceptibility $\chi_{QD}^{(1)}(\omega_{vis})$ of the QDs, which was resonant around the semiconductor gap at 488 nm, proving the generality of the first observations [29]. However, contrary to the ligand modes which vanish when the visible wavelength deviated from 488 nm (Figure 3a, 2900–3000 cm^{-1} IR spectral range), the vibration amplitude a_{ar} was much less altered at the other four visible wavelengths (Figure 3a, 3062 cm^{-1} IR wave number). This means that the ability of the QDs to modulate the vibrational response of PhTES was weaker than for the ligands.

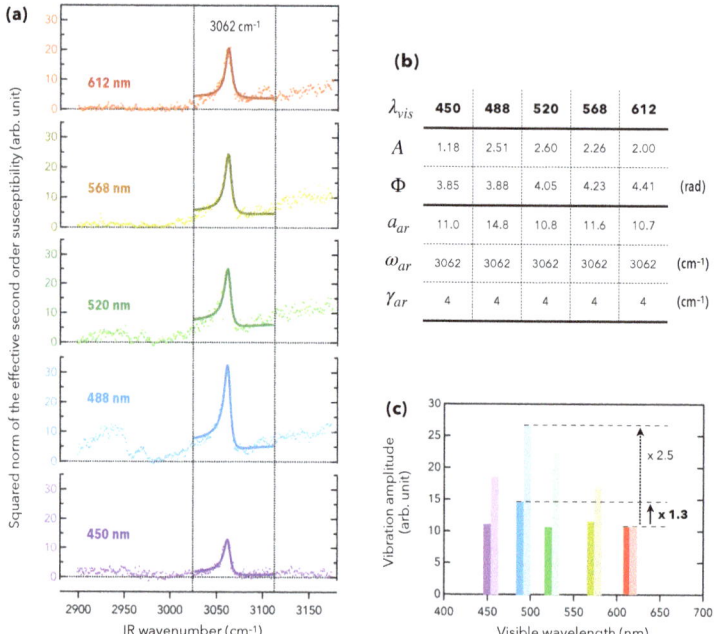

Figure 3. (**a**) SFG spectra of the Prism/PhTES/QD interface. These spectra consist in performing the vibrational spectroscopy of the sample over the IR range 2900–3200 cm^{-1} for five different fixed visible wavelengths, as indicated in nanometers on the left. The bold curves are fits to the experimental data. (**b**) Table gathering the fitting parameters corresponding to the fit curves of Figure 3a. They refer to Equation (1). (**c**) Superposition of, i, the vibration amplitudes a_{ar} of aromatic rings (left-handed color bars), extracted from the fitting procedure, and, ii, the mean vibration amplitudes a_{lig} of the five vibration modes of ligands (right-handed color bars), extracted from [29]. To be compared to a_{ar}, the vibration amplitudes a_{lig} are rescaled so that $a_{\text{lig}}(612\,\text{nm}) = a_{\text{ar}}(612\,\text{nm})$.

Arising from a second-order optical process, SFG is driven by the second-order susceptibility tensor of the sample, $\chi^{(2)}_{ijk}(\omega_{\text{vis}}, \omega_{\text{IR}})$, with $\{i, j, k\} = \{x, y, z\}$. Taking into account the planar geometry of the Prism/PhTES/QD interface, it is possible to reduce this tensor to only four components (zzz, xxz, xzx, zxx), which combine themselves into an effective second-order susceptibility [31,37,38]. Indeed, as calculated in Ref. [29], in [p:pp] polarization combination (for SFG, Vis, IR beams, respectively), only the zzz-Local Field factor prevailed in such experiments with an ATR prism; the three other Local Field factors involved (xxz, xzx, zxx) were significantly weaker, and their values were almost constant over the entire visible spectral range. In these conditions, only the zzz-component was considered in order to distinguish it from the vibroelectronic coupling between QDs and molecules in our calculations of the vibration mode amplitudes from 2C-SFG experimental data. It is quite logical because this Local Field factor is associated to the z-electric field components of the IR and Visible beams, which are the only ones that probe the sample layer in depth, in the normal direction to the prism base, including therefore the QDs. This leads to consider the well-known following expression of the effective second-order susceptibility to fit the SFG data:

$$\chi^{(2)}_{\text{eff}}(\omega_{\text{vis}}, \omega_{\text{IR}}) = A(\omega_{\text{vis}})\,e^{i\Phi(\omega_{\text{vis}})} + \frac{a_{\text{ar}}(\omega_{\text{vis}})}{\omega_{\text{ar}} - \omega_{\text{IR}} + i\gamma_{\text{ar}}}, \tag{1}$$

thus modeled as the sum of a non IR-resonant term associated to the substrate, whose amplitude and phase are A and Φ, and an IR-resonant term associated to the PhTES molecules, consisting in a Lorentzian function centered at $\omega_{ar} = 3062$ cm^{-1} with the amplitude a_{ar} and the damping constant γ_{ar}. From the SFG spectra of Figure 3a that give $|\chi_{eff}^{(2)}(\omega_{vis}, \omega_{IR})|^2$ as a function of ω_{IR}, it is possible to extract the vibration amplitudes $a_{ar}(\omega_{vis})$ of the aromatic rings for the five visible wavelengths. The results of the fitting procedure are gathered in Figure 3b. Figure 3c then reports the five values of $a_{ar}(\omega_{vis})$ with respect to the visible wavelength (left-handed color bars). According to the UV-visible absorption spectrum of Figure 2a, the QDs did not absorb at 612 nm, so that we can choose $a_{ar}(612$ nm$)$ as a reference value for which there is no enhancement due to the optoelectronic activity of QDs. The enhancement factor F_{ar} at 488 nm is written as follows:

$$F_{ar} = \frac{a_{ar}(488 \text{ nm})}{a_{ar}(612 \text{ nm})} = 1.3, \tag{2}$$

which is 1.9 times lower than that of the ligands $F_{lig} = 2.5$ established in Ref. [29] (Figure 3c).

4. Discussion

In order to explain the spectral correlation between $a_{lig/ar}(\omega_{vis})$ and $\chi_{QD}^{(1)}(\omega_{vis})$, we assume the existence of a dipolar coupling between QDs and molecules, stating that the molecules feel the local electric field $\mathbf{E}_\ell(\omega_{vis})$ produced by the QDs as a response of their excitation by the visible laser beam [29]:

$$\mathbf{E}_\ell(\omega_{vis}) \propto \boldsymbol{\kappa}(r) \cdot \chi_{QD}^{(1)}(\omega_{vis}) \cdot \mathbf{E}(\omega_{vis}), \tag{3}$$

where the tensor $\boldsymbol{\kappa}$ relates the local electric field produced by the QDs to their dipole moment $\mathbf{p}$:

$$\mathbf{E}_\ell(\omega_{vis}) = \boldsymbol{\kappa}(r) \, \mathbf{p}(\omega_{vis}), \quad \kappa_{ij}(r) = \frac{3 r_i r_j - \delta_{ij} r^2}{4\pi\varepsilon_0 r^5}, \tag{4}$$

and $\mathbf{E}(\omega_{vis})$ is the electric field of the input visible beam: $\mathbf{p}(\omega_{vis}) \propto \chi_{QD}^{(1)}(\omega_{vis}) \mathbf{E}(\omega_{vis})$. The dipole–dipole interaction is thus encoded by the tensor $\boldsymbol{\kappa}(r)$, depending on the distance r between QDs and molecules. Considering the QDs are isotropic, it is then possible to demonstrate that the vibration amplitudes of the surrounding molecules follow [29]:

$$a_{lig/ar}(\omega_{vis}) \propto \left| \kappa(r) \, \chi_{QD}^{(1)}(\omega_{vis}) \right|, \quad \kappa(r) = \frac{1}{2\pi\varepsilon_0 r^3}. \tag{5}$$

Consequently,

$$\frac{F_{lig}}{F_{ar}} = \frac{a_{lig}(488 \text{ nm})}{a_{ar}(488 \text{ nm})} = \left(\frac{r_{ar}}{r_{lig}} \right)^3 \left| \frac{\chi_{QD/lig}^{(1)}(488 \text{ nm})}{\chi_{QD/ar}^{(1)}(488 \text{ nm})} \right| = 1.9. \tag{6}$$

First, we can estimate the QD–ligand distance r_{lig} by the mean radius $r_0 = 1.7$ nm of QDs [33], and the QD–PhTES distance r_{ar} by $r_0 + L_{lig}$, where L_{lig} is the length of mercaptocarboxylic acids. Second, the ratio between the two linear susceptibilities is not equal to 1. Indeed, they are the macroscopic susceptibilities of the QD layers (not the polarizability of an individual QD), and are thus proportional to the QD density within the thick layer. From UV–visible measurements, we extracted a coverage density of 7.68 nm^{-2} for the Prism/PhTES/QD sample. In Ref. [29], we measured a density of 6.6 nm^{-2} for a Prism/QD sample. Hence,

$$\left| \frac{\chi_{QD/lig}^{(1)}(488 \text{ nm})}{\chi_{QD/ar}^{(1)}(488 \text{ nm})} \right| = \frac{6.6}{7.68} = 0.86. \tag{7}$$

Since $F_{\text{lig}}/F_{\text{ar}} = 1.9$, Equation (6) then leads to

$$L_{\text{lig}} = r_0 \left(\sqrt[3]{\frac{1.9}{0.86}} - 1 \right) = 0.51 \text{ nm.} \tag{8}$$

Given that the QD ligands are mercaptocarboxylic acids of type HS-$(CH_2)_n$-COOH, with $n \leqslant 3$, this value of 0.51 nm must be compared to the lengths of thioglycolic acid, 0.43 nm ($n = 1$), mercaptopropionic acids, 0.54 nm ($n = 2$), and mercaptobutyric acid, 0.65 nm ($n = 3$). As a result, our estimation of $L_{\text{lig}} = 0.51$ nm, based on the hypothesis of a dipolar interaction between QD and molecules, is compatible with the chain length of mercaptopropionic acid, which is actually the most commonly used [4,13,39]. In addition, studying the general case of an r^N-dependence, Figure 4 tells us that the couple of parameters $(n, N) = (2, 3)$ is the most consistent. These constitute decisive arguments in favor of an r^3-dependence of the vibroelectronic coupling occurring at QD/molecule interface.

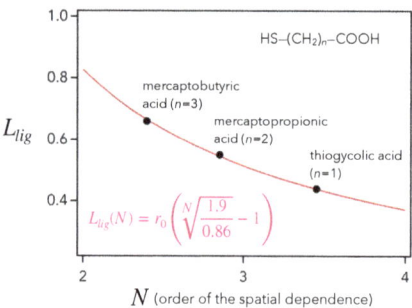

Figure 4. Drawing of the QD ligand chain length L_{lig} (nm) as a function of the order N of the spatial dependence (red curve). The black dots indicate the lengths of the mercaptocarboxylic acids HS-$(CH_2)_n$-COOH ($n \leqslant 3$).

5. Conclusions

The strength of a dipolar coupling between semiconductor nanocrystals and phenyl probe molecules was quantified thanks to 2C-SFG spectroscopy performed in ATR configuration. From the measurement of the amplitudes of specific molecular vibration modes as functions of the distance between the QDs and, first, their chemical ligands then, second, a further PhTES monolayer, this study quantitatively evidenced the spatial dependence in $\sim 1/r^3$ of the dipole–dipole interaction. As a collateral result from this observation, 2C-SFG allowed to deduce that, in the present case, the QD ligands are mercaptopropionic acids, information not always given or known by the suppliers whatever the investigated system. Therefore, 2C-SFG spectroscopy proved to be well-suited for molecular recognition by taking profit of such a dipolar coupling from excitons to molecular vibrations. However, it also confirms that neat synthesis protocols and control experiments are mandatory when ligand-capped QDs are operated at the industrial level. Besides, in these extreme conditions, 2C-SFG spectroscopy revealed its potential to be used as an analytical probe for biosensing applications at the nanoscale level. Such an optical technique could therefore be used in the future for any type of sensor based on metal, semiconductor, or hybrid nanocrystals.

Author Contributions: T.N., L.D. and C.H. designed the sample configuration for UV–vis and 2C-SFG spectroscopy, and performed the 2C-SFG measurements. T.N. performed the UV–visible measurements, analyzed all the data, and wrote the original draft. T.N. also derived the analytical calculation of the dipole–dipole interaction to account for 2C-SFG measurements. T.N., L.D., A.T. and C.H. participated in the analysis and interpretation of the data and contributed to discussions and corrections during the writing process. L.D. and C.H. initiated and supervised the project. All authors have read and agreed to the published version of the manuscript.

Funding: Research leading to these results has received funding from the International Scientific Cooperation Program of the CNRS (Centre National de la Recherche Scientifique) under Grant agreement number PICS07339.

Data Availability Statement: The data presented in this study are available on reasonable request from the corresponding author.

Acknowledgments: The authors acknowledge Assistant Engineer B. Rieul (Université Paris-Saclay, Institut de Chimie Physique, CNRS, 91405 Orsay, France) for his technical assistance on the pilot control development of the SFG spectroscopy setup.

Conflicts of Interest: The authors declare no conflicts of interest.

Abbreviations

The following abbreviations are used in this manuscript:

QD	Quantum Dot
2C-SFG	Two-color Sum-Frequency Generation
ATR	Attenuated Total Reflection
PhTES	Triethoxyphenylsilane
APTES	3-aminopropyltriethoxysilane

References

1. Brus, L.E. Electron-electron and electron-hole interactions in small semiconductor crystallites: The size dependence of the lowest excited electronic states. *J. Chem. Phys.* **1984**, *80*, 4403–4409. [CrossRef]
2. Masumoto, Y.; Sonobe, K. Size-dependent energy levels of CdTe quantum dots. *Phys. Rev. B* **1997**, *56*, 9734–9737. [CrossRef]
3. Wang, X.; Yu, W.W.; Zhang, J.; Aldana, J.; Peng, X.; Xiao, M. Photoluminescence upconversion in colloidal CdTe quantum dots. *Phys. Rev. B* **2003**, *68*, 125318–125323. [CrossRef]
4. Wuister, S.F.; Swart, I.; van Driel, F.; Hickey, S.G.; de Mello Donegá, C. Highly Luminescent Water-Soluble CdTe Quantum Dots. *Nano Lett.* **2003**, *3*, 503–507. [CrossRef]
5. Sapra, S.; Sarma, D.D. Evolution of the electronic structure with size in II-VI semiconductor nanocrystals. *Phys. Rev. B* **2004**, *69*, 125304–125310. [CrossRef]
6. Law, M.; Beard, M.C.; Choi, S.; Luther, J.M.; Hanna, M.C.; Nozik, A.J. Determining the Internal Quantum Efficiency of PbSe Nanocrystal Solar Cells with the Aid of an Optical Model. *Nano Lett.* **2008**, *8*, 3904–3910. [CrossRef] [PubMed]
7. Zhao, H.; Fan, Z.; Liang, H.; Selopal, G.S.; Gonfa, B.A.; Jin, L.; Soudi, A.; Cui, D.; Enrichi, F.; Natile, M.M.; et al. Controlling photoinduced electron transfer from PbS@CdS core@shell quantum dots to metal oxide nanostructured thin films. *Nanoscale* **2014**, *6*, 7004. [CrossRef]
8. Cao, S.W.; Yuan, Y.P.; Fang, J.; Shahjamali, M.M.; Boey, F.Y.C.; Barber, J.; Loo, S.C.J.; Xue, C. In-situ growth of CdS quantum dots on g-C$_3$N$_4$ nanosheets for highly efficient photocatalytic hydrogen generation under visible light irradiation. *Int. J. Hydrog. Energy* **2013**, *38*, 1258–1266. [CrossRef]
9. Xiao, F.X.; Miao, J.; Liu, B. Layer-by-Layer Self-Assembly of CdS Quantum Dots/Graphene Nanosheets Hybrid Films for Photoelectrochemical and Photocatalytic Applications. *J. Am. Chem. Soc.* **2014**, *136*, 1559–1569. [CrossRef]
10. Liu, J.; Zhang, H.; Navarro-Pardo, F.; Selopal, G.S.; Sun, S.; Wang, Z.M.; Zhao, H.; Rosei, F. Hybrid surface passivation of PbS/CdS quantum dots for efficient photoelectrochemical hydrogen generation. *Appl. Surf. Sci.* **2020**, *530*, 147252. [CrossRef]
11. Heuff, R.F.; Swift, J.L.; Cramb, D.T. Fluorescence correlation spectroscopy using quantum dots: Advances, challenges and opportunities. *Phys. Chem. Chem. Phys.* **2007**, *9*, 1870–1880. [CrossRef]
12. Hottechamps, J.; Noblet, T.; Brans, A.; Humbert, C.; Dreesen, L. How Quantum Dots Aggregation Enhances Förster Resonant Energy Tranfer. *ChemPhysChem* **2020**, *21*, 853–862. [CrossRef] [PubMed]
13. Medintz, I.L.; Uyeda, H.T.; Goldman, E.R.; Mattoussi, H. Quantum dot bioconjugates for imaging, labelling and sensing. *Nat. Mater.* **2005**, *4*, 435–446. [CrossRef]
14. Yong, K.T.; Law, W.C.; Roy, I.; Jing, Z.; Huang, H.; Swihart, M.T.; Prasad, P.N. Aqueous phase synthesis of CdTe quantum dots for biophotonics. *J. Biophotonics* **2011**, *4*, 9–20. [CrossRef]
15. Li, J.; Zhu, J.J. Quantum dots for fluorescent biosensing and bio-imaging applications. *Analyst* **2013**, *138*, 2506–2515. [CrossRef]
16. Tyrakowski, C.M.; Snee, P.T. A primer on synthesis, water-solubilization, and functionalization of quantum dots, their use as biological sensing agents, and present status. *Phys. Chem. Chem. Phys.* **2014**, *16*, 837–855. [CrossRef]
17. Wegner, K.D.; Hildebrandt, N. Quantum dots: Bright and versatile in vitro and in vivo fluorescence imaging biosensors. *Chem. Soc. Rev.* **2015**, *44*, 4792–4834. [CrossRef]
18. Dubertret, B. Quantum dots: DNA detectives. *Nat. Mater.* **2005**, *4*, 797–798. [CrossRef] [PubMed]
19. Liu, P.; Wang, Q.; Li, X. Studies on CdSe/L-cysteine Quantum Dots Synthesized in Aqueous Solution for Biological Labeling. *J. Phys. Chem. C* **2009**, *113*, 7670–7676. [CrossRef]

20. Zahavy, E.; Freeman, E.; Lustig, S.; Keysary, A.; Yitzhaki, S. Double Labeling and Simultaneous Detection of B- and T Cells Using Fluorescent Nano-Crystal (q-dots) in Paraffin-Embedded Tissues. *J. Fluoresc.* **2005**, *15*, 661. [CrossRef] [PubMed]

21. Goldman, E.R.; Clapp, A.R.; Anderson, G.P.; Uyeda, H.; Mauro, J.M.; Medintz, I.L.; Mattoussi, H. Multiplexed Toxin Analysis Using Four Colors of Quantum Dot Fluororeagents. *Anal. Chem.* **2004**, *76*, 684–688. [CrossRef] [PubMed]

22. Susha, A.S.; Javier, A.M.; Parak, W.J.; Rogach, A.L. Luminescent CdTe nanocrystals as ion probes and pH sensors in aqueous solutions. *Colloids Surfaces A Physicochem. Eng. Asp.* **2006**, *281*, 40–43. [CrossRef]

23. Generalova, A.N.; Oleinikov, V.A.; Zarifullina, M.M.; Lankina, E.V.; Sizova, S.V.; Artemyev, M.V.; Zubov, V.P. Optical sensing quantum dot-labeled polyacrolein particles prepared by layer-by-layer deposition technique. *J. Colloid Interface Sci.* **2011**, *357*, 265–272. [CrossRef]

24. Mrad, R.; Poggi, M.; Chaâbane, R.B.; Negrerie, M. Role of surface defects in colloidal cadmium selenide (CdSe) nanocrystals in the specificity of fluorescence quenching by metal cations. *J. Colloid Interface Sci.* **2020**, *571*, 368–377. [CrossRef] [PubMed]

25. Zhang, H.; Zhou, Z.; Yang, B. The Influence of Carboxyl Groups on the Photoluminescence of Mercaptocarboxylic Acid-Stabilized CdTe Nanoparticles. *J. Phys. Chem. B* **2003**, *107*, 8–13. [CrossRef]

26. Frederick, M.T.; Amin, V.A.; Weiss, E.A. Optical Properties of Strongly Coupled Quantum Dot-Ligand Systems. *J. Phys. Chem. Lett.* **2013**, *4*, 634–640. [CrossRef]

27. Liang, Y.; Thorne, J.E.; Parkinson, B.A. Controlling the Electronic Coupling between CdSe Quantum Dots and Thiol Capping Ligands via pH and Ligand Selection. *Langmuir* **2012**, *28*, 11072–11077. [CrossRef] [PubMed]

28. Jin, S.; Harris, R.D.; Lau, B.; Aruda, K.O.; Amin, V.A.; Weiss, E.A. Enhanced Rate of Radiative Decay in CdSe Quantum Dots upon Adsorption of an Exciton-Delocalizing Ligand. *Nano Lett.* **2014**, *14*, 5323–5328. [CrossRef] [PubMed]

29. Noblet, T.; Dreesen, L.; Boujday, S.; Méthivier, C.; Busson, B.; Tadjeddine, A.; Humbert, C. Semiconductor quantum dots reveal dipolar coupling from exciton to ligand vibration. *Commun. Chem.* **2018**, *1*, 76. [CrossRef]

30. Noblet, T.; Boujday, S.; Méthivier, C.; Erard, M.; Hottechamps, J.; Busson, B.; Humbert, C. Two-Dimensional Layers of Colloidal CdTe Quantum Dots: Assembly, Optical Properties, and Vibroelectronic Coupling. *J. Phys. Chem. C* **2020**, *124*, 25873–25883. [CrossRef]

31. Humbert, C.; Noblet, T. A Unified Mathematical Formalism for First to Third Order Dielectric Response of Matter: Application to Surface-Specific Two-Colour Vibrational Optical Spectroscopy. *Symmetry* **2021**, *13*, 153. [CrossRef]

32. Barbillon, G.; Noblet, T.; Busson, B.; Tadjeddine, A.; Humbert, C. Localised detection of thiophenol with gold nanotriangles highly structured as honeycombs by nonlinear Sum Frequency Generation spectroscopy. *J. Mater. Sci.* **2018**, *53*, 4554–4562. [CrossRef]

33. Noblet, T.; Dreesen, L.; Hottechamps, J.; Humbert, C. A global method for handling fluorescence spectra at high concentration derived from the competition between emission and absorption of colloidal CdTe quantum dots. *Phys. Chem. Chem. Phys.* **2017**, *19*, 26559–26565. [CrossRef]

34. Dalstein, L.; Haddada, M.B.; Barbillon, G.; Humbert, C.; Tadjeddine, A.; Boujday, S.; Busson, B. Revealing the Interplay between Adsorbed Molecular Layers and Gold Nanoparticles by Linear and Nonlinear Optical Properties. *J. Phys. Chem. C* **2015**, *119*, 17146–17155. [CrossRef]

35. Humbert, C.; Pluchery, O.; Lacaze, E.; Tadjeddine, A.; Busson, B. Optical spectroscopy of functionalized gold nanoparticles assemblies as a function of the surface coverage. *Gold Bull.* **2013**, *46*, 299–309. [CrossRef]

36. Tourillon, G.; Dreesen, L.; Volcke, C.; Sartenaer, Y.; Thiry, P.A.; Peremans, A. Total internal reflection sum-frequency generation spectroscopy and dense gold nanoparticles monolayer: A route for probing adsorbed molecules. *Nanotechnology* **2007**, *18*, 415301–415307. [CrossRef]

37. Chen, F.; Gozdzialski, L.; Hung, K.K.; Stege, U.; Hore, D.K. Assessing the Molecular Specificity and Orientation Sensitivity of Infrared, Raman, and Vibrational Sum-Frequency Spectra. *Symmetry* **2021**, *13*, 42. [CrossRef]

38. Zhuang, X.; Miranda, P.B.; Kim, D.; Shen, Y.R. Mapping molecular orientation and conformation interfaces by surface nonlinear optics. *Phys. Rev. B* **1999**, *59*, 12632–12640. [CrossRef]

39. Sperling, R.A.; Parak, W.J. Surface modification, functionalization and bioconjugation of colloidal inorganic nanoparticles. *Phil. Trans. R. Soc. A* **2010**, *368*, 1333–1383. [CrossRef]

Article

Density Functional Theory Study of Substitution Effects on the Second-Order Nonlinear Optical Properties of Lindquist-Type Organo-Imido Polyoxometalates

Emna Rtibi [1,2] and Benoit Champagne [2,*]

[1] Laboratory of Materials Molecules and Applications, Preparatory Institute for Scientific and Technical Studies, Carthage University, B.P. 51 La Marsa, Tunis 2075, Tunisia; emna.rtibi@unamur.be
[2] Laboratory of Theoretical Chemistry, Unit of Theoretical and Structural Physical Chemistry, Namur Institute of Structured Matter, University of Namur, Rue de Bruxelles, 61, 5000 Namur, Belgium
* Correspondence: benoit.champagne@unamur.be; Tel.: +32-081-724-554

Abstract: Density functional theory and time-dependent density functional theory have been enacted to investigate the effects of donor and acceptor on the first hyperpolarizability of Lindquist-type organo-imido polyoxometalates (POMs). These calculations employ a range-separated hybrid exchange-correlation functional (ωB97X-D), account for solvent effects using the implicit polarizable continuum model, and analyze the first hyperpolarizabilities by using the two-state approximation. They highlight the beneficial role of strong donors as well as of π-conjugated spacers (CH=CH rather than C≡C) on the first hyperpolarizabilities. Analysis based on the unit sphere representation confirms the one-dimensional push-pull π-conjugated character of the POMs substituted by donor groups and the corresponding value of the depolarization ratios close to 5. Furthermore, the use of the two-state approximation is demonstrated to be suitable for explaining the origin of the variations of the first hyperpolarizabilities as a function of the characteristics of a unique low-energy charge-transfer excited state and to attribute most of the first hyperpolarizability changes to the difference of dipole moment between the ground and that charge-transfer excited state.

Keywords: polyoxometalates; donor/acceptor substituents; first hyperpolarizability; (time-dependent) DFT

Citation: Rtibi, E.; Champagne, B. Density Functional Theory Study of Substitution Effects on the Second-Order Nonlinear Optical Properties of Lindquist-Type Organo-Imido Polyoxometalates. *Symmetry* **2021**, *13*, 1636. https://doi.org/10.3390/sym13091636

Academic Editors: Christophe Humbert and Thomas Noblet

Received: 14 July 2021
Accepted: 24 August 2021
Published: 6 September 2021

Publisher's Note: MDPI stays neutral with regard to jurisdictional claims in published maps and institutional affiliations.

1. Introduction

Polyoxometalates (POMs) are nanomolecular metal-oxides made of metal atoms (M) from groups VB (often, V) and VIB (often Mo or W) in a high oxidation state. These anionic nanoclusters are built from MO_x^{y-} oxyanion polyhedra linked together by shared O atoms. Much is known about their redox properties, leading to interesting catalytic activities [1], while they also found applications in life sciences [2]. Moreover, recent experimental investigations have demonstrated that POM units can be combined with organic moieties, leading to hybrid organic-inorganic compounds that exhibit nonlinear optical (NLO) properties [3–7]. Though reference [6] deals with third-order NLO effects, the other investigations as well as the current contribution focus on the second-order NLO effects and, more precisely, on second harmonic generation (SHG). These experimental studies [3–5,7] extended the field of organic and organometallic compounds, which can present large second-order NLO responses combined with short response times [8–25]. In particular, refs. [3,4] demonstrated that POMs may provide a new generation of high performance, high transparency, and potentially redox-switchable NLO materials. In the case of Lindqvist-type organo-imido-substituted hexamolybdates bearing π-conjugated ligands, these investigations demonstrated that the polyanion clusters act as electron acceptors because the first hyperpolarizability (β), which characterizes the SHG response at the molecular scale, is enhanced when these organic linkers are substituted by electron donors, in other words, when they present a strong non-centrosymmetry. These experimental characterizations have been carried out using the hyper-Rayleigh scattering (HRS) technique [26]. Though these interpretations were in contradiction with previous quantum chemical calculations [27,28], a recent contribution by the authors [29] showed that the polyanions of these Lindqvist-type POMs play the role of electron acceptor and that the use of an inappropriate density functional theory (DFT) exchange-correlation functional (XCF) was responsible for the incorrect structure-property relationships in refs. [27,28]. In reference [29], a striking difference with respect to the previous theoretical studies results from the use of a range-separated hybrid XCF, known to describe reliably the hyperpolarizabilities. Indeed, (linear and) nonlinear electric-field-induced polarization effects, which determine the β responses, are intrinsically nonlocal and require the use of XCFs that contain nonlocal (Hartree-Fock) exchange [30]. On the contrary, local density approximation (LDA) and generalized-gradient approximation (GGA) suffer from shortsightedness to the electric field perturbations, as previously demonstrated and analyzed [31–33].

Following reference [4], 11 hexamolybdate compounds (labeled **0–10**) have been selected in reference [29] and a detailed quantum chemical investigation has been enacted. Besides the selection of reliable methods to predict their geometrical structures, linear and nonlinear optical responses, that work provided an interpretation of the second-order NLO responses in agreement with the experimental data, bringing additional tools to deduce structure-property relationships and to support the design of new POM derivatives with large NLO responses. In this work, we extend our previous investigation by addressing one aspect of the structure-NLO property relationships in Lindqvist-type POMs: the modulation of the donor/acceptor character of the organic linker either by changing the substituent on the terminal phenyl ring or by changing the π-conjugated character by replacing the CC triple bond by a CC double bond (Figure 1).

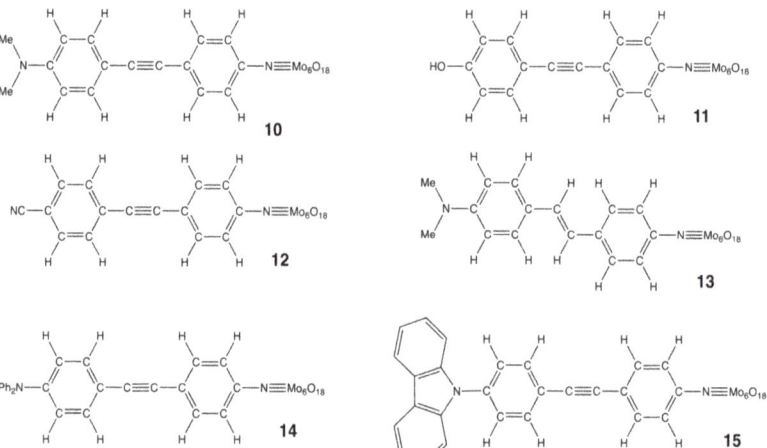

Figure 1. Structure of POM derivatives **10–15**. POMs **0–10** have been studied in our previous work (reference [29]), and a consistent notation has been adopted for easing the discussion.

The first point is tackled by starting from compound **10** and by changing its dimethylamino substituent, either by small groups, a hydroxyl substituent (**11**), or a cyano one (**12**). This will further confirm the contrasted role of acceptor and donor groups (CN versus OH and NMe$_2$). Then, the comparison between **10** and **13** aims at comparing the role of the linker, containing an ethynyl (**10**) or an ethenyl (**13**) spacer. Finally, based on reference [5], other donor groups are considered. These are bulkier than in **10**, a diphenylamino (**14**) or a carbazole (**15**) substituent.

2. Computational Methods

DFT and TDDFT calculations were carried out using the Gaussian16 package [34]. Geometry optimizations were performed using ωB97X-D XCF [35], which includes 100% of long-range exact exchange, a small fraction (about 22%) of short-range exact exchange, a modified B97 XCF for short-range interaction, the B97 correlation density functional [36] and empirical atom−atom London dispersion corrections. The default range-separating parameter ω = 0.2 Bohr^{-1} was used. The atomic basis set consists of 6-311+G(d,p) for C, H, N, O, and LANL2TZ for the Mo atoms. The reliability of this ωB97X-D/6-311+G(d,p)/LANL2TZ method for the geometry optimization of POM derivatives was demonstrated in comparison with other XC functionals in our previous work [29] and was confirmed here by comparison with experimental data from reference [3]. To better describe the impact of the solvent effects, geometry optimizations were performed in solution using the integral equation formalism (IEF) of the polarizable continuum model (PCM) (IEF-PCM), which represents the solvent by a dielectric continuum characterized by its dielectric permittivity (ε) [37]. Using the optimized geometries, the SHG β tensor components were calculated employing the time-dependent density functional theory (TDDFT) method [38,39] with the ωB97X-D XC functional, the 6-311G(d)/LanL2TZ basis set, and the IEF-PCM scheme to account for solvent effects. Both static and dynamic responses were evaluated for an incident wavelength of 1064 nm. Computing β has always been a challenge, in particular, for large compounds and for compounds having donor and/or acceptor substituents because of the intrinsic nonlocal nature of the response. ωB97X-D falls in a new class of DFT functional known as range-separated functionals, which are capable of capturing both short-range and long-range interactions.

To allow comparisons with the experiment, the HRS first hyperpolarizabilities, $\beta_{HRS}(-2\omega;\omega,\omega)$, were evaluated from the β tensor components. These are reported as well as the depolarization ratios (DR), which reflects the NLOphore shape. Full expressions for $\beta_{HRS}(-2\omega;\omega,\omega)$ and DR are available from refs. [40,41]. In the case of one-dimensional push-pull π-conjugated systems, the β tensor is dominated by a single diagonal component, β_{zzz}, where z is the charge-transfer axis. In that case, there is a simple relationship between β_{HRS} and that component [4]:

$$\beta_{zzz} = \sqrt{35/6}\,\beta_{HRS} \qquad (1)$$

To describe the first hyperpolarizability, the unit sphere representation (USR) was adopted [42]. It consists (i) in evaluating an effective induced dipole:

$$\vec{\mu}_{ind} = \overset{\leftrightarrow}{\beta} : \vec{E}^2(\theta,\phi) \qquad (2)$$

where $\overset{\leftrightarrow}{\beta}$ is the first hyperpolarizability tensor and $\vec{E}(\theta,\phi)$ is a unit vector of the electric field, of which the polarization is defined in spherical coordinates by the θ and ϕ angles, and (ii) then in representing the induced dipoles on a sphere centered at the molecule center of mass. The interpretation of the β values can further be performed by resorting to perturbation theory, where β is expressed under the form of a summation over the excited states (SOS) [43,44]. In particular, the reliability of the two-state approximation (TSA) has been demonstrated for push-pull π-conjugated systems [45]. In that scheme, the β response is dominated by a single low-energy charge-transfer excited state and, for the diagonal component along the charge-transfer axis, $\beta_{zzz} = \beta$:

$$\beta = 6\frac{\Delta\mu_{ge}\mu_{ge}^2}{\Delta E_{ge}^2} = 9\,f_{ge}\,\frac{\Delta\mu_{ge}}{\Delta E_{ge}^3} \qquad (3)$$

where $\Delta E_{ge} = E_e - E_g$, the excitation energy from the ground state g to the excited state e, is the lowest-energy dipole-allowed excited state, $\Delta\mu_{ge} = \mu_e - \mu_g$ is the corresponding difference in dipole moment, and μ_{ge} is the transition dipole moment, related to the oscilator strength f_{ge} of the excitation:

$$f_{ge} = \frac{2}{3}\Delta E_{ge}\mu_{ge}^2 \tag{4}$$

3. Results and Discussion

3.1. Ground State Equilibrium Geometries

Selected ground state equilibrium geometrical parameters of compounds **10–15**, which have been optimized with the IEF-PCM/ωB97X-D/6-311G*/LanL2TZ method, are displayed in Table 1 and compared with the experimental results from X-ray diffraction (XRD) (**10**, **14**, and **15**).

Table 1. Selected equilibrium bond lengths (in Å) and valence angles (deg.) of POMs derivatives as obtained at the IEF-PCM/ωB97X-D/6-311G*/LanL2TZ level in comparison with experimental results from X-ray diffraction [1,2].

Compounds	10		11	12	13	14		15	
Method	DFT [29]	XRD [4]	DFT	DFT	DFT	DFT	XRD [5]	DFT [3]	XRD [5]
R-C_1	1.367	1.368	1.352	1.432	1.371	1.403	1.385	1.413	1.447
C_1-C_2	1.413	1.411	1.395	1.398	1.412	1.401	1.406	1.395	1.390
C_2-C_3	1.382	1.385	1.386	1.383	1.382	1.383	1.388	1.385	1.392
C_3-C_4	1.400	1.403	1.401	1.401	1.401	1.401	1.395	1.400	1.388
C_4-C_5	1.424	1.430	1.427	1.427	1.462	1.426	1.448	1.428	1.474
C_5-C_6	1.208	1.208	1.207	1.206	1.342	1.207	1.198	1.207	1.210
C_6-C_7	1.425	1.433	1.426	1.426	1.465	1.426	1.438	1.427	1.489
C_7-C_8	1.403	1.385	1.402	1.402	1.404	1.403	1.400	1.402	1.389
C_8-C_9	1.384	1.384	1.382	1.383	1.382	1.383	1.362	1.383	1.391
C_9-C_{10}	1.397	1.391	1.400	1.400	1.400	1.400	1.417	1.402	1.390
C_{10}-N	1.373	1.395	1.375	1.374	1.374	1.374	1.382	1.378	1.373
N-Mo	1.727	1.737	1.729	1.730	1.727	1.728	1.755[5]	1.734	1.750
Mo-O	1.980	1.946	1.983	1.981	1.984	1.981	1.952	1.985	1.955
Mo-Mo	3.303	3.237	3.303	3.303	3.303	3.305	3.245	3.301	3.230
C_{10}-N-Mo	169.6	168.3	170.0	169.9	174.9	176.7	172.3	168.3	160.6
BLA [4]	0.024	0.023	0.012	0.016	0.024	0.018	0.012	0.012	−0.003

[1] When they are several equivalent atoms in the molecule or more than one molecule in the unit cell, the reported values are averages. [2] The C_5 and C_6 atoms of the general structure correspond either to ethenyl or ethynyl C atoms. [3] In compound **15**, the calculated torsion angle between the carbazole and the attached phenyl ring amounts to 55.6° while in the crystal it attains 69.9°. [4] BLA is defined as $\frac{1}{2}$[2 d $(C_2$-$C_3)$—d $(C_1$-$C_2)$—d $(C_3$-$C_4)$]. [5] The average is not reported here since the equivalent bond length for the other molecule of the unit cell amounts to 2.038 Å, which is beyond what could be expected for such an N-Mo bond.

The agreement is globally suitable, though the medium effects are different, i.e., the calculations do not account for crystal packing effects but for an isotropic dielectric medium (which is consistent with the calculations of the NLO responses, compared to measurements carried out in solution). Differences in bond lengths are generally of the order of 0.02 Å or less. For the C_{10}-N-Mo valence angle, the difference can attain 4–8°, which is attributed to the crystal environment.

Comparing **10** and **13**, besides the ethenyl versus ethynyl linker, the differences of geometry are very small (0.005 Å or less on the bond lengths and the same BLA value). This is consistent with their similar charge distributions in the ground state (vide infra). Then, comparing the optimized geometries of compounds with a CC triple bond as a spacer, differences in BLA are obvious. In the case of **10**, the BLA amounts to 0.024 Å and decreases to 0.018 Å in **14** (R = NPh$_2$) and 0.012 Å in **15** (R = carbazole). In fact, the BLA is a probe of the donor or acceptor strength of the substituent. When the substituent is a H atom (compound **0** from reference [29]), the BLA reduces to 0.008 Å while with the dimethylamino group (**10**), which is a strong donor, the quinoid character of the ring increases, and the BLA increases to 0.024 Å. So, on the basis of the BLA, the donor character decreases in the order NMe$_2$ > NPh$_2$ > carbazole. When R = OH (**11**), the BLA also amounts to 0.012 Å. When the substituent is a cyano group (**12**), it is slightly larger (0.016 Å), highlighting the acceptor character of that group. Note that in the case of **15**, the BLA is similar to that found in compounds **4** and **8** of reference [29], which involve a pyrrolyl substituent. Indeed, such as the pyrrolyl substituent, the carbazole of **15** is tilted (by 56°) with respect to the plane of the attached phenyl ring, reducing the donor character of the N atom. Moreover, the phenyl rings of the NPh$_2$ substituent in **14** are also tilted with respect to the phenyl of the π-conjugated linker, but the tilt angle is smaller than in **15** and goes down to 33°.

These BLA variations and the subsequent interpretation of the donor strengths are corroborated by the C$_1$-N bond lengths, which increase in the order NMe$_2$ < NPh$_2$ < carbazole (both from XRD data and from calculations). The substituent effects on the other geometrical parameters are much smaller because these units (CC triple bond, the other phenyl ring, and the POM moiety) are farther away.

3.2. Natural Population Analysis (NPA) Charge Distributions

Natural population analysis (NPA) was carried out for the different segments of the POMs, as defined in Table 2. The NPA charge on the POM moiety is always close to -1.9 e, while for the linking N atom (**E** moiety) and the nearby phenyl ring (**D** moiety), they amount to -0.3 e and 0.2 e. These sum up to -2 e, which is the global anion charge. The ethynyl/ethenyl spacer can be considered neutral, with negligible impact on the substituent. Thus, the global charge of the **A** and **B** units is also zero, and the differences refer to the donor/acceptor strengths. In the case of **10**, both **A** and **B** bear a quasi-zero charge. When replacing the NMe$_2$ substituent with NPh$_2$ and then a carbazole, the substituent becomes more negative. This can be explained by the fact that its donor (mesomer) character does not compensate anymore for the acceptor (inductive) effect of the N atom. In the case of **11**, the donor character of the hydroxyl group is smaller than that of the NMe$_2$ in **10**, while the acceptor character of the cyano group appears small, with a charge of -0.04 e.

Table 2. Natural Population Analysis charge distributions (in e) in the **A–F** moieties of compounds **10–15**, as obtained from calculations performed at the IEF-PCM/ωB97X-D/6-311G*/LanL2TZ level of approximation. The **A–F** moieties are defined in the scheme below.

Compounds	A	B	C	D	E	F
10 (A = −NMe$_2$, C = C≡C)	0.01	0.04	−0.01	0.19	−0.30	−1.93
11 (A = −OH, C = C≡C)	−0.19	0.22	−0.01	0.20	−0.30	−1.91
12 (A = −CN, C = C≡C)	−0.04	0.01	0.02	0.21	−0.31	−1.89
13 (A = NMe$_2$, C = CH=CH)	0.00	0.04	0.02	0.18	−0.29	−1.95
14 (A = −NPh$_2$, C = C≡C)	−0.12	0.14	0.00	0.20	−0.30	−1.92
15 (A = −Carb., C = C≡C)	−0.21	0.21	0.01	0.21	−0.31	−1.91

3.3. First Hyperpolarizabilities

The first hyperpolarizabilities of compounds 10−15 are listed in Table 3. Besides the β_{HRS} values and their depolarization ratios, the $\beta_{zzz} = \sqrt{35/6}\beta_{HRS}$ values are reported to allow straightforward comparisons with the experiment. To a suitable extent, variations of the β values are consistent with the BLA values: a large BLA leads to a large β value. This is substantiated by the relative β values of the compounds bearing an amino substituent: β(10, NMe$_2$) > β(14, NPh$_2$) > β(15, carbazole). On this basis, the dimethylamino group is a better donor than the diphenylamino one, both being stronger than carbazole. The weaker donor character of carbazole can be associated with its steric interactions with the phenyl ring, leading to a twist by about 56° and a subsequent reduction in π-conjugation. The intermediate value of 14 is then associated with the twist of the phenyl rings (33°). This BLA-β relationship is also verified by the differences between compounds 11 (R = OH) and 10 (R = NMe$_2$). Nevertheless, the BLA is not the only criterion to take into account. So, compound 12 bearing a cyano group has a much smaller β value than reference compound 10 in comparison to compound 11. This is attributed to the acceptor character of the cyano substituent, which, although it affects the BLA of the phenyl ring, is poorly conjugated with the POM acceptor moiety (vide infra). In addition, compounds 10 and 13 have similar BLA values, but the β value of compound 13 is 21% (41%) larger than that of compound 10 in the static limit (at 1064 nm). This is explained by the nature of the spacer between the phenyl rings: a single-double-single bond pattern enables better the propagation of the donor effect than a single-triple-single bond pattern.

Table 3. HRS first hyperpolarizabilities (in 10^3 au) of the POM derivatives as calculated at the IEF-PCM(solvent = acetonitrile)/TDDFT/ωB97X-D/6-311G*/LanL2TZ level in comparison with experimental data from reference [5]. Depolarization ratios are given in parentheses. Columns 4,5 report the β_{zzz} values (in 10^{-30} esu, B convention, i.e., the values are divided by two with respect to the T convention values) while column 6 reports the corresponding β_{zzz} experimental values.

Compounds	β_{HRS}		β_{zzz}		β_{zzz}, Exp.
	$\lambda = \infty$	$\lambda = 1064$ nm	$\lambda = \infty$	$\lambda = 1064$ nm	$\lambda = 1064$ nm
10	20.8 (4.75)	42.4 (4.94)	217	443	440 $\pm$ 55
11	11.3 (4.75)	19.2 (4.94)	118	200	/
12	3.2 (4.55)	5.4 (4.92)	34	56	/
13	25.2 (4.77)	58.5 (4.96)	263	611	/
14	17.0 (4.49)	36.6 (4.52)	177	382	590 $\pm$ 20
15	8.8 (4.37)	16.6 (4.50)	92	173	150 $\pm$36

The DR values are generally close to 5, which is the typical value for one-dimensional push-pull π-conjugated systems, which whom the β tensor is dominated by a single diagonal component (along the charge-transfer axis, called here β_{zzz}). This ratio gets also closer to 5 when going from the static value to the response at 1064 nm. The DR is also slightly smaller for compounds 14 and 15, which is attributed to the more extended nature of the donor substituents. The USRs of the β tensor further describe the second-order responses of these POM derivatives (Figure 2). All USRs highlight the non-centrosymmetry of the second-order NLO response as well as the strong one-dimensional push-pull character of these compounds. The arrows go from the acceptor (POM moiety) to the donor groups. Their lengths are proportional to the amplitude of the β response in a given direction. Note that in the case of the cyano group, the arrows are much smaller but still oriented in the same direction, which attributes to the POM a stronger acceptor character than to the cyano group.

Comparisons to the experiment confirm that the carbazole group is the weakest donor among the three amino substituents because the β_{HRS} response is substantially smaller for compound 15 than for 10 and 14. On the other hand, there is an inversion between the relative values of compounds 10 and 15. First, the quantitative agreement between theory and experiment is very suitable for **10**, but for **15**, calculations predict a decrease by 14%, while experiments show an increase by 34% with respect to **10**. This difference might result from the combination of the limitations of the method of calculation (the XCF and the treatment of the solvent are approximate), together with the experimental error bars.

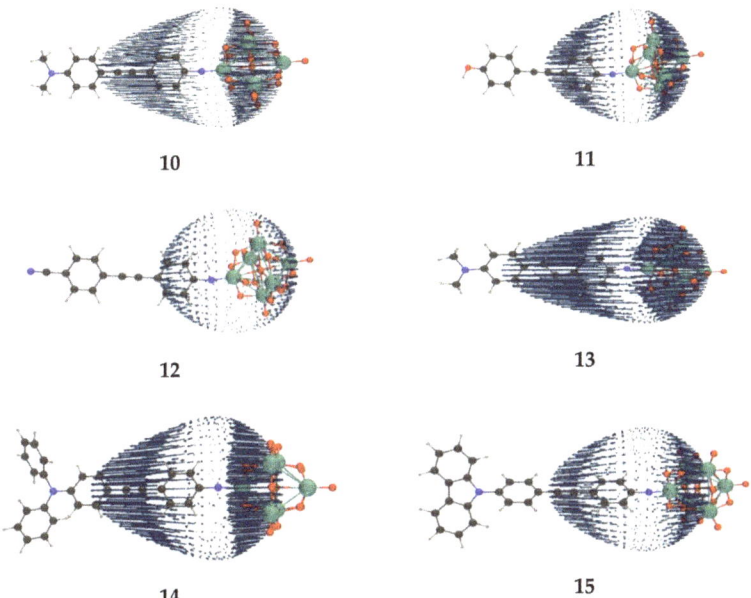

Figure 2. Unit sphere representation of the static first hyperpolarizability tensor of compounds **10–15**, as calculated at the TDDFT/ωB97X-D level of approximation (USR factor of 0.0001).

3.4. UV-Absorption Spectra and Interpretation of the β Values

The UV/visible absorption spectra of POMs **10–15** were simulated at the TDDFT level and are drawn in Figure 3. At large wavelengths (330–450 nm), they are dominated by a single transition, which corresponds to the second excited state. The characteristics of that state are listed in Table 4. Besides the excitation energy and oscillator strength, the charge-transfer distance (d_{CT}) and amplitude (q_{CT}), together with the change of dipole moment upon excitation ($\Delta\mu_{CT}$) are listed.

Starting from **10**, the lowest excitation energy band is blue-shifted by ~0.2 eV for compounds **11** and **12** while it is red-shifted by almost 0.2 eV for compound **13**, characterized by a better π-conjugated spacer between the phenyl rings. In the case of the amino-like substituents, comparison with the experiment is possible. Their calculated vertical excitation energies are systematically larger than the photon energies corresponding to the maximum of absorption (by 0.22–0.31 eV). This is consistent with the difference of nature between these two quantities and, subsequently, the fact that the maximum absorption is lowered in energy by about 0.2 eV with respect to the vertical excitation energy, as calculated recently for fluorescent protein chromophores [46]. Among these three amino-like compounds, POM **10** presents the smallest calculated (experimental) excitation energy, 2.98 eV. It is blue-shifted by 0.04 eV (experimentally, 0.04 eV as well) when the substituent is NPh$_2$ (**14**) and by 0.17 eV (experimentally, 0.26 eV) when it is a carbazole (**15**). Among these, **14** presents the largest calculated oscillator strength (f) and experimental extinction coefficient. **10** and **13**, which differ by the π-spacer, present similar oscillator strengths, which are larger than those of POMs **11** and **12**.

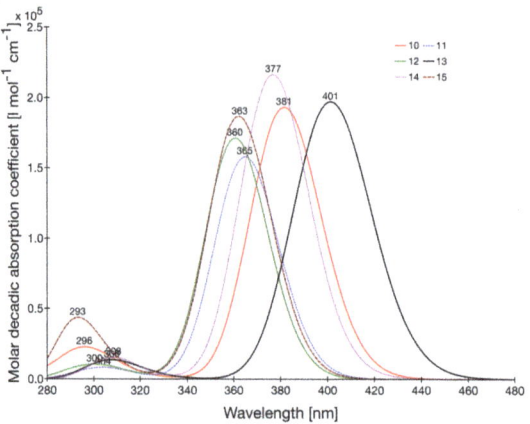

Figure 3. UV/visible absorption spectra of compounds **10–15** as obtained at the IEF-PCM/TDDFT/ωB97X-D/6-311G*/LanL2TZ level of approximation. Each transition is described by a Gaussian having an HWHM = 0.3 eV.

Table 4. UV/visible spectra characteristics of compounds **10–15** as determined at the IEF-PCM(solvent = acetonitrile)/TDDFT/ωB97X-D/6-311G*/LanL2TZ level of approximation. The β_{HRS} and β_{HRS} quantities have been evaluated using the two-state approximation (in 10^3 a.u.) and the CPKS β_{HRS} values are also given for comparison.

POMs	ΔE (eV) (λ, *nm*) [Root]	ΔE (Exp.)	f	d_{CT} (Å)	q_{CT} (e)	$\Delta\mu$ (D)	$\beta_{zzz}^{TSA}=9\frac{f\Delta\mu}{\Delta E^3}$	β_{HRS}^{TSA}	β_{HRS}^{CPKS}
10	3.25 (382) [2]	2.94 [5]	2.15	4.78	0.66	15.2	67.9	28.1	20.8
11	3.40 (365) [2]	-	1.76	3.56	0.57	9.8	31.1	12.9	11.3
12	3.44 (361) [2]	-	1.90	1.97	0.50	4.7	15.7	6.5	3.2
13	3.09 (401) [2]	-	2.19	4.83	0.66	15.4	81.6	33.8	25.2
14	3.29 (377) [2]	2.98 [5]	2.41	4.38	0.62	13.0	62.6	25.9	17.0
15	3.42 (362) [2]	3.20 [5]	2.08	3.08	0.54	8.0	29.6	12.2	8.8

For the dominant electronic excitation, the change of electron density, $\Delta\rho\left(\overrightarrow{r}\right) = \rho_{excited}\left(\overrightarrow{r}\right) - \rho_{ground\ state}\left(\overrightarrow{r}\right)$, was calculated (Figure 4). The patterns are similar: they highlight the acceptor character of the POM moiety and the donor character of the terminal organic moiety. Moreover, their extents differ among the compounds. For **12**, the $\Delta\rho$ hardly spreads over the phenyl ring that bears the acceptor cyano group. For the other compounds, the terminal phenyl ring is involved. For **15**, only the N atom of the carbazole takes part as donating moiety. The donating contribution of the amino groups is larger in **14** and even more in **10** and **13**. By integration of the volumes with positive or negative $\Delta\rho$, the changes of dipole moment upon excitation, $\Delta\mu$, were evaluated. Their ordering is opposite to the corresponding excitation energies: **13** < **10** < **14** < **11** < **15** < **12**. This change of dipole moment, which can be expressed as the product between a charge-transfer distance (d_{CT}) and the amount of charge transfer (q_{CT}), is dominated by the former. Indeed, the range of q_{CT} values is narrow, 0.50–0.66 e, while the range of d_{CT} values is much broader, from 1.97 Å in **12** to more than twice as much in **10**, **14**, and **15**.

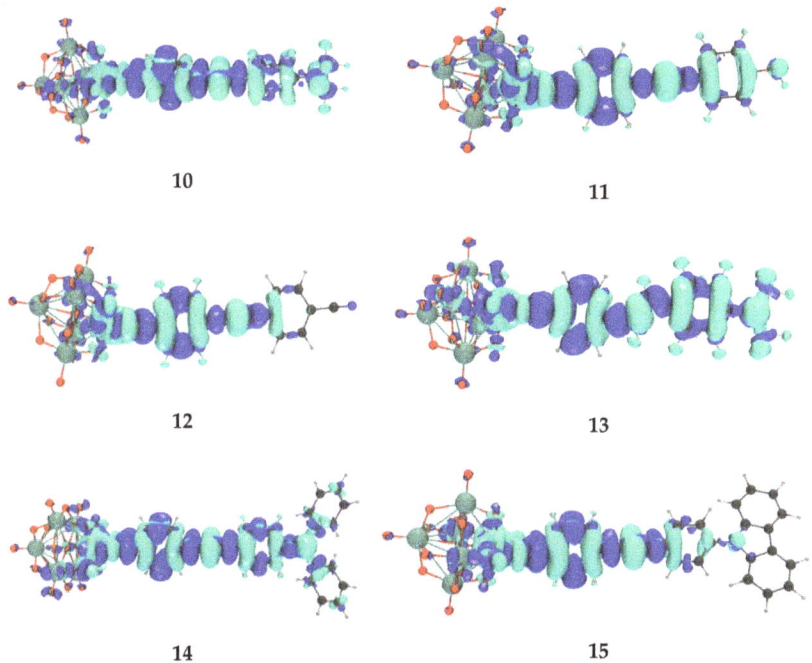

Figure 4. Excitation-induced electron density difference ($\Delta\rho\left(\vec{r}\right)$) as calculated for the key excited state of POMs **10–15** at the IEF-PCM/TDDFT/ωB97X-D/6-311G*/LanL2TZ level of approximation (iso-value = 0.0005 a.u.; light/dark blue corresponds to negative/positive $\Delta\rho\left(\vec{r}\right)$ so that the excitation-induced electron transfer goes from the light to the dark blue).

In the case of **10**, **14**, and **15**, these TDDFT/ωB97X-D UV/vis absorption characteristics are not straightforward to compare with those reported in reference [5], obtained at the TDDFT level with the SAOP (statistical average of orbital potential) XCF because their lowest excitation energy absorption bands result from more than one electronic transition with non-negligible oscillator strength, while in our case, there is only one transition. The comparison with the Stark spectroscopy data of reference [5] is also difficult for the same reason (more than one excited state) as well as owing to the specific experimental conditions (butyronitrile glasses at 77 K).

The linear optical properties were then employed to calculate the first hyperpolarizabilities within the TSA, [45] in fact the assumed dominant diagonal component of the β tensor in the direction of the CT axis, β_{zzz}^{TSA}, and from these the β_{HRS}^{TSA} values (Table 4). This assumption has been demonstrated to be valid because the DRs are close to the reference value of 5. A comparison between the TSA and CPKS static β_{zzz} values is provided in Figure 5. The agreement between the two sets of β_{zzz} values is excellent, with a correlation factor of 0.97. The slope of the least-squares fit linear relationship amounts to 1.31, indicating that the TSA overestimates, on average, the CPKS values by 31%. Such an overestimation of the TSA approach has been observed in other quantum chemistry investigations [47]. For our target compounds, the TSA is, therefore, a reliable model to explain the variations of β_{HRS} values and, the data of Table 4 points out that their variations are mostly governed by $\Delta\mu$ (and specifically, d_{CT}), then, on an equal foot, by the excitation energies and oscillator strengths (transition dipoles).

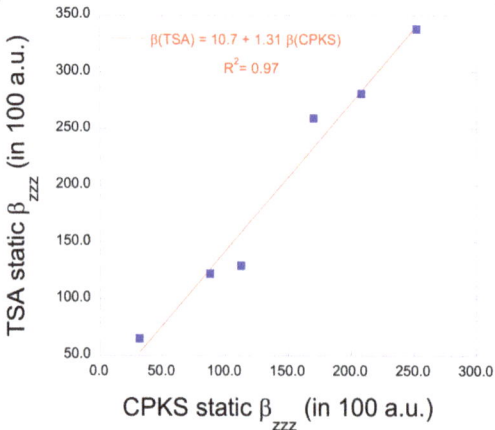

Figure 5. Comparison between static β_{zzz} values obtained within the two-state approximation and the full values calculated at the response TDDFT level (CPKS in the static limit). All β quantities have been obtained at the IEF-PCM/TDDFT/ωB97X-D/6-311G*/LanL2TZ level of approximation and are expressed in 10^2 a.u.

4. Conclusions and Outlook

Following reference [29], density functional theory and time-dependent calculations have been performed on an extended series of Lindquist-type organo-imido polyoxometa-lates derivatized with ligands bearing donor or acceptor groups to unravel the relationships between their structures and first hyperpolarizabilities. The electron acceptor character of the hexamolybdate moiety has been confirmed by these new quantum chemical analyses, highlighting that when associated with a donor substituent, its first hyperpolarizability increases, and stronger donor leads to larger first hyperpolarizabilities. By adopting a range-separated hybrid XC functional (ωB97X-D) and by describing solvent effects with the polarizable continuum model, a set of consistent data has been obtained: a stronger donor substituent on the terminal phenyl ring (i) increases its quinoid character (larger bond length alternation), (ii) augments the charge transfer between the substituent and that phenyl ring in the electronic ground state, (iii) decreases the excitation energy corresponding to the dominant low-energy excitation band, (iv) increases the oscillator strength, and (v) strongly enhances the excitation-induced change of dipole moment. In particular, in comparison to an ethynyl, the presence of an ethenyl π-spacer between the phenyl rings is favorable to achieve a large first hyperpolarizability. A larger first hyperpolarizability and corresponding consistent differences in the linear optical responses are also achieved in the case of a dimethylamino donor group, in comparison to a hydroxyl substituent, and even more in comparison to a cyano acceptor group.

Calculations have also enabled comparisons with recent experimental investigations [5], involving dimethylamino, diphenylamino, and carbazole moieties as donor groups. Calculations and experimental data highlight the weaker donor character of the carbazole moiety, which is attributed to the torsion angle between the carbazole and the attached phenyl ring, leading to a reduction in π-conjugation. On the other hand, calculations and experiments provide different conclusions on the comparison between POM bearing the dimethylamino or diphenylamino donor group. This difference is associated with the combination of the limitations of the method of calculation (the XCF and the treatment of the solvent are approximate) and of the experimental error bars.

Other structural effects of the POM on the first hyperpolarizability can be considered, such as the combination of two POM moieties with one organic linker, as proposed in reference [6], or the opposite, two organic ligands on one POM moiety. In both cases, the NLO performance of these Λ-shape compounds could be compared to those of their push-pull one-dimensional derivatives. Another direction would be to consider POM containing two types of metal atoms, such as the combination of W and Mo atoms in reference [48].

Author Contributions: Conceptualization, B.C.; formal analysis, E.R. and B.C.; investigation, E.R.; writing—original draft preparation, E.R. and B.C.; writing—review and editing, B.C.; supervision, B.C.; project administration, B.C.; funding acquisition, B.C. Both authors have read and agreed to the published version of the manuscript.

Funding: This research was funded by the University of Namur, the FNRS-FRFC (Conventions No. GEQ U.G006.15, U.G018.19, and RW/GEQ2016), and the Walloon Region (Convention RW/GEQ2016).

Data Availability Statement: Data are stored on the computers of the HPC platform of UNamur.

Acknowledgments: The calculations were performed on the computers of the Consortium des Équipements de Calcul Intensif and particularly those of the High-Performance Computing Platform, which are supported by the FNRS-FRFC, the Walloon Region, and the University of Namur (Conventions No. GEQ U.G006.15, U.G018.19, 1610468, and RW/GEQ2016).

Conflicts of Interest: The authors declare no conflict of interest. The funders had no role in the design of the study, in the collection, analyses, or interpretation of data, in the writing of the manuscript, or in the decision to publish the results.

References

1. Pope, M.T.; Müller, A. Polyoxometalate Chemistry: An Old Field with New Dimensions in Several Disciplines. *Angew. Chem. Int. Ed. Engl.* **1991**, *30*, 34–48. [CrossRef]
2. Anyushin, A.V.; Kondinski, A.; Parac-Vogt, T.N. Hybrid Polyoxometalates as Post-functionalization Platforms: From Fundamentals to Emerging Applications. *Chem. Soc. Rev.* **2020**, *49*, 382–432. [CrossRef]
3. Al-Yasari, A.; Van Steerteghem, N.; El Moll, H.; Clays, K.; Fielden, J. Donor—Acceptor Organo-Imido Polyoxometalates: High Transparency, High Activity Redox-Active NLO Chromophores. *Dalton Trans.* **2016**, *45*, 2818–2822. [CrossRef]
4. Al-Yasari, A.; Van Steerteghem, N.; Kearns, H.; El Moll, H.; Faulds, K.; Wright, J.A.; Brunschwig, B.S.; Clays, K.; Fielden, J. Organoimido-Polyoxometalate Nonlinear Optical Chromophores: A Structural, Spectroscopic, and Computational Study. *Inorg. Chem.* **2017**, *56*, 10181–10194. [CrossRef]
5. Al-Yasari, A.; Spence, P.; El Moll, H.; Van Steerteghem, N.; Horton, P.N.; Brunschwig, B.S.; Fielden, J. Fine-Tuning Polyoxometalate Non-Linear Optical Chromophores: A Molecular Electronic "Goldilocks" Effect. *Dalton Trans.* **2018**, *47*, 10415–10419. [CrossRef] [PubMed]
6. Al-Yasari, A.; El Moll, H.; Purdy, R.; Vincent, B.K.; Spence, P.; Malval, J.P.; Fielden, J. Optical Third Order Non-Linear Optical And Electrochemical Properties Of Dipolar, Centrosymmetric and C2v Organoimido Polyoxometalate Derivatives. *Phys. Chem. Chem. Phys.* **2021**, *23*, 11807–11817. [CrossRef]
7. Boulmier, A.; Vacher, A.; Zang, D.; Yang, S.; Saad, A.; Marrot, J.; Oms, O.; Mialane, P.; Ledoux, I.; Ruhlmann, L.; et al. Anderson-Type Polyoxometalates Functionalized by Tetrathiafulvalene Groups: Synthesis, Electrochemical Studies, and NLO Properties. *Inorg. Chem.* **2018**, *57*, 3742–3752. [CrossRef]
8. Perez-Moreno, J.; Zhao, Y.; Clays, K.; Kuzyk, M.G.; Shen, Y.; Qiu, L.; Hao, J.; Guo, K. Modulated Conjugation as a Means of Improving the Intrinsic Hyperpolarizability. *J. Am. Chem. Soc.* **2009**, *131*, 5084–5093. [CrossRef]
9. Castet, F.; Rodriguez, V.; Pozzo, J.L.; Ducasse, L.; Plaquet, A.; Champagne, B. Design and Characterization of Molecular Nonlinear Optical Switches. *Acc. Chem. Res.* **2013**, *46*, 2656–2665. [CrossRef] [PubMed]
10. Karamanis, P.; Otero, N.; Pouchan, C. Unleashing the Quadratic Nonlinear Optical Responses of Graphene by Confining White-Graphene (h-BN) Sections in Its Framework. *J. Am. Chem. Soc.* **2014**, *136*, 7464–7473. [CrossRef] [PubMed]
11. Nayak, A.; Park, J.; De Mey, K.; Hu, X.; Duncan, T.V.; Beratan, D.N.; Therien, M.J. Large Hyperpolarizabilities at Telecommunication-Relevant Wavelengths in Donor-Acceptor-Donor Nonlinear Optical Chromophores. *ACS Cent. Sci.* **2016**, *2*, 954–966. [CrossRef]
12. Coe, B.J.; Rusanova, D.; Joshi, V.D.; Sanchez, S.; Vavra, J.; Khobragade, D.; Severa, L.; Cisarova, I.; Saman, D.; Pohl, R.; et al. Helquat Dyes: Helicene-like Push—Pull Systems with Large Second-Order Nonlinear Optical Responses. *J. Org. Chem.* **2016**, *81*, 1912–1920. [CrossRef]
13. Lacroix, P.G.; Malfant, I.; Lepetit, C. Second-Order Nonlinear Optics in Coordination Chemistry: An Open Door towards Multi-Functional Materials and Molecular Switches. *Coord. Chem. Rev.* **2016**, *308*, 381–394. [CrossRef]
14. Knoppe, S.; Hakkinen, H.; Verbiest, T.; Clays, K. Role of Donor and Acceptor Substituents on the Nonlinear Optical Properties of Gold Nanoclusters. *J. Phys. Chem. C* **2018**, *122*, 4019–4028. [CrossRef]
15. Van Bezouw, S.; Koo, M.J.; Lee, S.C.; Lee, S.H.; Campo, J.; Kwon, O.P.; Wenseleers, W. Three-Stage pH-Switchable Organic Chromophores with Large Nonlinear Optical Responses and Switching Contrasts. *Chem. Commun.* **2018**, *54*, 7842–7845. [CrossRef]

16. Tonnelé, C.; Champagne, B.; Muccioli, L.; Castet, F. Second-Order Nonlinear Optical Properties of Stenhouse Photoswitches: Insights from Density Functional Theory. *Phys. Chem. Chem. Phys.* **2018**, *20*, 27658–27667. [CrossRef] [PubMed]
17. Lou, A.J.T.; Marks, T.J.A. Twist on Nonlinear Optics: Understanding the Unique Response of π-Twisted Chromophores. *Acc. Chem. Res.* **2019**, *52*, 1428–1438. [CrossRef] [PubMed]
18. Rigamonti, L.; Forni, A.; Cariati, E.; Malavasi, G.; Pasini, A. Solid-State Nonlinear Optical Properties of Mononuclear Copper (II) Complexes with Chiral Tridentate and Tetradentate Schiff Base Ligands. *Materials* **2019**, *12*, 3595. [CrossRef]
19. Rothe, C.; Neusser, D.; Hoppe, N.; Dirnberger, K.; Vogel, W.; Gámez-Valenzuela, S.; Ludwigs, S. Push-Pull Chromophores for Electro-Optic Applications: From 1D Linear to β-branched Structures. *Phys. Chem. Chem. Phys.* **2020**, *22*, 2283–2294. [CrossRef]
20. Qiu, S.; Morshedi, M.; Kodikara, M.S.; Du, J.; de Coene, Y.; Zhang, C.; Humphrey, M.G. Organometallic complexes for nonlinear optics. 66. Synthesis and quadratic nonlinear optical studies of trans-[Ru{C C {2, 5-C4H2S-(E)-CHCH} n-2, 5-C4H2S (NO2)} Cl (dppe) 2](*n* = 0–2). *J. Organomet. Chem.* **2020**, *919*, 121306. [CrossRef]
21. Cesaretti, A.; Foggi, P.; Fortuna, C.G.; Elisei, F.; Spalletti, A.; Carlotti, B. Uncovering Structure—Property Relationships in Push–Pull Chromophores: A Promising Route to Large Hyperpolarizability and Two-Photon Absorption. *J. Phys. Chem.* **2020**, *124*, 15739–15748. [CrossRef]
22. Ramos, T.N.; Canuto, S.; Champagne, B. Unraveling the Electric Field-Induced Second Harmonic Generation Responses of Stilbazolium Ion Pairs Complexes in Solution Using a Multiscale Simulation Method. *J. Chem. Inf. Model.* **2020**, *60*, 4817–4826. [CrossRef] [PubMed]
23. Idney, B.; Tertius, L.F.; Leandro, R.F.; Herbert, C.G.; Marcos, A.C. Applicability of DFT Functionals for Evaluating the First Hyperpolarizability of Phenol Blue in Solution. *J. Chem. Phys.* **2021**, *154*, 094501. [CrossRef]
24. Moris, M.; Van Den Eede, M.P.; Koeckelberghs, G.; Deshaume, O.; Bartic, C.; Clays, K.; Cleuvenbergen, S.; Verbiest, T. Solvent Role in the Self-Assembly of Poly (3-alkylthiophene): A Harmonic Light Scattering Study. *Macromolecules* **2021**, *54*, 2477–2484. [CrossRef]
25. Castet, F.; Gillet, A.; Bureš, F.; Plaquet, A.; Rodriguez, V.; Champagne, B. Second-Order Nonlinear Optical Properties of Λ-Shaped Pyrazine Derivatives. *Dye. Pigment.* **2021**, *184*, 108850. [CrossRef]
26. Verbiest, T.; Clays, K.; Rodriguez, V. *Second-Order Nonlinear Optical Characterizations Techniques: An Introduction*; CRC Press: New York, NY, USA, 2009.
27. Yan, L.; Yang, G.; Guan, W.; Su, Z.; Wang, R. Density Functional Theory Study on the First Hyperpolarizabilities of Organoimido Derivatives of Hexamolybdates. *J. Phys. Chem. B* **2005**, *109*, 22332–22336. [CrossRef]
28. Janjua, M.R.S.A.; Liu, C.G.; Guan, W.; Zhuang, J.; Muhammad, S.; Yan, L.K.; Su, Z.M. Prediction of Remarkably Large Second-Order Nonlinear Optical Properties of Organoimido-Substituted Hexamolybdates. *J. Phys. Chem.* **2009**, *113*, 3576–3587. [CrossRef]
29. Rtibi, E.; Abderrabba, M.; Ayadi, S.; Champagne, B. Theoretical Assessment of the Second-Order Nonlinear Optical Responses of Lindqvist-Type Organoimido Polyoxometalates. *Inorg. Chem.* **2019**, *58*, 11210–11219. [CrossRef]
30. Lescos, L.; Sitkiewicz, S.; Beaujean, P.; Blanchard-Desce, M.; Champagne, B.; Matito, R.E.; Castet, F. Performance of DFT Functionals for Calculating the Second-Order Nonlinear Optical Properties of Dipolar Merocyanines. *Phys. Chem. Chem. Phys.* **2020**, *22*, 16579–16594. [CrossRef]
31. Champagne, B.; Perpète, E.A.; Jacquemin, D.; van Gisbergen, S.J.A.; Baerends, E.J.; Soubra-Ghaoui, C.; Kirtman, B. Assessment of Conventional Density Functional Schemes for Computing the Dipole Moment and (Hyper)polarizabilities of Push–Pull π-Conjugated Systems. *J. Phys. Chem.* **2000**, *104*, 4755–4763. [CrossRef]
32. Bulat, F.A.; Toro-Labbé, A.; Champagne, B.; Kirtman, B.; Yang, W. Density-Functional Theory (hyper) polarizabilities of Push-Pull π-Conjugated Systems: Treatment of Exact Exchange and Role of Correlation. *J. Chem. Phys.* **2005**, *123*, 014319. [CrossRef] [PubMed]
33. Sun, H.; Autschbach, J. Influence of the Delocalization Error and Applicability of Optimal Functional Tuning in Density Functional Calculations of Nonlinear Optical Properties of Organic Donor-Acceptor Chromophores. *ChemPhysChem* **2013**, *14*, 2450–2461. [CrossRef] [PubMed]
34. Frisch, M.J.; Trucks, G.W.; Schlegel, H.B.; Scuseria, G.E.; Robb, M.A.; Cheeseman, J.R.; Scalmani, G.; Barone, V.; Petersson, G.A.; Nakatsuji, H.; et al. *Gaussian 16, Revis. C.01*; Gaussian Inc.: Wallingford, CT, USA, 2016.
35. Chai, J.D.; Head-Gordon, M. Long-range Corrected Hybrid Density Functionals with Damped Atom-Atom Dispersion Corrections. *Phys. Chem. Chem. Phys.* **2008**, *10*, 6615–6620. [CrossRef] [PubMed]
36. Becke, A.D. Density-Functional Thermochemistry. V. Systematic Optimization of Exchange-Correlation Functionals. *J. Chem. Phys.* **1997**, *107*, 8554–8560. [CrossRef]
37. Tomasi, J.; Mennucci, B.; Cammi, R. Quantum Mechanical Continuum Solvation Models. *Chem. Rev.* **2005**, *105*, 2999–3094. [CrossRef]
38. Van Gisbergen, S.J.A.; Snijders, J.G.; Baerends, E.J. Calculating Frequency-Dependent Hyperpolarizabilities Using Time-Dependent Density Functional Theory. *J. Chem. Phys.* **1998**, *109*, 10644–10656. [CrossRef]
39. Helgaker, T.; Coriani, S.; Jørgensen, P.; Kristensen, K.; Olsen, J.; Ruud, K. Recent Advances in Wave Function-Based Methods of Molecular-Property Calculations. *Chem. Rev.* **2012**, *112*, 543–631. [CrossRef]
40. Bersohn, R.; Pao, Y.H.; Frisch, H.L. Double-Quantum Light Scattering by Molecules. *J. Chem. Phys.* **1966**, *45*, 3184–3198. [CrossRef]
41. Castet, F.; Bogdan, E.; Plaquet, A.; Ducasse, L.; Champagne, B.; Rodriguez, V. Reference Molecules for Nonlinear Optics: A Joint Experimental and Theoretical Investigation. *J. Chem. Phys.* **2012**, *136*, 024506. [CrossRef]

42. Tuer, A.; Krouglov, S.; Cisek, R.; Tokarz, D.; Barzda, V. Three-Dimensional Visualization of the First Hyperpolarizability Tensor. *J. Comput. Chem.* **2011**, *32*, 1128–1134. [CrossRef]

43. Orr, B.J.; Ward, J.F. Perturbation Theory of the Non-Linear Optical Polarization of an Isolated System. *Mol. Phys.* **1971**, *20*, 513–526. [CrossRef]

44. Bishop, D.M. Explicit Non-divergent Formulas for Atomic and Molecular Dynamic Hyperpolarizabilities. *J. Chem. Phys.* **1994**, *100*, 6535–6542. [CrossRef]

45. Oudar, J.L.; Chemla, D.S. Hyperpolarizabilities of the Nitroanilines and Their Relations to the Excited State Dipole Moment. *J. Chem. Phys.* **1977**, *66*, 2664–2668. [CrossRef]

46. Zutterman, F.; Liégeois, V.; Champagne, B. Simulation of UV/visible Absorption Spectra of Fluorescent Protein Chromophore Models. *ChemPhotoChem* **2017**, *1*, 281–297. [CrossRef]

47. Champagne, B.; Kirtman, B. Alternative Sum-Over-States Expressions for the First Hyperpolarizability of Push-Pull π-Conjugated Systems. *J. Chem. Phys.* **2006**, *125*, 024101. [CrossRef]

48. Wei, Y.; Lu, M.; Cheung, C.F.-C.; Barnes, C.L.; Peng, Z. Functionalization of $[MoW_5O_{19}]^{2-}$ with Aromatic Amines: Synthesis of the First Arylimido Derivatives of Mixed-Metal Polyoxometalates. *Inorg. Chem.* **2001**, *40*, 5489–5490. [CrossRef]

Review

Characterisation and Manipulation of Polarisation Response in Plasmonic and Magneto-Plasmonic Nanostructures and Metamaterials

Pritam Khan, Grace Brennan, James Lillis, Syed A. M. Tofail, Ning Liu and Christophe Silien *

Department of Physics and Bernal Institute, University of Limerick, V94 T9PX Limerick, Ireland;
Pritam.Khan@ul.ie (P.K.); grace.brennan@ul.ie (G.B.); james.lillis@ul.ie (J.L.); tofail.syed@ul.ie (S.A.M.T.);
ning.liu@ul.ie (N.L.)
* Correspondence: christophe.silien@ul.ie

Received: 9 July 2020; Accepted: 12 August 2020; Published: 17 August 2020

Abstract: Optical properties of metal nanostructures, governed by the so-called localised surface plasmon resonance (LSPR) effects, have invoked intensive investigations in recent times owing to their fundamental nature and potential applications. LSPR scattering from metal nanostructures is expected to show the symmetry of the oscillation mode and the particle shape. Therefore, information on the polarisation properties of the LSPR scattering is crucial for identifying different oscillation modes within one particle and to distinguish differently shaped particles within one sample. On the contrary, the polarisation state of light itself can be arbitrarily manipulated by the inverse designed sample, known as metamaterials. Apart from polarisation state, external stimulus, e.g., magnetic field also controls the LSPR scattering from plasmonic nanostructures, giving rise to a new field of magneto-plasmonics. In this review, we pay special attention to polarisation and its effect in three contrasting aspects. First, tailoring between LSPR scattering and symmetry of plasmonic nanostructures, secondly, manipulating polarisation state through metamaterials and lastly, polarisation modulation in magneto-plasmonics. Finally, we will review recent progress in applications of plasmonic and magneto-plasmonic nanostructures and metamaterials in various fields.

Keywords: plasmonics; LSPR scattering; polarisation manipulation; metamaterials; Faraday effect (rotation); magneto-optic Kerr effect (MOKE); magnetoplasmonics

1. Introduction

Of late, thanks to their unique chemical, electrical and optical properties, nanomaterials have been the subject of extensive research in the frame of nanoscience and nanotechnology from the point of view of both fundamental science and practical applications. Among the family of nanomaterials, metallic nanostructures are of particular interest because of their remarkable optical properties that leads to a plethora of novel phenomena, mediated by elementary excitations, known as plasmons [1,2]. Localised surface plasmon resonance (LSPR) takes place from the collective oscillations of conduction electrons near metallic nanoparticles following light excitation [3]. LSPR in metallic nanoparticles allows to manipulate light at the nanoscale that gives rise to exotic phenomena, e.g., optical near-field enhancement at resonant wavelength, hot-electron generation [4,5], etc. Likewise, such effects find tremendous potential applications in photocarrier generators [6], optical holography [7], plasmonic routers [8], biosensors [9,10], surface-enhanced Raman scattering (SERS) [11], etc. LSPR of the plasmonic nanostructures can be readily tuned by the geometry, i.e., shape and size of the plasmonic nanostructures which in turn can be correlated with the polarisation state of the incident light [1,12]. It is well known that polarisation is a key attribute of light that describes the oscillation direction of the electromagnetic wave, that plays an important role in the light–matter interactions [13,14].

In particular, the resonant light scattering from plasmonic nanostructures (Figure 1) is expected to show the symmetry of the plasmon mode and the particle shape [15]. Therefore, detailed knowledge of the scattered light polarisation from plasmonic nanostructures is very important to understand the fundamental physics and practical applications of such nanostructures. At the same time, it also helps to differentiate several oscillation modes within one particle as well as distinguish particles of different shape within one nanostructure. For example, smallest unit of nanostructures like silver/gold nanosphere (diameter less than 50 nm) or nanoparticle dimer has high symmetry with only one dipole plasmon [16,17].

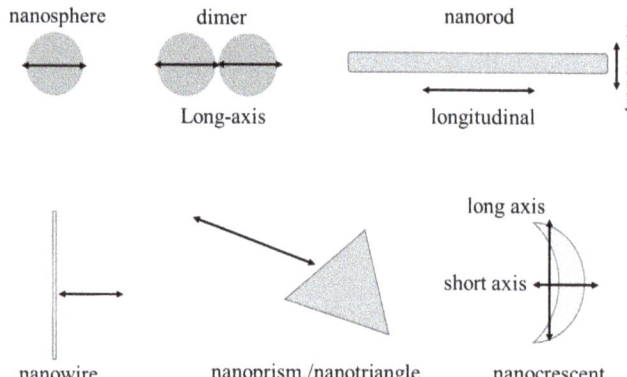

Figure 1. Plasmonic nanostructures of various shape. The arrow indicates the axis of symmetry of the nanostructures for the excitation of LSPR.

Moving on to nanoparticle trimer with broken symmetry in their geometry, they exhibit a polarisation response that is altogether different from the dipolar response of a dimer [17,18]. Similarly, in nanorods, instead of one dipole, two dipolar peaks, transverse and longitudinal [19] appear. Further complicated nanostructures like triangular Ag nanoparticles [20,21] or nanocrescents [22] possess in- and out-of-plane dipole, quadrupole and even higher multipoles. Several techniques, including dark-field (DF) extinction [17,23], SERS scattering [24,25], infrared absorption [22,26] have been used to extract the optical response of plasmonic nanostructures to get information on the polarisation state. In the first part of the review, we aim to tailor between LSPR scattering and symmetry of plasmonic nanostructures by going through polarisation sensitive optical measurements in such nanostructures. On the contrary, in another end of the spectrum, artificial plasmonic nanostructures are inversed designed to control the polarisation state of the light wave [27,28]. This new set of artificial materials are classified as metamaterials, that are composed of periodically arranged subwavelength dielectric elements or structured metallic components [29,30]. The metamaterials can arbitrarily manipulate the polarisation state of the electromagnetic waves with multiple degrees of freedom, that has found tremendous potential application in nanophotonics [31,32]. We will discuss the designing of such metamaterial strictures and their excellent application prospective in the second part of the review. In the last section, we will discuss magneto-optics and magnetoplasmonics with particular emphasis on the role of polarisation in a number of experiments including the Faraday effect, inverse Faraday effect, magneto-optical Kerr effect, magnetic second-harmonic generation and magnetic circular dichroism. Finally, we will explore a number of relevant applications.

2. Tailoring between LSPR Scattering and Symmetry of Plasmonic Nanostructures

In this section, we will discuss the polarisation dependent LSPR response of various plasmonic nanostructures of different shape and size. It is well known that axis of symmetry of plasmonic nanostructures plays an important role and by exciting along the favourable symmetry axis LSPR response can be enhanced significantly. Below we will analyse several plasmonic nanostructures and their LSPR response by polarisation sensitive measurements.

2.1. Single Nanosphere and Dimer

The smallest unit of plasmonic nanostructure is a single nanoparticle or nanosphere. The scattering spectra of a single Ag/Au nanosphere has one major peak, originated from the interaction of electromagnetic waves with the free electrons of the nanospheres. For single nanoparticles, the LSPR does not exhibit any marked polarisation dependence [33]. It can be seen from Figure 2a that LSPR of two isolated Au nanoparticles occurs at 573 nm and it is indistinguishable for two orthogonal light polarisations. However, if these two nanoparticles are brought closer, they get dimerised because of plasmonic coupling and a strong polarisation anisotropy takes place. For polarisation perpendicular to the long axis of the dimer, LSPR peak at 573 nm overlaps with that of a single particle [34], however, for polarisation parallel to the long axis of the dimer, we observed a strongly red-shifted spectrum with LSPR at 588 nm which is ascribed to the "long axis" mode of dimer. The position of the LSPR of a dimer corresponding to both parallel and perpendicular polarisation depends strongly on the interparticle distance (*d*) as well as their relative interaction [34]. In Figure 2b when *d* changes from 10 (1) to 25 nm (3), LSPR position of Ag dimer for parallel polarisation redshifts approximately by 100 nm. In contrast, for perpendicular polarisation LSPR exhibits very weak blueshift. It is important to note that, for very large *d* ~ 250 nm, LSPR of the dimer (5) is comparable to that of an individual particle (6). This observation indicates that when the separation is large between the pair of particles, it becomes complicated to resolve the effects of particle interactions.

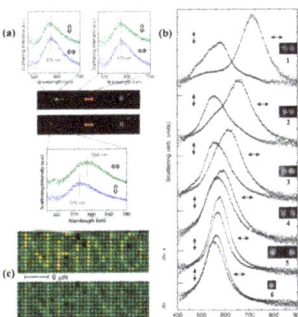

Figure 2. (**a**) Alignment of a dimer composed of two ~80 nm gold nanoparticles. The upper graphs are spectra for the immobilised particle (left) and the optically trapped particle (right) before dimerisation. The lower spectra correspond to the case when the two particles have been brought into near-field coupling range. All the figures were reprinted (adapted) with permission from [33], Copyright 2010, American Chemical Society. (**b**) DF spectra and SEM micrographs from isolated particle pairs with varying separations in parallel and perpendicular polarisation, as indicated by arrows. The separations (gaps) between the particles are *d* ~ (1) 10, (2) 15, (3) 25, (4) 50, and (5) 250 nm. Spectrum 6 from a single particle is included for comparison. The vertical bars indicate the baselines for the different spectra. (**c**) DF images form an array of "identical" silver disks with a diameter of 80 nm and a height of 25 nm. The text "NANO" is written with pairs of such particles with an interparticle distance of approximately 110 nm. In the top image, the array is illuminated with light polarised parallel to the particle pair axis. In the bottom image, the polarisation is perpendicular to the pair axis. All the figures were reprinted (adapted) with permission from [34], Copyright 2005, American Chemical Society.

The effect of parallel and perpendicular polarisations on the dimer composed of Ag particles array can be readily seen from the DF images shown in Figure 2c. For the top panel, under parallel polarisation, the text "NANO" written with dimers appears red compared to green single particles.

In contrast, for perpendicular polarisation the text appears blue in the green single particle background. Such observation is in line with the results shown in Figure 2b.

Next, we discuss the detailed polarisation response of single Ag nanosphere dimer (Figure 3a). The dimer is oriented at 40° with respect to the normal. In this regard, Figure 3b,c demonstrates the polar plot of Raman scattering intensity profile and depolarisation ratio (ρ) of the dimer, respectively against the polarisation angle at two dominant Raman bands of the dimer. Both the Raman scattering intensity and depolarisation ratio varies between ±1, at parallel and perpendicular to the dimer axis, respectively [18]. Therefore, clearly indicating that scattering from the dimer is linearly polarised in line with the results from Tian et al. [17]. Figure 3c also reveals that the depolarisation ratio of a dimer is wavelength independent.

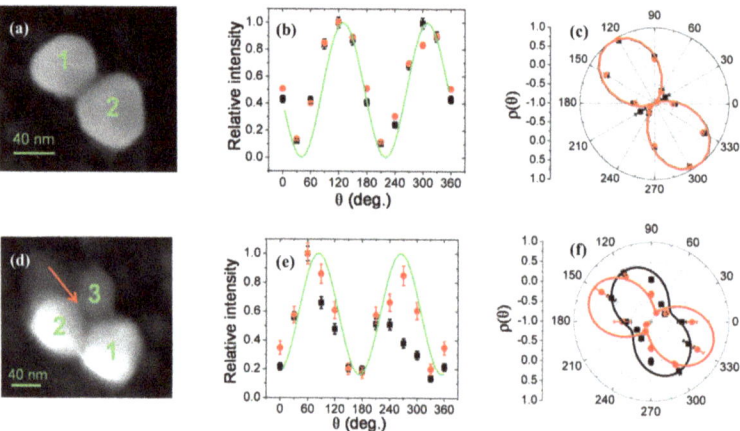

Figure 3. Polarisation response of a nanoparticle dimer and trimer. SEM image of the (**a**) dimer and (**d**) trimer of nanoparticles. The red arrow in (**d**) indicates the position of the molecule that leads to the best agreement between experiment and calculation. Normalised RS intensity at 555 (black squares) and 583 nm (red circles) as a function of the angle of rotation of the incident polarisation for (**b**) dimer and (**e**) trimer. Depolarisation ratio (ρ) measured at 555 (black squares) and 583 nm (red circles) for (**c**) dimer and (**f**) trimer. All the figures were reprinted (adapted) with permission from [18], Copyright 2008, National Academy of Sciences, USA.

2.2. Nanosphere Trimer

When an additional third particle (1) is added at the junction of a dimer formed by particles 2 and 3, it breaks the axial symmetry (Figure 3d) to form a trimer and the polarisation response of a symmetry-broken trimer is altogether different from that of a dimer. Figure 3e represents the Raman scattering profile of the trimer at the same wavelengths of that of the dimer, with varying incident polarisation angle. The maximum signal is obtained at 75° which does not match with the alignment of any of the pairs. The polar plot of the depolarisation ratio for a trimer shown in Figure 3f exhibits strong wavelength dependence, i.e., for different wavelengths it is rotated at different angles from the Raman intensity profile [18]. Unlike dimer, the scattered intensity in trimer never reaches ±1, signifying elliptically polarised light scattering from a trimer, which could arise from the presence of broken symmetry, after a third particle is added to a symmetric dimer to form a trimer. Apart from the results above, there are several other studies which also represent similar polarisation dependent optical response of plasmonic dimer [17,23,35] and trimer nanostructures [36,37].

2.3. Nanorod

Nanorods are the perfect example of "antenna-like" plasmonic structures, therefore the polarisation pattern of the scattered light holds paramount importance for practical applications [15]. Especially, gold nanorods have shown extremely strong light scattering due to the combination of lightning rod effect [38] and the suppression of interband damping [39]. In this regard, Figure 4a reveals the comparison between the single-particle scattering spectra of a nanosphere and a nanorod which shows that LSPR of the sphere at 2.19 eV and for the long-axis mode of the rod at 1.82 eV [39]. By extracting the linewidth (Γ) of the LSPR of nanosphere and nanorod, it is evident that Γ for nanorod is significantly lower than that of nanosphere which leads to lower plasmon damping for nanorods owing to their small volume.

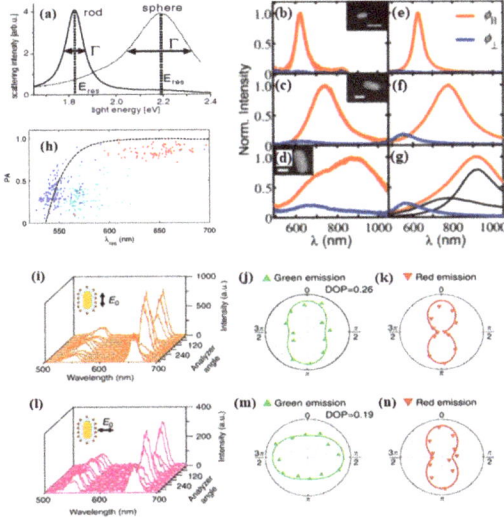

Figure 4. (**a**) Light-scattering spectra from a gold nanorod and gold nanosphere measured under identical conditions (light polarised along the long rod axis). All the figures were reprinted (adapted) with permission from [39], Copyright 2002, American Physical Society. Scattering spectra of single AuNRs with (**b**) d = 32 nm, (**c**) d = 81 nm, and (**d**) d = 100 nm, all having AR of ~2.2 ± 0.1, and the corresponding DDA calculations (**e–g**), respectively. All the figures were reprinted (adapted) with permission from [40], Copyright 2010, American Chemical Society. The spectra were recorded for scattered light polarised parallel (red) and perpendicular (blue) to the orientation of the main rod axis. A fit to a sum of two Lorentzian curves is included as black lines in (**g**). In all images, the scale bar represents 100 nm. (**h**) The polarisation at the longitudinal plasmon resonance wavelength λ_{res} is shown as a function of the resonance wavelength for three different gold particle samples (blue dots, nominally spherical gold particles with 60 nm diameter; 87 nm diameter, teal dots; and red dots, gold nanorods). The dashed black line is a theoretical prediction from simulations of gold rods of different aspect ratios and sizes embedded in water. All the figures were reprinted (adapted) with permission from [15], Copyright 2008, American Chemical Society. (**i**) UC emission spectra obtained as the analyser angle varied from 0 to 2 π under excitation polarisation parallel to the long axis of the hybrid nanostructure. From these spectra, the polar plots were extracted for the green (**j**) and red (**k**) emissions. (**l**) UC emission spectra under perpendicular excitation and corresponding polar plots for green (**m**) and red (**n**) emissions. The lines in the polar plots are cosine-squared fits of the experimental data. All the figures were reprinted (adapted) with permission from [41], Copyright 2017, Springer Nature.

Symmetry 2020, 12, 1365

It is well known that nanorods exhibit two LSPR modes, one that exhibits a strong polarisation response along the long axis (length), known as longitudinal LSPR and the other one with very weak polarisation response along the short axis (width) of nanorods, referred as transverse LSPR [40].

Longitudinal LSPR is of particular interest because it is tunable across the whole visible and near-infrared region by precisely tailoring the length (l), width (d), and/or aspect ratio (AR) of the nanorod as demonstrated in [40]. Figure 4 depicts the scattering spectra of AuNR for different d and l with fixed AR of 2.2 (±0.1). For the AuNR with (d, l) = 32 × 69 nm, a narrow longitudinal dipole LSPR is observed at 620 nm with no transverse component. When the size of AuNR increases to (d, l) = 84 × 174 nm and (d, l) = 100 × 227 nm, a clear redshift is observed in longitudinal LSPR to 740 and 900 nm, respectively as shown Figure 4c,d. Apart from that, a weak transverse LSPR peak appears in Figure 4c,d at 600 and 660 nm, respectively, because of the larger width of the AuNR [42,43]. Till now, the AuNRs discussed have a low AR of 2.2. Increasing the AR of a slim AuNR to 3.1 (24 × 74 nm) can lead to the similar redshift of the longitudinal LSPR. Experimental scattering spectra of these AuNR shows good agreement with the DDA calculations as depicted in Figure 4e–g. The longitudinal LSPR is highly anisotropic, i.e., it only favourably gets excited for polarisation along the long axis of the rod, and remains unexcited otherwise. Likewise, the scattered light from AuNR exhibits a dipolar response, in line with a cosine-squared function [44].

The strong polarisation dependent optical response in plasmonic nanosphere and nanorods in turn can be exploited to reveal the nanoparticle symmetry. In this context, wavelength-dependent polarisation anisotropy (PA(λ)) serves as an efficient parameter to distinguish nanoparticles with different symmetry [15]. In general, PA(λ) = ($I_{major} - I_{minor}$)/($I_{major} + I_{minor}$), where I_{major} and I_{minor} are defined as the scattering intensity of light polarised parallel to the major and minor axes, respectively [45]. For this purpose, PA is extracted at the resonance wavelength λ_{res}. Figure 4h shows that for an AuNR of (d, l) = 28 × 57 nm shows a high degree of PA(λ_{res}) ~ 0.84 [39], whereas for spherical AuNP of diameters 60 and 87 nm had an average PA(λ_{res}) ~ 0.35. It is important to note that AuNP and AuNR exhibit contrasting PA(λ) spectra. For AuNR, it is strongly wavelength dependent, i.e., the long-axis plasmon mode is only excited at the resonance wavelength, whereas for AuNP, PA(λ) is independent of excitation wavelength. It is also found that LSPR linewidth scales inversely with PA(λ_{res}), i.e., linewidth is lower for particles with high PA(λ_{res}). Likewise, we can conclude from Figure 4a AuNR with lower linewidth has high PA(λ_{res}) compared to AuNP at resonance wavelength [15].

AuNRs are an important plasmonic nanostructure which can strongly enhance as well as influence the polarisation state of fluorescence from organic fluorophores or upconversion nanocrystals (UCNC) [41]. It has been shown that, similar to bare AuNR, in hybrid nanostructures of AuNR-fluorophore (oxazine 725), the fluorescent emission is also polarised along the long axis of the NR and exhibits a dipolar pattern. However, the polarisation response of the emission pattern is bit compiled for hybrid plasmonic UCNCs. By measuring the emission spectra of UCNC hybrid nanostructures at polarisation angles from 0° to 360°, by keeping the excitation laser either parallel (Figure 4i) or perpendicular (Figure 4l) to the long axis of the hybrid nanostructure, two dominant emission bands are observed cantered at 540 (green) and 660 nm (red). In this regard, Figure 4j,k,m,n shows the polar plot of red and green emission, respectively. Clearly, red emission is independent of the excitation polarisation, i.e., for both parallel and perpendicular polarisation, red emission follows the scattering pattern of AuNR. In stark contrast, green emission follows the excitation polarisation and oriented along and perpendicular to the long axis of AuNR for parallel and perpendicular excitation polarisation, respectively. The observed results are explained on the basis of Förster resonance energy transfer (FRET) between the emission dipole of the UCNC and the plasmonic dipole of the AuNR [41].

Similar polarisation sensitive measurements on the LSPR of plasmonic Au nanorods and their arrays can be found in the following articles [46–49].

2.4. Nanowire

One-dimensional nanowires (NW) with length of tens of microns stand apart thanks to their easy microscopic directionality [50,51] compared to other counterparts like dimer or NR, where because of diffraction limit it is difficult to estimate the direction of the dimer axis or the long axis of the nanorod. The LSPR response of a NW can be easily tuned by varying the polarisation angle between incident polarisation and NW axis orientation. The excitation of LSPR in NW leads to well-known phenomenon of surface-enhanced Raman scattering (SERS) [25,52,53] that has been explored extensively for chemical and biological sensing. Mohanty et al. [54] demonstrated experimentally as well as from finite difference time domain (FDTD) simulation that SERS signal in the AgNW system reached maximum when the incident laser is perpendicular to NW axis. Similar results are also obtained by Li et al. [55] which shows that when the SERS spectra of R6G is measured at one spot on a NW at different polarisation angles it exhibits maximum at $\theta = 90$, i.e., for vertical polarisation as shown in the polar plot of Figure 5a. The results remain consistent when measured at different spots of the sample. They also demonstrated the dimerisation of 4-nitrobenzenethiol (4NBT) to p,p'-dimercaptoazobenzene (DMAB), arising from LSPR and monitored via SERS. It is shown in Figure 5b that when the polarisation angle θ changes from 0 to 90, new peaks, e.g., ν_4, ν_5, ν_6 gradually increase, indicating the catalytical transformation of 4NBT to DMAB. The above results are further substantiated with DF measurements (Figure 5c) which shows that LSPR scattering increases with increase in polarisation angle and becomes maximum for vertical polarisation, i.e., $\theta = 90$. In another study, Wei and co-workers [25] have shown that SERS of AgNW can be further enhanced by the presence of another metallic nanoparticle (AuNP) adjacent to the wire. The magnitude of this coupling is shown to be independent of the NP shape following the theoretical prediction. However, a strong polarisation dependence is expected owing to strong local and polarisation sensitive electric field enhancements at the NP-NW junctions [56] as shown by the SERS spectra in Figure 5d for different probe positions (Figure 5e) using Malachite green isothiocyanate (MGITC). SERS is inherently a plasmonic property, and therefore remains absent from Si substrate without Ag nanostructures, although the probe molecule MGITC is strongly resonant at 633 nm excitation. When SERS is probed on the trunk of the AgNW, a weak SERS signal is observed. Surprisingly, a remarkable enhancement is observed in the SERS signal when an AuNP is placed near the NW, thanks to the coupling between the AuNP-AgNW plasmons. A polarisation dependent study of the SERS signal in AuNP-AgNW system reveals that when the laser is polarised perpendicularly to the NW, the SERS intensity increases and remains weak for parallel polarisation [56]. The polarisation pattern of the composite system shown in Figure 5f exhibits a dipolar pattern similar to the observation by Mohanty [54] and Li [55].

Apart from SERS, one-photon photoluminescence (PL) is also found to be enhanced significantly by the plasmon coupling between Ag nanowire on top of an Au film in the presence of a ~6 nm dielectric spacer (gap plasmon mode) that supports a localised resonance. In their work, Hu and colleagues [57] further demonstrated that the PL associated with the gap plasmon mode depends strongly on the polarisation angle between the incident laser polarisation and the nanowire orientation, thus exhibits a dipolar emission profile. In this regard, Figure 5g depicts the DF scattering spectra peaking at 655 nm, which is attributed to the gap plasmon mode. Clearly, for perpendicular polarisation (red curve) the peak is much stronger than parallel polarisation (black curve). Such observation confirms that gap plasmon mode is associated with the transverse charge oscillations across nanowire-film junction. PL spectra in Figure 5h follow similar trend like DF scattering, i.e., maximum for perpendicular polarisation ($\theta = 90°$), which almost disappears under parallel polarisation ($\theta = 0°$). Like excitation polarisation, analyser or detection polarisation also plays a significant role in PL or SERS signal. It is found that when the analyser polarisation (Figure 5i) is parallel with excitation polarisation, the detected signal becomes strongest and diminishes when they are perpendicular to each other. In short, LSPR in nanowires can be favourably excited when the incident laser is directed perpendicular to the nanowire axis thanks to the spatial confinement of the electrons at the nanowire and the neighbouring medium interface. Such polarisation dependence is in strong contrary to the case of spherical nanoparticle,

Symmetry **2020**, *12*, 1365

where plasmon excitation is polarisation independent due to spherical geometry [58]. Apart from the above-mentioned results, there are many other studies [59–62] which also discuss the polarisation response LSPR response of plasmonic NWs.

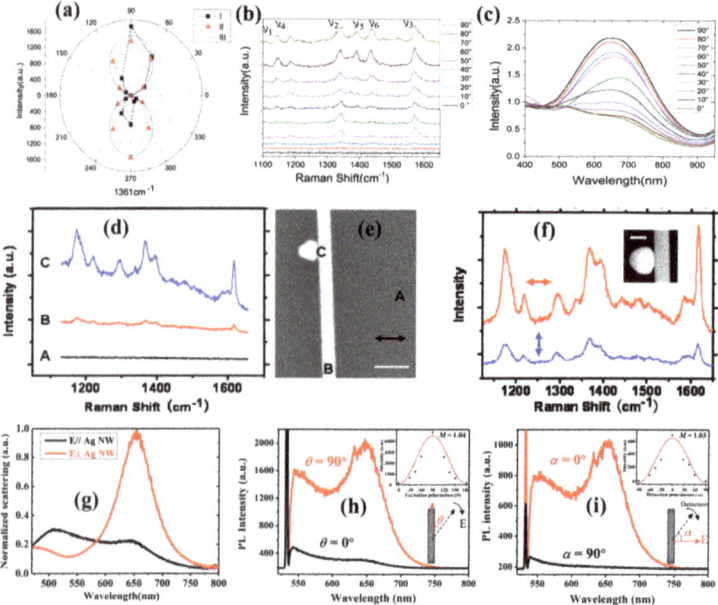

Figure 5. (**a**) Polar plot of SERS intensity at different polarisation angles (I), at different spots (II) and (III) Sin$^2\theta$ function for comparison. (**b**) SERS spectrum of 4NBT on the NW at different polarisation angles θ. (**c**) Experimentally measured DF scattering spectra with single NWs at different polarisation angles. All the figures were reprinted (adapted) with permission from [54], Copyright 2018, Royal Society of Chemistry. (**d**) Raman spectra of MGITC from different positions of the sample as shown in (**e**). The scale bar is 400 nm. The arrow in the SEM image shows the incident polarisation. (**f**) SERS spectra of MGITC at two different polarisations for the wire-particle shown in the inset. The scale bar in the inset is 200 nm. All the figures were reprinted (adapted) with permission from [25], Copyright 2008, American Chemical Society. (**g**) The scattering spectra were obtained under horizontal (red) and perpendicular (black) conditions. The strong and sharp resonant peak at 653 nm is due to the gap plasmon resonance, which is barely present under parallel illumination. (**h**) and (**i**) represent the excitation and detection polarisation dependences of PL intensity under 532 nm lasers, respectively. The absolute peak intensities as a function of excitation and collection polarisation are shown in the insets in (**h**) and (**i**), respectively, exhibiting a good dipole behaviour in photon absorption and emission All the figures were reprinted (adapted) with permission from [57], Copyright 2013, Royal Society of Chemistry.

2.5. Nanohole and Nanoellipse

Among the family of plasmonic nanostructures of different symmetry, elliptical geometry has particular importance because of its inherent anisotropy [63,64]. Therefore, the LSPR of elliptical plasmonic nanostructures is expected to be highly polarisation dependent. In this regard, Figure 6a shows the reflectance spectra of Au ellipsoidal cylinders with axes 80 and 110 nm, inside an array with a lattice constant of 200 nm under unpolarised and linearly polarised light parallel to two different axes [65]. The inset depicts the SEM image of the nanoparticle array. The broad LSPR observed for unpolarised excitation can be easily resolved by polarised illumination parallel to two axes, found to be located near 630 and 730 nm. Experimental observations are further verified with DDA simulations in the sample with the same dimension, however, with a larger lattice constant of 300 nm. The DDA simulations confirm the presence of two distinct resonance peaks even with unpolarised excitation when there is no coupling between neighbouring particles due to a larger lattice constant. Nevertheless, selective polarisation parallel to axes can lead to the excitation of the individual LSPR as evident from Figure 6b. Of late, Xia and co-workers [66] exploited the inherent asymmetry of elliptical graphene disks (Figure 6c) and showed that two orthogonal plasmonic modes along minor and major axes can be excited together or separately by choosing the incident light polarisation. The polarisation response is shown in Figure 6d,e for minor and major axis excitation, respectively, that reveals that resonant high frequency modes are favourably excited for minor axis polarisation. Apart from that, with an increase in AR, LSPR frequency for the eigenmode along the minor axis shows a blueshift, while it remains almost unchanged for the eigenmode along the major axis. Such observation indicates that the LSPR frequency of the mode along the minor axis is more sensitive to its length. To understand the role of incident light polarisation, first, the results are shown for a round graphene disk in Figure 6f,i. Expectedly, polarisation independent isotropic response is observed due to spherical symmetry of the round disk. On the other hand, Figure 6g,h shows polarisation dependent scattering spectra of two different sized ellipses by varying the polarisation direction from the minor axis (0°) to the major axis (90°). The relative strength of minor and major axes modes is shown by the polar plots for two ellipses in Figure 6j,k. They found that for both the ellipses, scattered intensity along the major axis (blue curve) is larger than that along the minor axis (red curve), thereby suggesting that light–matter interaction takes place predominantly along the major axis. Notably, the frequency difference between major and minor axes plasmon modes increases with increase in size difference between them, therefore provides more degrees of freedom for light manipulation. A similar kind of polarisation dependent response in plasmonic elliptical nanoholes can also be found elsewhere [67–69].

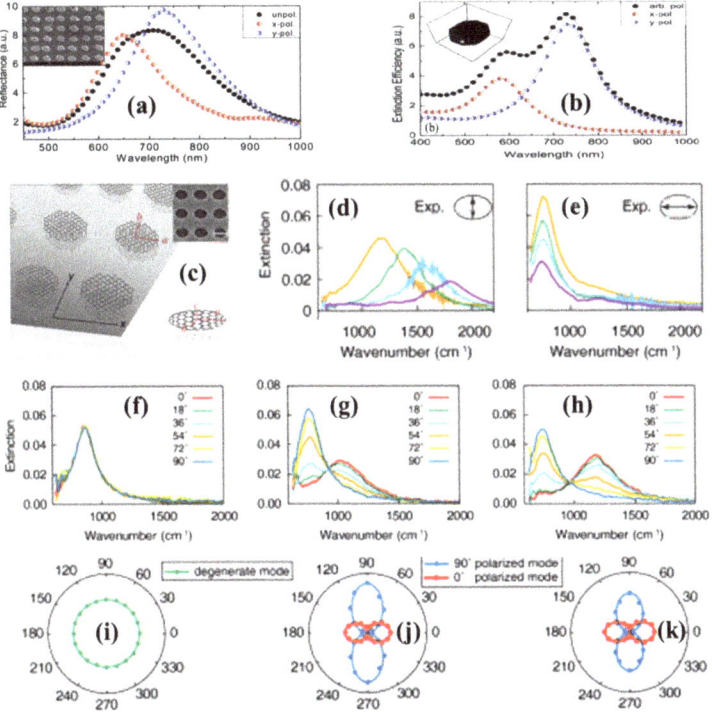

Figure 6. (**a**) The reflectance spectra of an array of ellipsoidal Au nanoparticles with axes of 80 and

110 nm, with a lattice constant of 200 nm over ITO coated glass under unpolarised illumination and linear polarisations parallel to short (x-pol) and large (y-pol) axes. The inset gives SEM images of the corresponding ellipsoid nanoparticle array. (**b**) DDA simulation results for the extinction efficiency of a single Au nanoparticle with 80 and 110 nm axes standing on ITO/Air interface. All the figures were reprinted (adapted) with permission from [65], Copyright 2010, The Optical Society. (**c**) The schematic diagram and the SEM image of periodic graphene ellipse arrays on BaF$_2$. The length of semi-major and semi-minor axes are a and b, respectively. Scale bar of the SEM image: 140 nm. Experimental extinction spectra at normal incidence with the polarisation along (**d**) minor and (**e**) major axes, respectively. From yellow line to purple line, the sizes of ellipse are a = 77:5 nm, b = 30 nm (orange); a = 72:5 nm, b = 25 nm (green); a = 67:5 nm, b = 20 nm (blue); a = 62:5 nm, b = 15 nm (purple), respectively. Polarisation-dependent extinction spectra of three different ellipticity structures. The extinction spectra of normal incident light with polarisations varied from 0° to 90° for (**f**) round graphene disk with 45 nm radius. (**g**) Ellipse with a = 70 nm, b = 38 nm; (**h**) ellipse with a = 70 nm, b = 32 nm. (**i–k**) are polar plots showing the extinction intensities for all polarisation direction of the two resonant plasmonic modes corresponding to (**f–h**), respectively. All the figures were reprinted (adapted) with permission from [66], Copyright 2019, The Optical Society.

2.6. Nanoprism and Nanotriangle

Triangular nanoprisms are a special type of plasmonic nanostructure where the combination of LSPR excitation and lightning rod effects leads to strong field enhancement [70,71]. Triangular Au and Ag nanoprisms hold advantages over flat and round surfaced nanostructures thanks to the presence of the sharp tips and edges, known as "hot spots" which favours strong enhancement in their LSPR [20,72] and allows high sensitivity to bulk and local dielectric changes. Several theoretical calculations by DDA simulation have shown the excitation of multipolar (l = 1, 2 and 3) LSPR modes in nanotriangles [20,73–75]. In their work, Félidj et al. [21] used far-field extinction spectroscopy to study in-plane multipolar LSPR modes on regular arrays of Au triangular particles (Figure 7a). Figure 7b depicts the extinction spectra corresponding to the arrays of different lateral size. For the array A with smallest lateral size, the LSPR response consists of a single peak at 590 nm, which is redshifted to 665 nm with increasing intensity for array B. With an increase in lateral size to arrays C and D, the first peak further redshifts with an additional weak peak appearing on the blue side of the spectrum. The strong peak in the longer wavelength regime is assigned to dipolar resonance (l = 1) while the weaker peak in the shorter wavelength regime is ascribed to quadrupolar mode (l = 2). It is shown that the theoretically calculated extinction cross-sections match well with the experimental results within ± 10 nm. For further large triangle of edge length a = 360 nm and grating constant of 840 nm (array E), l = 1 and l = 2 peak further redshifted to 974 and 672 nm while an additional new mode of l = 3 appears at 615 nm. In a rather unconventional work, Gao at co-workers [74] theoretically demonstrated that when the tips and edges, i.e., hotspots of lateral triangular nanoprisms are exposed to the environment directly, their LSPR characteristics are predominantly controlled by the polarisation over propagation.

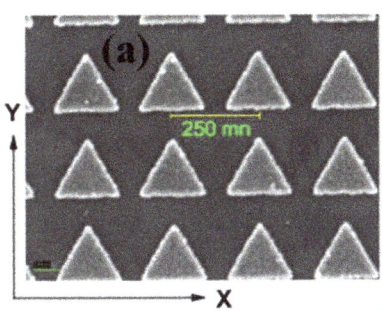
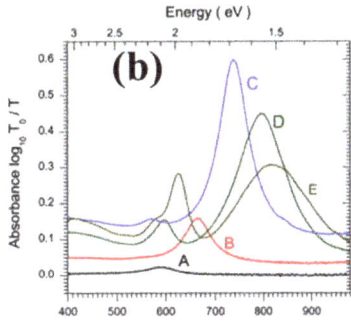

Figure 7. (**a**) Scanning electron microscopy image of the array A, constituted of gold nanotriangles on ITO. (**b**) Experimental extinction spectra of gold nanotriangles. The spectra correspond to triangle arrays with five different lateral sides. (A) 50 nm, (B) 100 nm, (C) 150 nm, (D) 200 nm, and (E) 260 nm. All the figures were reprinted (adapted) with permission from [21], Copyright 2008, American Institute of Physics.

2.7. Nanocrescent

Nanocrescents (NC) are a very special type of nanostructures which are fabricated using nanosphere template lithography (NTL) [76,77]. Bukasov and Shumaker-Parry [22] demonstrated that Polystyrene spheres (PS) of varying diameters can be exploited as templates to fabricate NCs with well-defined shape and size using NTL, as shown in Figure 8a–e. The NCs have sharp corners that can induce strong electromagnetic field enhancement. The LSPR of NCs is easily tunable by structural parameters like thickness, tip sharpness, tip gap angle, orientation [22,78]. Apart from that, due to the asymmetry of the crescent structure, LSPR is believed to be highly polarisation dependent. Figure 8f shows the extinction spectra consists of several peaks of the NCs produced from PS templates of different diameters [22]. For all the NCs the weakest peaks appeared in the visible range around 600 ± 50 nm range which is ascribed to the out-of-plane LSPR mode that is less sensitive to the NC orientation as well as to the incident polarisation. The dominating longitudinal LSPR peaks for all NCs appear in the longer wavelength side, e.g., at 2640 and 2470 nm for 410 and 356 nm diameter templates when the incident light is polarised along the long axis of the NC. On the other hand, transverse LSPR peak dominates for polarisation along the short axis of NC, e.g., 1450 nm peak for the templates of diameter 356 nm. Notably, both the longitudinal and transverse LSPR peaks of the NCs redshift with an increase in the template diameter as depicted in Figure 8g. The longitudinal LSPR peaks are found to be very sensitive to the incident polarisation as it reduced by 300–500% with unfavourable polarisation, while the transverse peaks are less sensitive which changes only by 10–30% against the variation of incident polarisation. In this regard, Cooper et al. [79] studied the polarisation sensitive LSPR response of open-structure NCs (Figure 8h). As shown in Figure 8i, LSPR extinction spectra of open-tip AuNCs upon unpolarised light excitation, consists of four distinct peaks, each of which is associated with particular mode.

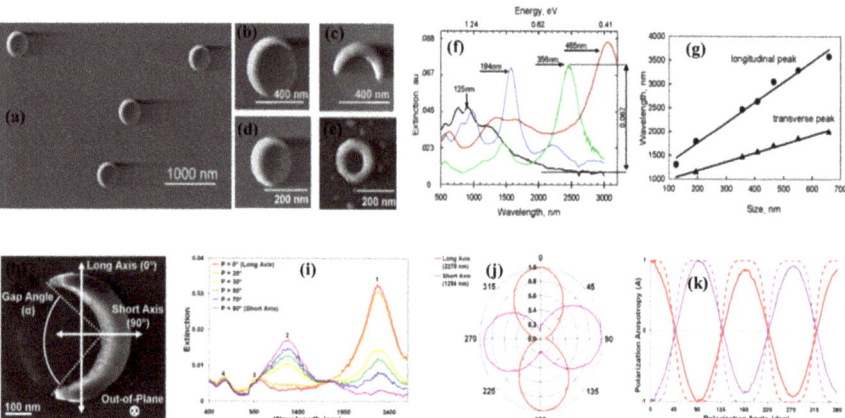

Figure 8. SEM images of nanocrescents template with PS beads with diameters of (**a–c**) 356 nm, (**d**) 194 nm beads, and (**e**) nanorings template with 125 nm diameter PS beads. (**f**) Ensemble extinction spectra with the PS bead template diameter shown near the longitudinal peaks. (**g**) The linear dependence of nanocrescent LSPR peaks on the diameter of the PS template used to fabricate the nanocrescents. All the figures were reprinted (adapted) with permission from [22], Copyright 2007, American Chemical Society. (**h**) Illustration of the direction of electric field polarisation with respect to nanocrescent axes for distinct resonance modes. (**i**) Extinction spectra of 356 nm diameter template AuNC. The varying polarisation angles (P) demonstrate selective excitation, co-excitation or non-excitation of resonances at specific angles. Peak labels correspond to unique resonance modes described in text: 1, long axis dipole; 2, short axis dipole; 3, long axis quadrupole; 4, out-of-plane dipole. (**j**) Polar plot of normalised extinction values for the LA-D (red) and SA-D (purple) resonance modes, demonstrating the anisotropy of 356 nm diameter AuNCs. (**k**) Experimental (solid) and calculated (dashed) polarisation anisotropy values (A) for LA-D (red) and SA-D (purple) resonances of the same AuNC sample. All the figures were reprinted (adapted) with permission from [79], Copyright 2013, American Chemical Society.

The peaks shown in Figure 8f under different polarisation can be assigned to particular resonance mode. The position of these peaks can be tuned by changing the angle between the incident light polarisation and the nanostructure orientation. By setting the incident light polarisation along the long and short axes of the nanocrescents, various resonance modes can be excited selectively and likewise can be assigned to long axis dipole (LA-D), short axis dipole (SA-D), long axis quadrupole (LA-Q), and out-of-plane dipole (OOPD) modes, as shown in Figure 8i. Both LA-D and LA-Q resonance modes are selectively excited when the incident light polarisation is along the long axis of the nanocrescent (0°). Notably, LA-D resonance mode shows strong electric field enhancement and appears between the near- to mid-infrared regime. On the other hand, the LA-Q mode is much weaker compared to LA-D and likewise produces a weaker peak with lower field enhancement. On the other hand, when light is polarised along the short axis (SA) of the nanocrescent (90°), i.e., orthogonal to LA, SA-D mode is excited, which is although strong, however less dominant than LA-D, thus not coupled with incident light most efficiently. The last one, i.e., out-of-plane weak dipole (OOP-D) mode can be excited irrespective of the incident polarisation, in a direction perpendicular to the plane of the nanocrescent around the visible wavelength range. Notably, while LA-D and SA-D modes redshift with increasing template diameter, OOP-D mode remains invariant against the variation of template diameter, similar to observations by Bukasov et al. [22]. The polarisation dependence of the nanocrescent LSPR can be visualised from the 360° polar plot as shown in Figure 8j. For LA-D mode maximum intensity is obtained for 0° and 180°, whereas SA-D shows maxima for 90° and 270°, thus indicates that these two modes are orthogonal to each other. Likewise, PA discussed before can be calculated for long axis as $PA_{LA} = (I_{LA} - I_{SA})/(I_{LA} + I_{SA})$ [80]. Here I_{LA} and I_{SA} are defined as the normalised intensities of the LA-D and SA-D resonance modes, respectively, for any given angle. From Figure 8k it is apparent that both calculated and measured normalised extinction for LA-D mode at 2278 nm and SA-D mode at 1284 nm become 1 at 0° and 90° for PA_{LA} and PA_{SA}, respectively. In addition, Goerlitzer et al. [81] and Zhang et al. [82] also demonstrated that LSPR of NCs depends strongly on the polarisation of the excitation light.

2.8. Hybrid Plasmonic Nanostructures

The quest for an enhanced electromagnetic field with superior signal-to-noise ratio from the optical signal leads to the idea of engineered plasmonic nanostructures [83]. Two-dimensional (2D) materials, thanks to their reduced symmetry provides ample controllability over physical properties, thus become an ideal candidate in the field of optics, optoelectronics and nanophotonics [84–86]. The integration of a 2D material with a plasmonic nanomaterial leads to a new generation of hybrid nanostructures which can efficiently manipulate the light through LSPR, that leads to exotic spectroscopy enhancement phenomenon, including SERS, PL, enhanced transmission, etc. [87–89]. Among the family of 2D materials/plasmonic hybrid nanostructures, black phosphorus (BP) [90,91] and GaSe metal chalcogenides [92] need special mention thanks to their tunable optical, electrical and electronic properties. In a recent theoretical framework, Deng and co-workers [26] demonstrated that excitation of surface plasmon polaritons (SPP) at the metal/BP array interface leads to broadband enhanced transmission which is found to be strongly polarisation dependent because of the inherent anisotropy of BP structure, coming from x-(armchair) and y-(zigzag) directions. A schematic diagram of gold patch arrays with a BP sheet hybrid structure is shown in Figure 9a. Clearly in both x-(armchair) and y-(zigzag) directions, transmission enhanced significantly (Figure 9b) through gold slit arrays after the BP incorporation, when LSPR at gold/BP interface couples with the SSP modes of BP. Interestingly, enhancement of transmissions is strongly wavelength dependent and also occurs differently for different polarisations, which leads to anisotropic polarisation response.

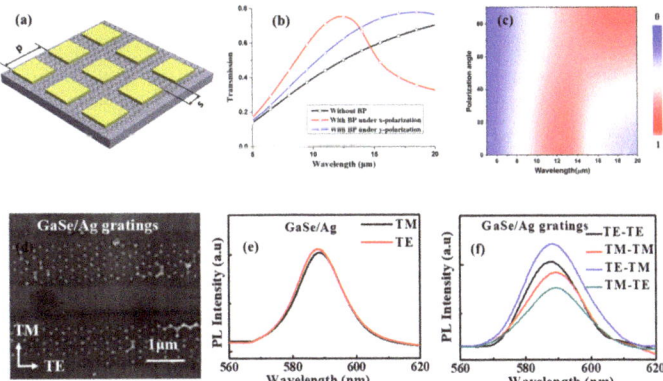

Figure 9. (**a**) Schematic of continuous BP sheet at the bottom of the gold patch arrays and (**b**) transmission of the structure with and without the BP sheet. (**c**) Transmission spectra of the gold patch arrays structures with BP under different polarisation angles. All the figures were reprinted (adapted) with permission from [26], Copyright 2019, The Optical Society. (**d**) SEM image of the Ag nanoprism gratings on GaSe layers. (**e**) Measured PL spectra with TM and TE polarisations for the normal GaSe/Ag hybrid structure. (**f**) Measured PL spectra for the GaSe/Ag grating structure, along two detection polarisation directions, TM and TE, with TM and TE excitation polarisations, respectively. The "TE–TE" ("TM–TM", "TE–TM", and "TM–TE") indicates the spectrum pumped with the TE (TM, TE, and TM) polarised incidence and detected along the TE (TM, TM, and TE) polarisation direction. All the figures were reprinted (adapted) with permission from [93], Copyright 2019, American Chemical Society.

To obtain a clear picture, Figure 9c shows the polarisation dependent transmission spectra at different wavelengths. It can be seen that for varying polarisation angle from 0° to 90°, at shorter wavelengths transmission slightly decreases, while transmission gets higher at longer wavelengths [26]. Such observation can be understood from wavelength dependence of x- and y-polarisation transmission. Below 15 μm, for both the x- and y-polarisation, the transmission with BP is almost indistinguishable. However, for above 15 μm, as the excitation of the propagating SPPs is not possible in the x-direction, transmission is reduced significantly. Nevertheless, transmission remains high in the y-direction (Figure 9b). Hence, a strong polarisation-dependent wave transmission is observed in the proposed hybrid nanostructures. In another similar work, Wan et al. [93] fabricated hybrid plasmonic nanostructures by designing a periodic array of Ag metallic nanostructures on typical 2D GaSe layers. Experimental results indicate that both SERS and PL signal enhanced significantly in the hybrid nanostructures compared to pristine one and the effect is found to be strongest for thinnest GaSe layer. Based on the plasmonic-enhanced optical response, they tried to manipulate the optical properties on the GaSe/Ag hybrid nanostructure. To realise the optical anisotropy, it is desirable to have broken structural symmetry in the x-y plane, which allows selective excitation of transverse and longitudinal surface plasmons by varying incident polarisation. For practical application, Ag nanoprisms with patterned gratings were imprinted on the GaSe layer, along the x axis with a periodicity of 1176 nm, which can be clearly seen from the SEM image in Figure 9d. To experimentally observe the optical anisotropy, PL spectra are recorded at TE (⊥ to x-axis)) and TM (∥ to x axis) polarisation as shown in Figure 9e,f. We learnt from Figure 9e that PL spectra in normal GaSe/Ag hybrid structure is polarisation-independent because of the presence of low anisotropy in geometric configuration. In stark contrast, a strong polarisation dependent PL spectrum is obtained for the GaSe/Ag grating structure. For example, under TM excitation polarisation, the PL at TM- and TE-polarised detections show a 9.3% polarisation which remains 8.2% for TE polarised excitation. Both the excitation and detection of PL signal show strong polarisation dependence which indicates anisotropic polarisation response. Precisely, for both TE and TM excitations, PL signals are detected to be higher along the TM polarisation [93]. On the other hand, when detected in two different polarisation directions, band edge emissions are more favourably excited for TE polarised excitation compared to TM polarisation. In short, polarisation sensitive, selective excitation and emission in GaSe/Ag grating structure confirms the role of Ag nanoprism gratings in inducing anisotropic plasmonic pumping in GaSe luminescence, which holds tremendous potential application in fabricating anisotropic 2D nanodevices.

2.9. Selected Applications

Manipulation of the polarisation state of light at the nanoscale by plasmonic nanostructures of various shape and size discussed above has led to notable applications in photonics, optoelectronic devices, plasmonic circuits and optical sensing techniques [94–98]. Of late, key functional elements of optoelectronic devices and nanophotonic circuitry have been realised utilising plasmonic structures, providing proof of principle devices at scales, which is otherwise not achievable with conventional photonics [95,99,100]. Plasmonics also continues to demonstrate progressing utility in biological and chemical fields, with plasmonic sensing methods providing single-molecule sensitivity at nanoscale dimensions [101–103]. The unique structural orientation and favourable polarisation direction of individual nanostructures have given rise to many diverse applications. For example, LSPRs in nanoparticles have been utilised to locally enhance Raman scattering, with dimer, trimer and quadrumer nanoparticle arrangements demonstrating confined Raman enhancement hot-spots, with marked polarisation dependence [104–106]. Nanorods, due to their polarisation dependent longitudinal LSPR modes, have been employed as orientation sensors, also allowing for precise alignment and rotation using polarised laser tweezer techniques [33,107]. Recently, one-dimensional nanowires have found wide-ranging applications, most notably in the development of novel plasmonic circuitry as plasmonic waveguides, routers, multiplexers and logic gates, etc. [60,100,108,109].

Photonic devices have been proposed as the foundation for the next generation of semiconductor-based computing thanks to their remarkable speed, bandwidth and energy efficiency as compared to their electronic counterparts. Plasmonic analogues of optical components can be replicated at nanoscale dimensions, and many of the functional elements required for plasmon-based integrated circuits have been developed recently, including Plasmonic waveguides, multiplexers, de-multiplexers, emitters, detectors, gain media and Boolean logic gates, etc. [60,100,108,109]. Among the variety of plasmonic nanostructures, Ag nanowires (NWs) are of particular interest because of the low loss propagation of surface plasmons (SPs) along the wire in the visible to near-infrared spectral range [110,111]. The coupling of far-field light to propagating SPs can be achieved when light is incident on metal NW terminals, allowing for subwavelength confinement as the SP travels along the NW before being emitted as a photon at the distal end. This in/out coupling process requires a scattering mechanism to take place and, as such, is found to occur only at areas of symmetry breaking within the wire, such as wire ends or sharp discontinuities [112]. Coupling of light to the AgNW in Figure 10a(i) by focused laser illumination is illustrated in Figure 10a(ii), launching a propagating SP that is re-emitted as scattered light from the NW terminal. These propagating SP distributions can be successfully imaged by coating the NWs with fluorescent quantum dots (QDs), which are excited by energy transfer from the propagating SPs [8]. Unique near-field distribution patterns are observed as a result of the superposition of different SP modes within the NW. It can be seen that these distributions change as the polarisation of the incident light is varied, with Figure 10a(iii,iv) demonstrating the patterns obtained for orthogonal polarisations using QD imaging.

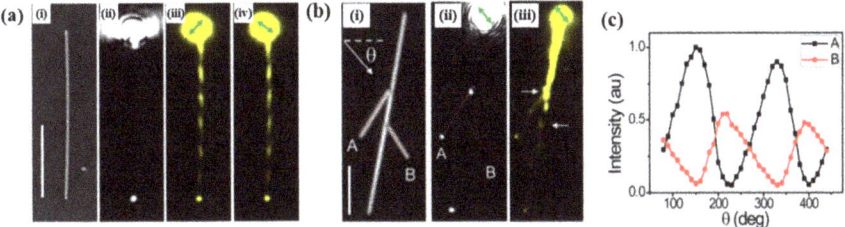

Figure 10. (a) (i) SEM image of an AgNW, scale bar is 5 μm. (ii) Scattering image during focused laser illumination of the NW terminal. (iii,iv) Quantum dot fluorescence imaging of the NW's propagating SP field distribution for different incident polarisations indicated by the green arrows. **(b)** (i) White light image, (ii) scattering image, and (iii) QD fluorescence image of a branched NW structure during polarised illumination. θ indicates the angle of polarisation of the incident light. **(c)** Output intensity of branch terminals A and B as the incident polarisation angle θ is varied. Selective routing into either branch can be achieved by tuning of the incident polarisation. All the figures were reprinted (adapted) with permission from [8], Copyright 2015, Royal Society of Chemistry.

Coupling of light to NWs at regions other than terminals or discontinuities is observed only as a result of near-field interactions and cannot occur through far-field illumination [61]. However, these near-field interactions were shown to facilitate the transfer of propagating SPs from one NW to an adjacent NW due to near-field coupling, allowing SPs to propagate through branched NW networks [60]. The successful coupling of propagating SPs from one NW to another depends on the near-field intensity at the junction between the two, with the SP either being routed into the adjacent wire or continuing in the original wire. The near-field patterns observed in these NWs are found to be strongly dependent on the polarisation of incident light. For example, the simple branched NW network shown in Figure 10b(i,ii) allows selective routing of propagating SPs into either branch A or B by tuning the incident polarisation. The near-field coupling to branch A from the main wire occurs due to the large near-field intensity at the junction between the two (marked by the upper white arrow in Figure 10b(iii)), while the weak near-field intensity at the junction with branch B (lower white arrow) does not lead to successful coupling. Figure 10c shows the output intensity from both A and B as the polarisation is rotated. A polarisation angle of $\theta \approx 150°$ exhibits a maximum scattering intensity from A and a minimum from B, while an angle of $\theta \approx 230°$ exhibits a maximum from B and minimum from A, demonstrating the polarisation selective routing behaviour. The routing process is also found to be dependent on the incident wavelength, leading to light at different frequencies being routed into different branches within the network, allowing for de-multiplexing of multi-wavelength signals [60].

In another pioneer work, Wei and co-workers demonstrated that, in simple AgNW networks, interference of plasmons between primary and secondary/branched NWs modulates the near-field distribution to control the output optical signal, which can be exploited to realise the complete family of Boolean logic gates [108,113]. NW networks with two input terminals (I1 and I2) were used to combine propagating SPs within the main wire, where both the phase difference and polarisation angle led to interference that dictated the output (O) of the NW network as shown in Figure 11a. Polarisation control allows coupling between wires to be maximised while tuning the relative phase difference between the propagating SPs allows their interaction to lead to constructive or destructive interference. Specific input phase and polarisations demonstrate a maximum to minimum intensity ratio larger than 10, allowing for simple binary classification of 'ON' and 'OFF' states, and the performance of basic logical functions (Figure 11a). For example, when inputs I1 and I2, separately or together, leads to maximum output at O, an "OR" gate is realised. On the other hand, when the output signal is obtained only for individual inputs and disappears (OFF) when two SPs propagate together owing to destructive interference between them, the NW network behaves as XOR gate. Further complicated NW networks with two inputs, I1 and I2, and two output terminals, O1 and O2, (Figure 11b) are also exploited to realise the additional logic gates. It can be seen from Figure 11b that for simultaneous inputs from I1 and I2, the outputs O1 and O2 are complementary to each other. An "AND" gate can be realised by considering O2 as the gate output, setting the output intensity threshold for the 'ON' state to 450 au, and tuning the relative phase delay so that simultaneous inputs at I1 and I2 lead to a maximum output at O2. In this case, inputs at I1 and I2 individually lead to a sub-threshold output at O2 (~100 and ~350 au, respectively) yielding a 'low' output, but simultaneous inputs at I1 and I2 leads to an output at O2 that exceeds the threshold (~800 au) yielding a 'high' output. Similar four-terminal NW networks are also proposed to demonstrate other logical functionalities like 'NOT', 'NAND' and binary 'Adder' operations as illustrated in Figure 11c.

Wei et al. further demonstrated the ability of AgNW networks to cascade basic logic functions to create more complex logic functions [109]. In their work, a four-terminal branched AgNW network was exploited to realise a universal logical 'NOR' gate by cascading 'OR' and 'NOT' gates as illustrated in Figure 11d. Operation of both the 'OR' and 'NOT' gates can be tuned by varying the intensity, polarisation and phase of I1 and I2. The 'NOR' gate is illustrated by considering terminals I1 and I2 as inputs where C serves as control terminal which inverts the signal, resulting in the binary 'high/low' states. The first section of the network consists of a primary and branched NW, with inputs I1 and I2 that operate as an 'OR' gate (as before), with inputs from I1 and I2 separately or together leading to a 'high' output from the gate. The second section takes the output from the first and, using a control input C from the second NW branch, uses destructive interference to realise a logical 'NOT' gate, inverting the output of the 'OR' gate. The realisation of the 'NOR' gate can be understood clearly by looking into the scattering images of the NW network with different combination of the inputs I1, I2, and C as shown in Figure 11f–k. For example, following inputs from I1 and I2 separately or together, the output is 'high' (as depicted by the yellow circle), indicating the 'OR' functionality (Figure 11f–h). Alternatively, when I1 and I2 are 'low' and C is enabled, the network output is 'high', thus depicting the 'NOT' operation (i). Finally, the 'NOR' gate is demonstrated when the 'NOT' gate acts upon the 'OR' gate, i.e., when the output is inverted to 'low' with both or either I1 and I2 being 'high', due to the control input C (j,k).

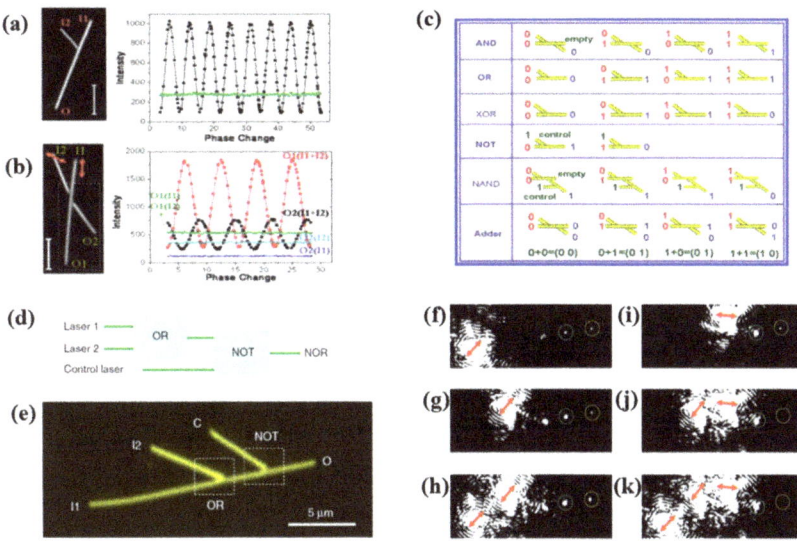

Figure 11. (**a**) Optical image of a simple branched NW network with two inputs (I1 and I2), and one output (O). The graph shows the output scattering intensity at O as a function optical phase delay when input is either I1 or I2 (green), and for simultaneous inputs I1 and I2 (black). Phase change does not impact output intensity for single inputs, however, for dual inputs, relative phase delay between I1 and I2 leads to interference that modulates the intensity at output O. (**b**) Optical image of a two-input (I1, I2) two output (O1, O2) NW network. The graph shows the variation in output intensity as a function of phase delay for both outputs with various input combinations. As before, no change in output intensity is observed as the phase of single inputs are varied (green, blue, dark blue). When propagating SPs are launched in both inputs simultaneously, the relative phase between I1 and I2 dictates the output intensity at O1 (red) and O2 (black). (**c**) Proposed schematics for various other interferometric logic operations in simple NW networks. All the figures were reprinted (adapted) with permission from [108], Copyright 2011, American Chemical Society. (**d**) Schematic of an optical cascaded logic gate in a four terminal AgNW network. (**e**) Optical image of the network. Propagating SPs can be launched at inputs I1 and I2 to perform the OR operation using phase-dependent interference before the output interferes with the control C to perform the interferometric NOT operation. (**f**–**k**) Scattering images illustrating the operation of the OR and NOT gates (with the green and yellow circles locating the outputs of the OR and NOT gates, respectively, while the red arrows indicate polarisation orientation). Launching propagating SPs at inputs I1 or I2 individually (**f**,**g**) or simultaneously (**h**) leads to a high output intensity from the OR gate. A low input to the NOT gate leads to a high output (**i**), while a high input leads to a low output (**j**,**k**). All the figures were reprinted (adapted) with permission from [109], Copyright 2011, Springer Nature.

'NOR' and 'NAND' gates are universal logic gates and form the foundation of Boolean logic networks central to electronic circuitry. Complex phase and polarisation dependent NW networks constitute a realistic route for plasmonic circuitry to overcome fundamental size limitations of optical computing devices, allowing for analogous plasmonic integrated circuits to be scaled down to sizes comparable with standard electronic ICs. Phase and polarisation dependent logic operations are a promising foundation for future on-chip integrated optical computing.

Manipulation of nanoscale objects by intense laser field through optical trapping and guided transport in plasmonic nanostructures has found tremendous applications in the field of hydrodynamics, microfluidics and lab-on-a-chip studies [114–117]. Strong electromagnetic field gradients and resulting optical gradient forces in localised LSPR of plasmonic nanostructures allows for trapping and manipulation of nearby nano-objects. Several plasmonic nanostructures of different shapes have been proposed for trapping and guided transport of single nanoparticles [114–117]. However, we are particularly interested in the work by Yang et al. who demonstrated for the first time the guided transport of TiO_2 nanoparticles (NP) in AgNW in aqueous solution at single-particle levels with dedicated applications in microfluidics [118]. Using focused laser illumination of NW terminals, they successfully demonstrated the trapping of TiO_2 nanoparticles on NW surfaces in fluids. It was found that plasmonic trapping also leads to the transport of the nanoparticles along the wire toward the incident terminal. It is important to note that the nanoparticle trajectory is explicitly determined by the combination of the nanostructure shape and direction of incident laser polarisation. For example, in a V-shaped NW dimer, polarisation parallel to the left branch of the NW induces the movement of the NP along the left branch only (Figure 12a), whereas polarisation parallel to the right branch guides the NP along the right branch only (Figure 12b). Far-field optical manipulation methods like laser tweezers have become widely used for particle trapping and transport, however, plasmonic nanostructures provide a route towards precise control at nanoscale dimensions, with a unique versatility provided by various nanostructure shapes.

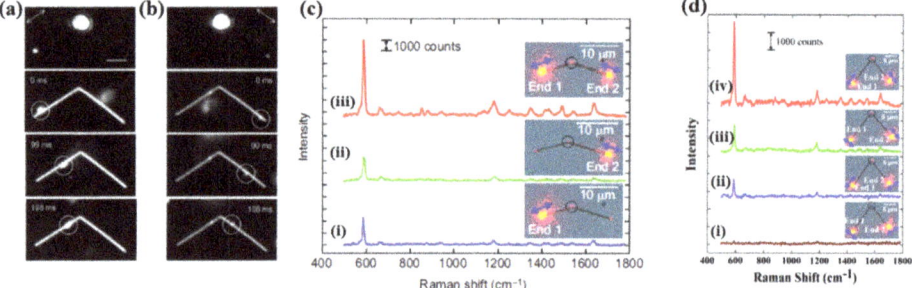

Figure 12. Images of trapping and guided transport of a TiO_2 nanoparticle along a v-shaped NW dimer structure (scale bar is 1 μm). Images in (**a**) illustrate the transport of a nanoparticle along the left branch for an incident polarisation orientation parallel to the left branch (marked by the white arrow). Images in (**b**) demonstrate transport along the right branch for orientation parallel to the right branch. Transport can be tuned to either the left or right branch by varying the incident polarisation. All the figures were reprinted (adapted) with permission from [118], Copyright 2016, Royal Society of Chemistry. Similar NW dimer structures were used to perform polarisation tuneable Remote SERS. (**c**) Comparison of the Remote SERS signal generated in NW dimer structures when propagating SPs are generated in (i) the left branch only (8 mW), (ii) the right branch only (8 mW) and (iii) both branches simultaneously (4 mW per branch). Incident polarisations are marked by the blue arrows. (**d**) Tuning of SERS signal intensity by varying the incident polarisation orientations. (iv) Polarisations parallel to their respective branches generated the greatest signal enhancement, whereas enhancement was reduced when polarisation in one branch was perpendicular (iii,ii), with the enhancement effect disappearing when both polarisations were perpendicular to their respective branches (i). All the figures were reprinted (adapted) with permission from [119], Copyright 2013, American Institute of Physics.

Plasmonic nanostructures have also led to notable advancements in various biosensing techniques [98]. Most notably, Surface Enhanced Raman Spectroscopy (SERS) has demonstrated the practical abilities of plasmon based sensing methodologies and has been shown to provide up to a 10^{10}–10^{11} enhancement over conventional Raman Spectroscopy [120–122]. Plasmonic nanostructures have been utilised as SERS probes for nanoscale Raman measurements, as LSPRs provide enhanced electromagnetic field strengths in nanoscale hot-spots regions. SERS has also been employed in NW structures, utilising propagating surface plasmons to transport incident light and perform Raman spectroscopy at distances several microns from the laser illumination. Remote SERS, while weaker than conventional SERS methods, provides notable advantages as the nanoscale volume probed avoids background noise due to the incident illumination while also isolating heat from the incident light source reducing photodamage experienced by samples at high illumination intensities [123]. Following the work by Dasgupta and co-workers, two AgNWs are coupled serially to form a NW-dimer, where remote SERS is achieved by performing dual-path illumination at both distal ends of the NW-dimer [119]. They observed that the SERS signal was enhanced significantly when propagating SPs were excited simultaneously in both NWs (dual-path) compared to single-path excitation, at identical excitation powers. This observation can be understood clearly from Figure 12c, where single path excitation was performed in each branch with an incident power of 8 mW (i,ii), before dual-path excitation was performed by exciting both branches simultaneously with 4 mW laser power (iii). Dual-path excitation led to a 70% enhancement in the SERS signal when compared to single-path excitation with the same total excitation power.

This dual path SERS enhancement was found to be strongly dependent on the incident polarisation of both excitation beams. For polarisation perpendicular to the NWs (Figure 12d(i)), no SERS signal is obtained. Rotating the polarisation parallel to either of the NW branches led to a noticeable signal enhancement (ii, iii), however, a maximum SERS enhancement was observed only when both incident polarisations were parallel to their respective NW branches (iv). Tuning of the incident polarisations alters the near-field intensity at the junction hot-spot, allowing for control and modulation of the SERS intensity generated at the junction between wires.

Polarisation sensitive optical response of plasmonic nanostructures have also been proposed for use in novel SERS-based security labels [124,125]. These labels are constructed from arrays of short Ag coated plasmonic NWs orientated orthogonally in specific pattern designs, with embedded molecular probes that allow information to be read out through pixel-by-pixel SERS analysis of the target molecules. The polarisation dependence of these nanostructure arrays allows separate images to be simultaneously encoded and later revealed through polarised SERS imaging. The pixel-by-pixel SERS response for an individual NW coated in 4-MBT target molecules for horizontal and vertical polarisations is shown in Figure 13a,b, with the SERS intensity being collected from the 1079 cm^{-1} band. 2D SERS imaging shows a strong Raman enhancement around the edges and tips of the NW for horizontally polarised light, while for vertically polarised light enhancement is only seen at the NW tips. Figure 13c–f represents a few examples of custom made plasmonic nanostructures that demonstrate the capacity for covert security labels based on polarisation sensitive SERS imaging. Simple arrays in (c) show how horizontally polarised light (ii) leads to illumination of vertically aligned NWs, while vertically polarised light (iii) leads to illumination of horizontal NWs. Orthogonally polarised SERS imaging allow specific designs to be separately resolved by selective excitation of horizontal or vertical NWs (d,e). Based on this idea the images in Figure 13f demonstrate a more sophisticated encryption of molecular information from complex plasmonic structures composed of horizontal and vertical NWs. In short, SERS based plasmonic structures demonstrate the capacity to be utilised as advanced anti-counterfeiting labels for next-generation securities that are difficult to replicate yet easily verified.

Other than the NW structures described above, basic nanoparticle dimer, as well as trimer and quadrumer structures have shown to create polarisation dependent local hot-spots in the region between nanoparticles due to plasmonic coupling within sufficiently close interparticle separation [102,104–106]. Nanodisk Au dimers, for example, have been used to design nanoscale plasmonic cavities in which SERS measurements of graphene suspended on cavity exhibits an enhancement of 10^3 within the cavity [126] for certain polarisations. The sample configuration is depicted in Figure 13g. It is also shown that the SERS signal depends strongly on the incident polarisation of 638 nm excitation (Figure 13h,i). For polarisations parallel to the nanodisk dimer axis, 2D Raman peak (2670 cm^{-1}) exhibits strong enhancement and reaches a maximum (Figure 13h). However, when the polarisation is rotated by 90° the nanodisks get decoupled and as the localisation is lifted, Raman signal (Figure 13i) drops by a factor of 20.

Anisotropic polarisation responses of plasmonic nanostructures have also found applications as novel orientation sensors DF microscopy at single-particle level [107]. For example, LSPR scattering of Au nanorods shown in Figure 14a is strongly polarised along the long axis of the nanorod, which makes them an ideal candidate for orientation sensors. At the same time, AuNRs demonstrate compelling advantages over conventional fluorescent methods, based on fluorophore dyes in terms of the photostability of the scattering intensity.

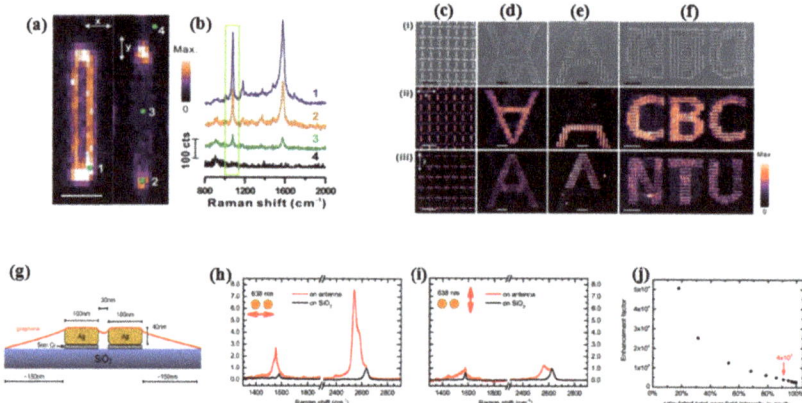

Figure 13. (**a**) SERS imaging of a single Ag NW under horizontal and vertical polarised light (scale bar is 1 μm). The NW is coated in 4-MBT target molecules, and the pixel intensities in the image are collected from the 1079 cm^{-1} band of the SERS spectra. (**b**) The SERS spectra obtained at points 1, 2, 3 and 4 in (**a**), demonstrating much stronger enhancement for light polarised perpendicularly to the NW. (**c**–**f**) Encrypted designs formed from horizontal and vertical AgNWs (scale bar is 1 μm). (i) SEM images, (ii) horizontally polarised and (iii) vertically polarised SERS images. All the figures were reprinted (adapted) with permission from [124], Copyright 2014, Royal Society of Chemistry. (**g**) Diagram of the polarisation dependent nanodisk dimer structure with the Raman hot-spot located in the nanogap between disks. (**h**,**i**) SERS spectra obtained from the hot-spot region for polarisation parallel and perpendicular to the longitudinal dimer mode at an incident wavelength of 638 nm. Maximum enhancement is obtained when the longitudinal LSPR of the dimer structure is excited with parallel polarisation, with this enhancement reducing when polarisation is orientated perpendicular to the long dimer axis and the nanodisks de-couple. (**j**) The enhancement factor is calculated by estimating the calculated integrated near-field intensity within the cavity and comparing it to the laser spot size. Here, the nanogap region is estimated to account for 90% of the enhancement, leading to a local enhancement factor of 4×10^3 for polarisations parallel to the longitudinal dimer mode. All the figures were reprinted (adapted) with permission from [126], Copyright 2013, American Chemical Society.

For plasmonic AuNRs, scattering intensity remains constant over the period of measurement (Figure 14b), whereas fluorescent dyes and quantum dots suffer from photobleaching, thereby reducing the emitted intensity over time and limiting timescales over which images can be recorded. For Au nanorods, the scattering intensity (I_{sca}) recorded for a certain polarisation orientation is proportional to the square of the cosine of the angle θ between the rod's longitudinal axis and the incident polarisation. The NR orientation can, therefore, be back-calculated from the recorded intensity, where $\theta = \arccos\left(\sqrt{I_{sca}}\right)$, and monitored as the NR rotates (Figure 14b).

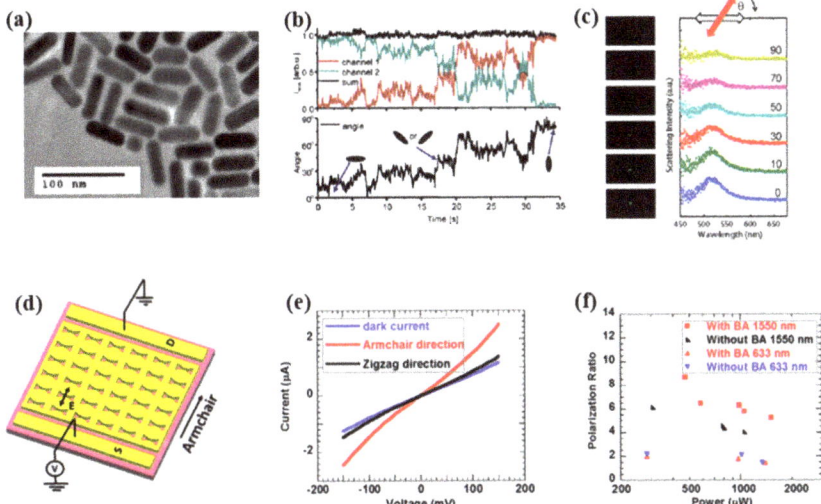

Figure 14. (**a**) SEM image of the Au nanorod orientation sensors (**b**) Scattered light intensity time traces recorded for orthogonal polarisations (channels 1 and 2) observed during DF imaging of a single rotating Au nanorod. Maximum signals are recorded in a channel when the nanorod orientation is parallel to the channel's polarisation axis. The sum of both channels illustrates a constant scatter intensity as the nanorod rotates. From these intensities, the orientation angle can be calculated. All the figures were reprinted (adapted) with permission from [107], Copyright 2005, American Chemical Society. (**c**) DF images and corresponding scattering intensities of an AgNR rotated using a polarised laser tweezers. A maximum intensity is recorded when the angle θ between the nanorod and the illumination polarisation is 0° (blue line), decreasing as θ increases, and reaching a minimum when θ is 90° (yellow line). As such, NR rotation and alignment using focused tweezers can be investigated and verified. All the figures were reprinted (adapted) with permission from [33], Copyright 2010, American Chemical Society. (**d**) Diagram of the polarisation-sensitive BP hybrid plasmonic photodetector. (**e**) Photodetector current vs. applied voltage for no illumination (blue), illumination polarised in the armchair illumination (red) and polarised in the zigzag direction (black) at 580 μW (1550 nm wavelength). (**f**) Polarisation ratios (photocurrent for armchair to zigzag directions) for various illumination powers at 150 mV bias. At 1550 nm illumination, devices with the bowtie apertures (BA) show an increased polarisation ratio compared to those without. This effect is wavelength dependent as 633 nm illumination shows similar ratios with and without the plasmonic apertures. All the figures were reprinted (adapted) with permission from [127], Copyright 2018, American Chemical Society.

Optical alignment and rotation of nanostructures has also been demonstrated using polarised light, as structures with one dominant LSPR mode, such as the long-axis longitudinal mode in nanorods, tend to align parallel to the incident laser polarisation [33]. Tong et al. utilised this phenomenon to rotate and align Ag nanorods using polarised laser tweezers. Rotation of the incident laser polarisation induces similar rotation of the AuNR to maintain alignment, which was verified using polarised white light DF imaging (Figure 14c). Maximum scattering is observed when the NR is orientated parallel to the white light polarisation, whereas for perpendicular polarisations, it reaches a minimum. Precise control and rotation of nanostructures allow nanoscale manipulation which may aid in the construction of nano-architectures, the driving of nano-pumps in fluidic devices, or even the testing of particle adhesion through rotational forces.

Polarisation sensitive LSPR response of hybrid plasmonic nanostructures discussed earlier have also found tremendous potential applications. For example, enhanced light absorption in 2D materials leads to enhanced performance of 2D devices [128]. Likewise, very recently Venuthurumilli et al.

demonstrated that hybrid plasmonic nanostructures made from Black Phosphorous (BP) that can be exploited for polarisation dependent photodetector devices to enhance polarisation sensitivity at NIR wavelengths [127]. Their design consists of bowtie nanoapertures in gold film deposited on 2D BP materials (Figure 14d) to enhance the photocurrent ratio of orthogonal polarisations in BP photodetectors. BP has gained interest for use in photodetectors owing to its thickness-dependent direct bandgap, while its intrinsic anisotropic properties, i.e., linear dichroism arising from its higher absorption along armchair axis compared to its zigzag axis, have been exploited for polarisation-sensitive detection [129]. The bowtie apertures utilised in the hybrid devices (Figure 14e) also exhibit polarisation dependence, allowing transmission of light polarised along the aperture's short-axis while suppressing light polarised along the aperture's long-axis [130]. By orientating the aperture's long-axis parallel to the BP's zigzag axis they further suppress the absorption in the zigzag direction, thus leading to an enhanced polarisation ratio (armchair to zigzag) for the photodetector. Measured currents through the photodetector are notably enhanced when the detector is illuminated with 1550 nm light polarised in the armchair direction, with little enhancement along the zigzag direction (Figure 14e). The polarisation ratio (defined as the ratio of photocurrent in the armchair direction to that in the zigzag direction) was then investigated for various illumination powers (Figure 14f) with and without bowtie apertures (BA). In general, the polarisation ratio is seen to decrease as the illumination power increases (possibly owing to saturation of the photocurrent in the armchair direction) for both structures with and without BA. Comparing structures with and without BA, the polarisation ratio in the device exhibits an increase from 4 without BA to 5.8 with BA at 1.05 mW illumination. At a lower power of 470 mW, the ratio reaches an even higher value of 8.7 for BA structures. For applications with lower power requirements such as IR polarimetry imaging, hybrid nanostructures provide avenues for enhanced sensitivity and selectivity for novel optical devices.

Plasmonic nanostructures provide unprecedented access to light manipulation at nanoscale dimensions while demonstrating the flexibility and control required for advancing photonic technologies. Continued research has motivated advances in optoelectronics, integrated photonics, telecommunications, biological sensing and nanoparticle manipulation, both furthering fundamental research and presenting proof of principle devices. Nanoparticles and nanostructures serve as optical antennas, exhibiting strong local field enhancements while plasmonic nanowires serve as novel waveguides and plasmon routers allowing for sub-wavelength manipulation and transport of light. The polarisation dependent responses of many nanostructures have brought about novel techniques to control and tune plasmon propagations and interactions, while also providing access to sensitive information through optical probing. The continued development and optimisation of plasmonic devices promises further advances in efficiency and sensitivity while continuing to integrate Plasmonics into conventional applications. Plasmonics promises to be at the centre of many notable future advances in optics, providing a realistic route toward the next generation of optical technologies.

3. Manipulating Polarisation State via Metamaterials

Polarisation state is an important characteristic of electromagnetic waves (EMW) which serves as a cornerstone in many optical phenomena. Therefore, the ability to control the polarisation state of EMW has attracted tremendous potential applications in the field of optical polarisation and wavefront manipulation [131,132], optical communication [133], THz photonics [134,135] and spin-hall effect of light [136,137], etc. Conventionally, bulky waveplates made of birefringent crystalline solids [138] or liquid crystals [139] are exploited to manipulate the polarisation state of the EMW. However, due to their large size, operational bandwidth, their application gets limited in optical system miniaturisation and integration. Therefore, it remains an important challenge to manipulate the polarisation state of the EMW at nanoscale for applications in nanophotonics.

Recently, after the emergence of metamaterials, we can unprecedently control the EMWs over a broad wavelength range from microwave to optical frequencies with multiple degrees of freedom e.g., polarisation, phase, and amplitude, which was beyond the scope of natural materials [140–142]. Similar to metamaterials, their two-dimensional counterpart, single-layered nanostructured metasurfaces also provide adequate functionalities of polarisation manipulation in an ultrathin, planar platform [143–145]. In comparison to the volumetric metamaterial, fabrication of metasurfaces requires less complexity and also, they offer reduced loss. To date, although different anisotropic building blocks including crossed nanodipoles [146,147], nanorods [148], L- or S-shaped nanostructures [149–151] and elliptical nanoholes [67] have been employed to fabricate metasurfaces-based waveplates to manipulate the polarisation state of the EMWs, they suffer from the optical anisotropy of the individual building blocks which ends up with limited bandwidth and low efficiency. Chiral metamaterials require special mention because they can arbitrarily manipulate polarisation state of EMWs at nanoscale by combining additional mirror symmetry breaking and by taking advantage of the fact that chirality in EM resonance is handedness sensitive [152,153]. In the second part of the review, we will discuss the designing of metamaterials to control or switch the polarisation states of light, for example by rotating linearly polarised light, ellipticity and chirality, etc.

In a recently published book chapter in 2017, Chen et al. [30] have demonstrated some of the important aspects of polarisation manipulation which we will discuss briefly in the following section. Jiang and co-workers [154] demonstrated anisotropic metasurface of nanorod resonators for high-efficiency, angle-insensitive polarisation rotation over a broadband wavelength regime. They design the metasurface structures by optimising by tailoring the interference of light at the subwavelength scale and the metasurface-based half-wave plate (HWP) and quarter-wave plate (QWP) work over large bandwidth from 640 to 1290 nm near-visible to IR regime, which converts linear polarisation to its cross polarisation and circular to linear polarisation, respectively. The book chapter also includes the observation of Kruk et al. [29], who designed and demonstrated transparent all-dielectric metadevices for highly efficient polarisation manipulation based on HWP and QWPs that can operate across several telecom bands. Their system has an advantage to interact with electromagnetic waves at extremely confined spots without any heat dissipation. Their work paves the idea of reflection-less HWP, QWP and q-plates with high transmittivity that can operate across multiple telecom bands with ~99% polarisation conversion efficiency. Similarly, Wu and colleagues [155] experimentally demonstrate Fano resonances with quality factors as high as Q > 100 in silicon-based planar chiral infrared metasurfaces. They further demonstrated that by designing silicon-based metasurfaces planar (2D) chiral metamaterial high (50%) linear-to-circular polarisation conversion efficiency can be achieved experimentally.

3.1. Multifunctional QWP

Chiral metamaterials designed so far have been exploited for a specific functionality to do with rotating LP, ellipticity of handedness of circularity. In a very recent work, Liu and co-workers [145] inverse designed chiral material with multifunctional polarisation manipulation including Meta-quarter-wave plate (Type 1), bifunctional chiral metamaterial (Type 2) and abnormal meta-quarter-wave plate (Type 3), all of which we will discuss in this section. The results are validated through theoretical calculation, numerical simulation and experimental measurements. They inverse designed the cascaded chiral metamaterials for different polarisation controls, starting from the scattering matrix *S*, defining the scattering properties of metamaterials. For an incident wave along *j*-polarisation, the reflection and transmission coefficients along *i*-polarisation are denoted as r_{ij} and t_{ij}. The forward (T_f) and backward (T_b) propagating transmission matrices are expressed as:

$$T_f = \frac{1}{\sqrt{2}} \begin{pmatrix} 1 & e^{j\theta} \\ -i & e^{j(\theta + \frac{\pi}{2})} \end{pmatrix} \tag{1}$$

$$T_b = \frac{1}{\sqrt{2}} \begin{pmatrix} 1 & -i \\ e^{j\theta} & e^{j(\theta + \frac{\pi}{2})} \end{pmatrix} \tag{2}$$

Here θ is arbitrary real number and by choosing several typical values of θ, the metamaterials will be exploited for abundant functionalities of polarisation control. To quantitatively evaluate the performance of the metamaterials as an m-QWP, first the Stokes parameters are introduced as [156]:

$$S_0 = |t_x|^2 + |t_y|^2, \ S_1 = |t_x|^2 - |t_y|^2, \ S_2 = 2|t_x||t_y|cos\Delta\varphi \text{ and } S_3 = 2|t_x||t_y|sin\Delta\varphi \tag{3}$$

Here $|t_x|$ and $|t_y|$ are the amplitude of transmitted electric fields along x and y directions and $\Delta\varphi = \angle t_y - \angle t_x$ is transmission phase difference. The ellipticity angle χ is defined as:

$$\chi = \frac{1}{2}arcsin(S_3/S_0) \tag{4}$$

When χ is $\pm45°$, the transmitted waves are perfect RCP and LCP, whereas $\chi = 0°$ represents a LP wave. In the following section, we will discuss three extreme cases of polarisation control:

Type 1. Meta-quarter-wave plate ($\theta = -\pi/2$)

When the variable $\theta = -\pi/2$, the forward and backward propagating matrices are expressed as:

$$T_f = T_b = \frac{1}{\sqrt{2}} \begin{pmatrix} 1 & -i \\ -i & 1 \end{pmatrix} \tag{5}$$

Type 2. Bifunctional chiral metamaterial ($\theta = 0$)

For this functionality, a four-layer chiral metamaterial (FLCM) is inverse designed by combining two TLMs which are oriented from each other at a twist angle of 45° and separated by an identical dielectric broad. For $\theta = 0$, the forward and backward propagating matrices are expressed as:

$$T_f = \frac{1}{\sqrt{2}} \begin{pmatrix} 1 & 1 \\ -i & i \end{pmatrix} \tag{6}$$

$$T_b = \frac{1}{\sqrt{2}} \begin{pmatrix} 1 & -i \\ 1 & i \end{pmatrix} \tag{7}$$

Equation (6) reveals that for forward propagating LP waves, m-QWP is realised for linear-to-circular polarisation conversion. On the other hand, following Equation (7) the structure works as a 45° polarisation rotator for backward propagating LP waves. It is quite evident from Figure 15b that for the forward propagating LP waves in x- and y-directions, both co-($|\vec{t_{xx}}|$, $\vec{t_{yy}}$) and cross-polarised transmission ($|\vec{t_{yx}}|$, $|\vec{t_{xy}}|$) exhibit high transmission of 0.7, which makes the total transmission $|\vec{T_x}|$ and $|\vec{T_y}|$ close to 1.

Likewise, a traditional m-QWP is realised that converts x- or y-polarised waves into LCP or RCP waves, for both forward and backward propagation direction. The m-QWP can be designed from a two-layer metamaterial (TLM), by keeping two metallic split ring resonators (SRRs) on each side of an F4B board. The schematic diagram of such optimised unit cell structure is shown in Figure 15a(i). Simulated results show that for normal incident LP waves, the co-polarised transmissions are greater than 0.8 (Figure 15a(ii)) with zero cross-polarisation transmission coefficients because of the mirror-symmetry of the TLM structure with respect to x-z plane. Figure 15a(iii) shows that the phase difference $\angle t_y - \angle t_x$ is ~90° ± 10°. Figure 15a(iv) illustrates that the simulated ellipticity angle $\chi > 40°$ is within the broadband frequency range of 10.5–12.5 GHz. This clearly demonstrate a nearly perfect high transmission RCP wave output, for an incident LP wave at 45° with respect to the x and y axes.

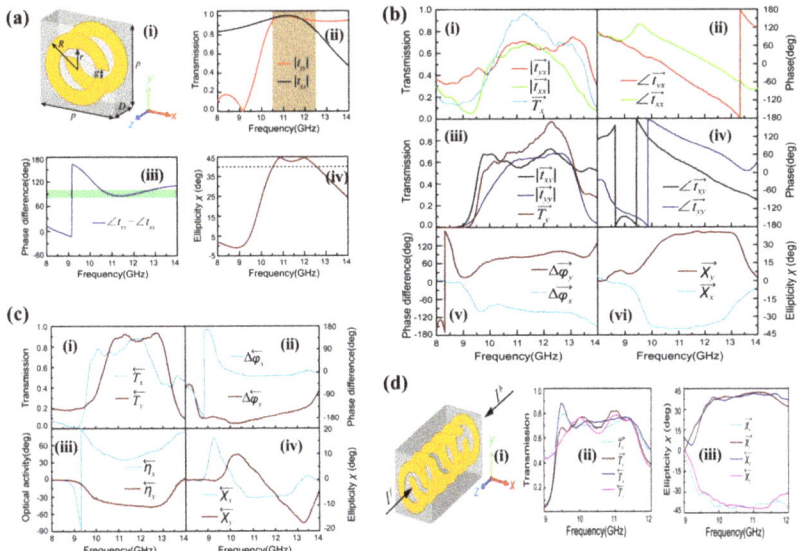

Figure 15. (**a**) (**i**) TLM as an m-QWP. The Schematic and geometric dimensions of the unit cell: p = 7.0 mm, D = 3.5 mm, r = 1.75 mm, R = 3.0 mm, and g = 0.75 mm. (ii) Simulated transmission spectra and (iii) phase difference for x- and y-polarised incident waves. (iv) Calculated ellipticity angle χ. (**b**) Experimental results of the FLCM for the forward propagating x- and y-polarised waves. ((i) and (iii)) Transmission spectra, ((ii) and (iv)) transmission phases, (v) transmission phase differences, and (vi) ellipticity angles χ of the transmitted waves. (**c**) Experimental results of the FLCM for the backward propagating x- and y-polarised waves. (i) Transmission spectra, (ii) transmission phase differences, (iii) polarisation azimuth rotation angles η, and (iv) ellipticity angles χ of the transmitted waves. (**d**) Multilayer chiral metamaterial as an abnormal m-QWP. (i) Schematic of the unit cell. Experimental results of (ii) transmission spectra and (iii) ellipticity angles. All the figures were reprinted (adapted) with permission from [27], Copyright 2019, Springer Nature.

For x and y polarised LP waves, ellipticity angle χ was found to be −40° and 40°, respectively, therefore indicting nearly perfect LCP and RCP output wave. The phase difference of −90° ± 10° and +90° ± 10° for x and y polarised waves support the observation further. Experimental results match well with the simulation.

For backward propagating LP waves, following reciprocity theorem, when the propagation direction is reversed, although the transmission coefficients of co-polarisation remain unchanged, it gets interchanged for cross-polarisation. The experimental results in Figure 15c show that the transmission phase difference $\Delta\overleftarrow{\varphi}_x$ and $\Delta\overleftarrow{\varphi}_y$ are calculated to be 0° and −180°, polarisation azimuth rotation angle η is +45° and −45° and the ellipticity angle is ~−6.3° and 8.3°, and for x and y polarised waves, respectively, which indicates a nearly linear polarisation.

Type 3. Abnormal meta-quarter-wave plate ($\theta = \pi/2$)

When the variable $\theta = \pi/2$, the forward and backward propagating matrices are expressed as

$$T_f = \frac{1}{\sqrt{2}}\begin{pmatrix} 1 & i \\ -i & -1 \end{pmatrix} \tag{8}$$

$$T_b = \frac{1}{\sqrt{2}}\begin{pmatrix} 1 & -i \\ i & 1 \end{pmatrix} \tag{9}$$

Clearly, such structures can convert the forward x-polarised or y-polarised wave into LCP or RCP wave, respectively; while it realises an inverse function, i.e., converts the backward x-polarised or y-polarised wave into RCP or LCP wave, respectively.

To realise this functionality, three m-QWPs are cascaded together as shown in Figure 15d(i). Two of them form an m-HWP, that together with the back m-QWP, oriented at 45° from the x-axis, gives rise to mirror symmetry breaking in the propagation direction. In line with the predicted theory, experimental results shown in Figure 4 match with each other for the forward and backward propagating LP waves. As can be seen from the Figure 15d(ii–iii) that for forward propagating x and y polarised wave ellipticities are −40° and 40°, respectively, thus output waves are LPC and RCP, respectively, with very strong transmission efficiency over a broadband. In contrast, backward propagating x and y polarised wave ellipticities are 40° and −40°, respectively, i.e., polarisation conversation is reversed to RCP and LCP, respectively. The proposed chiral metamaterials in this study show potential advantages of high transmission, broad bandwidth, and multi-functionality, and may find potential applications in polarisation-controlled devices.

3.2. Linear to Cross Polarisation Conversion

The multifunctional structure proposed by Liu et al. [145] missed an important component of 90° polarisation rotation of LP waves. In this regard, Yuqian Ye and Sailing He [157] proposed a bilayer chiral metamaterial (CMM) to realise 90° polarisation rotation with a resonant polarisation conversion efficiency over 90%. Figure 16a shows the schematic diagram of one-unit cell of the present bilayered CMM, while the whole sample is composed of 20 × 20 unit cells as depicted by Figure 16b. In their experiment, the incident wave is polarised in x-direction and normally impinged on the sample. The experimental and simulation results are shown in Figure 16c. The co-polarised transmission (dotted blue line) defined by $|t_{xx}| = \left|E_x^{out}\right|/\left|E_x^{in}\right|$ is below −5 dB in the given frequency range which suppressed below −20 dB around 12 GHz (Figure 16c). On the other hand, the cross polarised transmission (dotted red line), defined as $|t_{yx}| = \left|E_y^{out}\right|/\left|E_x^{in}\right|$ exhibits a resonant peak around 11.4 GHz with maximum amplitude of -2 dB. This clearly indicates polarisation conversion efficiency of over 90% is achieved through the strong rotatory strength in this bilayered CMM. The simulated results shown by solid blue and red lines agree well with the experimental observation. To understand the polarisation rotation in detail, polarisation state of the transmitted signal is studied at six different frequencies as shown in Figure 16e. The polarisation spectrum is shown in Figure 16d.

At low frequency of 10 GHz the transmission is relatively low and the polarisation is slightly off the x-axis with an azimuth of 20°. As the frequency increases, transmission polarisation rotates counterclockwise towards the y-axis followed by increased transmission. At 11.86 GHz maximum transmission is obtained with a polarisation azimuth angle of 86°. With further increase in frequency transmission starts reducing. It is important to note that within the frequency range 11.66–12.10 GHz, output polarisation is aligned in the y-axis. Eventually, at higher frequency the polarisation reverses back toward the x-axis (Figure 16e) in line with the Gaussian profile of the polarisation azimuth spectra of Figure 16d. Such observation confirms the 90° polarisation rotation by the bilayered CMM. In this context, it is also important to mention that in addition to the chiral metamaterial described above, anisotropic metamaterials also can be used for highly efficient conversions from a linear polarisation to its cross polarisation as proposed by Chin et al. [158] and Cui et al. [159]. Following the work by Chin, as shown in Figure 16f that around 10 GHz frequency range, the field intensity of the cross polarisation is close to 0 dB (p1 to p2) and that of the original polarisation (p1 to p1) is less than −20 dB. Such observation clearly depicts cross polarisation conversions with high efficiency.

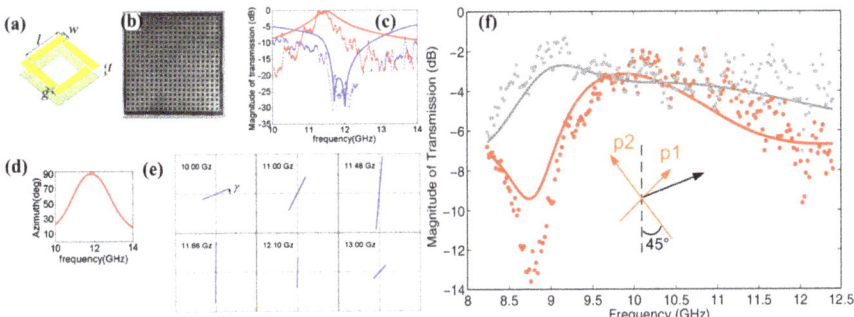

Figure 16. (**a**) Unit cell of the present bilayered CMM for transmission calculation. (**b**) The top view of the fabricated microwave-scale sample. (**c**) Co-polarised and cross-polarised transmission of electric field through the present bilayered CMM by both simulation (solid lines) and experimental measurement (dotted lines). (**d**) Polarisation azimuth of the transmitted wave as the frequency varies. (**e**) Polarisation states at six different frequencies. All the figures were reprinted (adapted) with permission from [157], Copyright 2010, American Institute of Physics. (**f**) The simulated (solid lines) and measured (dots) transmission of electric fields from p1 to p1 (yellow) and from p1 to p2 (blue). The inset shows the orientation for p1 and p2. All the figures were reprinted (adapted) with permission from [158], Copyright 2008, American Institute of Physics.

3.3. Linear to Left and Right Circular Polarisation Conversion

Most of the modern photonics devices are based on the terahertz (THz) technique with numerous significant applications, e.g., homeland security [160], communications and sensing [161], switching [162], etc. Therefore, it is desirable to design polarisation-controlling metamaterial in the THz regime to manipulate the polarisation state of THz wave and can be used as polarisers [163], a polarisation rotator [164] and waveplates [165], etc. Most of those structures suffer from low transmission, limited bandwidth, high cost, size constraint, etc. These shortcomings are overcome by Cong et al. [166] who designed broadband and highly efficient m-QWP fabricated on a free-standing flexible dielectric polymide layer that is sandwiched between the metamaterial layers (metallic grating) as shown in Figure 17a. The first metallic grating is oriented at −45° with respect to the x axis, while the second one is along the x-axis.

In addition, the structure is further capped with two additional polymide layers on the top and bottom of the first and second metallic grating, respectively. For all experiments and simulation, the incident THz wave is linearly polarised along the x-axis. The experimental scheme is based on broadband THz time domain experiment. Similar to the work by Liu et al. [27] polarisation states are numerically determined by Stokes parameter [156]. The ellipticity χ is redefined as $\chi = S_3/S_0$, where $\chi = 1$ and -1 represent LCP and RCP, respectively. It can be seen from Figure 17b that within 1–1.4 THz regime, orthogonal components of transmission, i.e., both co- and cross-polarised transmission, $\left|\overrightarrow{t_{xx}}\right|$ and $\left|\overrightarrow{t_{yx}}\right|$, respectively, have similar amplitude. In the same regime, the phase retardance data in Figure 17c exhibit around 90° (±5°) change, the signature of the functionality of QWP. The results are further substantiated with the ellipticity of $\chi \sim 0.99$ (Figure 17d) between 1 and 1.4 THz, thus depicting nearly perfect broadband LCP. To realise RCP, the first metasurface is oriented to 45°, to make the new m-QWP which is exactly the mirror-symmetry of the pristine QWP. The new QWP is named as negative m-QWP that can introduce −180°/180° phase retardance between the orthogonal components. It can be seen from Figure 17e that like the original m-QWP, orthogonal transmission components for negative m-QWP also reveal a similar transmission value. However, phase retardance is found to be -90° (Figure 17f) and ellipticity gives the value $\chi \sim -0.99$ (Figure 17g) over the broadband, the signature of RCP. The structure has an added advantage on the tunability of the operational THz bandwidth which can easily be adjusted by changing the dimensions of the two metal strips. Apart from that, the structure is found to be very robust against crude handling which makes it ideal for practical device applications. It is important to note that broadband THz linear to circular polarisation conversation also has been theoretically demonstrated by Jiang and co-workers using monolayer black phosphorus (phosphorene) metamaterial [167].

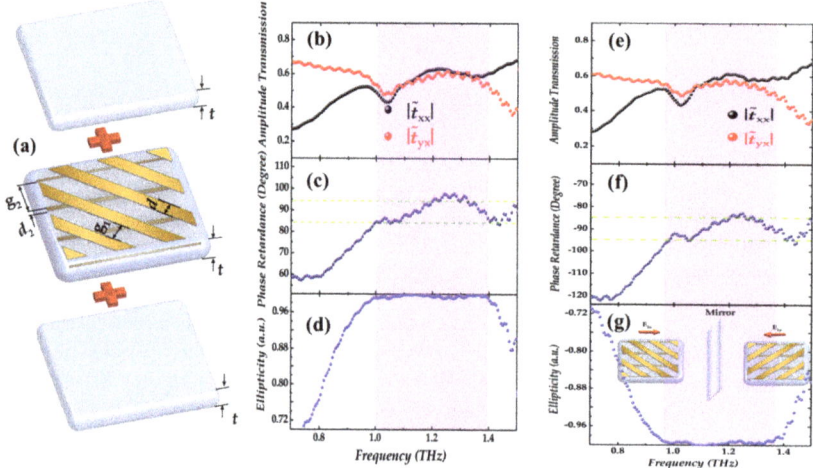

Figure 17. (a) Schematic diagram of the sandwiched metamaterial structure with labelled dimensions. (b) Amplitude transmissions (c) phase retardance between orthogonal components and corresponding (d) ellipticities change. (e) Amplitude transmissions (f) phase retardance between orthogonal components and corresponding (g) ellipticities change for the mirror symmetry sample shown in the inset of (g). All the figures were reprinted (adapted) with permission from [166], Copyright 2014, Wiley-VCH.

3.4. Circular Polarisation Conversion Using Helical Metamaterials

Thus, we are left with the one last important polarisation functionality of the metamaterial, i.e., the circular polarisation switching, in other words, conversion of the handedness of the circular polarisation, i.e., LCP to RCP or vice-versa. Helical metamaterials have been used extensively for this functionality because they exhibit inherent circular dichroism over an unmatched bandwidth above one octave. Depending on the handedness of the circular beam, a helix can either transmit or reflect the incident wave. When the handedness of the helix matches with that of the incoming circular beam, it gets reflected unperturbed whereas for opposite handedness no coupling takes place and light gets transmitted. Different helix structures have been proposed as circular polarisers with high extinction ratio and enhanced bandwidth in the mid-IR region. However, research on the asymmetric circular polarisation conversion has been started of late with generally very narrow operation bandwidths. There are very few experimental designs for circular polarisation conversions over broadband, however, conversion efficiency is well below 50% throughout the operational band, thus making the application limited. For example, Pan and co-workers [168] demonstrated circular polarisation conversion with 20% overall transmission (Figure 18a) using G-shaped chiral metamaterial whereas, Pfeiffer et al. [169] showed conversion from RCP to LCP with a low extinction ratio of 20:1 (Figure 18b). To overcome these shortcomings, Johannes Kaschke [28] proposed a novel helical metamaterial based on unit cells with a single helix. The uniqueness of the structure lies in the fact that the helix changes its handedness halfway through the helix axis. The device can perform high circular polarisation conversion (up to 80%) from RCP to LCP over a bandwidth of more than one octave.

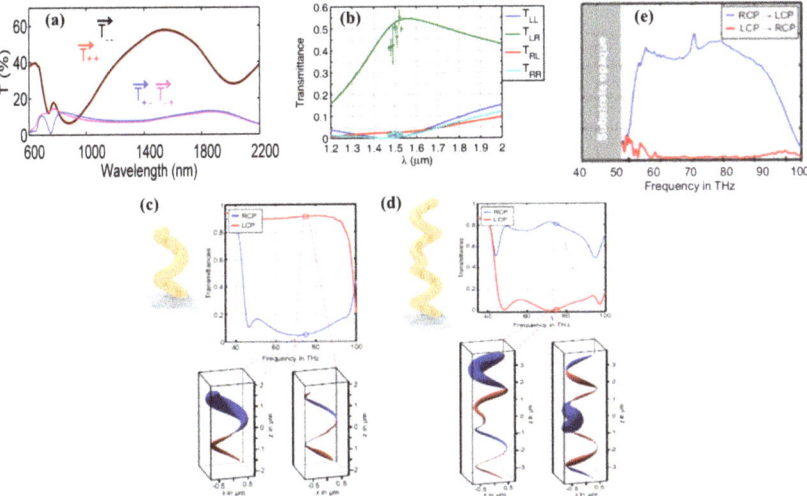

Figure 18. (**a**) Transmission spectra for circular polarisation conversion in G-shaped chiral metamaterial. All the figures were reprinted (adapted) with permission from [168], Copyright 2014, American Institute of Physics. (**b**) Measured (circles) and simulated (solid lines) Jones matrix of the bianisotropic metasurface. All the figures were reprinted (adapted) with permission from [169], Copyright 2014, American Physical Society. The top panels in (**c**,**d**) depict the numerically calculated transmittance spectra for both incident circular polarisations not differentiating between emerging polarisations. In the bottom panels, the calculated normalised current densities are shown for one frequency within the operation band (f = 75 THz). (**e**) Experimental data showing polarisation conversions. All the figures were reprinted (adapted) with permission from [28], Copyright 2015, WILEY-VCH.

To start with, for a single right-handed helix (Figure 18c) an incoming RCP light matches with the helix handedness, couples strongly to it and is reflected with the same handedness. On the contrary, for an incoming LCP light, handedness mismatch leads to no coupling between LCP light and the helix structure, thus gets transmitted as shown in Figure 18c. Following the same logic, for a left-handed helix, the transmitted light will be dominantly RCP. To substantiate this idea, they numerically calculated the current density at f = 75 THz along the helix wire (bottom panel of Figure 18c). For incident RCP, strong coupling leads to large currents at the top end of the helix with little to no transmission, whereas for incident LCP, weak coupling between light and helix structure results in comparably smaller current along the entire helix. Next, they performed the same measurement on the helix structure of both handedness's as shown in Figure 18d. For incoming LCP, the right-handed lower part of the overall structure does not play a role, it transmits to the upper left-handed part. At the top end of the left-handed helix, LCP light undergoes strong coupling and most of the light is therefore reflected. Thus, transmission remains less for incoming LCP. However, for an incoming RCP strong coupling takes place with the bottom right-handed helix, which generates large current that transfers from bottom right- to the top left-handed section of the helix. As a result, the left-handed helix, gets excited and behaves like a helical antenna. Consequently, owing to time-reversal symmetry, the left-handed antenna in the far-field emits LCP, consistent with its handedness. Therefore, the double helix structure converts an incoming RCP to LCP with high efficiency of 75% over a broadband from 50 to 100 THz (Figure 18e). However, for LCP to RCP, the conversion rate remains very low (<10%), over the same frequency regime. Apart from that, Sonsilphong and Wongkasem [170] also demonstrated numerically circular polarisation switching in helical metamaterial.

3.5. Selected Applications of Metamaterials

As discussed in the previous section, metamaterials can arbitrarily manipulate the polarisation state of electromagnetic waves which paves the way to design novel devices for real life applications. Much of the interest in metamaterial devices has stemmed from their potential to overcome fundamental size and bandwidth limitations in conventional optical materials by specific tuning of metamaterial properties, allowing for not only selective manipulation, but also completely novel optical phenomena unseen in natural materials. Engineered metamaterials have advanced research in superlenses, cloaking, holography, while also demonstrating compelling advantages over conventional optical devices [171–173]. The arbitrary wavefront manipulation provided by subwavelength nanostructures affords researchers unparalleled design opportunities for artificial materials, leading to vast and varied approaches to metamaterial devices. Metasurfaces, in particular, have prompted research into the field of flat optics, whereby ultra-thin metadevices provide functionalities previously available only through bulky waveplates and lenses [174]. Functional flat optics would allow for continued miniaturisation of optical systems and devices as well as integration into emerging nanophotonic technologies.

The design flexibility provided by novel metadevices has also allowed researchers to combine multiple optical functionalities into one device, allowing for novel multitasking which would previously require multiple discrete components [175–177]. Very recently, Wang et al. experimentally demonstrated simultaneous beam shaping and focusing using metasurface devices based on silicon nanobricks (Figure 19a) [178]. Careful engineering of the device allowed them to fabricate an optical vortex metalens (OVM) that can produce and focus a vortex beam from incident circularly polarised plane wave. This focusing behaviour is found to vary with the handedness of the polarised light, however, by merging two polarity-inverse OVMs a new device can be created to focus both LCP and RCP light to the same position (Figure 19b–e). Similarly, merging OVMs with different focal points leads to the creation of a new bifocal OVM, allowing the vortex beam to be focused at (Figure 19f) 2 μm and (Figure 19g) 5 μm. Other metadevices allow multiple functions to be performed for light at different wavelengths. Cheng et al. created a multifunctional metasurface based on arrays of plasmonic nanorods (Figure 19h) that demonstrate nearly perfect absorption, linear cross-polarisation and linear-to-circular polarisation conversion for different wavelengths of incident linearly polarised light [179]. For wavelengths ~770nm the device demonstrates absorption (Figure 19i), while at longer wavelengths, the device operates as a polarisation converter, exhibiting linear cross-polarisation at $\lambda = 1227$ nm (Figure 19j) and linear-to-circular polarisation conversion at $\lambda = 1380$ nm (Figure 19k).

Engineered metasurface optics also enable the construction of dynamically tunable and active devices not possible with conventional materials. Many metadevices have been demonstrated to dynamically change their optical properties in response to external stimuli. Thermal, electromagnetic, electromechanical and optical influences have all been shown to dynamically alter metasurface functionalities, allowing for metadevices to be precisely tuned to illicit desired effects, without prefabrication of the device [180]. Microelectromechanical systems (MEMS) fabricated in CMOS compatible materials have been employed as reconfigurable metasurfaces, using the deflection of microcantilever arrays to alter polarisation response.

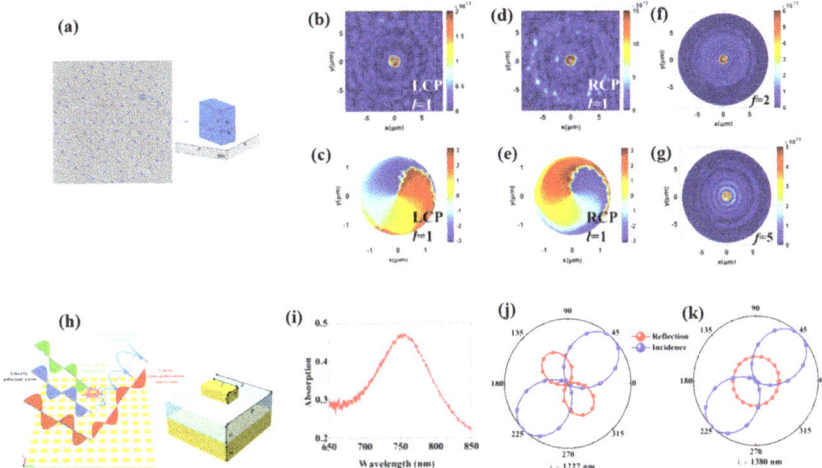

Figure 19. A multifunctional metasurface fabricated from silicon nanobricks functioning as an optical vortex metalens (OVM) allowing for simultaneous beam shaping and focusing ($\lambda = 1500$ nm). (**a**) Schematic of the metasurface and constituent nanobricks. Intensity (**b**,**d**) and phase (**c**,**e**) distributions for left and right circularly polarised light demonstrating the ability to shape and focus light of opposite handedness. Intensity distributions for the bifocal OVM, demonstrating focusing at (**f**) f = 2 μm and (**g**) f = 5 μm. All the figures were reprinted (adapted) with permission from [178], Copyright 2020, Elsevier. (**h**) A multifunctional metasurface consisting of nanorod arrays demonstrating nearly perfect absorption, cross-polarisation and linear-to-circular polarisation conversion for different wavelengths of incident light. (**i**) Measured absorption showing maximum absorption at ~ 770nm. Measured intensity at different polarisations for incident and reflected light illustrating (**j**) cross polarisation and (**k**) linear-to-circular polarisation conversion at $\lambda = 1227$ nm and 1380 nm, respectively. All the figures were reprinted (adapted) with permission from [179], Copyright 2017, American Institute of Physics.

Work by Ma et al. demonstrated structurally reconfigurable metasurfaces based on MEMS resonator arrays to create polarisation sensitive terahertz filters (Figure 20a). Deflection of the curved microcantilevers by an applied electric field allows for dynamic tuning of the device's resonant frequency, leading to tuning of transmitted light for *e*-polarisation while *o*-polarised light remains unaltered. A similar device operating on a thermoelectric principle was demonstrated by Ho et al. [181]. In their device current through the microactuator arrays leads to Joule heating that deflects the microcantilevers, altering the polarisation response at terahertz frequencies (Figure 20b). Further polarisation manipulation and control using MEMS metadevices was demonstrated by Zhao et al. as they realised tunable circular-to-linear polarisation conversion through voltage based microcantilever actuation (Figure 20c) [182]. Novel metadevices have recently been created using other materials and techniques. Nouman and others utilised the insulator to metal transition in vanadium dioxide to create a tunable metasurface device operating at terahertz frequencies. The metasurface is created from wire grating array on VO_2 thin film patches (Figure 20d). Varying the current through the device triggers the insulator to metal transition, altering the resonant frequency of the device for incident polarisations perpendicular to the wire grating and modulating the phase of transmitted light. Parallel polarisations, however, do not experience a current dependent phase shift, allowing phase to be independently varied for orthogonal polarisations. As such, specific tuning of the device enables circular-to-linear polarisation conversion at THz frequencies. A novel liquid metal-based metasurface device was demonstrated by Wu et al. to allow for reconfigurable polarisation response within a microfluidic platform [183]. The device consisted of individually addressable L-shaped microfluidic resonators filled with liquid Galinstan (Figure 20e). The length of both arms in the L-shaped resonators can be varied by tuning the pressure at both outlets, leading to changes in the polarisation response of orthogonal polarisations. Accordingly, tuning of their device allowed for linear-to-linear, linear-to-circular and linear-to-elliptical polarisation conversions. The versatility provided by engineered metamaterials gives metadevices a unique advantage over conventional optics. Ultrathin metasurfaces continue to demonstrate their utility for wavefront shaping and manipulation, demonstrating functional flat optics in proof of principle devices. Merging, stacking and cascading of separate 2D devices has led to multifunctional metasurface devices, allowing for simultaneous control of multiple optical parameters or specified functions for specified wavelengths. Individually addressable and tunable elements in metadevice arrays lead to tuning of the metadevice, allowing for active metasurfaces to be controlled and reconfigured in a variety of ways. Future devices based on engineered metamaterials will afford users unparalleled versatility in numerous applications through tunable, multifunctional and ultrathin optical wavefront manipulation.

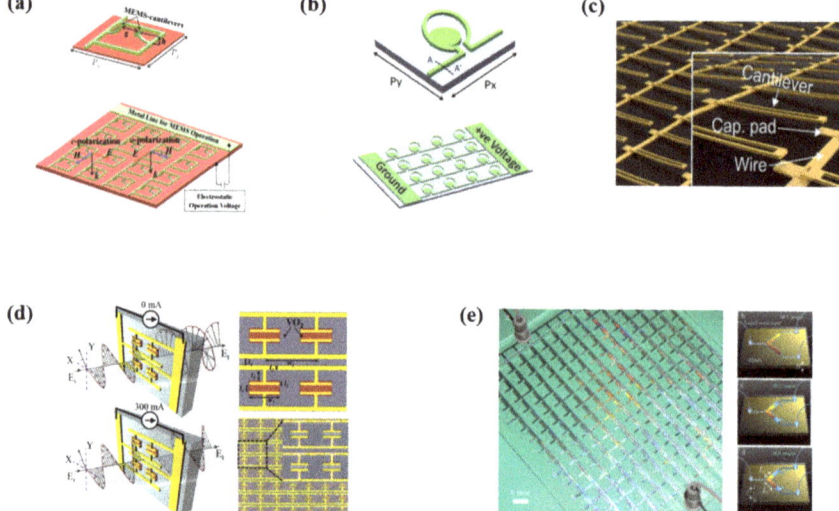

Figure 20. (**a–c**) Tuneable MEMS metasurfaces created using CMOS compatible materials operating at terahertz frequencies. Polarisation filter devices achieved through electromechanical (**a**) and electrothermal (**b**) actuation of microcantilever arrays. All the figures were reprinted (adapted) with permission from [181,184], Copyright 2014 and Copyright 2013, American Institute of Physics, respectively. (**c**) Reconfigurable linear-to-circular polarisation conversion whereby voltage based actuation of the microcantilevers allows tuning of the metasurface polarisation response. All the figures were reprinted (adapted) with permission from [182], Copyright 2018, The Optical Society. (**d**) Switchable, voltage-operated quarter wave plate metadevices operating via the insulator to metal transition in Vanadium Dioxide. All the figures were reprinted (adapted) with permission from [185], Copyright 2018, The Optical Society. (**e**) Tuneable polarisation converter metadevice based on a liquid-metal microfluidic platform whereby polarisation response is varied by tuning the length of L-shaped resonator metasurface-elements. All the figures were reprinted (adapted) with permission from [183], Copyright 2017, WILEY-VCH.

4. Polarisation Measurements of Magnetic-Plasmonic Nanostructures

In this third and final section, we will discuss the role of polarisation in magnetic-plasmonic nanostructures. Beginning with a general introduction to magneto-optics and magnetoplasmonics, we will then discuss the role of plasmonics in the Faraday effect, inverse Faraday effect and magneto-optical Kerr effect. Next, we will briefly discuss magnetic plasmon resonances. Then magnetic second-harmonic generation and magnetic circular dichroism will be reviewed. Finally, several magnetoplasmonics-based applications will be explored.

The study of magneto-optical (MO) effects dates back to 1845 when Michael Faraday discovered that the plane of polarisation of light is rotated when passing through an optically transparent dielectric material under an external magnetic field (Faraday rotation). This effect, later called the Faraday effect, was the first experimental evidence of the connection between light and electromagnetism [186]. The Faraday effect is a result of the left and right circularly polarised (LCP and RCP) light propagating at different speeds through the material (phase difference). Later, John Kerr found that light reflected from a magnetic surface could change intensity and polarisation, which was later named the Kerr effect. In reflection, linearly polarised light was seen to rotate (Kerr rotation) and reflected light can become elliptically polarised (Kerr ellipticity). Microscopically, MO effects require both exchange splitting and spin–orbit interactions [187]. Macroscopically, these MO effects depend on the off-diagonal (antisymmetric) elements of the permittivity tensor associated with the material. Magneto-optic technologies have been applied to microscopy (Kerr microscope) [188], magneto-optic memory devices [189], optical isolators [190], wave modulators [191] and magnetic field sensors [192].

The fields of plasmonics and magnetics merged about 100 years later when Chiu and Quinn discovered that external magnetic fields affect the surface plasmon on metal [193]. Later, with the progression of nanofabrication, complex nanoarchitectures could be developed to further exploit this interaction, bringing forth exciting new physics and applications. In this section, we will discuss magnetoplasmonics, with a special emphasis on a vital component of its measurement—polarisation. The polarisation state of light is integral to magneto-optic measurements, as in MO materials the magnetic field causes optical anisotropy. This optical anisotropy can be quantified by the non-diagonal terms of the permittivity tensor of the material, which leads to variations in the intensity and polarisation state of light.

A plasmon can be used to enhance MO effects, as at the LSPR, diagonal and off-diagonal terms of the permittivity tensor are enhanced. A simple coupled oscillator model has recently been proposed by Floess and Giessen to explain the magnetoplasmonic interaction [194]. Typically, noble metals like silver and gold are selected for plasmonic applications thanks to their low optical losses in the visible and near-infrared spectral range, giving rise to a sharp plasmon peak. These efficient plasmonic materials usually have minimal MO activity, and thus are not suited for MO applications alone. Conversely, some magnetic materials have strong MO effects but cannot sustain a strong plasmon due to optical losses. For this reason, most magnetoplasmonic structures combine a noble metal and a magnetic material, typically a ferromagnetic material, into a hybrid structure. Ferromagnetic materials, unlike paramagnetic materials, possess spontaneous magnetisation resulting from the long-range ordering of unpaired electron spins, and when magnetised, the bulk magnetisation is strong and retained by the material. Most ferromagnetic materials have optical losses too large to sustain a plasmon, except nickel nanoparticles, which have exhibited both localised surface plasmon and ferromagnetism [195].

There are two main reasons to design magnetoplasmonic structures, firstly, to modulate the LSPR response by using external magnetic fields and secondly, to increase the MO effects using the LSPR. These two scenarios, i.e., magnetic field modulation of the LSPR and plasmon-enhanced MOs, are both referred to as magnetoplasmonics; however, the term magnetoplasmonic is also often used to describe systems that combine magnetic and plasmonic materials without the direct study of the magnetic–plasmon interaction [196,197]. By combining MO and plasmonic activity into a single nanostructure, electronic hybridisation between the magnetic and plasmonic material is anticipated, and localisation of the magnetic field near to the plasmonic material takes place [198]. In ferromagnetic materials, the conduction electron spins are spin-polarised, which can affect the free electrons of the plasmonic material (electronic hybridisation). Therefore, the magnetic material must be metallic in nature. Secondly, for magnetic field localisation near the plasmon, the magnetic field of the material must be sufficiently strong and does not necessarily need to interact with the free electrons of the plasmonic material (no hybridisation) and therefore, does not need to be metallic [198]. Without hybridisation, the LSPR and MO response must be spectrally distinct; otherwise, the magnetoplasmonic response at the plasmon frequency would not be distinguishable from other frequencies [198]. The plasmon-enhancement of the MO effects can be improved by introducing the plasmon-associated enhanced local electric field near to the MO material and/or by changing the reflectivity of the material to maximise the reflected/transmitted optical signal.

4.1. Faraday Effect and Inverse Faraday Effect

Measurement of the Faraday effect is straightforward, linearly polarised light is passed through the sample subject to an external magnetic field (parallel with light propagation) which then passes through an analyser and is detected. In 2005, enhanced Faraday (polarisation) rotation was observed in $CoFe_2O_4$-Ag, dumbbell-like nanoparticles. An enhancement of the Faraday effect was observed for nanoparticles with the plasmonic component (dimer) compared to the $CoFe_2O_4$ monomer [199]. For this experiment, six different laser wavelengths (385, 421, 455, 532, 633 and 850 nm) were used with varying magnetic fields from −1000 to 1000 Oe to collect a Faraday rotation (FR) loop as a function of the magnetic field. Both the $CoFe_2O_4$ nanoparticles with and without Ag exhibited a maximum absorption for the 385 nm laser. Both samples gave a large FR of about 0.75°, but the Ag dimer had a marginally larger rotation. The difference between the samples became more pronounced at longer wavelengths. Beyond 633 nm, the FR for monomer $CoFe_2O_4$ changed sign, i.e., instead of positive FR at positive magnetic fields, negative FRs were observed at positive magnetic fields. Such sign reversal was not observed for the plasmonic hybrid nanostructures (see Figure 21a). Plasmon-enhanced FR has also been observed in magnetic-plasmonic, γ-Fe_2O_3-Au, core-shell nanoparticles suspended in solution [200]. Using a tunable laser, an improved spectral resolution was obtained compared to the $CoFe_2O_4$ that used select laser wavelengths. Here, a clear peak in the FR spectrum was observed for the gold-coated γ-Fe_2O_3 at the LSPR (~540 nm), which was not observed in uncoated nanoparticles (Figure 21b). Later, the FR was also found to be dependent on the cobalt core radius with silver shells when the total diameter is fixed [201]. As the LSPR blue-shifted due to higher silver content, the FR maximum also blue-shifted with higher magnitude.

The FR is not limited to nanoparticle form. Chin et al. studied yttrium and bismuth iron garnet films with gold nanowires deposited periodically, maintaining high transparency [202]. Polarisation rotation due to the Faraday effect was enhanced by one order of magnitude owing to the plasmonic structures, with spectral dependency on the period of the nanowires (see Figure 21c). Plasmon-enhanced FR was also observed in Bi:YIG films with a gold nanoparticle coating [203]. The measurements were conducted between 500 and 700 nm, with a plasmon-associated absorption observed at ~630 nm. When the angle of rotation of the light polarisation was studied using an external magnetic field of 5 kOe, a clear peak is observed at the SPR maximum which was not observed in the sample without gold coating. Floess et al. observed a tunable and switchable polarisation rotation in gold nanowire coated EuSe thin films [204]. In these structures, the period and the width of the gold nanowires allowed wavelength selectivity; and rotations up to 8.4° were observed. Recently, Kuzmichev et al. studied Bi-substituted iron garnet films with gold nanodisks at different depths [205]. They found that the Faraday effect was most enhanced by the gold nanodisk plasmon when submerged near the upper surface of the magnetic film (see Figure 21d). This finding may aid the future design of plasmon-enhanced FR materials.

Along with noble metal plasmons, single and multilayer graphene deposited on SiC substrate demonstrated large FR, as a result of either the cyclotron effect or inter-Landau-level transitions [206]. Large magnetic fields of 7 T were used to achieve FR of ~6° within 2–4 THz range. Later, Tymchenko et al. calculated large FR in graphene microribbon arrays at higher frequencies (>10 THz) and with smaller magnetic fields than in continuous graphene sheets [207], thus opening up new possibilities in ultrathin tunable MO devices.

Magnetisation can also be induced in purely metallic structures through illumination with circularly polarised light; this is called the inverse Faraday effect. This measurement is typically conducted using time-resolved pump-probe, with the pump beam circularly polarised and the probe beam linearly polarised. The scheme is similar to standard Faraday effect measurements, but with the absence of an external magnetic field and the filtering out of the pump beam. First observed in DyFeO$_3$ [208], inverse Faraday effect was seen in various films [209,210]. Recently, the inverse Faraday effect was observed in gold nanoparticles in solution [211].

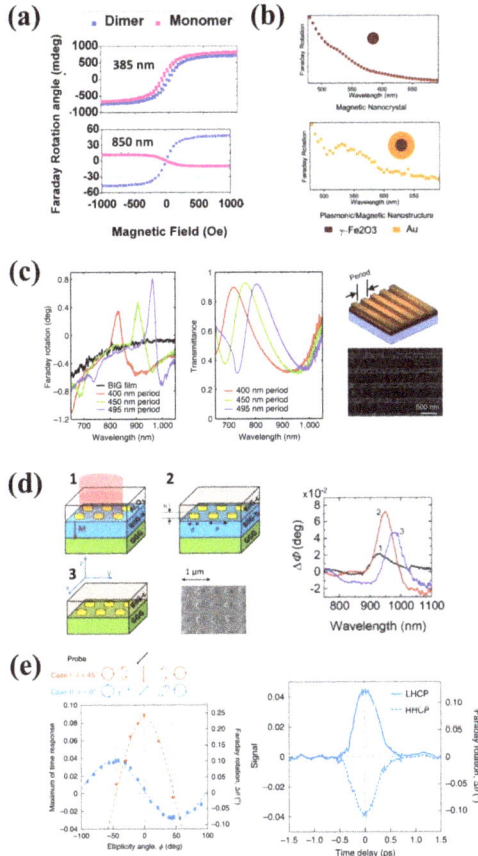

Figure 21. (**a**) FR of CoFe$_2$O$_4$ nanoparticles (monomer, pink) and CoFe$_2$O$_4$-Ag nanoparticles (dimer, blue) at 385 (top) and 850 nm (bottom), showing a reversal in the magnetisation loop only for the monomer nanoparticles at long wavelengths. Adapted with permission from [199], Copyright 2005, American Chemical Society. (**b**) FR of iron oxide nanoparticles (top) enhanced by gold coating (bottom), with a peak corresponding to the LSPR of the nanoparticle. Adapted with permission from [200], Copyright 2009, American Chemical Society. (**c**) FR and transmittance dependency on gold nanowire period atop a magnetic film. Adapted with permission from [202], Copyright 2013, Springer Nature. (**d**) Plasmon-enhanced FR of samples (1–3) with different depths of gold nanodisks in films, with sample 2 where nanodisks are submerged inside the magnetic film achieving the highest rotation. Adapted with permission from [205], Copyright 2020, Wiley-VCH. (**e**) Inverse Faraday effect in gold nanoparticles measured using a pump-probe setup. Left, FR for different ellipticity angles (φ) of the pump, for two different polarisation angles between the pump beam and probe (δ), with a maximum for δ = 45° at linear polarisation (Kerr effect) and at δ = 0° for circular polarisation (φ = 45°) (inverse Faraday effect). Right, time response of Faraday rotation, showing picosecond regime magnetisation and demagnetisation. Adapted with permission from [211], Copyright 2020, Springer Nature.

In this work, a pump-probe setup was used. The linearly polarised probe beam was passed through the sample and detected with an analyser, while the pump beam was circularly polarised to induce the inverse Faraday effect. The ellipticity angle (φ), handedness and polarisation angle between the pump beam and probe (δ) were varied to confirm the inverse Faraday effect (see Figure 21e). Where δ = 0°, increased pump ellipticity led to increased FR, with maximums for pure LCP and RCP light; while for δ = 45°, the maximum rotation was observed for linear polarisation (arising from the Kerr effect). Furthermore, the time-response indicated the mechanism was related to the coherent circular motion of the electrons in the gold nanoparticles as opposed to the spin dynamics as seen in ferromagnetic materials, shown in the right panel of Figure 21e.

4.2. Magneto-Optic Kerr Effect

There are three types of magneto-optic Kerr effect (MOKE) measurement techniques, which are classified by the sample's magnetisation vector direction with respect to the sample surface and the incident light [188]. Polar MOKE (PMOKE) denotes the measurement where magnetisation vector is orthogonal to the surface and parallel to the incident light plane, longitudinal MOKE (LMOKE) corresponds to a magnetisation vector in parallel with the surface and incident light plane and lastly, the transverse MOKE (TMOKE) involves the magnetisation vector orthogonal to the light plane and parallel to the surface [188]. All three types of MOKE measurements have been employed in magneto-plasmonic measurement. P/LMOKE are used to study the effects of the plasmon on the reflected light polarisation, while TMOKE involves a plasmon-enhancement of the reflected light intensity.

Plasmonic nickel nanoferromagnet discs have shown plasmon-controlled Kerr rotation, in LMOKE configuration [212]. Three differently sized nanodisks with distinct LSPR responses were studied with two excitation lasers (405 and 670 nm), with MOKE rotation exhibiting contrasting characteristics for the differently sized discs. For the smallest disc diameter, the magnetisation loop shows a maximum MOKE rotation for negative magnetic fields for both wavelengths, while the largest disc shows a maximum MOKE rotation for positive magnetic fields for both wavelengths. Conversely, for the intermediate disc size, the MOKE magnetisation loop shows an excitation wavelength-dependent sign change (see Figure 22a). Considering nickel-based magnetoplasmonics avoid the complex chemistry and fabrication techniques often required for hybrid plasmonic-ferromagnetic structures, this observation opened up a more straightforward method to study and apply plasmon-enhanced MO.

Surface plasmons have been shown to enhance the PMOKE effect in Au/Co/Au multilayer films [213], then later in Au/Co/Au nanodisks [214]. The optical and MO properties of the latter could be tuned by varying the nanoparticle disk size and shape. Recently, asymmetric geometry magnetoplasmonic nanocavities were designed which support multipolar dark plasmons [215]. In this work, gold nanoring arrays had a permalloy nanoparticle disc added inside, either in the centre to create the symmetric nanocavity (CRD) or off centre, forming the asymmetric cavity (NCRD) (see Figure 22b). The authors showed unprecedented MO enhancement in the broken symmetry structure, facilitating effective control of light polarisation using weak magnetic fields. This enhancement was explained by dark multipolar Fano resonance modes (at ~820 nm, see Figure 22b middle and bottom panel) in the ring nanostructure hybridising and enhancing the magnetic-field-induced radiant dipole of the permalloy, measured using PMOKE configuration.

Kreilkamp et al. reported 1.5% modulation of transmitted light intensity, using plasmonic gold nanowire enhanced TMOKE while maintaining transparency of ~45% [216]. The 1.5% modulation occurred when the localised plasmon hybridised with the propagating waveguide mode of the nanowire. By reducing the period of the nanowires, the resonance seen in the transmission and TMOKE spectra could be blue-shifted, with a gradual reduction in the TMOKE signal (see Figure 22c). MO activity was also detected in gold nanoparticles sputtered on glass in TMOKE configuration, which was also applied to SPR refractive index sensing [217]. Rizal et al. recently compared the efficiency of Ti/Au/Co/Au against Ti/Ag/Co/Au by using two plasmonic sensing schemes (TMOKE vs.

SPR) [218] (see Figure 22d). Both of the samples showed TMOKE enhancement over the SPR, while the Ag-based one gave overall higher TMOKE and SPR activity. They found that the TMOKE sensor had a Q-factor more than twice that of the SPR sensor, and suggested this enhanced sensitivity could be used to detect lower analyte concentrations.

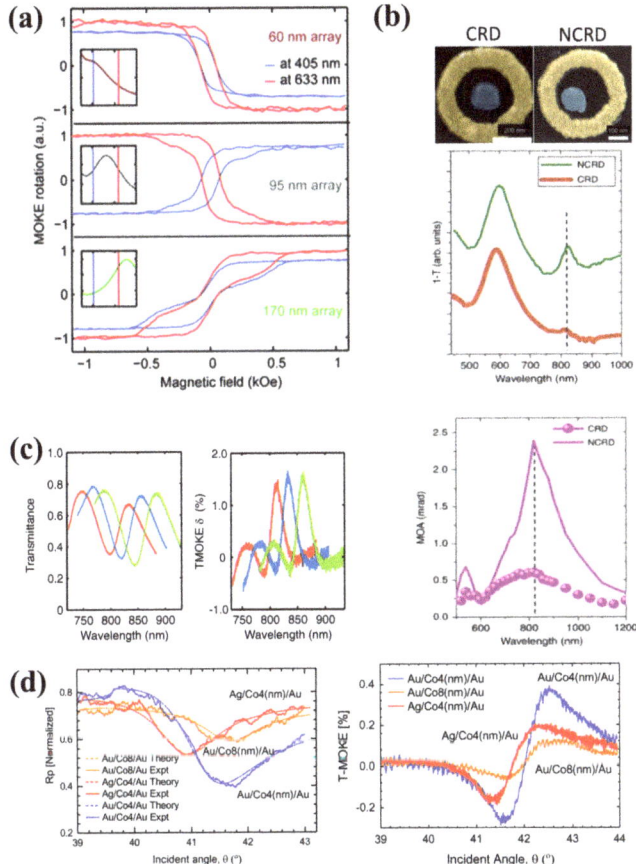

Figure 22. (**a**) LMOKE rotation studies of nickel nanodisks with varying diameters (60, 95 and 170 nm) at 405 and 633 nm, with insets of the extinction spectrum of the nanodisks arrays. A clear wavelength-dependent MOKE magnetisation loop reversal can be seen for the 95 nm array. Adapted with permission from [212], Copyright 2011, American Chemical Society. (**b**) Scanning electron microscopy images of magnetoplasmonic concentric ring disks (CRD) and non-concentric ring disk (NCRD) composed of a gold ring and $Fe_{20}Ni_{80}$ enclosed disk, the transmittance spectra are shown below in the middle panel. The green transmittance spectra correspond to NCRD which has a second peak that can be observed at 820 nm. MO activity (measured by PMOKE) of the nanocavities is shown in the bottom panel, with a large enhancement at 820 nm in the asymmetric cavity. Adapted from [215], CC BY 3.0 2020, Springer Nature. (**c**) Transmittance and TMOKE of iron garnet films with gold nanowires deposited atop with varying period, 450 nm (red), 475 nm (blue), and 500-nm period (green). The TMOKE peak can be seen to redshift with increased period. Adapted from [216], CC BY 2013, American Physical Society. (**d**) P-polarisation reflectivity and TMOKE profiles for Au/Co/Au or Ag/Co/Au samples, used to find the quality factor of the different sensing schemes. Adapted with permission from [218], Copyright 2020, IOP Publishing.

4.3. Magnetic Plasmon Resonances

At optical frequencies, the magnetic permeability of most materials is small and, therefore, the magnetic interaction is typically less than electric interaction, likewise; magnetic plasmon resonances at optical frequencies are more challenging to achieve in natural materials. Pendry et al. [219] demonstrated resonance of the magnetic plasmon incident on double split-ring resonator structures, tuning the effective magnetic permeability of nonmagnetic material to negative values. Furthermore, the permeability could be tuned by changing the geometry of the nanostructure, but the resonance was limited to the microwave region. These split ring structures were modelled as a LC circuit, with a capacitance (C) and inductance (L). In this model, the ring structure can be considered a coil winding, while the branches of the horseshoe are capacitor plates. By scaling down the dimensions of the nanostructure, the inductance and capacitance of the structure also scale down. As the resonant frequency of an LC circuit is inversely proportional to the product of the inductance and capacitance, scaling down the structure was assumed to lead to an increased resonance frequency. Klein et al. [220] demonstrated a breakdown of this rule, achieving a magnetic plasmon resonance in more compact horseshoe split rings at 900 nm. The authors attribute this to the metal deviating from "ideal" metal explained by the Drude model (LC resonance frequency << plasma frequency of the metal), and instead the complex dielectric function of the metal was needed to support the experimental results theoretically. Horizontal light polarisation at normal incidence may be used to excite the magnetic resonance by the electric field component by inducing a circulating circuit in the structure, provided it is perpendicular to the branches of the horseshoe-like, split ring structure. For vertical polarisation at normal incidence, neither the electric nor magnetic field can excite the LC resonance. However, both linear polarisations may excite the electric resonance of the structure, and so the different polarisation schemes can be used to identify the magnetic and electric plasmon resonances.

Bao et al. [221] studied gold split ring hexamer nanostructures using scattering spectroscopy, showing magnetic and electric plasmon modes appearing depending on the illumination polarisation, shown in Figure 23a. Two electrical dipolar modes were observed at 650 and 775 nm. The magnetic dipole mode was observed at 900 nm, which results from the x-component of the electric field and could only be detected using azimuthally polarised light. This magnetic mode was most prominent for 0° (parallel to split) and decreased in magnitude with increased angle of incidence. These experimental findings were supported by finite-difference time-domain (FDTD) simulations, supporting the authors' experimental determination of the magnetic and electric resonances by polarisation resolved scattering spectroscopy. Furthermore, these split-ring hexamer structures were then assembled into 6-piece and 12-piece ring structures that exhibited narrowband single and double Fano resonance, respectively. The narrow FWHM of these Fano resonances is noteworthy for lineshape engineering applications.

Kuznetsov et al. partially cut gold and silver nanoparticles into split-ball resonator structures shown in the top panel of Figure 23b [222]. These split-ball resonators are similar to upright split-ring resonators, but these structures facilitate coupling of the incident light to the magnetic resonance mode yielding higher efficiency owing to a combined electric and magnetic field contribution (LC mode). These split balls were capable of sustaining a magnetic plasmon at 600 nm in gold and 565 nm in silver. To study the electric and magnetic plasmons, s- and p-polarised light was used. P-polarised light was expected to couple with the electric dipole resonance, whereas the s-polarisation excited both the electric and magnetic dipole (LC) (see Figure 23b). Simulations showed that the deeper the depth of the cut in the nanosphere, the more blue-shifted the LC resonance while increasing the width of the cut led to a red-shifting of the LC resonance.

DNA-origami-based strategies have been used by Wang et al. to assemble gold nanoparticles into hexagon rings and then combining these rings into more complex nanoarchitectures, which were subsequently coated with silver [223], as depicted in the left panel of Figure 23c. In the single DNA origami ring composed of six nanoparticles, the peak at ~520 nm is the electric dipole whereas the smaller peak at ~570 nm is attributed to the magnetic dipole, which could be isolated by using a cross-analyser. Combining these rings into more complex structures, yielded scattering spectra with multiple modes, and magnetic SPPs could be supported in ring chain-like structures. For further details about magnetic plasmons, a comprehensive review on optical magnetism was carried out by Monticone and Alù [224] and by Calandrini et al. on magnetic hot-spots [225].

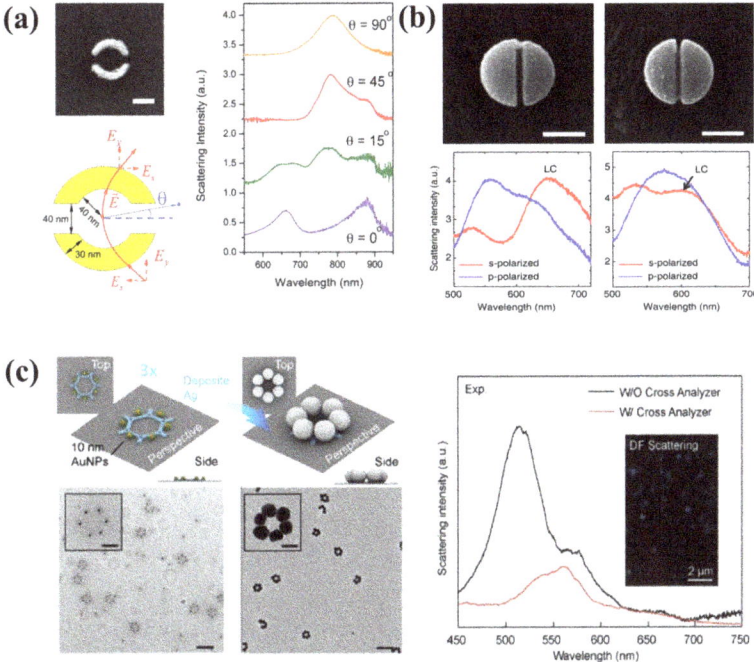

Figure 23. (**a**) Split ring nanostructure image and geometry, right, scattering spectra of nanorings with differing angles of incidence. At $0°$, two resonances are observed 650 (electric) and 870 nm (magnetic), then at $15°$ a third mode at 750 nm (electric) appears and becomes prominent for the larger angles. Adapted with permission from [221], Copyright 2015, Wiley-VCH. (**b**) Electron microscopy image of split ball resonators, gold nanoparticles with a cut width of 15 nm, with different depths (where left is deeper). Below, their respective scattering spectra where s-polarisation light polarisation perpendicular to the cut and p-polarisation is parallel. The marked LC resonance is the combined electric and magnetic resonance, while the p-polarised peak is attributed to electric resonance. Adapted with permission from [222], Copyright 2014, Springer Nature. (**c**) Simplified construction of gold nanoparticles assembled using DNA origami, which are subsequently coated with silver, scattering spectra of the nanostructure, with the electric (520 nm) and magnetic dipolar contributions (570 nm). Adapted with permission from [223], Copyright 2019, Wiley-VCH.

4.4. Second-Harmonic Generation (SHG)

Second-harmonic generation (SHG) is a nonlinear optical phenomenon where two photons of coherent light with the same frequency interact with a material and combine to generate a new photon that has twice the frequency of the incident photons. SHG is sensitive to breaks in the spatial or temporal inversion symmetry of material, and so has been applied to study magnetics (MSHG) by adding the application of an external magnetic field. MSHG has better sensitivity to interfaces than linear MOKE, owing to the increased sensitivity to breaks in symmetry. In the simplest form, SHG setups consist of a fundamental laser focused onto the sample that generates the SHG signal, the fundamental signal is filtered out and the SHG signal is sent to the detector, in either reflection or transmission.

Symmetry **2020**, *12*, 1365

Purely plasmonic nanostructures have demonstrated plasmon-enhanced (non-magnetic) SHG [226] and third harmonic generation, (non-magnetic) THG [227]. Similarly, magnetic-dipole plasmons have been shown to enhance (non-magnetic) SHG activity in metal–dielectric–metal disk nanoparticles [228] and colloidal gold nanocups [229]. Silicon nanodiscs that exhibit both electric and magnetic dipolar resonances were shown to have enhanced third-harmonic generation near the magnetic dipolar resonance [230].

Nickel nanorods have exhibited plasmon-enhanced MOKE, both linear and nonlinear (MSHG) [231]. The geometric anisotropy of the nanorods led to differing contributions to the second-order susceptibility tensor that has magnetisation and crystallographic dependent components. Linear measurements (TMOKE) were performed using p-polarised light at an incident angle of 68° and was varied between 300 and 850 nm. The TMOKE spectrum exhibits a peak at 380 nm, corresponding to the transverse plasmon of the nanorods. A second peak emerged at 600 nm in the TMOKE spectrum, which was also seen as a minimum in the reflectivity spectra, and therefore was attributed to the Fabry–Perot resonance mode of the material. Magnetic and nonmagnetic SHG measurements were conducted using s- and p-polarised light at various angles of incidence. Nonmagnetic SHG showed no resonant features, while its magnetic counterpart showed a maximum at 760 nm (twice the fundamental wavelength) for the s-polarised pump beam, but was not observed in the p-polarised pump beam spectra and thus, is not an effect of interference (see Figure 24a). The 100 nm gold nanoparticle arrays covered with a 90 nm thick layer of iron garnet exhibited MSHG which could be spectrally shifted (by up to 5 nm) by changing the magnetic field direction [232] (see Figure 24b). This spectral shift is not attributed to shifting of the LSPR, but rather due to interference of resonant and nonresonant MSHG signals of both crystallographic and magnetic origin.

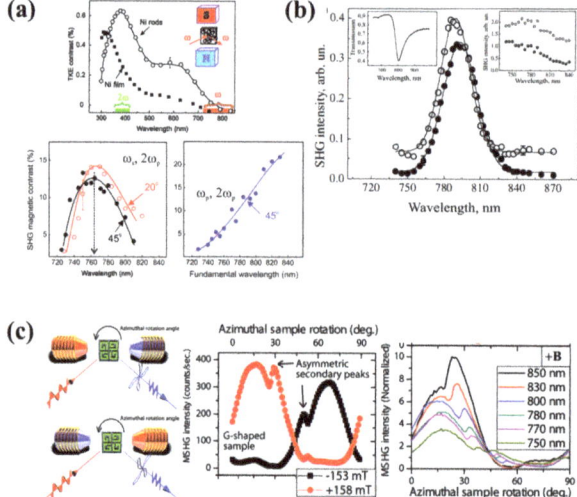

Figure 24. (**a**) MOKE spectrum obtained for nickel nanorod (open circles) vs. film material (filled squares) with fundamental and doubled frequency marked. Below left, MSHG magnetic contrast spectrum of the nickel nanorod is given for two angles of incidence of s-polarised light, a maximum is observed for 760 nm, where the SHG emission matches the LSPR maximum of 380 nm. Below right, the same for p-polarised light with an absence of peak. Adapted with permission from [231], Copyright 2013, American Physical Society. (**b**) MSHG spectra for gold nanoparticle array coated by an iron garnet

layer with an applied magnetic field of varied sign (positive open circle, negative filled circle), showing a spectral shift. Insets show the transmission spectra and MSHG for a non-plasmonic film. Adapted with permission from [232], Copyright 2016, The Optical Society. (c) MSHG of G-shaped nickel nanostructures to determine magnetisation direction, where the sample is rotated azimuthally in different magnetic field directions. The four-fold polarisation profile is asymmetric (secondary peaks) and resembles a ratchet wheel. Middle, MSHG intensity as a function of rotation angle for two magnetic fields, a clear asymmetry can be seen. Right, the MSHG for different wavelengths, with longer wavelengths yielding high MSHG intensity. Adapted with permission from [233], Copyright 2011, American Chemical Society.

Valev et al. used the plasmon contributions to the MSHG to find the magnetisation direction in G-shaped Ni nanostructures [233]. Here, the surface plasmons could create asymmetries in the rotational dependant MSHG response, similar to a ratchet wheel, so that directionality could be inferred (see Figure 24c). In this work, the magnetic field is in the plane of optical incidence, with the polariser and analyser along the vertical direction. In this configuration, a single odd element of the effective nonlinear susceptibility tensor contributes to the signal. Asymmetric peaks and magnetic field direction dependence can be seen in the MSHG intensity as a function of azimuthal sample rotation. Furthermore, the position of the secondary peak depends on the wavelength. The asymmetric MSHG response is therefore attributed to the plasmon, where incident light selectively couples to the plasmon modes of the nanostructure at certain sample rotation angles.

4.5. Magnetic Circular Dichroism

Magnetic circular dichroism (MCD), an extension of circular dichroism (CD), is a technique where the difference between a sample's absorption of right and left circularly polarised light is measured in the presence of an external magnetic field. MCD has been used to study circularly propagating magnetoplasmonic modes in symmetric gold nanospheres, where MCD signal is a derivative-like, bisignated curve with the x-axis crossover point aligning spectrally with the LSPR [234] (see Figure 25a).

The MCD bisignated curve is a result of the differing response of the electrons in the nanoparticle to the incoming LCP and RCP light, with the polarisations shifted in energy per the right panel in Figure 25a. Thanks to the sensitivity of the LSPR to the refractive index of the surrounding medium and the strong dependency of the MCD signal on this LSPR, MCD measurements utilising plasmonic nanoparticles have good potential in refractometric sensing. MCD was also used to monitor the linking of silver-coated gold nanorods to supramolecular J-aggregates [235]. When the J-band exciton and plasmons coupled at resonance, enhancements were observed in the MCD signal. This finding opened up the possibility of magnetic-based chemo- and biosensing.

Shiratsu and Yao demonstrated that the bisignated MCD dipolar response of Ag nanocubes depends strongly on the nanocube edge length, with the zero crossover point in the MCD spectra corresponding to the LSPR maximum [236]. Furthermore, the smallest nanocube exhibited the highest MCD as shown in Figure 25b, and this size dependency arises from spectral inhomogeneity in the LSPR extinction. In stark contrast, MCD signal attributed to higher-order multipolar LSPR modes did not correspond to the optical extinction spectra and was size-independent, which the authors hypothesised was as a result of an unequal response to the RCP and LCP light under the magnetic field.

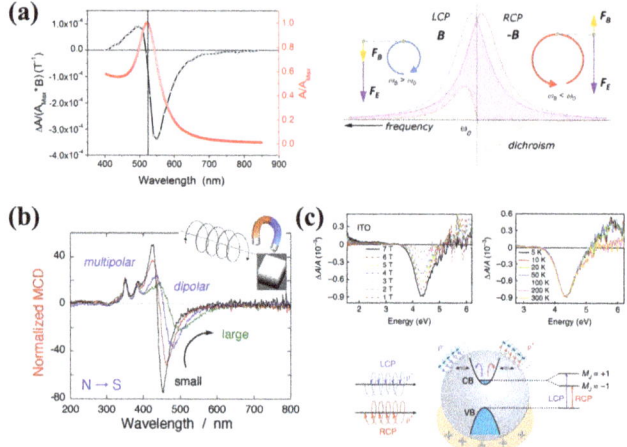

Figure 25. (**a**) Left, MCD/absorbance spectrum of gold nanoparticles, with MCD y-crossover at the LSPR wavelength. Right, schematic showing the differing response for RCP and LCP light, due to different electric (F$_E$) and magnetic (F$_B$) contributions of the Lorentz force on the electrons. Adapted with permission from [234], Copyright 2013, American Chemical Society. (**b**) MCD spectra for silver nanocubes of varied size, exhibiting dipolar and higher-order multipolar resonances. MDC dipolar response decreases with increased size, but multipolar effects are less size-dependent. Adapted with permission from [236], Copyright 2018, Elsevier. (**c**) Electron polarisation scheme for Doped-ITO nanoparticles. Top left, MCD spectrum at different field strengths is given in dashed coloured lines. Right, the temperature dependency of the MCD signal. Lastly the schematic of the conduction band splitting due to the angular momentum of the magnetoplasmonic modes due to RCP and LCP excitation. Adapted with permission from [237], Copyright 2018, Springer Nature.

Yin et al. used MCD to study the excitonic properties of degenerately doped (Sn/Mo) In$_2$O$_3$ nanocrystals [237]. The measured MCD signal for the ITO nanocrystals was temperature-independent and linearly dependent on the magnetic field (see Figure 25c), and thus specific to the cyclotron motion of the nanocrystals free electrons (magnetoplasmon) leading to splitting of the electronic band state, as opposed to interband sublevels, because the electrons are spin polarised. This result was noteworthy as the spin polarisation coupling is non-resonant; with magnetoplasmons resonant in the near-infrared, whereas the excitons at the bandgap are resonant in the ultraviolet. Furthermore, the charge carrier polarisation could be controlled in the IMO nanocrystals by varying the doping level and magnetic field strength, thus, the magnetoplasmonic mode could be harnessed as a new degree of freedom. This finding opens up a new field, plasmontronics, involving intrinsic plasmon-exciton and plasmon-spin interaction phenomena.

Spin-polarisation transfer from iron oxide to gold has been observed using X-ray magnetic circular dichroism (XMCD) [238]. A magnetic moment arose in the 5d band of gold-iron oxide, core-shell nanoparticles observed at the gold L edge in the XMCD spectrum. The phase of the iron oxide was demonstrated to be crucial for spin polarisation transfer.

4.6. Applications of Magneto-Plasmonics

In this final section, we will explore selected applications of magnetoplasmonic materials, in particular sensing and nanophotonic devices. SPR sensors (e.g., Biacore) are a common biosensing tool used to measure biomolecular interaction. These sensors detect variation in the refractive index at the sensor surface using total internal reflection of plane polarised light incident on a liquid–metal film interface. At the opposite side of the metal face, the photon-induced plasmon propagates which is sensitive to the refractive index that varies with analyte binding. Combining SPR and MO technology into MOSPR devices, an enhancement of p-polarised light can be achieved due to MO Kerr enhancements. Sepúlveda et al. [239] and Rizal et al. [240] showed an improvement of MOSPR biosensor technology over SPR sensor by a factor of 3–4. Figure 26a demonstrates the superiority of MOSPR sensitivity (compared to conventional SPR) to isopropanol vapours at different concentrations [241].

Magnetoplasmonics have also been applied to measure nanoscale distances [242]. The distance between nickel nanodiscs was measured using Kerr polarisation rotation, with a precision ~2 orders of magnitude higher than state-of-the-art plasmon rulers. Moreover, the system allowed intrinsic spatial orientation adoptability for optimising the nanogap measurement orientation. Figure 26b shows the effect of the spatial orientation of the ruler with respect to the electric and magnetic field direction (90°, 45° and 0°) on the Kerr rotation angle in the 625–635 nm spectral region. When the electric and magnetic fields are 90° to the ruler (p-short) a figure-of-merit (FOM, the ratio between sensitivity and the width of the resonance peak) of 1.5 was achieved. For the electric and magnetic fields at 45° (p-45) a FOM of 1 was attained. When the electric and magnetic fields were aligned parallel with the ruler, the best separation in the Kerr rotation angle for the different ruled distances was achieved with a FOM of 26.7. Considering a standard plasmon ruler could reach a FOM of 0.67, all magnetoplasmonic ruler orientations were superior.

Iron oxide nanorods coated in silica and gold, have been designed by Wang et al. [243] that can be oriented using an external magnetic field, which in turn elicits a varied optical polarisation response. Furthermore, a device was created based on the hybrid nanorods, capable of sensing the magnetic field orientation based on the optical response.

Along with sensing, magnetoplasmonics can also be utilised in photonic applications. Pancaldi et al. fabricated arrays of elliptical Au-Py-Au layered nanoparticles on glass to study the plasmonic photo-heating of nanomagnets using specific light polarisations for selective element heating [244]. Figure 26c shows the extinction spectrum (1-T) using light polarisation along the major/minor axis of the elliptical nanoparticles and the spectral position of the pump and probe. This pump beam was used to measure LMOKE hysteresis loops using polarisation along the long axis of the nanoparticle. A higher power pump led to a decreased coercive field and increased photo-heating, with the magnitude depending on the aspect ratio of the particular nano-ellipse. This finding supports thermally triggered magnetisation reversal in single nanostructures. This technology has interesting applications for selective thermalisation in say, multisystem chips.

Belotelov et al. reported light intensity modulation of 24% by varying the transparency of a magneto-plasmonic crystal [245]. By using in-plane magnetic fields to excite a perpendicularly polarised waveguide mode to vary the transmission spectrum of a magneto-plasmonic crystal [245]. The authors theorise that the effect could exceed 100% using higher quality material. Zubritskaya et al. reported a magneto-chiral trimer nanoantenna surface that consisted of gold and nickel nanodisks. The structure could tune the chiroptical transmission up to 150% using an external magnetic field perpendicular to the nanoantennas plane [246] as depicted in Figure 26d.

Under an applied magnetic field, magnetic nanoparticles can assemble into 1D chains due to magnetic dipolar interaction forces. Song et al. utilise this phenomenon by assembling iron oxide coated silver nanoparticles into long chain-like structures for eventual applications in optical filtering [247]. By varying the polarisation of light, the longitudinal and transverse LSPR can be tuned from visible to near-infrared wavelength regime (see Figure 26e). The redshift of the longitudinal LSPR is caused by near field coupling of neighbouring plasmonic NPs, whereas a blueshift of the transverse LSPR arises from far-field coupling. A summary of the polarisation-based applications of magnetic-plasmonic materials is shown in Table 1.

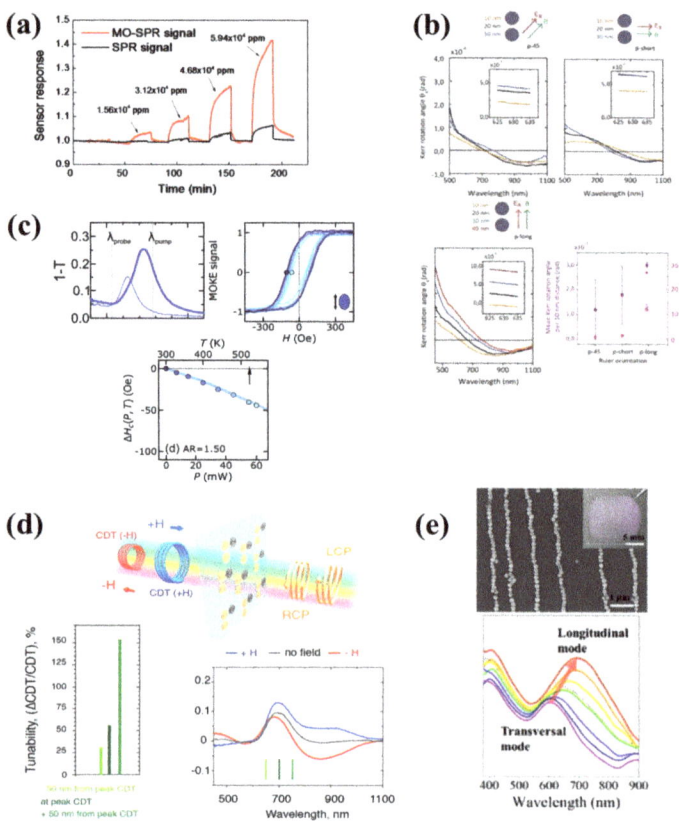

Figure 26. (**a**) Signal response of SPR and MOSPR to isopropanol vapours of different concentrations, with MOSPR showing a clear superiority. Adapted with permission from [241], Copyright 2012, American Institute of Physics. (**b**) Magnetoplasmonic ruler based on nickel nanodiscs, the distance between the nanodiscs can be calculated from the Kerr rotation angle. The Kerr rotations for electric and magnetic field directions (with respect to ruler orientation) are shown, with the parallel fields yielding superior rotations. Bottom right compares figure-of-merit and error bars for the various orientations compared to standard plasmonic rulers (dashed line). Adapted with permission from [242], Copyright 2015, American Chemical Society. (**c**) Left, Extinction spectrum of tri-layer Au–Py–Au elliptical nanostructure along the long axis (thick line) and short-axis (thin line), with pump and probe wavelengths marked. Right, thermoplasmonic heating effects on the magnetic properties obtained by LMOKE, with increased power leading to a decreased coercive field (light blue lines), below, the power-dependent decrease in the coercive field against the calculated temperature increase. Adapted with permission from [244], Copyright 2019, Royal Society of Chemistry. (**d**) Shows the scheme of Au–Au–Ni trimer nanoantennas arrays to study chiral differential transmission (CDT) under magnetic field application. Below left, the tunability of up to 150% for a specific geometry shown in CDT spectrum to the right with a varied external magnetic field. Adapted with permission from [246], Copyright 2018, American Chemical Society. (**e**) Assembled silver-magnetite nanoparticles electron microscopy image and photograph inset, where the LSPR extinction peak varies with the change in the polarisation angle. Adapted with permission from [247], Copyright 2017, American Chemical Society.

Table 1. Overview of the polarisation dependent applications of magnetic, plasmonic materials.

Material	Mechanism	Possible Application	References
Plasmonic nanowire on magnetic film	Faraday effect	Tunable and switchable polarisation rotation for optical isolators	[202,204]
Gold nanoparticles in solution	Inverse Faraday effect	Optical isolation without external magnetic fields	[211]
Plasmonic—magnetic film	Kerr effect	Magneto-optical surface plasmon resonance	[218,239]
Nickel nanodiscs	Kerr effect	Active ruler utilising polarisation, monitoring polarisation-selective photo-heating	[242,244]
Plasmonic resonator structures	Magnetic plasmon resonance	Surface-enhanced Raman scattering, nanoantennas	[221,222]
G-shaped nickel nanostructures	Magnetic second-harmonic generation	Probing the magnetisation direction	[233]
Plasmonic nanoparticles	Magnetic circular dichroism	Sensing by monitoring the intensity of circularly polarised light	[235]
Assembled chains of magnetic-plasmonic nanoparticles	Dipole–dipole magnetic interaction	Optical filtering	[247]

5. Conclusions and Perspectives

In this review, we covered three important aspects of polarisation response from plasmonic nanostructures. In the first section, we discussed the tailoring between LSPR scattering and symmetry of various plasmonic nanostructures with potential applications in optics and optoelectronics. Numerous techniques including SERS scattering, DF extinction and IR transmission/absorption have been employed to investigate the polarisation response, starting from the simplest nanostructure of single nanoparticle to complicated nanoprisms or nanocrescents. In general, all such measurements allow to identify the symmetry of the plasmon modes and distinguish differently shaped particles in a nanoparticle cluster. Moving forward, the strong optical anisotropy and polarisation response obtained from differently shaped plasmonic nanostructures intrigued much interest to exploit such effects SPR sensing. Most of the established SPR sensing relies on the dip or shift in reflected intensity (amplitude) profile at certain wavelength or incident angle. However, we believe that polarisation sensitive selective excitation and detection of particular plasmonic mode and measuring phase shift between them opens up more contrasting sensing opportunities which is yet to be explored. In the second section, we discussed how the artificially fabricated new generation metamaterials can manipulate the polarisation state of light in different ways, e.g., linear polarisation rotation to its cross polarisation, linear-to-circular (or vice versa) polarisation or handedness change for circular polarisation. It is always desirable to achieve all the functionalities within a single metamaterial structure. Although, Liu and co-workers inverse designed chiral metamaterials with multifunctional polarisation manipulation ability, it operates in the GHz regime and remains a real challenge to facilitate such structures to operate in the high frequency THz regime which have more potential applications in ultrafast photonics and optomagnetism. In the last section, we discussed the newly emerged field of magneto-plasmonics with particular emphasis on polarisation in magnetic-plasmonic nanoparticles and thin film structures. These nanostructures either consist of a magnetic material which can sustain a plasmon (e.g., nickel) or, more commonly, consist of hybridisation of a magnetic and plasmonic material (e.g., iron + gold). Various topics including Faraday and inverse Faraday effect, MOKE, magnetic plasmon resonance, magnetic second harmonic generation and magnetic circular dichroism are discussed, along with many potential applications. Magnetoplasmonics is a constantly evolving field, with new sub-fields such as plasmontronics emerging and nanofabrication advancing, it is safe to assume that many more interesting developments are on the horizon and it is likely that polarisation will be pivotal

Symmetry **2020**, *12*, 1365

to the measurement. Subsequently, many applications will emerge, particularly in sensing and nanophotonic devices.

Author Contributions: P.K., G.B. and J.L. wrote the paper. P.K., G.B. and J.L. edited the draft. P.K., G.B., J.L., S.A.M.T., N.L. and C.S. All authors have read and agreed to the published version of the manuscript.

Funding: This work was supported by Irish Research Council (GOIPD/2018/716), Science Foundation Ireland (SFI) centre CÚRAM, the European Regional Development Fund (Grant Number 13/RC/2073), Science Foundation Ireland's Career Development Award program (13CDA2221) and Science Foundation Ireland's National Access Programme (No. 444) and SFI 17/CDA/4733.

Conflicts of Interest: The authors declare no conflict of interest.

References

1. Jiang, N.; Zhuo, X.; Wang, J. Active Plasmonics: Principles, Structures, and Applications. *Chem. Rev.* **2018**, *118*, 3054–3099. [CrossRef] [PubMed]
2. Stockman, M.I.; Kneipp, K.; Bozhevolnyi, S.I.; Saha, S.; Dutta, A.; Ndukaife, J.; Kinsey, N.; Reddy, H.; Guler, U.; Shalaev, V.M.; et al. Roadmap on plasmonics. *J. Opt.* **2018**, *20*. [CrossRef]
3. Harutyunyan, H.; Martinson, A.B.; Rosenmann, D.; Khorashad, L.K.; Besteiro, L.V.; Govorov, A.O.; Wiederrecht, G.P. Anomalous ultrafast dynamics of hot plasmonic electrons in nanostructures with hot spots. *Nat. Nanotechnol.* **2015**, *10*, 770–774. [CrossRef]
4. Baffou, G.; Quidant, R. Nanoplasmonics for chemistry. *Chem. Soc. Rev.* **2014**, *43*, 3898–3907. [CrossRef] [PubMed]
5. Willets, K.A.; Van Duyne, R.P. Localized surface plasmon resonance spectroscopy and sensing. *Annu. Rev. Phys. Chem.* **2007**, *58*, 267–297. [CrossRef]
6. Huang, W.; Wang, J.; Bian, L.; Zhao, C.; Liu, D.; Guo, C.; Yang, B.; Cao, W. Oxygen vacancy induces self-doping effect and metalloid LSPR in non-stoichiometric tungsten suboxide synergistically contributing to the enhanced photoelectrocatalytic performance of WO3-x/TiO2-x heterojunction. *Phys. Chem. Chem. Phys.* **2018**, *20*, 17268–17278. [CrossRef]
7. Leonhardt, U. Optical conformal mapping. *Science* **2006**, *312*, 1777–1780. [CrossRef]
8. Wei, H.; Pan, D.; Xu, H. Routing of surface plasmons in silver nanowire networks controlled by polarization and coating. *Nanoscale* **2015**, *7*, 19053–19059. [CrossRef]
9. Mejia-Salazar, J.R.; Oliveira, O.N., Jr. Plasmonic Biosensing. *Chem. Rev.* **2018**, *118*, 10617–10625. [CrossRef]
10. Yu, C.; Irudayaraj, J. Multiplex Biosensor Using Gold Nanorods. *Anal. Chem.* **2007**, *79*, 572–579. [CrossRef]
11. Tian, F.; Bonnier, F.; Casey, A.; Shanahan, A.E.; Byrne, H.J. Surface enhanced Raman scattering with gold nanoparticles: Effect of particle shape. *Anal. Methods* **2014**, *6*, 9116–9123. [CrossRef]
12. Ringe, E.; Langille, M.R.; Sohn, K.; Zhang, J.; Huang, J.; Mirkin, C.A.; Van Duyne, R.P.; Marks, L.D. Plasmon Length: A Universal Parameter to Describe Size Effects in Gold Nanoparticles. *J. Phys. Chem. Lett.* **2012**, *3*, 1479–1483. [CrossRef] [PubMed]
13. Li, D. Femtosecond polarization switching. *Nat. Photonics* **2017**, *11*, 336–337. [CrossRef]
14. Yang, Y.; Kelley, K.; Sachet, E.; Campione, S.; Luk, T.S.; Maria, J.-P.; Sinclair, M.B.; Brener, I. Femtosecond optical polarization switching using a cadmium oxide-based perfect absorber. *Nat. Photonics* **2017**, *11*, 390–395. [CrossRef]
15. Schubert, O.; Becker, J.; Carbone, L.; Khalavka, Y.; Provalska, T.; Zins, I.; Sonnichsen, C. Mapping the polarization pattern of plasmon modes reveals nanoparticle symmetry. *Nano Lett.* **2008**, *8*, 2345–2350. [CrossRef]
16. Kumbhar, A.S.; Kinnan, M.K.; Chumanov, G. Multipole plasmon resonances of submicron silver particles. *J. Am. Chem. Soc.* **2005**, *127*, 12444–12445. [CrossRef]
17. Tian, X.; Zhou, Y.; Thota, S.; Zou, S.; Zhao, J. Plasmonic Coupling in Single Silver Nanosphere Assemblies by Polarization-Dependent Dark-Field Scattering Spectroscopy. *J. Phys. Chem. C* **2014**, *118*, 13801–13808. [CrossRef]
18. Shegai, T.; Li, Z.; Dadosh, T.; Zhang, Z.; Xu, H.; Haran, G. Managing light polarization via plasmon-molecule interactions within an asymmetric metal nanoparticle trimer. *Proc. Natl. Acad. Sci. USA* **2008**, *105*, 16448–16453. [CrossRef]

19. Luo, M.; Huang, H.; Choi, S.I.; Zhang, C.; da Silva, R.R.; Peng, H.C.; Li, Z.Y.; Liu, J.; He, Z.; Xia, Y. Facile Synthesis of Ag Nanorods with No Plasmon Resonance Peak in the Visible Region by Using Pd Decahedra of 16 nm in Size as Seeds. *ACS Nano* **2015**, *9*, 10523–10532. [CrossRef]

20. Shuford, K.L.; Ratner, M.A.; Schatz, G.C. Multipolar excitation in triangular nanoprisms. *J. Chem. Phys.* **2005**, *123*, 114713. [CrossRef]

21. Felidj, N.; Grand, J.; Laurent, G.; Aubard, J.; Levi, G.; Hohenau, A.; Galler, N.; Aussenegg, F.R.; Krenn, J.R. Multipolar surface plasmon peaks on gold nanotriangles. *J. Chem. Phys.* **2008**, *128*, 094702. [CrossRef] [PubMed]

22. Bukasov, R.; Shumaker-Parry, J.S. Highly tunable infrared extinction properties of gold nanocrescents. *Nano Lett.* **2007**, *7*, 1113–1118. [CrossRef] [PubMed]

23. Li, G.C.; Zhang, Y.L.; Lei, D.Y. Hybrid plasmonic gap modes in metal film-coupled dimers and their physical origins revealed by polarization resolved dark field spectroscopy. *Nanoscale* **2016**, *8*, 7119–7126. [CrossRef] [PubMed]

24. Chen, W.; Shi, H.; Wan, F.; Wang, P.; Gu, Z.; Li, W.; Ke, L.; Huang, Y. Substrate influence on the polarization dependence of SERS in crossed metal nanowires. *J. Mater. Chem. C* **2017**, *5*, 7028–7034. [CrossRef]

25. Wei, H.; Hao, F.; Huang, Y.; Wang, W.; Nordlander, P.; Xu, H. Polarization dependence of surface-enhanced Raman scattering in gold nanoparticle-nanowire systems. *Nano Lett.* **2008**, *8*, 2497–2502. [CrossRef]

26. Deng, G.; Dereshgi, S.A.; Song, X.; Aydin, K. Polarization dependent, plasmon-enhanced infrared transmission through gold nanoslits on monolayer black phosphorus. *J. Opt. Soc. Am. B* **2019**, *36*. [CrossRef]

27. Liu, C.; Bai, Y.; Zhou, J.; Zhao, Q.; Yang, Y.; Chen, H.; Qiao, L. High-performance bifunctional polarization switch chiral metamaterials by inverse design method. *npj Comput. Mater.* **2019**, *5*. [CrossRef]

28. Kaschke, J.; Blume, L.; Wu, L.; Thiel, M.; Bade, K.; Yang, Z.; Wegener, M. A Helical Metamaterial for Broadband Circular Polarization Conversion. *Adv. Opt. Mater.* **2015**, *3*, 1411–1417. [CrossRef]

29. Kruk, S.; Hopkins, B.; Kravchenko, I.I.; Miroshnichenko, A.; Neshev, D.N.; Kivshar, Y.S. Invited Article: Broadband highly efficient dielectric metadevices for polarization control. *APL Photonics* **2016**, *1*. [CrossRef]

30. Chen, S.; Liu, W.; Li, Z.; Cheng, H.; Tian, J. Polarization State Manipulation of Electromagnetic Waves with Metamaterials and Its Applications in Nanophotonics. In *Metamaterials—Devices and Applications*; IntechOpen Limited: London, UK, 2017. [CrossRef]

31. Bi, K.; Yang, D.; Chen, J.; Wang, Q.; Wu, H.; Lan, C.; Yang, Y. Experimental demonstration of ultra-large-scale terahertz all-dielectric metamaterials. *Photonics Res.* **2019**, *7*, 457–463. [CrossRef]

32. Soukoulis, C.M.; Wegener, M. Past achievements and future challenges in the development of three-dimensional photonic metamaterials. *Nat Photonics* **2011**, *5*, 523–530. [CrossRef]

33. Tong, L.; Miljkovic, V.D.; Kall, M. Alignment, rotation, and spinning of single plasmonic nanoparticles and nanowires using polarization dependent optical forces. *Nano Lett.* **2010**, *10*, 268–273. [CrossRef] [PubMed]

34. Gunnarsson, L.; Rindzevicius, T.; Prikulis, J.; Kasemo, B.; Kall, M.; Zou, S.; Schatz, G.C. Confined plasmons in nanofabricated single silver particle pairs: Experimental observations of strong interparticle interactions. *J. Phys. Chem. B* **2005**, *109*, 1079–1087. [CrossRef] [PubMed]

35. Dort, K.; Kroth, K.; Klar, P.J. A surface-enhanced Raman-spectroscopic study: Verification of the interparticle gap dependence of field enhancement by triangulation of spherical gold nanoparticle trimers. *J. Raman Spectrosc.* **2019**, *50*, 1807–1816. [CrossRef]

36. Steinigeweg, D.; Schutz, M.; Schlucker, S. Single gold trimers and 3D superstructures exhibit a polarization-independent SERS response. *Nanoscale* **2013**, *5*, 110–113. [CrossRef]

37. Wang, H.; Li, Z.; Zhang, H.; Wang, P.; Wen, S. Giant local circular dichroism within an asymmetric plasmonic nanoparticle trimer. *Sci. Rep.* **2015**, *5*, 8207. [CrossRef]

38. Mohamed, M.B.; Volkov, V.; Link, S.; El-Sayed, M.A. The 'lightning' gold nanorods: Fluorescence enhancement of over a million compared to the gold metal. *Chem. Phys. Lett.* **2000**, *317*, 517–523. [CrossRef]

39. Sonnichsen, C.; Franzl, T.; Wilk, T.; von Plessen, G.; Feldmann, J.; Wilson, O.; Mulvaney, P. Drastic reduction of plasmon damping in gold nanorods. *Phys. Rev. Lett.* **2002**, *88*, 077402. [CrossRef]

40. Slaughter, L.S.; Chang, W.-S.; Swanglap, P.; Tcherniak, A.; Khanal, B.P.; Zubarev, E.R.; Link, S. Single-Particle Spectroscopy of Gold Nanorods beyond the Quasi-Static Limit: Varying the Width at Constant Aspect Ratio. *J. Phys. Chem. C* **2010**, *114*, 4934–4938. [CrossRef]

41. He, J.; Zheng, W.; Ligmajer, F.; Chan, C.F.; Bao, Z.; Wong, K.L.; Chen, X.; Hao, J.; Dai, J.; Yu, S.F.; et al. Plasmonic enhancement and polarization dependence of nonlinear upconversion emissions from single gold nanorod@SiO2@CaF2:Yb(3+),Er(3+) hybrid core-shell-satellite nanostructures. *Light Sci. Appl.* **2017**, *6*, e16217. [CrossRef]

42. Khlebtsov, B.N.; Khlebtsov, N.G. Multipole Plasmons in Metal Nanorods: Scaling Properties and Dependence on Particle Size, Shape, Orientation, and Dielectric Environment. *J. Phys. Chem. C* **2007**, *111*, 11516–11527. [CrossRef]

43. Aizpurua, J.; Bryant, G.W.; Richter, L.J.; García de Abajo, F.J.; Kelley, B.K.; Mallouk, T. Optical properties of coupled metallic nanorods for field-enhanced spectroscopy. *Phys. Rev. B* **2005**, *71*, 235420. [CrossRef]

44. Ming, T.; Zhao, L.; Yang, Z.; Chen, H.; Sun, L.; Wang, J.; Yan, C. Strong polarization dependence of plasmon-enhanced fluorescence on single gold nanorods. *Nano Lett.* **2009**, *9*, 3896–3903. [CrossRef] [PubMed]

45. Yguerabide, J.; Yguerabide, E.E. Light-Scattering Submicroscopic Particles as Highly Fluorescent Analogs and Their Use as Tracer Labels in Clinical and Biological Applications: I. Theory. *Anal. Biochem.* **1998**, *262*, 137–156. [CrossRef]

46. Zijlstra, P.; Chon, J.W.; Gu, M. Five-dimensional optical recording mediated by surface plasmons in gold nanorods. *Nature* **2009**, *459*, 410–413. [CrossRef]

47. Diefenbach, S.; Erhard, N.; Schopka, J.; Martin, A.; Karnetzky, C.; Iacopino, D.; Holleitner, A.W. Polarization dependent, surface plasmon induced photoconductance in gold nanorod arrays. *Phys. Status Solidi (RRL)—Rapid Res. Lett.* **2014**, *8*, 264–268. [CrossRef]

48. Ruan, Q.; Fang, C.; Jiang, R.; Jia, H.; Lai, Y.; Wang, J.; Lin, H.Q. Highly enhanced transverse plasmon resonance and tunable double Fano resonances in gold@titania nanorods. *Nanoscale* **2016**, *8*, 6514–6526. [CrossRef]

49. Zhang, M.; Li, C.; Wang, C.; Zhang, C.; Wang, Z.; Han, Q.; Zheng, H. Polarization dependence of plasmon enhanced fluorescence on Au nanorod array. *Appl. Opt.* **2017**, *56*, 375–379. [CrossRef] [PubMed]

50. Sun, M.; Zhang, Z.; Wang, P.; Li, Q.; Ma, F.; Xu, H. Remotely excited Raman optical activity using chiral plasmon propagation in Ag nanowires. *Light Sci. Appl.* **2013**, *2*, e112. [CrossRef]

51. Kim, S.; Bailey, S.; Liu, M.; Yan, R. Decoupling co-existing surface plasmon polariton (SPP) modes in a nanowire plasmonic waveguide for quantitative mode analysis. *Nano Res.* **2017**, *10*, 2395–2404. [CrossRef]

52. Vasista, A.B.; Jog, H.; Heilpern, T.; Sykes, M.E.; Tiwari, S.; Sharma, D.K.; Chaubey, S.K.; Wiederrecht, G.P.; Gray, S.K.; Kumar, G.V.P. Differential Wavevector Distribution of Surface-Enhanced Raman Scattering and Fluorescence in a Film-Coupled Plasmonic Nanowire Cavity. *Nano Lett.* **2018**, *18*, 650–655. [CrossRef] [PubMed]

53. Zhang, Z.; Fang, Y.; Wang, W.; Chen, L.; Sun, M. Propagating Surface Plasmon Polaritons: Towards Applications for Remote-Excitation Surface Catalytic Reactions. *Adv. Sci. (Weinh)* **2016**, *3*, 1500215. [CrossRef] [PubMed]

54. Mohanty, P.; Yoon, I.; Kang, T.; Seo, K.; Varadwaj, K.S.K.; Choi, W.; Park, Q.H.; Ahn, J.P.; Suh, Y.D.; Ihee, H.; et al. Simple Vapor-Phase Synthesis of Single-Crystalline Ag Nanowires and Single-Nanowire Surface-Enhanced Raman Scattering. *J. Am. Chem. Soc.* **2007**, *129*, 9576–9577. [CrossRef] [PubMed]

55. Li, Z.; Gao, Y.; Zhang, L.; Fang, Y.; Wang, P. Polarization-dependent surface plasmon-driven catalytic reaction on a single nanowire monitored by SERS. *Nanoscale* **2018**, *10*, 18720–18727. [CrossRef] [PubMed]

56. Hao, F.; Nordlander, P. Plasmonic coupling between a metallic nanosphere and a thin metallic wire. *Appl. Phys. Lett.* **2006**, *89*, 103101. [CrossRef]

57. Hu, H.; Akimov, Y.A.; Duan, H.; Li, X.; Liao, M.; Tan, R.L.; Wu, L.; Chen, H.; Fan, H.; Bai, P.; et al. Photoluminescence via gap plasmons between single silver nanowires and a thin gold film. *Nanoscale* **2013**, *5*, 12086–12091. [CrossRef]

58. Yang, M.; Cai, W.; Wang, Y.; Sun, M.; Shang, G. Orientation-and polarization-dependent optical properties of the single Ag nanowire/glass substrate system excited by the evanescent wave. *Sci. Rep.* **2016**, *6*, 25633. [CrossRef]

59. Lee, S.J.; Baik, J.M.; Moskovits, M. Polarization-dependent surface-enhanced Raman scattering from a silver-nanoparticle-decorated single silver nanowire. *Nano Lett.* **2008**, *8*, 3244–3247. [CrossRef]

60. Fang, Y.; Li, Z.; Huang, Y.; Zhang, S.; Nordlander, P.; Halas, N.J.; Xu, H. Branched silver nanowires as controllable plasmon routers. *Nano Lett.* **2010**, *10*, 1950–1954. [CrossRef]

61. Liu, N.; Li, Z.; Xu, H. Polarization-dependent study on propagating surface plasmons in silver nanowires launched by a near-field scanning optical fiber tip. *Small* **2012**, *8*, 2641–2646. [CrossRef]

62. Chen, L.; Rong, Y.; Ren, M.; Wu, W.; Qin, M.; Pan, C.; Ma, Q.; Liu, S.; Wu, B.; Wu, E.; et al. Selective Polarization Modification of Upconversion Luminescence of NaYF4:Yb3+,Er3+ Nanoparticles by Plasmonic Nanoantenna Arrays. *J. Phys. Chem. C* **2018**, *122*, 15666–15672. [CrossRef]

63. Mobini, E.; Rahimzadegan, A.; Alaee, R.; Rockstuhl, C. Optical alignment of oval graphene flakes. *Opt. Lett.* **2017**, *42*, 1039–1042. [CrossRef] [PubMed]

64. Chen, J.; Zeng, Y.; Xu, X.; Chen, X.; Zhou, Z.; Shi, P.; Yi, Z.; Ye, X.; Xiao, S.; Yi, Y. Plasmonic Absorption Enhancement in Elliptical Graphene Arrays. *Nanomaterials* **2018**, *8*, 175. [CrossRef]

65. Guler, U.; Turan, R. Effect of particle properties and light polarization on the plasmonic resonances in metallic nanoparticles. *Opt. Express* **2010**, *18*, 17322–17338. [CrossRef] [PubMed]

66. Xia, Y.; Dai, Y.; Wang, B.; Chen, A.; Zhang, Y.; Zhang, Y.; Guan, F.; Liu, X.; Shi, L.; Zi, J. Polarization dependent plasmonic modes in elliptical graphene disk arrays. *Opt. Express* **2019**, *27*, 1080–1089. [CrossRef]

67. Gordon, R.; Brolo, A.G.; McKinnon, A.; Rajora, A.; Leathem, B.; Kavanagh, K.L. Strong Polarization in the Optical Transmission through Elliptical Nanohole Arrays. *Phys. Rev. Lett.* **2004**, *92*, 037401. [CrossRef]

68. Sepulveda, B.; Alaverdyan, Y.; Alegret, J.; Kall, M.; Johansson, P. Shape effects in the localized surface plasmon resonance of single nanoholes in thin metal films. *Opt. Express* **2008**, *16*, 5609–5616. [CrossRef]

69. Petronijevic, E.; Ali, H.; Zaric, N.; Belardini, A.; Leahu, G.; Cesca, T.; Mattei, G.; Andreani, L.C.; Sibilia, C. Chiral effects in low-cost plasmonic arrays of elliptic nanoholes. *Opt. Quantum Electron.* **2020**, *52*, 176. [CrossRef]

70. Hermoso, W.; Alves, T.V.; de Oliveira, C.C.S.; Moriya, E.G.; Ornellas, F.R.; Camargo, P.H.C. Triangular metal nanoprisms of Ag, Au, and Cu: Modeling the influence of size, composition, and excitation wavelength on the optical properties. *Chem. Phys.* **2013**, *423*, 142–150. [CrossRef]

71. Sherry, L.J.; Jin, R.; Mirkin, C.A.; Schatz, G.C.; Van Duyne, R.P. Localized Surface Plasmon Resonance Spectroscopy of Single Silver Triangular Nanoprisms. *Nano Lett.* **2006**, *6*, 2060–2065. [CrossRef]

72. Shahjamali, M.M.; Bosman, M.; Cao, S.; Huang, X.; Saadat, S.; Martinsson, E.; Aili, D.; Tay, Y.Y.; Liedberg, B.; Loo, S.C.J.; et al. Gold Coating of Silver Nanoprisms. *Adv. Funct. Mater.* **2012**, *22*, 849–854. [CrossRef]

73. Sweeney, C.M.; Stender, C.L.; Nehl, C.L.; Hasan, W.; Shuford, K.L.; Odom, T.W. Optical properties of tipless gold nanopyramids. *Small* **2011**, *7*, 2032–2036. [CrossRef] [PubMed]

74. Gao, M.; Zheng, X.; Khan, I.; Cai, H.; Lan, J.; Liu, J.; Wang, J.; Wu, J.; Huang, S.; Li, S.; et al. Resonant light absorption and plasmon tunability of lateral triangular Au nanoprisms array. *Phys. Lett. A* **2019**, *383*. [CrossRef]

75. Banholzer, M.J.; Harris, N.; Millstone, J.E.; Schatz, G.C.; Mirkin, C.A. Abnormally Large Plasmonic Shifts in Silica-Protected Gold Triangular Nanoprisms. *J. Phys. Chem. C* **2010**, *114*, 7521–7526. [CrossRef]

76. Love, J.C.; Gates, B.D.; Wolfe, D.B.; Paul, K.E.; Whitesides, G.M. Fabrication and Wetting Properties of Metallic Half-Shells with Submicron Diameters. *Nano Lett.* **2002**, *2*, 891–894. [CrossRef]

77. Lu, Y.; Liu, G.L.; Kim, J.; Mejia, Y.X.; Lee, L.P. Nanophotonic Crescent Moon Structures with Sharp Edge for Ultrasensitive Biomolecular Detection by Local Electromagnetic Field Enhancement Effect. *Nano Lett.* **2005**, *5*, 119–124. [CrossRef]

78. Shumaker-Parry, J.S.; Rochholz, H.; Kreiter, M. Fabrication of Crescent-Shaped Optical Antennas. *Adv. Mater.* **2005**, *17*, 2131–2134. [CrossRef]

79. Cooper, C.T.; Rodriguez, M.; Blair, S.; Shumaker-Parry, J.S. Polarization Anisotropy of Multiple Localized Plasmon Resonance Modes in Noble Metal Nanocrescents. *J. Phys. Chem. C* **2013**, *118*, 1167–1173. [CrossRef]

80. Won Ha, J.; Sun, W.; Wang, G.; Fang, N. Differential interference contrast polarization anisotropy for tracking rotational dynamics of gold nanorods. *Chem. Commun.* **2011**, *47*, 7743–7745. [CrossRef]

81. Goerlitzer, E.S.A.; Speichermann, L.E.; Mirza, T.A.; Mohammadi, R.; Vogel, N. Addressing the plasmonic hotspot region by site-specific functionalization of nanostructures. *Nanoscale Adv.* **2020**, *2*, 394–400. [CrossRef]

82. Zhang, Y.; Jia, T.Q.; Zhang, S.A.; Feng, D.H.; Xu, Z.Z. Dipole, quadrupole and octupole plasmon resonance modes in non-concentric nanocrescent/nanodisk structure: Local field enhancement in the visible and near infrared regions. *Opt. Express* **2012**, *20*, 2924–2931. [CrossRef] [PubMed]

83. Garoli, D.; Mosconi, D.; Miele, E.; Maccaferri, N.; Ardini, M.; Giovannini, G.; Dipalo, M.; Agnoli, S.; De Angelis, F. Hybrid plasmonic nanostructures based on controlled integration of MoS2 flakes on metallic nanoholes. *Nanoscale* **2018**, *10*, 17105–17111. [CrossRef]

84. Late, D.J.; Liu, B.; Luo, J.; Yan, A.; Matte, H.S.; Grayson, M.; Rao, C.N.; Dravid, V.P. GaS and GaSe ultrathin layer transistors. *Adv. Mater.* **2012**, *24*, 3549–3554. [CrossRef] [PubMed]

85. Hu, P.; Wang, L.; Yoon, M.; Zhang, J.; Feng, W.; Wang, X.; Wen, Z.; Idrobo, J.C.; Miyamoto, Y.; Geohegan, D.B.; et al. Highly Responsive Ultrathin GaS Nanosheet Photodetectors on Rigid and Flexible Substrates. *Nano Lett.* **2013**, *13*, 1649–1654. [CrossRef]

86. Gan, X.-T.; Zhao, C.-Y.; Hu, S.-Q.; Wang, T.; Song, Y.; Li, J.; Zhao, Q.-H.; Jie, W.-Q.; Zhao, J.-L. Microwatts continuous-wave pumped second harmonic generation in few- and mono-layer GaSe. *Light Sci. Appl.* **2018**, *7*, 17126. [CrossRef] [PubMed]

87. Ding, S.-Y.; Yi, J.; Li, J.-F.; Ren, B.; Wu, D.-Y.; Panneerselvam, R.; Tian, Z.-Q. Nanostructure-based plasmon-enhanced Raman spectroscopy for surface analysis of materials. *Nat. Rev. Mater.* **2016**, *1*, 16021. [CrossRef]

88. Seo, S.; Chang, T.-W.; Liu, G.L. 3D Plasmon Coupling Assisted Sers on Nanoparticle-Nanocup Array Hybrids. *Sci. Rep.* **2018**, *8*, 3002. [CrossRef]

89. Najmaei, S.; Mlayah, A.; Arbouet, A.; Girard, C.; Léotin, J.; Lou, J. Plasmonic Pumping of Excitonic Photoluminescence in Hybrid MoS2–Au Nanostructures. *ACS Nano* **2014**, *8*, 12682–12689. [CrossRef]

90. Rodin, A.S.; Carvalho, A.; Castro Neto, A.H. Strain-induced gap modification in black phosphorus. *Phys. Rev. Lett.* **2014**, *112*, 176801. [CrossRef]

91. Qiao, J.; Kong, X.; Hu, Z.X.; Yang, F.; Ji, W. High-mobility transport anisotropy and linear dichroism in few-layer black phosphorus. *Nat. Commun.* **2014**, *5*, 4475. [CrossRef]

92. Jappor, H.R. Electronic structure of novel GaS/GaSe heterostructures based on GaS and GaSe monolayers. *Phys. B Condens. Matter* **2017**, *524*, 109–117. [CrossRef]

93. Wan, W.; Yin, J.; Wu, Y.; Zheng, X.; Yang, W.; Wang, H.; Zhou, J.; Chen, J.; Wu, Z.; Li, X.; et al. Polarization-Controllable Plasmonic Enhancement on the Optical Response of Two-Dimensional GaSe Layers. *ACS Appl. Mater. Interfaces* **2019**, *11*, 19631–19637. [CrossRef] [PubMed]

94. Ozbay, E. Plasmonics: Merging photonics and electronics at nanoscale dimensions. *Science* **2006**, *311*, 189–193. [CrossRef] [PubMed]

95. Liang, Z.; Sun, J.; Jiang, Y.; Jiang, L.; Chen, X. Plasmonic Enhanced Optoelectronic Devices. *Plasmonics* **2014**, *9*, 859–866. [CrossRef]

96. Dionne, J.A.; Sweatlock, L.A.; Sheldon, M.T.; Alivisatos, A.P.; Atwater, H.A. 2010_Silicon-Based Plasmonics for On-Chip Photonics.pdf. *IEEE J. Sel. Top. Quantum Electron.* **2010**, *16*, 295–306. [CrossRef]

97. Špačková, B.; Wrobel, P.; Bocková, M.; Homola, J. Optical Biosensors Based on Plasmonic Nanostructures: A Review. *Proc. IEEE* **2016**, *104*, 2380–2408. [CrossRef]

98. Strobbia, P.; Languirand, E.; Cullum, B.M. Recent advances in plasmonic nanostructures for sensing: A review. *Opt. Eng.* **2015**, *54*, 100902. [CrossRef]

99. Guo, X.; Ma, Y.; Wang, Y.; Tong, L. Nanowire plasmonic waveguides, circuits and devices. *Laser Photonics Rev.* **2013**, *7*, 855–881. [CrossRef]

100. Fang, Y.; Sun, M. Nanoplasmonic waveguides: Towards applications in integrated nanophotonic circuits. *Light Sci. Appl.* **2015**, *4*, 1–11. [CrossRef]

101. Kleinman, S.L.; Ringe, E.; Valley, N.; Wustholz, K.L.; Phillips, E.; Scheidt, K.A.; Schatz, G.C.; Van Duyne, R.P. Single-molecule surface-enhanced raman spectroscopy of crystal violet isotopologues: Theory and experiment. *J. Am. Chem. Soc.* **2011**, *133*, 4115–4122. [CrossRef]

102. Zhang, Y.; Zhen, Y.R.; Neumann, O.; Day, J.K.; Nordlander, P.; Halas, N.J. Coherent anti-Stokes Raman scattering with single-molecule sensitivity using a plasmonic Fano resonance. *Nat. Commun.* **2014**, *5*, 1–7. [CrossRef] [PubMed]

103. Zheng, Y.; Soeriyadi, A.H.; Rosa, L.; Ng, S.H.; Bach, U.; Justin Gooding, J. Reversible gating of smart plasmonic molecular traps using thermoresponsive polymers for single-molecule detection. *Nat. Commun.* **2015**, *6*, 1–8. [CrossRef] [PubMed]

104. Brandl, D.W.; Mirin, N.A.; Nordlander, P. Plasmon modes of nanosphere trimers and quadrumers. *J. Phys. Chem. B* **2006**, *110*, 12302–12310. [CrossRef]

105. Lee, H.; Kim, G.H.; Lee, J.H.; Kim, N.H.; Nam, J.M.; Suh, Y.D. Quantitative Plasmon Mode and Surface-Enhanced Raman Scattering Analyses of Strongly Coupled Plasmonic Nanotrimers with Diverse Geometries. *Nano Lett.* **2015**, *15*, 4628–4636. [CrossRef] [PubMed]

106. Thomas, R.; Swathi, R.S. Linear and Polygonal Assemblies of Plasmonic Nanoparticles: Incident Light Polarization Dictates Hot Spots. *J. Phys. Chem. C* **2016**, *120*, 18733–18740. [CrossRef]

107. Sönnichsen, C.; Alivisatos, A.P. Gold nanorods as novel nonbleaching plasmon-based orientation sensors for polarized single-particle microscopy. *Nano Lett.* **2005**, *5*, 301–304. [CrossRef] [PubMed]

108. Wei, H.; Li, Z.; Tian, X.; Wang, Z.; Cong, F.; Liu, N.; Zhang, S.; Nordlander, P.; Halas, N.J.; Xu, H. Quantum dot-based local field imaging reveals plasmon-based interferometric logic in silver nanowire networks. *Nano Lett.* **2011**, *11*, 471–475. [CrossRef]

109. Wei, H.; Wang, Z.; Tian, X.; Käll, M.; Xu, H. Cascaded logic gates in nanophotonic plasmon networks. *Nat. Commun.* **2011**, *2*, 385–387. [CrossRef]

110. Ditlbacher, H.; Hohenau, A.; Wagner, D.; Kreibig, U.; Rogers, M.; Hofer, F.; Aussenegg, F.R.; Krenn, J.R. Silver nanowires as surface plasmon resonators. *Phys. Rev. Lett.* **2005**, *95*, 1–4. [CrossRef]

111. Ma, Y.; Li, X.; Yu, H.; Tong, L.; Gu, Y.; Gong, Q. Direct measurement of propagation losses in silver nanowires. *Opt. Lett.* **2010**, *35*, 1160–1162. [CrossRef] [PubMed]

112. Sanders, A.W.; Routenberg, D.A.; Wiley, B.J.; Xia, Y.; Dufresne, E.R.; Reed, M.A. Observation of plasmon propagation, redirection, and fan-out in silver nanowires. *Nano Lett.* **2006**, *6*, 1822–1826. [CrossRef] [PubMed]

113. Wei, H.; Xu, H. Controlling surface plasmon interference in branched silver nanowire structures. *Nanoscale* **2012**, *4*, 7149–7154. [CrossRef] [PubMed]

114. Righini, M.; Zelenina, A.S.; Girard, C.; Quidant, R. Parallel and selective trapping in a patterned plasmonic landscape. *Nat. Phys.* **2007**, *3*, 477–480. [CrossRef]

115. Daly, M.; Truong, V.G.; Chormaic, S.N. Evanescent field trapping of nanoparticles using nanostructured ultrathin optical fibers. *Opt. Express* **2016**, *24*, 14470. [CrossRef] [PubMed]

116. Tsai, W.Y.; Huang, J.S.; Huang, B.C. Selective trapping or rotation of isotropic dielectric microparticles by optical near field in a plasmonic archimedes spiral. *Nano Lett.* **2014**, *14*, 547–552. [CrossRef]

117. Wang, K.; Schonbrun, E.; Steinvurzel, P.; Crozier, K.B. Trapping and rotating nanoparticles using a plasmonic nano-tweezer with an integrated heat sink. *Nat. Commun.* **2011**, *2*. [CrossRef]

118. Yang, C.; Pan, D.; Tong, L.; Xu, H. Guided transport of nanoparticles by plasmonic nanowires. *Nanoscale* **2016**, *8*, 19195–19199. [CrossRef]

119. Dasgupta, A.; Singh, D.; Pavan Kumar, V.G. Dual-path remote-excitation surface enhanced Raman microscopy with plasmonic nanowire dimer. *Appl. Phys. Lett.* **2013**, *103*. [CrossRef]

120. Kumar, G.V.P. Plasmonic nano-architectures for surface enhanced Raman scattering: A review. *J. Nanophotonics* **2012**, *6*, 064503. [CrossRef]

121. Ru, L.E.C.; Blackie, E.; Meyer, M.; Etchegoin, P.G. Surface Enhanced Raman Scattering Enhancement Factors: A Comprehensive Study. *J. Phys. Chem. C* **2007**, *111*, 13794. [CrossRef]

122. Wang, A.X.; Kong, X. Review of recent progress of plasmonic materials and nano-structures for surface-enhanced raman scattering. *Materials* **2015**, *8*, 3024–3052. [CrossRef] [PubMed]

123. Huang, Y.; Fang, Y.; Zhang, Z.; Zhu, L.; Sun, M. Nanowire-supported plasmonic waveguide for remote excitation of surface-enhanced Raman scattering. *Light Sci. Appl.* **2014**, *3*. [CrossRef]

124. Cui, Y.; Hegde, R.S.; Phang, I.Y.; Lee, H.K.; Ling, X.Y. Encoding molecular information in plasmonic nanostructures for anti-counterfeiting applications. *Nanoscale* **2014**, *6*, 282–288. [CrossRef] [PubMed]

125. Cui, Y.; Phang, I.Y.; Lee, Y.H.; Lee, M.R.; Zhang, Q.; Ling, X.Y. Multiplex plasmonic anti-counterfeiting security labels based on surface-enhanced Raman scattering. *Chem. Commun.* **2015**, *51*, 5363–5366. [CrossRef]

126. Heeg, S.; Fernandez-Garcia, R.; Oikonomou, A.; Schedin, F.; Narula, R.; Maier, S.A.; Vijayaraghavan, A.; Reich, S. Polarized plasmonic enhancement by Au nanostructures probed through raman scattering of suspended graphene. *Nano Lett.* **2013**, *13*, 301–308. [CrossRef]

127. Venuthurumilli, P.K.; Ye, P.D.; Xu, X. Plasmonic Resonance Enhanced Polarization-Sensitive Photodetection by Black Phosphorus in Near Infrared. *ACS Nano* **2018**, *12*, 4861–4867. [CrossRef]

128. Li, Q.; Lu, J.; Gupta, P.; Qiu, M. Engineering Optical Absorption in Graphene and Other 2D Materials: Advances and Applications. *Adv. Opt. Mater.* **2019**, *7*, 1900595. [CrossRef]

129. Yuan, H.; Liu, X.; Afshinmanesh, F.; Li, W.; Xu, G.; Sun, J.; Lian, B.; Curto, A.G.; Ye, G.; Hikita, Y.; et al. Polarization-sensitive broadband photodetector using a black phosphorus vertical p-n junction. *Nat. Nanotechnol.* **2015**, *10*, 707–713. [CrossRef]

130. Kinzel, E.C.; Xu, X. Extraordinary infrared transmission through a periodic bowtie aperture array. *Opt. Lett.* **2010**, *35*, 992. [CrossRef]

131. Zheludev, N.I. Applied physics. The road ahead for metamaterials. *Science* **2010**, *328*, 582–583. [CrossRef]
132. Zheludev, N.I. Applied physics. Obtaining optical properties on demand. *Science* **2015**, *348*, 973–974. [CrossRef] [PubMed]
133. Li, J.; Yu, P.; Cheng, H.; Liu, W.; Li, Z.; Xie, B.; Chen, S.; Tian, J. Optical Polarization Encoding Using Graphene-Loaded Plasmonic Metasurfaces. *Adv. Opt. Mater.* **2016**, *4*, 91–98. [CrossRef]
134. Shen, N.H.; Massaouti, M.; Gokkavas, M.; Manceau, J.M.; Ozbay, E.; Kafesaki, M.; Koschny, T.; Tzortzakis, S.; Soukoulis, C.M. Optically implemented broadband blueshift switch in the terahertz regime. *Phys. Rev. Lett.* **2011**, *106*, 037403. [CrossRef]
135. Valmorra, F.; Scalari, G.; Maissen, C.; Fu, W.; Schönenberger, C.; Choi, J.W.; Park, H.G.; Beck, M.; Faist, J. Low-Bias Active Control of Terahertz Waves by Coupling Large-Area CVD Graphene to a Terahertz Metamaterial. *Nano Lett.* **2013**, *13*, 3193–3198. [CrossRef] [PubMed]
136. Liu, Y.; Ling, X.; Yi, X.; Zhou, X.; Chen, S.; Ke, Y.; Luo, H.; Wen, S. Photonic spin Hall effect in dielectric metasurfaces with rotational symmetry breaking. *Opt. Lett.* **2015**, *40*, 756–759. [CrossRef]
137. Shu, W.; Ke, Y.; Liu, Y.; Ling, X.; Luo, H.; Yin, X. Radial spin Hall effect of light. *Phys. Rev. A* **2016**, *93*, 013839. [CrossRef]
138. Barry, R.M. Fundamentals of Photonics, Second Edition. *J. Biomed. Opt.* **2008**, *13*, 1–4. [CrossRef]
139. She, J.; Shen, S.; Wang, Q. Optimal design of achromatic quarter-wave plate using twisted nematic liquid crystal cells. *Opt. Quantum Electron.* **2005**, *37*, 625–634. [CrossRef]
140. Shelby, R.A.; Smith, D.R.; Schultz, S. Experimental verification of a negative index of refraction. *Science* **2001**, *292*, 77–79. [CrossRef] [PubMed]
141. Pendry, J.B.; Schurig, D.; Smith, D.R. Controlling electromagnetic fields. *Science* **2006**, *312*, 1780–1782. [CrossRef]
142. Ni, X.; Wong, Z.J.; Mrejen, M.; Wang, Y.; Zhang, X. An ultrathin invisibility skin cloak for visible light. *Science* **2015**, *349*, 1310. [CrossRef] [PubMed]
143. Won, R. The rise of plasmonic metasurfaces. *Nature Photonics* **2017**, *11*, 462–464. [CrossRef]
144. Kildishev, A.V.; Boltasseva, A.; Shalaev, V.M. Planar photonics with metasurfaces. *Science* **2013**, *339*, 1232009. [CrossRef] [PubMed]
145. Liu, Z.; Li, Z.; Liu, Z.; Li, J.; Cheng, H.; Yu, P.; Liu, W.; Tang, C.; Gu, C.; Li, J.; et al. High-Performance Broadband Circularly Polarized Beam Deflector by Mirror Effect of Multinanorod Metasurfaces. *Adv. Funct. Mater.* **2015**, *25*, 5428–5434. [CrossRef]
146. Pors, A.; Nielsen, M.G.; Della Valle, G.; Willatzen, M.; Albrektsen, O.; Bozhevolnyi, S.I. Plasmonic metamaterial wave retarders in reflection by orthogonally oriented detuned electrical dipoles. *Opt. Lett.* **2011**, *36*, 1626–1628. [CrossRef]
147. Zhao, Y.; Alù, A. Tailoring the Dispersion of Plasmonic Nanorods to Realize Broadband Optical Meta-Waveplates. *Nano Lett.* **2013**, *13*, 1086–1091. [CrossRef]
148. Ellenbogen, T.; Seo, K.; Crozier, K.B. Chromatic plasmonic polarizers for active visible color filtering and polarimetry. *Nano Lett.* **2012**, *12*, 1026–1031. [CrossRef]
149. Li, T.; Liu, H.; Wang, S.-M.; Yin, X.-G.; Wang, F.-M.; Zhu, S.-N.; Zhang, X. Manipulating optical rotation in extraordinary transmission by hybrid plasmonic excitations. *Appl. Phys. Lett.* **2008**, *93*, 021110. [CrossRef]
150. Sung, J.; Sukharev, M.; Hicks, E.M.; Van Duyne, R.P.; Seideman, T.; Spears, K.G. Nanoparticle Spectroscopy: Birefringence in Two-Dimensional Arrays of L-Shaped Silver Nanoparticles. *J. Phys. Chem. C* **2008**, *112*, 3252–3260. [CrossRef]
151. Wu, S.; Zhang, Z.; Zhang, Y.; Zhang, K.; Zhou, L.; Zhang, X.; Zhu, Y. Enhanced Rotation of the Polarization of a Light Beam Transmitted through a Silver Film with an Array of Perforated S-Shaped Holes. *Phys. Rev. Lett.* **2013**, *110*, 207401. [CrossRef]
152. Zhang, S.; Zhou, J.; Park, Y.S.; Rho, J.; Singh, R.; Nam, S.; Azad, A.K.; Chen, H.T.; Yin, X.; Taylor, A.J.; et al. Photoinduced handedness switching in terahertz chiral metamolecules. *Nat. Commun.* **2012**, *3*, 942. [CrossRef] [PubMed]
153. Yin, X.; Schaferling, M.; Michel, A.K.; Tittl, A.; Wuttig, M.; Taubner, T.; Giessen, H. Active Chiral Plasmonics. *Nano Lett.* **2015**, *15*, 4255–4260. [CrossRef] [PubMed]
154. Jiang, Z.H.; Lin, L.; Ma, D.; Yun, S.; Werner, D.H.; Liu, Z.; Mayer, T.S. Broadband and wide field-of-view plasmonic metasurface-enabled waveplates. *Sci. Rep.* **2014**, *4*, 7511. [CrossRef] [PubMed]

155. Wu, C.; Arju, N.; Kelp, G.; Fan, J.A.; Dominguez, J.; Gonzales, E.; Tutuc, E.; Brener, I.; Shvets, G. Spectrally selective chiral silicon metasurfaces based on infrared Fano resonances. *Nat. Commun.* **2014**, *5*, 3892. [CrossRef]

156. Stokes, G.G. On the Composition and Resolution of Streams of Polarized Light from different Sources. *Trans. Camb. Philos. Soc.* **1851**, *9*, 399.

157. Ye, Y.; He, S. 90° polarization rotator using a bilayered chiral metamaterial with giant optical activity. *Appl. Phys. Lett.* **2010**, *96*, 203501. [CrossRef]

158. Chin, J.Y.; Lu, M.; Cui, T.J. Metamaterial polarizers by electric-field-coupled resonators. *Appl. Phys. Lett.* **2008**, *93*, 251903. [CrossRef]

159. Cui, J.; Huang, C.; Pan, W.; Pu, M.; Guo, Y.; Luo, X. Dynamical manipulation of electromagnetic polarization using anisotropic meta-mirror. *Sci. Rep.* **2016**, *6*, 30771. [CrossRef] [PubMed]

160. Federici, J.F.; Schulkin, B.; Huang, F.; Gary, D.; Barat, R.; Oliveira, F.; Zimdars, D. THz imaging and sensing for security applications—explosives, weapons and drugs. *Semicond. Sci. Technol.* **2005**, *20*, S266–S280. [CrossRef]

161. Piesiewicz, R.; Kleine-Ostmann, T.; Krumbholz, N.; Mittleman, D.; Koch, M.; Schoebel, J.; Kurner, T. Short-Range Ultra-Broadband Terahertz Communications: Concepts and Perspectives. *IEEE Antennas Propag. Mag.* **2007**, *49*, 24–39. [CrossRef]

162. Ho, I.C.; Guo, X.; Zhang, X.C. Design and performance of reflective terahertz air-biased-coherent-detection for time-domain spectroscopy. *Opt. Express* **2010**, *18*, 2872–2883. [CrossRef] [PubMed]

163. Cong, L.; Cao, W.; Tian, Z.; Gu, J.; Han, J.; Zhang, W. Manipulating polarization states of terahertz radiation using metamaterials. *New J. Phys.* **2012**, *14*, 115013. [CrossRef]

164. Cong, L.; Cao, W.; Zhang, X.; Tian, Z.; Gu, J.; Singh, R.; Han, J.; Zhang, W. A perfect metamaterial polarization rotator. *Appl. Phys. Lett.* **2013**, *103*, 171107. [CrossRef]

165. Zhao, Y.; Alù, A. Manipulating light polarization with ultrathin plasmonic metasurfaces. *Phys. Rev. B* **2011**, *84*, 205428. [CrossRef]

166. Cong, L.; Xu, N.; Gu, J.; Singh, R.; Han, J.; Zhang, W. Highly flexible broadband terahertz metamaterial quarter-wave plate. *Laser Photonics Rev.* **2014**, *8*, 626–632. [CrossRef]

167. Jiang, Y.; Zhao, H.; Wang, L.; Wang, J.; Cao, W.; Wang, Y. Broadband linear-to-circular polarization converter based on phosphorene metamaterial. *Opt. Mater. Express* **2019**, *9*. [CrossRef]

168. Pan, C.; Ren, M.; Li, Q.; Fan, S.; Xu, J. Broadband asymmetric transmission of optical waves from spiral plasmonic metamaterials. *Appl. Phys. Lett.* **2014**, *104*. [CrossRef]

169. Pfeiffer, C.; Zhang, C.; Ray, V.; Guo, L.J.; Grbic, A. High Performance Bianisotropic Metasurfaces: Asymmetric Transmission of Light. *Phys. Rev. Lett.* **2014**, *113*. [CrossRef]

170. Sonsilphong, A.; Wongkasem, N. Mid-infrared circular polarization switching in helical metamaterials. *J. Opt.* **2016**, *18*. [CrossRef]

171. Meinzer, N.; Barnes, W.L.; Hooper, I.R. Plasmonic meta-atoms and metasurfaces. *Nat. Photonics* **2014**, *8*, 889–898. [CrossRef]

172. Estakhri, N.M.; Alù, A. Recent progress in gradient metasurfaces. *J. Opt. Soc. Am. B* **2016**, *33*, A21. [CrossRef]

173. Zhu, A.Y.; Kuznetsov, A.I.; Luk'Yanchuk, B.; Engheta, N.; Genevet, P. Traditional and emerging materials for optical metasurfaces. *Nanophotonics* **2017**, *6*, 452–471. [CrossRef]

174. Yu, N.; Capasso, F. Flat optics with designer metasurfaces. *Nat. Mater.* **2014**, *13*, 139–150. [CrossRef] [PubMed]

175. Chen, S.; Liu, W.; Li, Z.; Cheng, H.; Tian, J. Metasurface-Empowered Optical Multiplexing and Multifunction. *Adv. Mater.* **2020**, *32*, 1805912. [CrossRef]

176. Pfeiffer, C.; Grbic, A. Cascaded metasurfaces for complete phase and polarization control. *Appl. Phys. Lett.* **2013**, *102*. [CrossRef]

177. Li, J.; Chen, S.; Yang, H.; Li, J.; Yu, P.; Cheng, H.; Gu, C.; Chen, H.T.; Tian, J. Simultaneous control of light polarization and phase distributions using plasmonic metasurfaces. *Adv. Funct. Mater.* **2015**, *25*, 704–710. [CrossRef]

178. Wang, W.; Guo, C.; Zhao, Z.; Li, J.; Shi, Y. Polarization multiplexing and bifocal optical vortex metalens. *Results Phys.* **2020**, *17*, 103033. [CrossRef]

179. Cheng, H.; Wei, X.; Yu, P.; Li, Z.; Liu, Z.; Li, J.; Chen, S.; Tian, J. Integrating polarization conversion and nearly perfect absorption with multifunctional metasurfaces. *Appl. Phys. Lett.* **2017**, *110*. [CrossRef]

180. Zheludev, N.I.; Plum, E. Reconfigurable nanomechanical photonic metamaterials. *Nat. Nanotechnol.* **2016**, *11*, 16–22. [CrossRef]

181. Ho, C.P.; Pitchappa, P.; Lin, Y.S.; Huang, C.Y.; Kropelnicki, P.; Lee, C. Electrothermally actuated microelectromechanical systems based omega-ring terahertz metamaterial with polarization dependent characteristics. *Appl. Phys. Lett.* **2014**, *104*. [CrossRef]

182. Zhao, X.; Schalch, J.; Zhang, J.; Seren, H.R.; Duan, G.; Averitt, R.D.; Zhang, X. Electromechanically tunable metasurface transmission waveplate at terahertz frequencies. *Optica* **2018**, *5*, 303. [CrossRef]

183. Wu, P.C.; Zhu, W.; Shen, Z.X.; Chong, P.H.J.; Ser, W.; Tsai, D.P.; Liu, A.Q. Broadband Wide-Angle Multifunctional Polarization Converter via Liquid-Metal-Based Metasurface. *Adv. Opt. Mater.* **2017**, *5*, 1–7. [CrossRef]

184. Ma, F.; Qian, Y.; Lin, Y.S.; Liu, H.; Zhang, X.; Liu, Z.; Ming-Lin Tsai, J.; Lee, C. Polarization-sensitive microelectromechanical systems based tunable terahertz metamaterials using three dimensional electric split-ring resonator arrays. *Appl. Phys. Lett.* **2013**, *102*. [CrossRef]

185. Nouman, M.T.; Hwang, J.H.; Faiyaz, M.; Lee, K.-J.; Noh, D.-Y.; Jang, J.-H. Vanadium dioxide based frequency tunable metasurface filters for realizing reconfigurable terahertz optical phase and polarization control. *Opt. Express* **2018**, *26*, 12922. [CrossRef] [PubMed]

186. Sugano, S.; Kojima, N. *Magneto-Optics*; Springer: Berlin/Heidelberg, Germany, 2000; ISBN 9783662041437.

187. Misemer, D.K. The effect of spin-orbit interaction and exchange splitting on magneto-optic coefficients. *J. Magn. Magn. Mater.* **1988**, *72*, 267–274. [CrossRef]

188. Stupakiewicz, A.; Chizhik, A.; Tekielak, M.; Zhukov, A.; Gonzalez, J.; Maziewski, A. Direct imaging of the magnetization reversal in microwires using all-MOKE microscopy. *Rev. Sci. Instrum.* **2014**, *85*, 103702. [CrossRef]

189. McDaniel, T. Magneto-optical data storage. *Commun. ACM* **2000**, *43*, 56–63. [CrossRef]

190. Shoji, Y.; Mizumoto, T.; Yokoi, H.; Hsieh, I.-W.; Osgood, R.M. Magneto-optical isolator with silicon waveguides fabricated by direct bonding. *Appl. Phys. Lett.* **2008**, *92*, 071117. [CrossRef]

191. Tien, P.K.; Martin, R.J.; Wolfe, R.; Le Craw, R.C.; Blank, S.L. Switching and modulation of light in magneto-optic waveguides of garnet films. *Appl. Phys. Lett.* **1972**, *21*, 394–396. [CrossRef]

192. Kim, S.; Hong, Y.-P.; Kim, Y.-G.; Lee, D.-J. Field-calibrated magneto-optic sensor based on off-axis optical probing of intense magnetic fields. *Appl. Opt.* **2017**, *56*, 1701. [CrossRef]

193. Chiu, K.W.; Quinn, J.J. Magnetoplasma Surface Waves in Metals. *Phys. Rev. B* **1972**, *5*, 4707–4709. [CrossRef]

194. Floess, D.; Giessen, H. Nonreciprocal hybrid magnetoplasmonics. *Rep. Prog. Phys.* **2018**, *81*, 116401. [CrossRef] [PubMed]

195. Chen, J.; Albella, P.; Pirzadeh, Z.; Alonso-González, P.; Huth, F.; Bonetti, S.; Bonanni, V.; Åkerman, J.; Nogués, J.; Vavassori, P.; et al. Plasmonic Nickel Nanoantennas. *Small* **2011**, *7*, 2341–2347. [CrossRef] [PubMed]

196. Tomitaka, A.; Arami, H.; Raymond, A.; Yndart, A.; Kaushik, A.; Jayant, R.D.; Takemura, Y.; Cai, Y.; Toborek, M.; Nair, M. Development of magneto-plasmonic nanoparticles for multimodal image-guided therapy to the brain. *Nanoscale* **2017**, *9*, 764–773. [CrossRef]

197. Urries, I.; Muñoz, C.; Gomez, L.; Marquina, C.; Sebastian, V.; Arruebo, M.; Santamaria, J. Magneto-plasmonic nanoparticles as theranostic platforms for magnetic resonance imaging, drug delivery and NIR hyperthermia applications. *Nanoscale* **2014**, *6*, 9230. [CrossRef]

198. Pineider, F.; Sangregorio, C. Nanomaterials for Magnetoplasmonics. In *Novel Magnetic Nanostructures*; Elsevier: Amsterdam, The Netherlands, 2018; pp. 191–220.

199. Li, Y.; Zhang, Q.; Nurmikko, A.V.; Sun, S. Enhanced Magnetooptical Response in Dumbbell-like Ag–CoFe 2 O 4 Nanoparticle Pairs. *Nano Lett.* **2005**, *5*, 1689–1692. [CrossRef]

200. Jain, P.K.; Xiao, Y.; Walsworth, R.; Cohen, A.E. Surface Plasmon Resonance Enhanced Magneto-Optics (SuPREMO): Faraday Rotation Enhancement in Gold-Coated Iron Oxide Nanocrystals. *Nano Lett.* **2009**, *9*, 1644–1650. [CrossRef]

201. Wang, L.; Clavero, C.; Huba, Z.; Carroll, K.J.; Carpenter, E.E.; Gu, D.; Lukaszew, R.A. Plasmonics and Enhanced Magneto-Optics in Core-Shell Co-Ag Nanoparticles. *Nano Lett.* **2011**, *11*, 37. [CrossRef]

202. Chin, J.Y.; Steinle, T.; Wehlus, T.; Dregely, D.; Weiss, T.; Belotelov, V.I.; Stritzker, B.; Giessen, H. Nonreciprocal plasmonics enables giant enhancement of thin-film Faraday rotation. *Nat. Commun.* **2013**, *4*, 1599. [CrossRef]

203. Fujikawa, R.; Baryshev, A.V.; Kim, J.; Uchida, H.; Inoue, M. Contribution of the surface plasmon resonance to optical and magneto-optical properties of a Bi:YIG-Au nanostructure. *J. Appl. Phys.* **2008**, *103*, 07D301. [CrossRef]

204. Floess, D.; Chin, J.Y.; Kawatani, A.; Dregely, D.; Habermeier, H.-U.; Weiss, T.; Giessen, H. Tunable and switchable polarisation rotation with non-reciprocal plasmonic thin films at designated wavelengths. *Light Sci. Appl.* **2015**, *4*, e284. [CrossRef]

205. Kuzmichev, A.N.; Sylgacheva, D.A.; Kozhaev, M.A.; Krichevsky, D.M.; Shaposhnikov, A.N.; Berzhansky, V.N.; Freire-Fernández, F.; Qin, H.J.; Popova, O.E.; Keller, N.; et al. Influence of the Plasmonic Nanodisk Positions Inside a Magnetic Medium on the Faraday Effect Enhancement. *Phys. Status Solidi Rapid Res. Lett.* **2020**, *14*, 1–4. [CrossRef]

206. Crassee, I.; Levallois, J.; Walter, A.L.; Ostler, M.; Bostwick, A.; Rotenberg, E.; Seyller, T.; van der Marel, D.; Kuzmenko, A.B. Giant Faraday rotation in single- and multilayer graphene. *Nat. Phys.* **2011**, *7*, 48–51. [CrossRef]

207. Tymchenko, M.; Nikitin, A.Y.; Martín-Moreno, L. Faraday Rotation Due to Excitation of Magnetoplasmons in Graphene Microribbons. *ACS Nano* **2013**, *7*, 9780–9787. [CrossRef]

208. Kimel, A.V.; Kirilyuk, A.; Usachev, P.A.; Pisarev, R.V.; Balbashov, A.M.; Rasing, T. Ultrafast non-thermal control of magnetization by instantaneous photomagnetic pulses. *Nature* **2005**, *435*, 655–657. [CrossRef]

209. Kruglyak, V.V.; Hicken, R.J.; Ali, M.; Hickey, B.J.; Pym, A.T.G.; Tanner, B.K. Ultrafast third-order optical nonlinearity of noble and transition metal thin films. *J. Opt. A Pure Appl. Opt.* **2005**, *7*. [CrossRef]

210. Hansteen, F.; Kimel, A.; Kirilyuk, A.; Rasing, T. Nonthermal ultrafast optical control of the magnetization in garnet films. *Phys. Rev. B—Condens. Matter Mater. Phys.* **2006**, *73*, 014421. [CrossRef]

211. Cheng, O.H.-C.; Son, D.H.; Sheldon, M. Light-induced magnetism in plasmonic gold nanoparticles. *Nat. Photonics* **2020**, 1–4. [CrossRef]

212. Bonanni, V.; Bonetti, S.; Pakizeh, T.; Pirzadeh, Z.; Chen, J.; Nogués, J.; Vavassori, P.; Hillenbrand, R.; Åkerman, J.; Dmitriev, A. Designer Magnetoplasmonics with Nickel Nanoferromagnets. *Nano Lett.* **2011**, *11*, 5333–5338. [CrossRef]

213. Safarov, V.I.; Kosobukin, V.A.; Hermann, C.; Lampel, G.; Peretti, J.; Marlière, C. Magneto-optical effects enhanced by surface plasmons in metallic multilayer films. *Phys. Rev. Lett.* **1994**, *73*, 3584–3587. [CrossRef]

214. González-Díaz, J.B.; García-Martín, A.; García-Martín, J.M.; Cebollada, A.; Armelles, G.; Sepúlveda, B.; Alaverdyan, Y.; Käll, M. Plasmonic Au/Co/Au Nanosandwiches with Enhanced Magneto-optical Activity. *Small* **2008**, *4*, 202–205. [CrossRef] [PubMed]

215. López-Ortega, A.; Zapata-Herrera, M.; Maccaferri, N.; Pancaldi, M.; Garcia, M.; Chuvilin, A.; Vavassori, P. Enhanced magnetic modulation of light polarisation exploiting hybridization with multipolar dark plasmons in magnetoplasmonic nanocavities. *Light Sci. Appl.* **2020**, *9*. [CrossRef] [PubMed]

216. Kreilkamp, L.E.; Belotelov, V.I.; Chin, J.Y.; Neutzner, S.; Dregely, D.; Wehlus, T.; Akimov, I.A.; Bayer, M.; Stritzker, B.; Giessen, H. Waveguide-Plasmon Polaritons Enhance Transverse Magneto-Optical Kerr Effect. *Phys. Rev. X* **2013**, *3*, 041019. [CrossRef]

217. Manera, M.G.; Colombelli, A.; Taurino, A.; Martin, A.G.; Rella, R. Magneto-Optical properties of noble-metal nanostructures: Functional nanomaterials for bio sensing. *Sci. Rep.* **2018**, *8*, 12640. [CrossRef] [PubMed]

218. Rizal, C.; Kapralov, P.O.; Ignatyeva, D.; Belotelov, V.; Pisana, S. Comparison of the effects of surface plasmon resonance and the transverse magneto-optic Kerr effect in magneto-optic plasmonic nanostructures. *J. Phys. D Appl. Phys.* **2020**, *53*, 02LT02. [CrossRef]

219. Pendry, J.B.; Holden, A.J.; Robbins, D.J.; Stewart, W.J. Magnetism from conductors and enhanced nonlinear phenomena. *IEEE Trans. Microw. Theory Tech.* **1999**, *47*, 2075–2084. [CrossRef]

220. Klein, M.W.; Enkrich, C.; Wegener, M.; Soukoulis, C.M.; Linden, S. Single-slit split-ring resonators at optical frequencies: Limits of size scaling. *Opt. Lett.* **2006**, *31*, 1259–1261. [CrossRef]

221. Bao, Y.; Hu, Z.; Li, Z.; Zhu, X.; Fang, Z. Magnetic Plasmonic Fano Resonance at Optical Frequency. *Small* **2015**, *11*, 2177–2181. [CrossRef]

222. Kuznetsov, A.I.; Miroshnichenko, A.E.; Hsing Fu, Y.; Viswanathan, V.; Rahmani, M.; Valuckas, V.; Ying Pan, Z.; Kivshar, Y.; Pickard, D.S.; Luk'Yanchuk, B. Split-ball resonator as a three-dimensional analogue of planar split-rings. *Nat. Commun.* **2014**, *5*, 1–8. [CrossRef]

223. Wang, P.; Huh, J.; Lee, J.; Kim, K.; Park, K.J.; Lee, S.; Ke, Y. Magnetic Plasmon Networks Programmed by Molecular Self-Assembly. *Adv. Mater.* **2019**, *31*, 1901364. [CrossRef]

224. Monticone, F.; Alù, A. The quest for optical magnetism: From split-ring resonators to plasmonic nanoparticles and nanoclusters. *J. Mater. Chem. C* **2014**, *2*, 9059–9072. [CrossRef]

225. Calandrini, E.; Cerea, A.; De Angelis, F.; Zaccaria, R.P.; Toma, A. Magnetic hot-spot generation at optical frequencies: From plasmonic metamolecules to all-dielectric nanoclusters. *Nanophotonics* **2018**, *8*, 45–62. [CrossRef]

226. Sandrock, M.L.; Pibel, C.D.; Geiger, F.M.; Foss, C.A. Synthesis and second-harmonic generation studies of noncentrosymmetric gold nanostructures. *J. Phys. Chem. B* **1999**, *103*, 2668–2673. [CrossRef]

227. Lippitz, M.; Van Dijk, M.A.; Orrit, M. Third-harmonic generation from single gold nanoparticles. *Nano Lett.* **2005**, *5*, 799–802. [CrossRef]

228. Kruk, S.; Weismann, M.; Bykov, A.Y.; Mamonov, E.A.; Kolmychek, I.A.; Murzina, T.; Panoiu, N.C.; Neshev, D.N.; Kivshar, Y.S. Enhanced Magnetic Second-Harmonic Generation from Resonant Metasurfaces. *ACS Photonics* **2015**, *2*, 1007–1012. [CrossRef]

229. Ding, S.J.; Zhang, H.; Yang, D.J.; Qiu, Y.H.; Nan, F.; Yang, Z.J.; Wang, J.; Wang, Q.Q.; Lin, H.Q. Magnetic Plasmon-Enhanced Second-Harmonic Generation on Colloidal Gold Nanocups. *Nano Lett.* **2019**, *19*, 2005–2011. [CrossRef]

230. Shcherbakov, M.R.; Neshev, D.N.; Hopkins, B.; Shorokhov, A.S.; Staude, I.; Melik-Gaykazyan, E.V.; Decker, M.; Ezhov, A.A.; Miroshnichenko, A.E.; Brener, I.; et al. Enhanced third-harmonic generation in silicon nanoparticles driven by magnetic response. *Nano Lett.* **2014**, *14*, 6488–6492. [CrossRef]

231. Krutyanskiy, V.L.; Kolmychek, I.A.; Gan'shina, E.A.; Murzina, T.V.; Evans, P.; Pollard, R.; Stashkevich, A.A.; Wurtz, G.A.; Zayats, A.V. Plasmonic enhancement of nonlinear magneto-optical response in nickel nanorod metamaterials. *Phys. Rev. B* **2013**, *87*, 035116. [CrossRef]

232. Kolmychek, I.A.; Shaimanov, A.N.; Baryshev, A.V.; Murzina, T. V Magnetization-induced effects in second harmonic generation under the lattice plasmon resonance excitation. *Opt. Lett.* **2016**, *41*, 5446. [CrossRef]

233. Valev, V.K.; Silhanek, A.V.; Gillijns, W.; Jeyaram, Y.; Paddubrouskaya, H.; Volodin, A.; Biris, C.G.; Panoiu, N.C.; De Clercq, B.; Ameloot, M.; et al. Plasmons reveal the direction of magnetization in nickel nanostructures. *ACS Nano* **2011**, *5*, 91–96. [CrossRef]

234. Pineider, F.; Campo, G.; Bonanni, V.; Fernández, C.D.J.; Mattei, G.; Caneschi, A.; Gatteschi, D.; Sangregorio, C. Circular magnetoplasmonic modes in gold nanoparticles. *Nano Lett.* **2013**, *13*, 4785–4789. [CrossRef] [PubMed]

235. Melnikau, D.; Govyadinov, A.A.; Sánchez-Iglesias, A.; Grzelczak, M.; Liz-Marzán, L.M.; Rakovich, Y.P. Strong Magneto-Optical Response of Nonmagnetic Organic Materials Coupled to Plasmonic Nanostructures. *Nano Lett.* **2017**, *17*, 1808–1813. [CrossRef]

236. Shiratsu, T.; Yao, H. Magnetic circular dichroism (MCD) in silver nanocubes with different sizes. *Chem. Phys. Lett.* **2018**, *706*, 607–612. [CrossRef]

237. Yin, P.; Tan, Y.; Fang, H.; Hegde, M.; Radovanovic, P.V. Plasmon-induced carrier polarisation in semiconductor nanocrystals. *Nat. Nanotechnol.* **2018**, *13*, 463–467. [CrossRef] [PubMed]

238. Pineider, F.; de Julián Fernández, C.; Videtta, V.; Carlino, E.; al Hourani, A.; Wilhelm, F.; Rogalev, A.; Cozzoli, P.D.; Ghigna, P.; Sangregorio, C. Spin-Polarisation Transfer in Colloidal Magnetic-Plasmonic Au/Iron Oxide Hetero-nanocrystals. *ACS Nano* **2013**, *7*, 857–866. [CrossRef]

239. Sepúlveda, B.; Calle, A.; Lechuga, L.M.; Armelles, G. Highly sensitive detection of biomolecules with the magneto-optic surface-plasmon-resonance sensor. *Opt. Lett.* **2006**, *31*, 1085. [CrossRef] [PubMed]

240. Rizal, C.; Pisana, S.; Hrvoic, I.; Fullerton, E.E. Microstructure and magneto-optical surface plasmon resonance of Co/Au multilayers. *J. Phys. Commun.* **2018**, *2*, 055010. [CrossRef]

241. Manera, M.G.; Colombelli, A.; Rella, R.; Caricato, A.; Cozzoli, P.D.; Martino, M.; Vasanelli, L. TiO 2 brookite nanostructured thin layer on magneto-optical surface plasmon resonance transductor for gas sensing applications. *J. Appl. Phys.* **2012**, *112*, 053524. [CrossRef]

242. Zubritskaya, I.; Lodewijks, K.; Maccaferri, N.; Mekonnen, A.; Dumas, R.K.; Åkerman, J.; Vavassori, P.; Dmitriev, A. Active Magnetoplasmonic Ruler. *Nano Lett.* **2015**, *15*, 3204–3211. [CrossRef] [PubMed]

243. Wang, X.; Feng, J.; Yu, H.; Jin, Y.; Davidson, A.; Li, Z.; Yin, Y. Anisotropically Shaped Magnetic/Plasmonic Nanocomposites for Information Encryption and Magnetic-Field-Direction Sensing. *Research* **2018**, *2018*, 1–13. [CrossRef]

244. Pancaldi, M.; Leo, N.; Vavassori, P. Selective and fast plasmon-assisted photo-heating of nanomagnets. *Nanoscale* **2019**, *11*, 7656–7666. [CrossRef] [PubMed]

245. Belotelov, V.I.; Kreilkamp, L.E.; Akimov, I.A.; Kalish, A.N.; Bykov, D.A.; Kasture, S.; Yallapragada, V.J.; Gopal, A.V.; Grishin, A.M.; Khartsev, S.I.; et al. Plasmon-mediated magneto-optical transparency. *Nat. Commun.* **2013**, *4*, 1–7. [CrossRef] [PubMed]

246. Zubritskaya, I.; Maccaferri, N.; Inchausti Ezeiza, X.; Vavassori, P.; Dmitriev, A. Magnetic Control of the Chiroptical Plasmonic Surfaces. *Nano Lett.* **2018**, *18*, 302–307. [CrossRef] [PubMed]

247. Song, Y.; Tran, V.T.; Lee, J. Tuning Plasmon Resonance in Magnetoplasmonic Nanochains by Controlling Polarisation and Interparticle Distance for Simple Preparation of Optical Filters. *ACS Appl. Mater. Interfaces* **2017**, *9*, 24433–24439. [CrossRef]

Review

Applications of Symmetry Breaking in Plasmonics

Grégory Barbillon [1,*], Andrey Ivanov [2] and Andrey K. Sarychev [2]

[1] EPF-Ecole d'Ingénieurs, 3 bis rue Lakanal, 92330 Sceaux, France
[2] Institute for Theoretical and Applied Electrodynamics, Russian Academy of Sciences,
    Moscow 125412, Russia; av.ivanov@physics.msu.ru (A.I.); sarychev@bioplasmonics.com (A.K.S.)
* Correspondence: gregory.barbillon@epf.fr

Received: 25 April 2020; Accepted: 19 May 2020; Published: 1 June 2020

Abstract: Plasmonics is one of the most used domains for applications to optical devices, biological and chemical sensing, and non-linear optics, for instance. Indeed, plasmonics enables confining the electromagnetic field at the nanoscale. The resonances of plasmonic systems can be set in a given domain of a spectrum by adjusting the geometry, the spatial arrangement, and the nature of the materials. Moreover, symmetry breaking can be used for the further improvement of the optical properties of the plasmonic systems. In the last three years, great advances in or insights into the use of symmetry breaking in plasmonics have occurred. In this mini-review, we present recent insights and advances on the use of symmetry breaking in plasmonics for applications to chemistry, sensing, devices, non-linear optics, and chirality.

Keywords: symmetry breaking; chiral plasmonics; non-linear optics; plasmonic devices; plasmonic sensing

1. Introduction

Since the 2000s, the plasmonic nanostructures or nanoparticles have been widely used for realizing optical [1–6] and photovoltaic devices [7–10], as well as sensors of biological and chemical molecules [11–27]. Indeed, these plasmonic systems have different modes such as dipolar resonances [28,29], multipolar resonances [28,29], surface lattice resonances [30], and coupled resonances [31–34]. All these resonances can be set by varying their geometries and the employed materials. Moreover, thanks to the modern tools of fabrication at the nanoscale such as optical and interference lithographies [35–40], focused ion-beam lithography [41], electron-beam lithography [42–45], Nanosphere Lithography (NSL) [46–49], and Nanoimprint Lithography (NIL) [50], the plasmonic systems can be realized by taking into account the different parameters cited above, with an excellent control and accuracy. In addition, another phenomenon can be used for improving the optical properties of plasmonic nanosystems or nanostructures. The latter is symmetry breaking. Indeed, the linear symmetry breaking in plasmonic nanostructures [51,52] has been recently used for studying asymmetric metallic/dielectric metamaterials in order to fabricate photonic devices [53]. To break the symmetry, the structural geometry is modified in order to have an asymmetric system (in-plane or out-of-plane) [54–57]. The alteration of the excitation conditions (light polarization or incidence angle) [58,59] can also induce broken symmetry. Moreover, the effect of the non-linear broken symmetry can be observed as well. For instance, a non-linear symmetry breaking of the Kerr-type has allowed the emergence of a new asymmetric non-linear mode [60]. Other examples of symmetry breaking in non-linear regimes have been observed and studied in non-linear couplers [61] and also in the non-linearity-induced localization of plasmon beams for more sophisticated settings [62].

During these last three years, great advances or insights into the use of symmetry breaking in plasmonics have occurred. Here, an overview of these recent insights and advances on the use of symmetry breaking in plasmonics is reported. We begin by a review of the applications of symmetry breaking to plasmonic devices. Next, we present the applications to non-linear optics, then those to chiral plasmonics. Finally, a review on the applications of symmetry breaking to chemistry and plasmonic sensing is summarized.

2. What Is Symmetry Breaking in Plasmonics?

The symmetry in plasmonic structures strongly affects their optical response. Any structure in gold, silver or another noble metal can be considered as a plasmon antenna where the incident light excites various plasmonic modes. For symmetric metal structures whose size is smaller than the wavelength, the dipolar Electromagnetic (EM) modes prevail. Spatial symmetry breaking induced by the changing of the geometry results in the excitation of other modes [52,54] with much larger local field enhancement since these modes could have small radiation losses. In low symmetry plasmon structures, the incident electromagnetic field achieves so-called dark modes. For instance, symmetry breaking in metallic nanoantenna dimers can induce Fano resonances caused by the interaction of narrow dark modes with broad radiating bright modes [51,52]. In this case, the resonance shape can be tuned by the incidence angle of impinging light. Symmetry breaking reduces degeneracy, and the resonance eigenmodes of the low-symmetry plasmon structures are distributed over all of the frequency space. The scattered field can be always expand in spherical harmonics; however, the coefficients of the expansion have a "geometric" part that can strongly depend on the direction and polarization of the incident light. Non-uniformity of the local field is important for non-linear effects. Another interesting case of symmetry breaking in plasmonics is chiral molecules deposited on a plasmon structure [63]. The plasmon resonance increases the natural chirality, so the whole system loses its symmetry.

3. Applications of Symmetry Breaking in Plasmonics

3.1. Applications to Plasmonic Devices

The first field of application for symmetry breaking is plasmonic devices. Several groups have worked on this first application field (see Table 1).

Table 1. Improved performances and applications due to symmetry breaking in the field of the plasmonic devices (HMM = Hyperbolic Metamaterials; EP = Exceptional Point).

Refs.	Improved Performances	Applications
[64]	Plasmon-induced transparency effect	Biosensing and spectral filters in the terahertz regime
[65]	Amplitude control of transmitted light	Security features for anticounterfeiting
[66]	Scattering directions	Polarization-dependent security patterns
[67]	Tunability of the multimode laser effect	Loss-compensated magnetoplasmonic devices
[68]	Polarization-dependent lasing responses	Optical sensing and communications
[69]	Optical feedback for nanolasing	Super-resolved imaging and on-chip circuitry
[70]	Laser effect with weak scattering	Optofluidic random laser
[71]	High transmission efficiency	Photodiodes and single-photon avalanche diodes
[72]	Generation of exceptional points	Active components with HMMs and EP
[73]	Transverse photo-induced voltage	Photodetection and chiral sensing
[74]	Non-Hermicity-induced strong coupling	Localized surface plasmon systems
[75]	Reversal of optical binding force	Sensors and particle clustering/aggregation
[76]	Optical spectral features	Ultrasensitive biosensing and efficient photocatalysis

Firstly, Jia et al. reported on obtaining a significant plasmon-induced transparency in THz metamaterials, which can be governed by breaking the structural symmetry [64]. Another example with plasmonic metasurfaces has been investigated where the amplitude and phase of the transmitted signal are controllable by symmetry breaking [65]. In addition, Esposito et al. studied how the symmetry and symmetry breaking of an oligomer allowed the control of the scattering directions [66]. Besides, other groups have demonstrated a laser effect by using symmetry breaking with plasmonic nanostructures such as Ni nanodisc arrays [67], Al nanoparticle arrays [68], and Au nanocrescent arrays [69]. Pourjamal et al. reported on the laser effect (at visible wavelengths) by using ferromagnetic Ni nanodisc arrays on which an organic gain medium was deposited. They observed laser modes (tunable) at different wavelengths by using symmetry breaking of the Ni nanodisc array [67].

Knudson et al. showed polarization-dependent plasmonic lasing responses with rhombohedral arrays of Al anisotropic nanoparticles. When a modification of the excitation beam polarization occurred, the symmetry of the Al nanoparticle array changed (symmetry breaking), and thus, a laser emission wavelength could be selected following the polarization of the pump beam (here, two wavelengths were possible; see Figure 1). The lasing thresholds obtained for these two wavelengths were very similar (see Figure 1d and [68]). Lin et al. described bright quadrupolar lattice plasmon modes obtained for gold nanocrescent arrays that had symmetry breaking could be used as optical feedback for the nanolaser effect. Moreover, if the polarization of the pump beam was changed, the laser effect could be activated or not [69]. Finally, the importance of a replica of broken symmetry was reported for a random laser with weak scattering in an optofluidic environment. The authors remarked that the laser effect coincided with Replica Symmetry Breaking (RSB) and Lévy flight statistics [70].

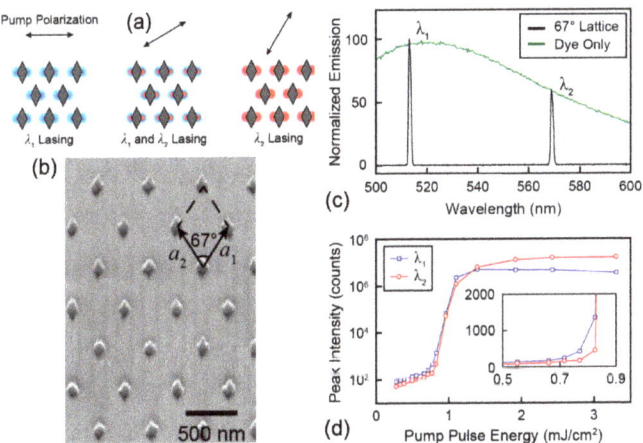

Figure 1. (**a**) Principle scheme of lasing at different wavelengths (λ_1 and λ_2) depending on the polarization of the pump beam. (**b**) SEM picture of a rhombohedral array of Al nanoparticles displaying the vectors of the lattice. (**c**) Normalized emission spectra for the Al nanoparticle array (lattice angle = 67°) on which dye molecules are deposited (in black) and for only dye molecules (in green). (**d**) Peak intensity versus pump pulse energy for the two wavelengths (λ_1 in blue and λ_2 in red). The zoom in (**d**) displays the lasing threshold for the two wavelengths better. All the figures were reprinted (adapted) with permission from [68], Copyright 2019, American Chemical Society.

Besides, Shah et al. showed a high transmission efficiency (44%) with a narrow linewidth (79 nm) from nanohole arrays in a metallic layer. The nanohole shapes used in this study were elliptical and circular, and the organization of the nanoholes was periodic with a periodicity a* (see Figure 2a). They also remarked that this high transmission efficiency was independent of the incidence beam polarization, and the narrow linewidth was caused by an interaction between the extraordinary optical transmission and the Fano resonance. This Fano resonance was realized by symmetry breaking of the nanoholes, which was obtained thanks to the polarization of the impinging beam. Moreover, the experimental transmission peak of 44% observed in Figure 2b is asymmetric, which is characteristic of a Fano resonance (see Figure 2b, the comparison between experiments, and the analytical Fano lineshape). The experimental result (transmission peak) was in good agreement with the analytical

Fano lineshape. Furthermore, from electric field mappings recorded at $\lambda_{peak} = 1642$ nm displayed in Figure 2b, a larger confinement of electric field ($|E|^2$) for elliptical holes was achieved compared to circular holes. Finally, a reflection mode confined within the substrate was observed at $\lambda = 1440$ nm (see Figure 2b and the electric field mapping at 1440 nm for ellipses) [71]. Vaianella et al. investigated the influence of dye molecules integrated in a dielectric medium composed of multilayers of hyperbolic metamaterials. They observed in the regime of strong coupling that strong alterations of plasmonic modes were generated by absorption and emission. These alterations were caused by the splitting of Rabi and the Parity–Time (PT)-symmetry breaking phase with production of Exceptional Points (EP) at certain frequencies [72]. In addition, Akbari et al. reported on the manipulation of the transverse photovoltage obtained with plasmonic triangle holes. This manipulation of the photovoltage (transverse) was elucidated by analyzing the broken symmetry of the mappings of the electric and magnetic fields for plasmonic triangle holes illuminated by a circularly-polarized incident light [73]. Lourenco-Martins et al. demonstrated theoretically and experimentally the strong coupling induced by the non-Hermicity between several plasmonic modes of different orders obtained with silver nanodaggers, which were localized plasmonic systems. This non-Hermicity stemmed from spatial symmetry breaking [74]. Furthermore, the last two examples presented in this mini-review were concerned with the optical properties of plasmonic nanostructures such as spherical heterodimers [75] and tetrahedral nanoparticles [76]. In the first of these two examples, Mahdy et al. reported that the control of the inversion of binding force (here, the force longitudinal component) could be done by varying the light direction or by manipulating its relative orientation with forced symmetry breaking spherical heterodimers [75]. Finally, in the second example, Zheng et al. proved that the tetrahedral shape of a plasmonic nanoparticle, which naturally has symmetry breaking, opens the way toward hybridizations between bright dipolar and quadrupolar modes [76].

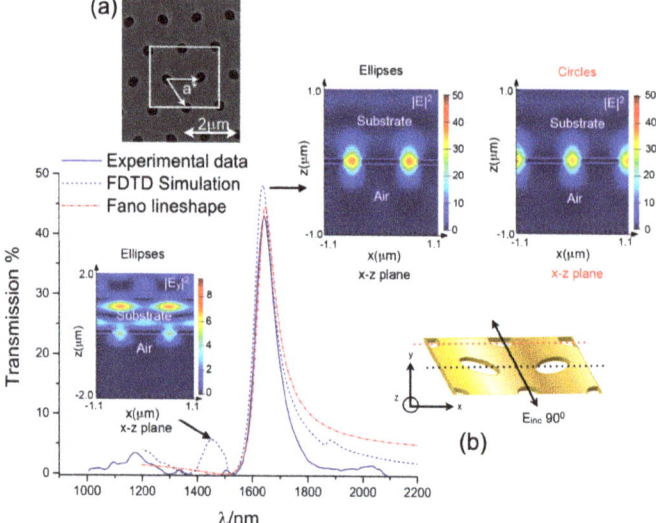

Figure 2. (**a**) SEM picture of periodic nanoholes. a* corresponds to the periodicity. (**b**) Comparison between experiments, FDTD simulations, and the analytical Fano lineshape for $E_{inc} = 90°$. From electric field mappings recorded at $\lambda_{peak} = 1642$ nm, $|E|^2$ for elliptical holes is larger than $|E|^2$ for circular holes. From the electric field mapping recorded at $\lambda = 1440$ nm, a reflection within the substrate is displayed. All the figures were reprinted (adapted) with permission from [71], Copyright 2018, American Chemical Society.

3.2. Applications to Non-Linear Optics

The second field of application for symmetry breaking is non-linear optics. Several groups have demonstrated that symmetry breaking can improve the optical performances of plasmonic systems applied to non-linear optics (see Table 2).

Table 2. Improved performances and applications due to symmetry breaking in the field of non-linear optics (SHG = Second Harmonic Generation; FWM = Four-Wave Mixing; TDMC = Transition Metal Dichalcogenides; SRR = Split-Ring Resonator; SFG = Sum Frequency Generation).

Refs.	Improved Performances	Applications
[77]	Polarization-dependent SHG signals	Detection of the symmetry of nanostructures/molecules
[78]	SHG and FWM non-linear processes	Identification of the role of high-order antenna modes
[79]	Second-order non-linear susceptibilities	Creation and active tuning of second-order non-linearities
[80]	Plasmon-enhanced SHG of TDMCs	Ideal integration platform for on-chip non-linear plasmonics
[81]	SHG of vertical SRRs	Photonics and sensing
[82]	SFG signals	Spectroscopic analysis and sensing of molecules

For instance, Rahmani et al. demonstrated that a novel type of non-linear broken symmetry in plasmonic nanosystems (oligomers) was observed by analyzing the Second Harmonic Generation (SHG) variations due to the change of the angle of impinging light polarization (see Figure 3). Figure 3 shows a scheme of the nanostructures investigated in this paper with the excitation conditions and also the SHG intensity versus the azimuthal angle of the linear polarization for the excitation light. This approach can enable the detection of the symmetry of oligomers or other molecules [77].

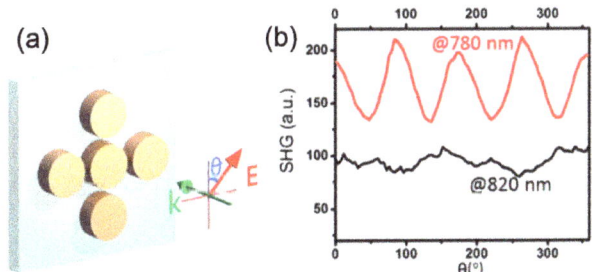

Figure 3. (**a**) Scheme of the studied pentamer on a glass substrate with the excitation conditions. (**b**) SHG intensity versus the azimuthal angle of the excitation polarization (in red, λ_{exc} = 780 nm, and in black, λ_{exc} = 820 nm). All the figures were reprinted (adapted) with permission from [77], Copyright 2017, American Chemical Society.

In addition, Gennaro et al. investigated the significance of higher order modes of antennas with metasurfaces having a non-linear gradient (broken symmetry) and based on the Pancharatnam–Berry phase by using SHG and Four-Wave Mixing (FWM) non-linear signals. They demonstrated that generalized diffraction rules (for the geometric phase) were found taking into account the higher order modes and the structural rotation in order to extend the geometric phase metasurfaces to non-linear signals with a broken symmetry [78]. Another different example of applications is the creation and the active control of second-order non-linearities as the second-order non-linear susceptibility $\chi^{(2)}$. Indeed, Taghinejad et al. demonstrated that inversion symmetry breaking by using hot-electron dynamics could be employed in order to have an all-optical tuning of effective responses for $\chi^{(2)}$. In this study, a hybrid system composed of an Au triangle on an amorphous TiO_2 film was used for conversion under the picosecond of an inactive dielectric material into a transient non-linear medium thanks to an ultrafast transfer of hot electrons [79]. Besides, Shi et al. observed a significant enhancement (~400) of the SHG signal by using a monolayer of Transition Metal Dichalcogenides (TMDCs; here tungsten disulfide WS_2) integrated on a silver nanogroove grating. One of the optical properties of TDMCs is a significant second-order non-linearity, which has a broken inversion symmetry in 2D crystals. However, this non-linearity is limited by a sub-nanometric thickness. Thus, this monolayer of WS_2 is deposited on plasmonic nanogrooves spatially arranged in a grating in order to enhance the SHG signal. The surface plasmon in nanogrooves is excited in a such way that the SHG frequency is in resonance with the C-exciton of the WS_2 film. The SHG enhancement is due to the significant electric field confinement in the nanogrooves [80].

In the following two examples, symmetry breaking inducing modifications of non-linear optical properties is dedicated to the sensing of molecules. For the first example, Tsai et al. demonstrated an enhancement factor of 2.6 for the SHG non-linearity obtained with vertical Split-Ring Resonators (vertical SRRs = U-shaped nanostructures of which the basis of U is only on the glass substrate; see more details in [81]) compared to the planar SRRs. In this study, plasmonic SRRs had geometries with broken centro-symmetries at the level of the interface between air and the plasmonic surface. This enhancement of the SHG signal was due to the fact that vertical SRRs could lift the localized fields (electric and magnetic) of surface plasmons, which were confined between the two vertical arms and did not "touch" the glass substrate [81]. In the second example, Dalstein et al. observed an improvement of the non-linear optical signal called Sum Frequency Generation (SFG) for gold spherical nanoparticles coated with dodecanethiol molecules by red-shifting the visible wavelength of excitation (see Figure 4). This enhancement was due to the plasmonic coupling involved in the SFG phenomenon when the excitation wavelength located in the visible spectral domain was red-shifted, and the fact that strong electric fields and a broken symmetry related to hotspots created in nanoparticle multimers (or aggregates) were involved in the plasmonic coupling, even if the presence of multimers or aggregates of Au nanospheres was weak [82]. Figure 4 displays a SEM image of gold nanospheres on Si substrate, where we observe a couple of multimers or aggregates. Then, SFG spectra recorded at 20 visible wavelengths of excitation are presented, and finally SFG intensity is displayed versus excitation wavelength. Indeed, from the SFG spectra displayed in Figure 4b,c, an increase of the SFG signal was observed when the visible wavelength of excitation was red-shifted, as explained previously.

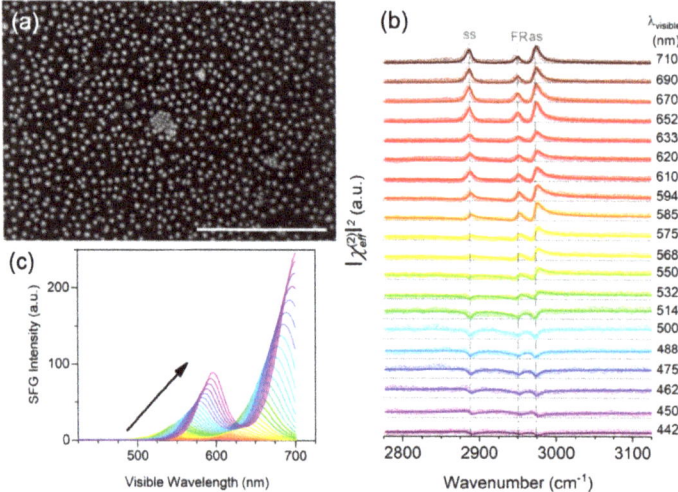

Figure 4. (**a**) SEM picture of Au nanospheres on Si substrate (scale bar = 500 nm). (**b**) SFG spectra recorded at 20 visible wavelengths of excitation (from 442 nm to 710 nm). (**c**) SFG intensity versus the visible wavelength of excitation. All the figures were reprinted (adapted) with permission from [82], Copyright 2019, American Chemical Society.

3.3. Applications to Chiral Plasmonics

The third field of application for symmetry breaking is chiral plasmonics. A couple of groups reported on chiral plasmonic nanostructures with symmetry breaking (see Table 3) such as Au nanorod equilateral trimers [83], chiral metamaterials composed of plasmonic slanted nanoapertures [84], plasmonic Λ-shaped nanostructures [85], plasmonic ramp-shaped nanostructures [86], 3D plasmonic crescents [87], and GaAS/Au nanowires [88].

Table 3. Improved performances and applications due to symmetry breaking in the field of chiral plasmonics.

Refs.	Improved Performances	Applications
[83]	Hybridized plasmon modes	Optical magnetic field enhancement
[84]	Circular dichroism in transmission	Chiral imaging, sensing, and spectroscopy
[85]	3D chiral effects	Study of complex plasmonic nanostructures
[86]	Circular dichroism	Nanoscale circular polarizers
[87]	Tailoring of circular dichroism	Chiral sensing and circular dichroism spectroscopy
[88]	Circular dichroism	Chiral sensing devices

In the first example, the bidimensional chiral effect was approached. Greybush et al. demonstrated that gold nanorod assemblies (see the examples in Figure 5a) enabled obtaining hybrid plasmonic modes, which were dependent on rotation and polarization. These hybrid plasmonic modes were also sensitive to the changes of the size, position, and orientation of gold nanorods that were conducive to the symmetry breaking of the geometry. The hybrid plasmonic modes (resonances) were characterized by using dark-field scattering spectroscopy under excitation for which the Polarization was Left-Circular (LCP) or Right-Circular (RCP) (see Figure 5b). The chiroptical response of gold nanorod assemblies was obtained by determining the percent of the Circular Differential Scattering (%CDS; see Figure 5c), which depended on the scattering intensities under LCP excitation and RCP excitation [83]. Figure 5b,c displays the scattering spectra with LCP and RCP excitation in which several peaks appear indicating a privileged excitation conducive to a "bisignate" lineshape of which the values of the chiroptical response %CDS could be negative or positive.

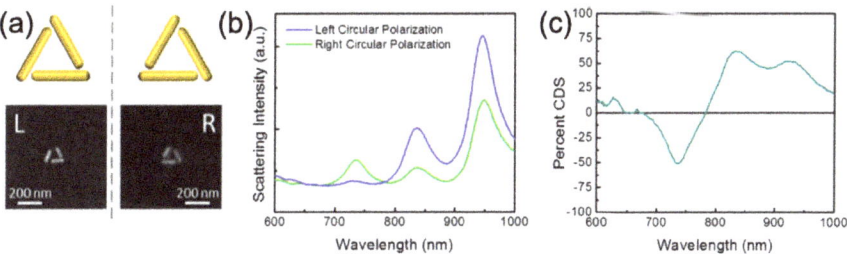

Figure 5. (**a**) Scheme and SEM pictures of a nanorod trimer oriented "at the left" (L) and oriented "at the right" (R). (**b**) Experimental scattering spectra for the trimer oriented "at the right" illuminated with a left circular (in blue) polarization and a right circular (in green) polarization of the excitation beam. (**c**) Circular Differential Scattering (CDS) versus the wavelength obtained with the scattering data of (**b**). All the figures were reprinted (adapted) with permission from [83], Copyright 2019, American Chemical Society.

Now, we report on the tridimensional chiral effect. Chen et al. reported on a novel design of chiral metamaterials based on the tilt of nanoapertures along a given direction (see Figure 6a,b) in order to break all the symmetries. This novel design consisted of slanted split-ring nanoapertures (SSRA) and allowed obtaining a giant Circular Dichroism in Transmission (CDT) in the spectral range of the near-infrared (78% at 760 nm; see Figure 6c), which depended on Transmissions recorded with a Left-Circular (T-LCP) or Right-Circular Polarization (T-RCP) of incident light. Moreover, this giant CDT came from a mode coupling between portions of the waveguide within slanted nanoapertures [84].

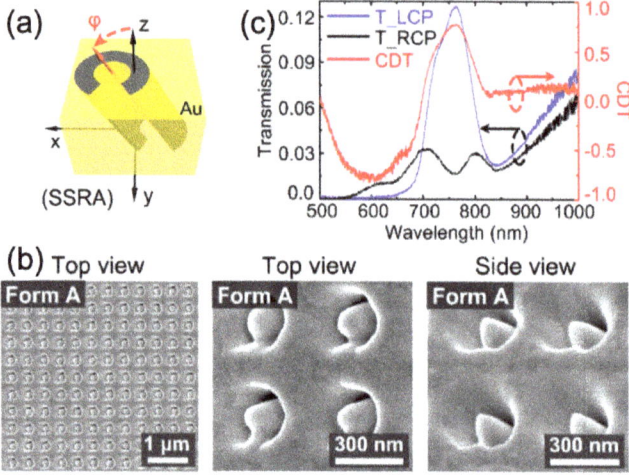

Figure 6. (**a**) Scheme of a slanted split-ring nanoaperture (SSRA). (**b**) SEM pictures of SSRA in Form A with an inclination angle of 40°. (**c**) Experimental spectra of transmission for SSRA (in Form A) with Transmissions recorded with a Left-Circular (T-LCP) (in blue color) or Right-Circular Polarization (T-RCP) (in black color) of incident light and the corresponding spectrum of Circular Dichroism in Transmission (CDT, in red color). All the figures were reprinted (adapted) with permission from [84], Copyright 2018, American Chemical Society.

Pham et al. demonstrated 3D chiral effects in Λ-shaped plasmonic nanoapertures due to the defects of symmetry breaking [85]. Besides, Rajaei et al. showed that the gradient depth for a plasmonic array of nanostructures with a ramp shape provided symmetry breaking that led to a significant value of the Circular Dichroism (CD) in the range of visible frequencies (CD = 64% at the wavelength of 678 nm) obtained by reflection spectroscopy [86]. Furthermore, Goerlitzer et al. showed the fabrication of 3D plasmonic crescents with tuning of chirality by using on-edge colloidal lithography. Indeed, the chirality could be tuned experimentally by moving the position of the deposition step of a silicon dioxide film on which metallic crescent-shaped structures were realized. This intermediate film of silicon dioxide permitted symmetry breaking of the crescent structure [87]. To finish this part on chiral plasmonics, Leahu et al. reported on the fabrication of GaAs/AlGaAs/GaAS nanowires partially overlayed with gold, which led to symmetry breaking and thus a chiral response (circular dichroism) [88].

3.4. Applications to Chemistry and Plasmonic Sensing

To finish this mini-review, the last fields of application presented here are chemistry and plasmonic sensing (see Table 4). The first four examples are devoted to chemistry [89–92], and the last six are dedicated to plasmonic sensing [93–98].

Table 4. Improved performances and applications due to symmetry breaking in the field of chemistry and plasmonic sensing (NP = Nanoparticle; EP = Exceptional Point).

Refs.	Improved Performances	Applications
[89]	Plasmonic resonances	Surface-enhanced Raman scattering sensing
[90]	Splitting of plasmon modes	Sensing
[91]	Optical properties of 1D plasmonic nanostructures	Solution-phase metamaterials
[92]	Dynamic process of H_2 dissociation on metallic NP	Tunable photochemistry
[93]	Splitting of plasmon modes for alloy nanodisc arrays	Biosensing technologies
[94]	Detection sensitivity	Modern biosensors
[95]	Magnetic Fano resonances	Bioanalytics via high precision sensing
[96]	Detection sensitivity with plasmonic EPs	Nanoscale devices and sensors
[97]	Circular dichroism	Detection of chiral molecules
[98]	Circular dichroism	Chiral sensors

In the first study, Topal et al. investigated the plasmonic modes in silver Nanohemispheres (NHSs) using an incident illumination with an *s*- and *p*-polarization for different angles. They showed that symmetry breaking by the shape of asymmetric nanoparticles (nanohemispheres) was conducive to dipole modes, which were parallel and also normal to the base. These dipole modes were extremely distinct in terms of electromagnetic coupling, energy, and dependence on polarization for the excitation. For instance, the principal parallel mode provided a couple of advantages in plasmonics compared to the classical case of nanospheres. Indeed, the very intense coupling of a parallel mode with the substrate gave the possibility of benefiting photovoltaics in thin films through an efficient coupling of light [89]. Furthermore, Smith et al. proved that the degenerated plasmonic modes of gold nanotriangles were responsive to symmetry breaking. Indeed, they demonstrated that the inclination of Au nanotriangles led to a substantial breaking of the degeneracy between plasmonic modes [90]. In addition, Jones et al. studied the optical properties of plasmonic nanostructures realized by using assembly by DNA, allowing a deterministic symmetry breaking. The symmetry breaking enabled the emergence of coupled modes of the π-type constituted by both dipolar and quadripolar modes [91]. To finish the applications to chemistry, Zhang et al. showed the dynamic process of H_2 dissociation on plasmonic nanoparticles (see Figure 7a), which was a plasmonic chemical process obtained by the intermediary of hot-carriers. Indeed, this process took place when the H_2 molecule was near to a unique plasmonic nanoparticle. When the H_2 molecule was situated at an equal distance between the two nanoparticles forming the dimer, the suppression of the H_2 dissociation occurred on account of a sequential charge transfer (see Figure 7a,b). If the H_2 molecule were moved asymmetrically in this gap, then the symmetry was broken, and the H_2 dissociation was restored due to the meaningful stop of the additional charge transfer (see Figure 7a,b). From Figure 7c, no dissociation occurred for this case where D = d = 5.82 Å(gray line). Moreover, this case was identically sensitive to that with D = d = 1.59 Å(green line). The only difference between these two cases was that the scale of the bond-fluctuation time was quicker for the case D = d = 5.82 Å. For the given distance D between the nanoparticle and the molecule of dihydrogen, the dissociation effectively started when the size d of the dimer exceeded some critical value d_c. It is interesting to note that the distance d_c for the effective H_2 dissociation increased when the resonance energy ω increased [92].

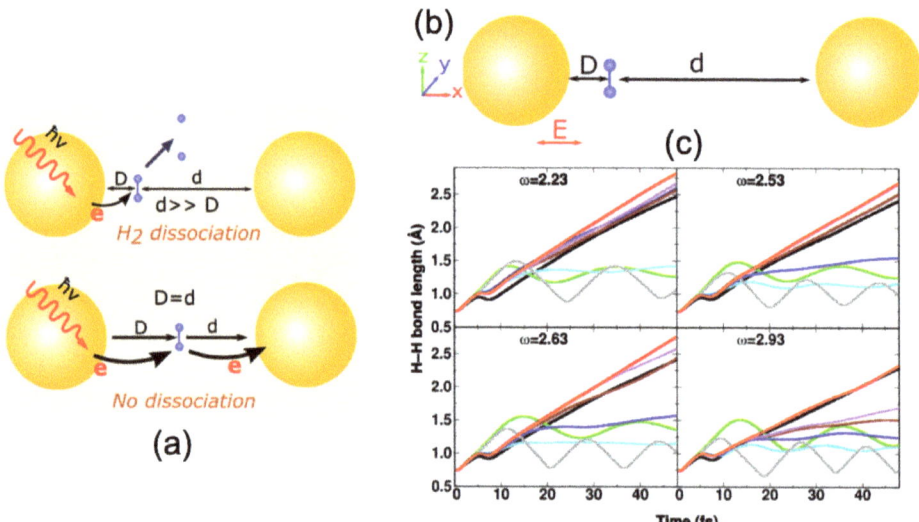

Figure 7. (**a**) Principle scheme of the dissociation of the H_2 molecule within a dimer. (**b**) Scheme of the configuration used for the case where H_2 is placed between the plasmonic nanoparticles, and the distance D is set at 1.59 Å. The other distance is d, which is not fixed. (**c**) Bond dynamics of H_2 within the dimer for several distances d (with D = 1.59 Å) for four resonant energies (ω): in black, for a monomer, for d = 1.59, 3.70, 5.82, 7.94, 10.05, 12.17 Å(in green, cyan, blue, brown, purple, red, respectively), and for the last case, in grey, for D = d = 5.82 Å. All the figures were reprinted (adapted) with permission from [92], Copyright 2018, American Chemical Society.

In the first example dedicated to plasmonic sensing, Misbah et al. showed the mode splitting induced by symmetry breaking for coupled Au-Ag Alloy Nanodisc Arrays (ANAs; see Figure 8a). In this ANA, two modes, of which one had low energy and the other had High Energy (HE mode), appeared due to the splitting of the original plasmonic mode of a single nanodisc. The resonance of the HE mode could be set at 540 nm by using alloy nanodiscs that were rich in silver. Then, the authors used this mode obtained with an ANA coupled in the far-field, because this mode was related to a higher sensitivity to local refractive index variations (344 nm/RIU; RIU = Refractive Index Unit) compared to classical plasmonic arrays for the same spectral range. This same mode was also of key significance for colorimetric sensing. By using this mode, the detection limit was 10^{-10} M for the concentration of streptavidin (see Figure 8b), a molecule used for testing these plasmonic ANAs, and for this same concentration, the Red/Green (R/G) ratio reduction was slightly inferior to 0.05 (see Figure 8b) [93].

Furthermore, Zhu et al. demonstrated that symmetry breaking of the 3D metallic nanoholes improved the sensitiveness to local refractive index changes up to 946 nm/RIU. This effect was due to the improvement of the electric field localized on corners, and the excitation of a supplemental plasmonic quadrupolar mode. Then, the authors demonstrated 3D Plasmonic Photonic Crystal (PPC) nanostructures, which were obtained from quasi-3D plasmonic nanoholes on which quasi-3D SU-8 nanosquares were reverse-imprinted in order to sustain gold nanosquares on the top. These gold nanosquares broke the symmetry of the quasi-3D plasmonic nanoholes. This mixture allowed a better EM field confinement from the spatial point of view. Moreover, they improved their 3D PPC by introducing point-defect cavities in order to enhance the confinement of the EM field around the defect zones. Thus, with this type of nanostructure, the sensitivity to local refractive index changes was 1376 nm/RIU. A detection limit of 10^4 particles per mL for the concentration of exosomes was obtained, characterized by a spectral shift of 9 nm for the resonance peak at 1082 nm [94]. Next, Wang et al.

investigated symmetric nanotrimer arrays with a high density in the infrared domain in order to obtain magnetic Fano resonances induced by symmetry breaking. The authors showed that the excitation of these resonances could occur when a coupling between neighboring cells involved a broken symmetry. The latter showed a sensitivity to local refractive index variations of around 300 nm/RIU [95]. Park et al. demonstrated that the refractive index sensitivity for plasmonic exceptional points was 4821 nm/RIU and enabled the detection of 15×10^{-12} g·L^{-1} for the concentration of anti-immunoglobulin G. The plasmonic exceptional points were found on the hybridized detuned resonators in a bilayered plasmon periodic edifice. The critical complex coupling led to the fusion of both losses and resonances. The broken symmetry performed the detuning by employing alike resonators within dissimilar optical media [96]. To finish this part on plasmonic sensing, a couple of groups demonstrated a plasmon-enhanced sensing of the chiral molecules [97,98]. In this case, the plasmon resonance of nanostructures increased the natural chirality of molecules so the whole system lost its symmetry. Indeed, the highly confined electromagnetic fields of plasmonic structures allowed a better interaction between these fields and chiral molecules, which were deposited on these plasmonic structures.

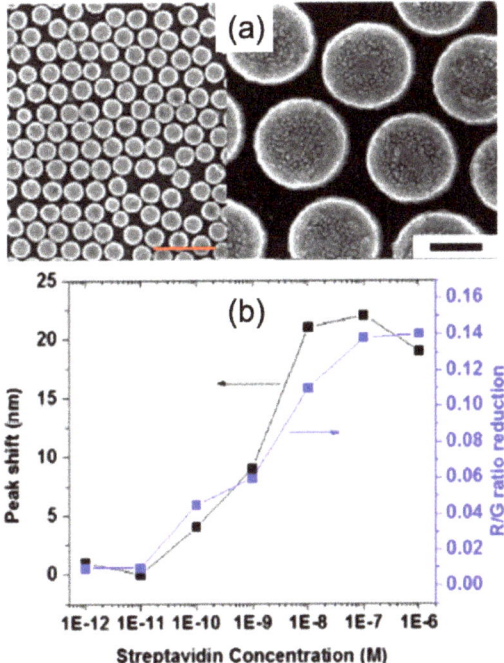

Figure 8. (**a**) SEM pictures of an alloy nanodisc array (scale bar = 1000 nm, and for the zoom, scale bar = 200 nm). (**b**) Spectral shift of the resonance peak at 540 nm (in black) and the Red/Green (R/G) ratio reduction (in blue) versus streptavidin concentration. All the figures were reprinted (adapted) with permission from [93], Copyright 2019, American Chemical Society.

4. Conclusions

In this mini-review, recent insights and advances concerning the applications of symmetry breaking in plasmonics were reported in four major parts: (i) plasmonic devices, (ii) non-linear optics, (iii) chiral plasmonics, and (iv) chemistry and plasmonic sensing. Indeed, symmetry breaking has a key role in many physical and chemical phenomena. In general, symmetry breaking is employed in order to enhance different properties or effects of plasmonic nanostructures such as transmission efficiency, nanolasing, second harmonic generation signals, sum frequency generation signals, circular dichroism, splitting of plasmonic modes, sensitivity to local refractive index changes for sensing applications, and H$_2$ dissociation. Thus, symmetry breaking is a phenomenon that is not to be neglected and to be used for a great number of fields such as those cited previously, for instance.

Author Contributions: G.B. wrote the whole paper, prepared the original draft, and edited the draft; A.I. wrote Section 2 and edited the draft; A.K.S. wrote Section 2 and edited the draft. All authors have read and agreed to the published version of the manuscript.

Funding: This research was partially supported by the Russian Science Foundation (Grant No. 16-14-00209).

Conflicts of Interest: The authors declare no conflict of interest.

References

1. Haffner, C.; Heni, W.; Fedoryshyn, Y.; Niegemann, J.; Melikyan, A.; Elder, D.L.; Baeuerle, B.; Salamin, Y.; Josten, A.; Koch, U.; et al. All-plasmonic Mach-Zehnder modulator enabling optical high-speed communication at the microscale. *Nat. Photonics* **2015**, *9*, 525–528. [CrossRef]

2. Ayata, M.; Fedoryshyn, Y.; Heni, W.; Baeuerle, B.; Josten, A.; Zahner, M.; Koch, U.; Salamin, Y.; Hoessbacher, C.; Haffner, C.; et al. High-speed plasmonic modulator in a single metal layer. *Science* **2017**, *358*, 630–632. [CrossRef] [PubMed]

3. Magno, G.; Bélier, B.; Barbillon, G. Gold thickness impact on the enhancement of SERS detection in low-cost Au/Si nanosensors. *J. Mater. Sci.* **2017**, *52*, 13650–13656. [CrossRef]

4. Salamin, Y.; Ma, P.; Baeuerle, B.; Emboras, A.; Fedoryshyn, Y.; Heni, W.; Cheng, B.; Josten, A.; Leuthold, J. 100 GHz Plasmonic Photodetector. *ACS Photonics* **2018**, *5*, 3291–3297. [CrossRef]

5. Thomaschewski, M.; Yang, Y.Q.; Bozhevolnyi, S.I. Ultra-compact branchless plasmonic interferometers. *Nanoscale* **2018**, *10*, 16178–16183. [CrossRef]

6. Sarychev, A.K.; Ivanov, A.; Lagarkov, A.; Barbillon, G. Light Concentration by Metal-Dielectric Micro-Resonators for SERS Sensing. *Materials* **2019**, *12*, 103. [CrossRef]

7. Chen, X.; Fang, J.; Zhang, X.D.; Zhao, Y.; Gu, M. Optical/Electrical Integrated Design of Core-Shell Aluminum-Based Plasmonic Nanostructures for Record-Breaking Efficiency Enhancements in Photovoltaic Devices. *ACS Photonics* **2017**, *4*, 2102–2110. [CrossRef]

8. Li, M.Z.; Guler, U.; Li, Y.A.; Rea, A.; Tanyi, E.K.; Kim, Y.; Noginov, M.A.; Song, Y.L.; Boltasseva, A.; Shalaev, V.M.; et al. Plasmonic Biomimetic Nanocomposite with Spontaneous Subwavelength Structuring as Broadband Absorbers. *ACS Energy Lett.* **2018**, *3*, 1578–1583. [CrossRef]

9. Shao, W.J.; Liang, Z.Q.; Guan, T.F.; Chen, J.M.; Wang, Z.F.; Wu, H.H.; Zheng, J.Z.; Abdulhalim, I.; Jiang, L. One-step integration of a multiple-morphology gold nanoparticle array on a TiO$_2$ film via a facile sonochemical method for highly efficient organic photovoltaics. *J. Mater. Chem. A* **2018**, *6*, 8419–8429. [CrossRef]

10. Vangelidis, I.; Theodosi, A.; Beliatis, M.J.; Gandhi, K.K.; Laskarakis, A.; Patsalas, P.; Logothetidis, S.; Silva, S.R.P.; Lidorikis, E. Plasmonic Organic Photovoltaics: Unraveling Plasmonic Enhancement for Realistic Cell Geometries. *ACS Photonics* **2018**, *5*, 1440–1452. [CrossRef]

11. Pichon, B.P.; Barbillon, G.; Marie, P.; Pauly, M.; Begin-Colin, S. Iron oxide magnetic nanoparticles used as probing agents to study the nanostructure of mixed self-assembled monolayers. *Nanoscale* **2011**, *3*, 4696–4705. [CrossRef] [PubMed]

12. He, Y.; Su, S.; Xu, T.T.; Zhong, Y.L.; Zapien, J.A.; Li, J.; Fan, C.H.; Lee, S.T. Silicon nanowires-based highly-efficient SERS-active platform for ultrasensitive DNA detection. *Nano Today* **2011**, *6*, 122–130. [CrossRef]

13. Huang, J.-A.; Zhao, Y.-Q.; Zhang, X.-J.; He, L.-F.; Wong, T.-L.; Chui, Y.-S.; Zhang, W.-J.; Lee, S.-T. Ordered Ag/Si Nanowires Array: Wide-Range Surface-Enhanced Raman Spectroscopy for Reproducible Biomolecule Detection. *Nano Lett.* **2013**, *13*, 5039–5045. [CrossRef] [PubMed]

14. Dalstein, L.; Ben Haddada, M.; Barbillon, G.; Humbert, C.; Tadjeddine, A.; Boujday, S.; Busson, B. Revealing the Interplay between Adsorbed Molecular Layers and Gold Nanoparticles by Linear and Nonlinear Optical Properties. *J. Phys. Chem. C* **2015**, *119*, 17146–17155. [CrossRef]

15. Bryche, J.-F.; Bélier, B.; Bartenlian, B.; Barbillon, G. Low-cost SERS substrates composed of hybrid nanoskittles for a highly sensitive sensing of chemical molecules. *Sens. Actuators B* **2017**, *239*, 795–799. [CrossRef]

16. Tian, X.; Lin, Y.; Dong, J.; Zhang, Y.; Wu, S.; Liu, S.; Zhang, Y.; Li, J.; Tian, Z. Synthesis of Ag Nanorods with Highly Tunable Plasmonics toward Optimal Surface-Enhanced Raman Scattering Substrates Self-Assembled at Interfaces. *Adv. Opt. Mater.* **2017**, *5*, 1700581. [CrossRef]

17. Chen, J.; Gan, F.; Wang, Y.; Li, G. Plasmonic Sensing and Modulation Based on Fano Resonances. *Adv. Opt. Mater.* **2018**, *6*, 1701152. [CrossRef]

18. Dolci, M.; Bryche, J.-F.; Leuvrey, C.; Zafeiratos, S.; Gree, S.; Begin-Colin, S.; Barbillon, G.; Pichon, B.P. Robust clicked assembly based on iron oxide nanoparticles for a new type of SPR biosensor. *J. Mater. Chem. C* **2018**, *6*, 9102–9110. [CrossRef]

19. Lu, G.; Xu, J.; Wen, T.; Zhang, W.; Zhao, J.; Hu, A.; Barbillon, G.; Gong, Q. Hybrid Metal-Dielectric Nano-Aperture Antenna for Surface Enhanced Fluorescence. *Materials* **2018**, *11*, 1435. [CrossRef]

20. Magno, G.; Bélier, B.; Barbillon, G. Al/Si nanopillars as very sensitive SERS substrates. *Materials* **2018**, *11*, 1534. [CrossRef]

21. Barbillon, G. Fabrication and SERS Performances of Metal/Si and Metal/ZnO Nanosensors: A Review. *Coatings* **2019**, *9*, 86. [CrossRef]

22. Humbert, C.; Noblet, T.; Dalstein, L.; Busson, B.; Barbillon, G. Sum-Frequency Generation Spectroscopy of Plasmonic Nanomaterials: A Review. *Materials* **2019**, *12*, 836. [CrossRef] [PubMed]

23. Zambrana-Puyalto, X.; Ponzellini, P.; Maccaferri, N.; Tessarolo, E.; Pelizzo, M.G.; Zhang, W.; Barbillon, G.; Lu, G.; Garoli, D. A hybrid metal-dielectric zero mode waveguide for enhanced single molecule detection. *Chem. Commun.* **2019**, *55*, 9725–9728. [CrossRef] [PubMed]

24. Barbillon, G.; Ivanov, A.; Sarychev, A.K. Hybrid Au/Si Disk-Shaped Nanoresonators on Gold Film for Amplified SERS Chemical Sensing. *Nanomaterials* **2019**, *9*, 1588. [CrossRef] [PubMed]

25. Graniel, O.; Iatsunskyi, I.; Coy, E.; Humbert, C.; Barbillon, G.; Michel, T.; Maurin, D.; Balme, S.; Miele, P.; Bechelany, M. Au-covered hollow urchin-like ZnO nanostructures for surface-enhanced Raman scattering sensing. *J. Mater. Chem. C* **2019**, *7*, 15066–15073. [CrossRef]

26. Tomyshev, K.A.; Tazhetdinova, D.K.; Manuilovich, E.S.; Butov, O.V. High-resolution fiber optic surface plasmon resonance sensor for biomedical applications. *J. Appl. Phys.* **2018**, *124*, 113106. [CrossRef]

27. Cai, S.S.; Gonzalez-Vila, A.; Zhang, X.J.; Guo, T.; Caucheteur, C. Palladium-coated plasmonic optical fiber gratings for hydrogen detection. *Opt. Lett.* **2019**, *44*, 4483–4486. [CrossRef]

28. Maier, S.A. *Plasmonics: Fundamentals and Applications*; Springer: New York, NY, USA, 2007; pp. 3–220.

29. Enoch, S.; Bonod, N. *Plasmonics: From Basics to Advanced Topics*; Springer: Heidelberg, Germany, 2012; pp. 3–317.

30. Kravets, V.G.; Kabashin, A.V.; Barnes, W.L.; Grigorenko, A.N. Plasmonic Surface Lattice Resonances: A Review of Properties and Applications. *Chem. Rev.* **2018**, *118*, 5912–5951. [CrossRef]

31. Li, Z.; Butun, S.; Aydin, K. Ultranarrow Band Absorbers Based on Surface Lattice Resonances in Nanostructured Metal Surfaces. *ACS Nano* **2014**, *8*, 8242–8248. [CrossRef]

32. Sarkar, M.; Besbes, M.; Moreau, J.; Bryche, J.-F.; Olivéro, A.; Barbillon, G.; Coutrot, A.-L.; Bartenlian, B.; Canva, M. Hybrid Plasmonic Mode by Resonant Coupling of Localized Plasmons to Propagating Plasmons in a Kretschmann Configuration. *ACS Photonics* **2015**, *2*, 237–245. [CrossRef]

33. Sobhani, A.; Manjavacas, A.; Cao, Y.; McClain, M.J.; Javier Garcia de Abajo, F.; Nordlander, P.; Halas, N.J. Pronounced Linewidth Narrowing of an Aluminum Nanoparticle Plasmon Resonance by Interaction with an Aluminum Metallic Film. *Nano Lett.* **2015**, *15*, 6946–6951. [CrossRef] [PubMed]

34. Yue, W.; Wang, Z.; Whittaker, J.; Lopez-Royo, F.; Yang, Y.; Zayats, A.V. Amplification of surface-enhanced Raman scattering due to substrate-mediated localized surface plasmons in gold nanodimers. *J. Mater. Chem. C* **2017**, *5*, 4075–4084. [CrossRef]

35. Barbillon, G.; Bijeon, J.-L.; Lérondel, G.; Plain, J.; Royer, P. Detection of chemical molecules with integrated plasmonic glass nanotips. *Surf. Sci.* **2008**, *602*, L119–L122. [CrossRef]

36. Dhawan, A.; Duval, A.; Nakkach, M.; Barbillon, G.; Moreau, J.; Canva, M.; Vo-Dinh, T. Deep UV nano-microstructuring of substrates for surface plasmon resonance imaging. *Nanotechnology* **2011**, *22*, 165301. [CrossRef] [PubMed]

37. Zhang, P.; Yang, S.; Wang, L.; Zhao, J.; Zhu, Z.; Liu, B.; Zhong, J.; Sun, X. Large-scale uniform Au nanodisc arrays fabricated via X-ray interference lithography for reproducible and sensitive SERS substrate. *Nanotechnology* **2014**, *25*, 245301. [CrossRef]

38. Guisbert Quilis, N.; Lequeux, M.; Venugopalan, P.; Khan, I.; Knoll, W.; Boujday, S.; Lamy de la Chapelle, M.; Dostalek, J. Tunable laser interference lithography preparation of plasmonic nanoparticle arrays tailored for SERS. *Nanoscale* **2018**, *10*, 10268. [CrossRef]

39. Hwang, J.S.; Yang, M. Sensitive and Reproducible Gold SERS Sensor Based on Interference Lithography and Electrophoretic Deposition. *Sensors* **2018**, *18*, 4076. [CrossRef]

40. Hentschel, M.; Schäferling, M.; Duan, X.; Giessen, H.; Liu, N. Chiral plasmonics. *Sci. Adv.* **2017**, *3*, e1602735. [CrossRef]

41. Henzie, J.; Lee, J.; Lee, M.H.; Hasan, W.; Odom, T.W. Nanofabrication of Plasmonic Structures. *Annu. Rev. Phys. Chem.* **2009**, *60*, 147–165. [CrossRef]

42. Yu, Q.; Guan, P.; Qin, D.; Golden, G.; Wallace, P.M. Inverted size-dependence of surface-enhanced Raman scattering on gold nanohole and nanodisc arrays. *Nano Lett.* **2008**, *8*, 1923–1928. [CrossRef]

43. Faure, A.C.; Barbillon, G.; Ou, M.; Ledoux, G.; Tillement, O.; Roux, S.; Fabregue, D.; Descamps, A.; Bijeon, J.-L.; Marquette, C.A.; et al. Core/shell nanoparticles for multiple biological detection with enhanced sensitivity and kinetics. *Nanotechnology* **2008**, *19*, 485103. [CrossRef] [PubMed]

44. Bryche, J.-F.; Gillibert, R.; Barbillon, G.; Sarkar, M.; Coutrot, A.-L.; Hamouda, F.; Aassime, A.; Moreau, J.; de La Chapelle, M.L.; Bartenlian, B.; et al. Density effect of gold nanodiscs on the SERS intensity for a highly sensitive detection of chemical molecules. *J. Mater. Sci.* **2015**, *50*, 6601–6607. [CrossRef]

45. Sarychev, A.K.; Bykov, I.V.; Boginskaya, I.A.; Ivanov, A.V.; Kurochkin, I.N.; Lagarkov, A.N.; Nechaeva, N.L.; Ryzhikov, I.A. Metal-dielectric optical resonance in metasurfaces and SERS effect. *Opt. Quantum Electron.* **2020**, *52*, 26. [CrossRef]

46. Masson, J.F.; Gibson, K.F.; Provencher-Girard, A. Surface-enhanced Raman spectroscopy amplification with film over etched nanospheres. *J. Phys. Chem. C* **2010**, *114*, 22406–22412. [CrossRef]

47. Bechelany, M.; Brodard, P.; Elias, J.; Brioude, A.; Michler, J.; Philippe, L. Simple Synthetic Route for SERS-Active Gold Nanoparticles Substrate with Controlled Shape and Organization. *Langmuir* **2010**, *26*, 14364–14371. [CrossRef] [PubMed]

48. Bryche, J.-F.; Tsigara, A.; Bélier, B.; Lamy de la Chapelle, M.; Canva, M.; Bartenlian, B.; Barbillon, G. Surface enhanced Raman scattering improvement of gold triangular nanoprisms by a gold reflective underlayer for chemical sensing. *Sens. Actuators B* **2016**, *228*, 31–35. [CrossRef]

49. Barbillon, G.; Noblet, T.; Busson, B.; Tadjeddine, A.; Humbert, C. Localised detection of thiophenol with gold nanotriangles highly structured as honeycombs by nonlinear sum frequency generation spectroscopy. *J. Mater. Sci.* **2018**, *53*, 4554–4562. [CrossRef]

50. Ding, T.; Sigle, D.O.; Herrmann, L.O.; Wolverson, D.; Baumberg, J.J. Nanoimprint lithography of Al Nanovoids for Deep-UV SERS. *ACS Appl. Mater. Interfaces* **2014**, *6*, 17358–17363. [CrossRef]

51. Luk'yanchuk, B.; Zheludev, N.I.; Maier, S.A.; Halas, N.J.; Nordlander, P.; Giessen, H.; Chong, C.T. The Fano resonance in plasmonic nanostructures and metamaterials. *Nat. Mater.* **2010**, *9*, 707–715. [CrossRef]

52. Halas, N.J.; Lal, S.; Chang, W.-S.; Link, S.; Nordlander, P. Plasmons in strongly coupled metallic nanostructures. *Chem. Rev.* **2011**, *111*, 3913–3961. [CrossRef]

53. Durach, M.; Rusina, A.; Stockman, M.I.; Nelson, K. Toward full spatiotemporal control on the nanoscale. *Nano Lett.* **2007**, *7*, 3145–3149. [CrossRef]

54. Hao, F.; Sonnefraud, Y.; Dorpe, P.V.; Maier, S.A.; Halas, N.J.; Nordlander, P. Symmetry breaking in plasmonic nanocavities: subradiant LSPR sensing and a tunable Fano resonance. *Nano Lett.* **2008**, *8*, 3983–3988. [CrossRef]

55. Liu, N.; Hentschel, M.; Weiss, T.; Alivisatos, A.P.; Giessen, H. Three-dimensional plasmon rulers. *Science* **2011**, *332*, 1407–1410. [CrossRef] [PubMed]

56. Kondratov, A.V.; Gorkunov, M.V.; Darinskii, A.N.; Gainutdinov, R.V.; Rogov, O.Y.; Ezhov, A.A.; Artemov, V.V. Extreme optical chirality of plasmonic nanohole arrays due to chiral Fano resonance. *Phys. Rev. B* **2016**, *93*, 195418. [CrossRef]

57. Dietrich, K.; Menzel, C.; Lehr, D.; Puffky, O.; Hübner, U.; Pertsch, T.; Tünnermann, A.; Kley, E.-B. Elevating optical activity: Efficient on-edge lithography of three-dimensional starfish metamaterial. *Appl. Phys. Lett.* **2014**, *104*, 193107. [CrossRef]

58. Camacho-Morales, R.; Rahmani, M.; Kruk, S.; Wang, L.; Xu, L.; Smirnova, D.A.; Solntsev, A.S.; Miroshnichenko, A.; Tan, H.H.; Karouta, F.; et al. Nonlinear generation of vector beams from AlGaAs nanoantennas. *Nano Lett.* **2016**, *16*, 7191–7197. [CrossRef]

59. Hao, F.; Nordlander, P.; Sonnefraud, Y.; Dorpe, P.V.; Maier, S.A. Tunability of subradiant dipolar and Fano-type plasmon resonances in metallic ring/disk cavities: implications for nanoscale optical sensing. *ACS Nano* **2009**, *3*, 643–652. [CrossRef]

60. Davoyan, A.R.; Shadrivov, I.V.; Kivshar, Y.S. Nonlinear plasmonic slot waveguides. *Opt. Express* **2008**, *16*, 21209–21214. [CrossRef]

61. Salgueiro, J.R.; Kivshar, Y.S. Nonlinear plasmonic directional couplers. *Appl. Phys. Lett.* **2010**, *97*, 081106. [CrossRef]

62. Kravtsov, V.; Ulbricht, R.; Atkin, J.M.; Raschke, M.B. Plasmonic nanofocused four-wave mixing for femtosecond near-field imaging. *Nat. Nanotechnol.* **2016**, *11*, 459–464. [CrossRef]

63. Nesterov, M.L.; Yin, X.; Schäferling, M.; Giessen, H.; Weiss, T. The role of Plasmon-Generated Near Fields for Enhanced Circular Dichroism Spectroscopy. *ACS Photonics* **2016**, *3*, 578–583. [CrossRef]

64. Jia, W.; Ren, P.; Jia, Y.; Fan, C. Active Control and Large Group Delay in Graphene-Based Terahertz Metamaterials. *J. Phys. Chem. C* **2019**, *123*, 18560–18564. [CrossRef]

65. Frese, D.; Wei, Q.; Wang, Y.; Huang, L.; Zentgraf, T. Nonreciprocal Asymmetric Polarization Encryption by Layered Plasmonic Metasurfaces. *Nano Lett.* **2019**, *19*, 3976–3980. [CrossRef] [PubMed]

66. Esposito, M.; Todisco, F.; Bakhti, S.; Passaseo, A.; Tarantini, I.; Cuscuna, M.; Destouches, N.; Tasco, V. Symmetry Breaking in Oligomer Surface Plasmon Lattice Resonances. *Nano Lett.* **2019**, *19*, 1922–1930. [CrossRef] [PubMed]

67. Pourjamal, S.; Hakala, T.K.; Necada, M.; Freire-Fernandez, F.; Kataja, M.; Rekola, H.; Martikainen, J.; Törmä, P.; van Dijken, S. Lasing in Ni Nanodisk Arrays. *ACS Nano* **2019**, *13*, 5686–5692. [CrossRef]

68. Knudson, M.P.; Li, R.; Wang, D.; Wang, W.; Schaller, R.D.; Odom, T.W. Polarization-Dependent Lasing Behavior from Low-Symmetry Nanocavity Arrays. *ACS Nano* **2019**, *13*, 7435–7441. [CrossRef]

69. Lin, Y.; Wang, D.; Hu, J.; Liu, J.; Wang, W.; Guan, J.; Schaller, R.D.; Odom, T.W. Engineering Symmetry-Breaking Nanocrescent Arrays for Nanolasing. *Adv. Funct. Mater.* **2019**, *29*, 1904157. [CrossRef]

70. Sarkar, A.; Shivakiran Bhaktha, B.N.; Andreasen, J. Replica Symmetry Breaking in a Weakly Scattering Optofluidic Random Laser. *Sci. Rep.* **2020**, *10*, 2628. [CrossRef]

71. Shah, Y.D.; Grant, J.; Hao, D.; Kenney, M.; Pusino, V.; Cumming, D.R.S. Ultra-narrow Line Width Polarization-Insensitive Filter Using a Symmetry-Breaking Selective Plasmonic Metasurface. *ACS Photonics* **2018**, *5*, 663–669. [CrossRef]

72. Vaianella, F.; Hamm, J.M.; Hess, O.; Maes, B. Strong Coupling and Exceptional Points in Optically Pumped Active Hyperbolic Metamaterials. *ACS Photonics* **2018**, *5*, 2486–2495. [CrossRef]

73. Akbari, M.; Gao, J.; Yang, X. Manipulating transverse photovoltage across plasmonic triangle holes of symmetry breaking. *Appl. Phys. Lett.* **2019**, *114*, 171102. [CrossRef]

74. Lourenço-Martins, H.; Das, P.; Tizei, L.H.G.; Weil, R.; Kociak, M. Self-hybridization within non-Hermitian localized plasmonic systems. *Nat. Phys.* **2018**, *14*, 360–364. [CrossRef]

75. Mahdy, M.R.C.; Danesh, M.; Zhang, T.; Ding, W.; Rivy, H.M.; Chowdhury, A.B.; Mehmood, M.Q. Plasmonic Spherical Heterodimers: Reversal of Optical Binding Force Based on the Forced Breaking of Symmetry. *Sci. Rep.* **2018**, *8*, 3164. [CrossRef] [PubMed]

76. Zheng, P.; Paria, D.; Wang, H.; Li, M.; Barman, I. Optical properties of symmetry-breaking tetrahedral nanoparticles. *Nanoscale* **2020**, *12*, 832–842. [CrossRef] [PubMed]

77. Rahmani, M.; Shorokhov, A.S.; Hopkins, B.; Miroshnichenko, A.E.; Shcherbakov, M.R.; Camacho-Morales, R.; Fedyanin, A.A.; Neshev, D.N.; Kivshar, Y.S. Nonlinear Symmetry Breaking in Symmetric Oligomers. *ACS Photonics* **2017**, *4*, 454–461. [CrossRef]

78. Gennaro, S.D.; Li, Y.; Maier, S.A.; Oulton, R.F. Nonlinear Pancharatnam–Berry Phase Metasurfaces beyond the Dipole Approximation. *ACS Photonics* **2019**, *6*, 2335–2341. [CrossRef]

79. Taghinejad, M.; Xu, Z.; Lee, K.-T.; Lian, T.; Cai, W. Transient Second-Order Nonlinear Media: Breaking the Spatial Symmetry in the Time Domain via Hot-Electron Transfer. *Phys. Rev. Lett.* **2020**, *124*, 013901. [CrossRef]

80. Shi, J.; Liang, W.-Y.; Raja, S.; Sang, Y.; Zhang, X.-Q.; Chen, C.-A.; Wang, Y.; Yang, X.; Lee, Y.-H.; Ahn, H.; et al. Plasmonic Enhancement and Manipulation of Optical Nonlinearity in Monolayer Tungsten Disulfide. *Laser Photonics Rev.* **2018**, *12*, 1800188. [CrossRef]

81. Tsai, W.-Y.; Chung, T.L.; Hsiao, H.-H.; Chen, J.-W.; Lin, R.J.; Wu, P.C.; Sun, G.; Wang, C.-M.; Misawa, H.; Tsai, D.P. Second Harmonic Light Manipulation with Vertical Split Ring Resonators. *Adv. Mater.* **2019**, *31*, 1806479. [CrossRef]

82. Dalstein, L.; Humbert, C.; Ben Haddada, M.; Boujday, S.; Barbillon, G.; Busson, B. The Prevailing Role of Hotspots in Plasmon-Enhanced Sum-Frequency Generation Spectroscopy. *J. Phys. Chem. Lett.* **2019**, *10*, 7706–7711. [CrossRef]

83. Greybush, N.J.; Pacheco-Pena, V.; Engheta, N.; Murray, C.B.; Kagan, C.R. Plasmonic Optical and Chiroptical Response of Self-Assembled Au Nanorod Equilateral Trimers. *ACS Nano* **2019**, *13*, 1617–1624. [CrossRef] [PubMed]

84. Chen, Y.; Gao, J.; Yang, X. Chiral Metamaterials of Plasmonic Slanted Nanoapertures with Symmetry Breaking. *Nano Lett.* **2018**, *18*, 520–527. [CrossRef] [PubMed]

85. Pham, A.; Jiang, Q.; Zhao, A.; Bellessa, J.; Genet, C.; Drezet, A. Manifestation of Planar and Bulk Chirality Mixture in Plasmonic Λ-Shaped Nanostructures Caused by Symmetry Breaking Defects. *ACS Photonics* **2017**, *4*, 2453–2460. [CrossRef]

86. Rajaei, M.; Zeng, J.; Albooyeh, M.; Kamandi, M.; Hanifeh, M.; Capolino, F.; Wickramasinghe, H.K. Giant Circular Dichroism at Visible Frequencies Enabled by Plasmonic Ramp-Shaped Nanostructures. *ACS Photonics* **2019**, *6*, 924–931. [CrossRef]

87. Goerlitzer, E.S.A.; Mohammadi, R.; Nechayev, S.; Banzer, P.; Vogel, N. Large-Area 3D Plasmonic Crescents with Tunable Chirality. *Adv. Optical Mater.* **2019**, *7*, 1801770. [CrossRef]

88. Leahu, G.; Petronijevic, E.; Belardini, A.; Centini, M.; Sibilia, C.; Hakkarainen, T.; Koivusalo, E.; Piton, M.R.; Suomalainen, S.; Guina, M. Evidence of Optical Circular Dichroism in GaAs-Based Nanowires Partially Covered with Gold. *Adv. Opt. Mater.* **2017**, *5*, 1601063. [CrossRef]

89. Özge Topal, Ç.; Jaradat, H.M.; Karumuri, S.; O'Hara, J.F.; Akyurtlu, A.; Kaan Kalkan, A. Plasmon Resonances in Nanohemisphere Monolayers. *J. Phys. Chem. C* **2017**, *121*, 23599–23608. [CrossRef]

90. Smith, K.W.; Yang, J.; Hernandez, T.; Swearer, D.F.; Scarabelli, L.; Zhang, H.; Zhao, H.; Moringo, N.A.; Chang, W.-S.; Liz-Marzan, L.M.; et al. Environmental Symmetry Breaking Promotes Plasmon Mode Splitting in Gold Nanotriangles. *J. Phys. Chem. C* **2018**, *122*, 13259–13266. [CrossRef]

91. Jones, M.R.; Kohlstedt, K.L.; O'Brien, M.N.; Wu, J.; Schatz, G.C.; Mirkin, C.A. Deterministic Symmetry Breaking of Plasmonic Nanostructures Enabled by DNA-Programmable Assembly. *Nano Lett.* **2017**, *17*, 5830–5835. [CrossRef]

92. Zhang, Y.; Nelson, T.; Tretiak, S.; Guo, H.; Schatz, G.C. Plasmonic Hot-Carrier-Mediated Tunable Photochemical Reactions. *ACS Nano* **2018**, *12*, 8415–8422. [CrossRef]

93. Misbah, I.; Zhao, F.; Shih, W.-C. Symmetry Breaking-Induced Plasmonic Mode Splitting in Coupled Gold–Silver Alloy Nanodisk Array for Ultrasensitive RGB Colorimetric Biosensing. *ACS Appl. Mater. Interfaces* **2019**, *11*, 2273–2281. [CrossRef] [PubMed]

94. Zhu, S.; Li, H.; Yang, M.; Pang, S.W. Highly sensitive detection of exosomes by 3D plasmonic photonic crystal biosensor. *Nanoscale* **2018**, *10*, 19927–19936. [CrossRef] [PubMed]

95. Wang, N.; Zeisberger, M.; Huebner, U.; Giannini, V.; Schmidt, M.A. Symmetry-breaking induced magnetic Fano resonances in densely packed arrays of symmetric nanotrimers. *Sci. Rep.* **2019**, *9*, 2873. [CrossRef] [PubMed]

96. Park, J.; Ndao, A.; Cai, W.; Hsu, L.; Kodigala, A.; Lepetit, T.; Lo, Y.; Kanté, B. Symmetry-breaking-induced plasmonic exceptional points and nanoscale sensing. *Nat. Phys.* **2020**, *16*, 462–468. [CrossRef]

97. Zhang, W.; Wu, T.; Wang, R.; Zhang, X. Surface-Enhanced Circular Dichroism of Oriented Chiral Molecules by Plasmonic Nanostructures. *J. Phys. Chem. C* **2017**, *121*, 666–675. [CrossRef]

98. Garcia-Guirado, J.; Svedendahl, M.; Puigdollers, J.; Quidant, R. Enantiomer-Selective Molecular Sensing Using Racemic Nanoplasmonic Arrays. *Nano Lett.* **2018**, *18*, 6279–6285. [CrossRef]

MDPI

St. Alban-Anlage 66

4052 Basel

Switzerland

Tel. +41 61 683 77 34

Fax +41 61 302 89 18

www.mdpi.com

Symmetry Editorial Office

E-mail: symmetry@mdpi.com

www.mdpi.com/journal/symmetry

www.ingramcontent.com/pod-product-compliance
Lightning Source LLC
LaVergne TN
LVHW070633100526
838202LV00012B/794